MANAGING PHYSICAL EDUCATION, FITNESS, AND SPORTS PROGRAMS

Second Edition

MANAGING PHYSICAL EDUCATION, FITNESS, AND SPORTS PROGRAMS

Second Edition

Jim H. Railey

*California Polytechnic State University
San Luis Obispo*

Peggy Railey Tschauner

*Director of Fitness, Kona Kai Club,
San Diego, California*

*Mayfield Publishing Company
Mountain View, California
London • Toronto*

Library of Congress Cataloging-in-Publication Data

Railey, Jim H.
    Managing physical education, fitness and sports programs / Jim H. Railey, Peggy Railey Tschauner. —2nd ed.
      p.   cm.
    Includes index.
    ISBN 1-55934-173-4
    1. Physical education and training—Administration. 2. Recreation leadership. 3. Sports—Organization and administration.
I. Tschauner, Peggy Railey. II. Title.
GV343.5.R35   1993
613.7′068—dc20   92-12796
                                 CIP

Manufactured in the United States of America
10   9   8   7   6

Mayfield Publishing Company
1240 Villa Street
Mountain View, California 94041

Sponsoring editor, Erin Mulligan; production editor, Lynn Rabin Bauer; manuscript editor, Colleen O'Brien; text designer, Wendy Calmenson; associate designer, Jean Mailander; cover designer, Terry Wright; illustrators, Kevin Opstedal, Susan Breitbard, and Marilyn Kreiger; manufacturing manager, Martha Branch. The text was set in 10/12 Century Old Style by Graphic Composition and printed on 50# Finch opaque by Maple-Vail Book Manufacturing Group.

Contents

Preface

Before we began the revision process for the second edition of *Managing Physical Education, Fitness, and Sports Programs,* we sent a questionnaire to many instructors who were using the first edition. We asked them to identify the strengths and weaknesses of the first edition as they perceived them. Those who completed and returned the questionnaire did a very thorough job in providing advice that has been very helpful for us in the revision process. We would like to thank these critics individually for the valuable information but most did not identify themselves as we failed to provide an appropriate space. So to those of you who were so thoughtful, we say "Thank you very much."

Most of the respondents asked us not to do a radical revision. Most liked the basic approach and our choice of topics. The following are the features that we hoped to provide and which they considered to be strengths which should be preserved in the new edition. Our first intention, then, in this revision is to continue to provide a text that:

- is easy to read and understand. Your students will be able to comprehend and learn what they really need to succeed in a management setting from the clearly presented material in the book.
- introduces students to the basic processes of leadership and management (planning, organizing, communicating, decision making, etc.) and then considers physical education and fitness-related applications. Students tackle subject-specific issues only after they have been exposed to general management strategies.
- includes coverage of physical education, fitness, and sports management in a wide variety of settings, not just schools. This appeals to the growing number of majors who will choose career options other than teaching or coaching (e.g., corporate fitness and private wellness club management).
- is full of useful pedagogy. Each chapter begins with chapter objectives and ends with key words and phrases, questions for review, a self-test, and a bibliography, enabling students to reinforce their reading and retain important information. Case studies at the end of every chapter help students put themselves in the shoes of working administrators and learn to solve real-life problems.
- features a chapter on computers and management (Chapter 16) with updated information to help future managers learn how to choose and use the right computers.

The major changes in the second edition, which will be obvious to those who are familiar with the first edition, are as follows:

All of the chapters have been carefully updated and many discussions expanded.

The chapters have been reorganized into three parts: Part I, Overview of Leadership and Management in Physical Education, Fitness, and Sports; Part II, The Basic Skills and Processes of Management; and Part III, Functions of Management Applied to Activity-Based Programs.

Additional photographs, cartoons, figures, and case studies have been incorporated.

Special effort was devoted to improving the quality of the self-tests at the end of each chapter.

We hope that this edition, like the last, will be a valuable tool in teaching effective leadership and administration in the broad field of physical education, recreation, fitness and sports management. In addition to the questionnaire respon-

dents, several people were kind enough to provide in-depth reviews of the first edition which helped us to make this second edition even better. Specifically we wish to acknowledge the following text reviewers: Michael J. Stewart, University of Nebraska, Omaha; Gary R. Gray, Iowa State University; Frederick Draper, Indiana State University; Dwayne Head, California Polytechnic State University; and William J. Considine, Springfield College. We especially thank William J. Considine and Betty L. Mann of Springfield College for revising Chapter 14; Stephen Frederick of Wright State University who was principally involved with the revision of Chapter 16; and Dwayne Head of California Polytechnic State University, San Luis Obispo for writing the section on ethics in administration in Chapter 1.

Introduction

This is a text about how to lead, administer, and manage programs in physical education, fitness, and sports. These programs include athletics, intramural competition, and recreation, and are referred to as activity-based programs throughout the text. Leadership is the driver of any organization. It is the most important factor in the success or failure of any activity-based program. If a weak link exists somewhere in the leadership or administrative chain, a program can still be successful if a strong and effective leader at some other level can adequately compensate for the weak link. For example, a school district with an ineffective superintendent may still be an effective enterprise if the principals and other administrators are strong enough to compensate for the weakness of the superintendent.

Because leadership and management are the essential factors in the success of any activity-based program, we discuss the nature of these two important processes in chapters one through three. But first, we want to suggest that problem-solving and case-study techniques be used in teaching the materials and concepts presented. Previously, we introduced the steps for using the two techniques in the chapter on decision making; however, because the opportunity arises to use the case-study before getting to that discussion, we believe it is important to present those steps at the beginning. The discussion of the problem-solving technique is presented in Chapter 4.

THE CASE-STUDY APPROACH

We present case studies at the end of each chapter in this book to provide you with an opportunity to feel the satisfaction of solving problems through your own independent and responsible thought processes. In the following paragraphs we will describe a method of approaching these case studies to practice decision-making skills. You should not become discouraged and give up on the method until you have given it a fair chance. It is not an easy method to master; in fact, it is quite difficult and demanding and requires self-discipline in the use of your time, interest, and thought. But in return, tremendous satisfaction is in store for you if you can get caught up with the case-study approach. After three to six weeks, you will begin to gain the insights of an administrator, be able to read between the lines, and generally get a feel for making effective decisions.

Be aware that there usually is more than one correct response as you move toward the case solution. The correct actions will, in most situations, be guided by established principles, policies, and rules, but not always. Sometimes you will suggest an action just because of your gut feelings, and if you can give some clue as to why you feel as you do, that is appropriate.

We suggest that you follow these steps in using the case-study method for improving your decision-making skills:

Step 1 Read the case first to enjoy. Do not analyze.

Step 2 Think deliberately about the case as a whole.

Step 3 Read the case again and look for the issues and/or problems.

Step 4 Look for the primary cause of the problems.

Step 5 Read the case again and make assumptions.

Step 6 Put yourself in the role of each character and try to understand why each acted as he or she did.

Step 7 Answer the questions at the end of each case:

a. What is (are) the issue(s)?

An issue is debatable and always stated in the form of a question. For example, the issue in Case 1.1 is: Should the administration course be a requirement in the major program?

b. What are the problems?

A problem is an existing reality that hinders the desired course of events. For example, one problem in Case 1.1 is that there were too many required courses.

c. What blocks or hurdles may be in the way of the best solution?

These are very similar to problems, but usually are identified as shortcomings, such as fear, impulsiveness, lack of knowledge or appreciation, or limited budget, of the decision maker or the or-

ganization. For example, in Case 1.1 the committee has a very limited perception of the values derived from taking a course in management.

d. What actions should be, or should have been, taken to solve the problems? (You must consider the consequences of your actions.)

In Case 1.1 Chris Janes should have presented an extended course outline to the committee members to better educate them as to the value of the course.

e. What decision or action guides led you to the suggested actions?

Decision and action guides may be principles, rules, policies, or generalizations that provide direction. For example, the action guide that relates to the above suggested action is: Every instructor should make an extended effort to inform the other instructors of the course content and objectives for the courses which he or she teaches. You will note that the action guide is a generalization that is applicable to other situations—not just to this case.

It is important to remember that for every problem there should be at least one suggested action, and for every action, there should be at least one action guide identified.

Chapters four through nine contain in-depth discussions of the six basic skills and processes of management or administration. Our perception is that an effective director needs to have three basic personal skills—communication, decision making, and time management excellence—as well as competence in three basic processes—planning, organizing, and controlling—that relate more to the system of management than to the director's personal makeup.

With this basic leadership background in hand, we move into the final chapters, ten through sixteen, where we discuss topics that are concerned with the more specific responsibilities of the manager, administrator, or leader. The general concepts, principles, and guides-to-action presented in the earlier chapters are applied to the various functions the leader is in touch with on a day-to-day and week-to-week basis, from staffing and budget problems to coping with conflicts and computers.

1

The Nature of Leadership and Management

No program can advance beyond the vision of those who administer it.

author unknown

Chapter Objectives

After reading this chapter and completing the exercises, you should be able to:

1 Define leadership, management, and administration and relate how they differ from and complement one another

2 Explain why undergraduate and graduate students should study management theory and application

3 Understand the difference between charismatic and positional leaders in sports and identify who may fall into each category

4 Define power and authority and explain how each complements the other in some sport or fitness situation

5 List the resources in sport and fitness over which the director has authority

6 Explain why a democratic-style management is preferred over other styles discussed

7 Identify the three areas that constitute the scope of management

8 Briefly discuss the two basic skills and the three basic processes of administration

THE MEANING OF LEADERSHIP, ADMINISTRATION, AND MANAGEMENT

Administration and *management* are often considered synonymous terms. But a survey of more than one hundred sports and fitness program directors throughout the nation revealed that many differentiate between the two terms. Some directors use the term *administration* to refer to the management function in schools and government agencies, and the term *management* to refer to the same function in the business and industrial world. One director in a corporate fitness setting referred to top-level management as administrators and lower- and middle-level management as managers. Another director's concept was directly opposite. In this book, the terms are used interchangeably, regardless of the level or setting being considered.

Leadership does differ from administration and management, and in fact can be considered to encompass them. Consequently, we discuss leadership first.

Leadership

Most dictionaries define leadership as the ability to lead; so what, exactly, does *lead* mean?

- to show the way to, or direct the course of, by going before or along with
- to conduct or guide
- to direct, as by persuasion or influence, to a course of action or thought.

Based upon the meaning of lead, the term *leadership* can be defined as the act of guiding or directing others to a course of action through persuasion or influence.

The persuasion or influence exerted by a leader is considered to be intentional; however, leadership can occur without intent. For example,

suppose that a fitness group meeting for the first time must select its activity leader. Whom are they more likely to select: an elderly, frail, stoop-shouldered person or someone who is young, strong, and healthy looking? The answer is obvious: If the two individuals' physical traits are the only known qualities, there is no contest. The young person will be chosen, even if she or he prefers not to be the leader, because of the charisma often associated with youth and the look of good health.

Leadership is a broader and more encompassing concept than management. All managers or administrators are leaders, but not all leaders are managers or administrators. Coaches, for example, are readily recognized as leaders by anyone who knows anything about athletics, but they are not considered managers or members of the administrative team even though they perform many managerial functions. For this reason, this text is intended not only for those who will be managing but for those who will be performing in other leadership roles as well.

Basically, there are two distinctly different types of leaders: the charismatic (natural) leader and the positional (appointed) leader. The most preferred leadership situation occurs when the charismatic leader is also the positional leader.

Charismatic Leaders   Charismatic leaders can be an influential force in the organization because people informally endow them with leadership power. This type of leader may or may not have made an intentional effort to be placed in the influencing role. In its purest form, the leadership role results totally from charisma. The person may be charismatic because of charm, wealth, wit, appearance, intelligence, or a combination of these qualities. Charisma sometimes escapes explanation and understanding, so that we may not always know why certain people are identified by their peers as the ones who guide and direct. However, positional leaders are unwise to ignore the reality that charismatic leaders do exist within

Leaders don't push, they steer.

their groups. Natural leaders, if properly recognized, can be of tremendous assistance to administrators, but if ignored, may be their downfall.

Positional Leaders   The positional leader is placed in a power position as the result of an election or appointment. The classic example of a positional leader is the prince who inherits a throne because he happened to be the firstborn son of a king or queen. A more familiar example for Americans is the leader we often must tolerate when the owner of an enterprise places a son or daughter in an authoritative position regardless of personal qualifications or ability. Because of the power assigned to the position, the person in the position has persuasive and influencing ability. When the positional leader has the expertise to manage and also possesses the power and influence derived from being the people's choice, successful administration is likely to result.

Administration/Management

The terms *administration* and *management,* as previously stated, are considered by us to be synonymous and are used interchangeably throughout this text. In its simplest form, management is the act of arranging and organizing materials and conditions so that the goals and purposes of an organization may be achieved. It is both an art and a science and consists of leading and working with people, planning for and providing resources, and then organizing and controlling those resources toward desired outcomes.

In considering management as both an art and a science, we can compare it to a two-sided coin. On the art side of the coin, management is the specific skill of adept performance, conceived as requiring the exercise of intuitive faculties that cannot be learned solely by study. Although management skills cannot be learned by study alone, they certainly can be improved by studying and employing a system of principles and methods. As a musician who is born with specific intuitive fac-

Coaches, readily recognized as leaders, are not considered administrative, even though they perform managerial functions.

ulties in music can become a better musician through hard work and study, so can the person who has specific intuitive skills in working with people become a more effective administrator through extended study and practice.

On the science side of the coin, management is classified as a social science, not an exact science. Through studying the existing system of concepts, premises, principles, and expert opinions, a person can more confidently and successfully relate to other people, which is absolutely essential in achieving worthy organizational goals. By using the logical reasoning and analytical methods of the scientific approach to problem solving, a manager can be most effective.

WHY STUDY ADMINISTRATION?

Why is the study of leadership and administration important? This is a very legitimate question, and

The exploding concern of Americans about personal health and fitness has created
a job market for physical educators and fitness experts unparalleled in history.

physical education students and some faculty members in higher education ask it quite often, especially when major curriculum revisions are being considered. Based upon reflection on past experiences and the reality of the currently accepted styles of leadership, we propose four reasons why an administration course in physical education, fitness, and sports should be a core requirement in the major curriculum.

To Gain a Theoretical Foundation

In talking with athletics directors, department chairs, and fitness directors about their preparation for the position they now hold, we have found that it is not difficult to tell those who have had solid course experience in administration from those who have not. Those who do not have formal training always talk about their on-the-job experience as being the key factor in their ability to manage. Experience is important, and it plays a pivotal role in anyone's maturation; but a basic foundation for managerial ability can also result from a good course in leadership, management skills, and theory. Repeatedly, those directors and administrators who have had a good course experience state that they still rely very heavily upon the administrative principles and concepts acquired from their undergraduate study of administration.

Students can acquire a feel for managing by applying learned administrative concepts to case studies in the classroom. Although all managers learn to some extent by trial and error, those whose education has included a practical and theoretical course in management rely on trial and error much less. Consequently, they make fewer errors early in their experience, and clientele services do not suffer while they are learning.

To Acquire Leadership Skills Required in Entry-Level Positions

Beginning professionals in the field of physical education, fitness, and recreation enter positions that from the very first day require proficiency in leadership skills. A fitness director in a corporation is not available, and does not have the time, to make the decisions that the aerobics and weight-training instructors encounter in their routine workday. Can you imagine a coach with a team on a broken-down bus thirty-five miles from the site of the contest and an equal distance from home throwing up her hands in despair because the athletics director is not there to make the decision as to what must be done? Of course not! The coach must decide how to proceed in correcting the predicament and how to occupy the team members until the problem is corrected. She becomes the decision maker and the administrator for her team. Studying administration will help prepare her to move through those administrative functions with confidence and wisdom.

To Improve as a Participant in the Group Process

Very few dictators survive as administrators of physical education or athletics departments, corporate or hospital fitness centers, or community and private sports clubs or associations. If you stay in the profession, unless you open your own business, you are likely to be employed in one of these work settings. In the United States, health, fitness, and physical education professionals have insisted on participating in their own governance. The democratic way is slow, sloppy, and frustrating at times, but it works because all people who so desire are involved in and have an opportunity for input into those decisions that affect their jobs and lives.

Participation carries with it the responsibility to understand the functions, processes, and principles of administration and to appreciate the difficult role of the leader or manager. With this understanding and appreciation, teachers, coaches, or exercise specialists can participate more effectively in the process that can significantly affect their own destinies. Participating members of an organizational unit who understand the role of committees, unit directors, and upper-level management have a more satisfying and rewarding experience while pursuing the goals of the enterprise.

To Manage Your Personal Life

The most important value derived from the study of administration may be related more to the activities of your private life than to job-related activities. A person's life away from work is in most cases more complex than within the organization. Relation to family, maintaining a home, and meeting family objectives can create more decision-making circumstances than professional obligations create. Planning, organizing, and problem-solving skills learned in an administration class will carry over into domestic life. These skills not only prepare you for, and assist you in coping with, life's demands, but they also are basic to the healthy, happy, and rewarding feeling of reaching life goals. Living with a spouse and sending children from elementary school through college, for example, do not flow smoothly along without someone's exercising effective managerial skills. Such skills as good communication and delegation are not restricted to your job.

LEADERSHIP OPPORTUNITIES IN ACTIVITY-BASED PROGRAMS

From the beginning of human history, competent leaders have been needed. No doubt during cave-dwelling times, leaders emerged to direct their tribes in the search for food and shelter, battles against other tribes, and the simple activities of government. Competition for leadership positions was surely as evident then as now. As long as the leader was competent and held a concern for his constituency above his own personal desires, dislodging him could have been difficult. But if personal greed became a priority and his leadership was without justice, then he might soon be replaced by whatever means necessary—possibly even a fight unto death.

Opportunities always have existed and always will exist for well-prepared, competent, and dedicated leaders.

In the field of physical education, fitness, and sports, the opportunities are more challenging than ever. The need for directors, department chairs, and coaches in the school systems will continue; and as the population increases, so will the need for leaders. Besides this continued need, the exploding concern of Americans about personal health and fitness has created a job market for physical educators and fitness experts unparalleled in history. The need for program and executive leaders or directors is so great now that the industry is hiring people with management training in executive roles whether they have adequate preparation in exercise science or not. The health and fitness industry needs executives and administrators with strong backgrounds in both exercise science and management. That need is not going to diminish, because fitness is not a passing fad. The benefits of exercise have been established, and the general public has been educated to understand those values.

POWER, AUTHORITY, AND THE DIRECTOR

Power and authority are tools of both charismatic and positional leaders and are directly related to their performances. For a director to be effective, power and authority are absolute essentials. Without authority, a director is only a record keeper and messenger between the organizational unit and the one who does hold authority. To understand the reality and importance of power and authority in the director's role, an in-depth discussion is needed.

The Nature of Power and Authority

Authority is defined as the right to control use of resources, to set program direction, and to enforce established policies and regulations of the organization. The director gains authority through the process of delegation. In a school setting, the board of education is empowered by the state legislature to operate and control the school system. In turn, the board delegates the responsibility and authority to the superintendent to serve as the chairman of the board, and the superintendent passes the authority to operate a particular school down to the principal. The principal who is responsible for the school delegates the power that originated in the state legislature to the physical education and athletics directors.

Corporate fitness directors and directors of private fitness clubs or YMCAs are officially granted their authority in a similar fashion, although in a smaller operation the route from owner to director may be a one-step authorization. The amount of authority that a director has is limited by the amount that the director's immediate superior has and by how much of that authority and responsibility the superior wishes to release. It may range from no power to full power.

Since power is attached to authority, we should

The director's duties may include control over things and people—personnel, programs, facilities.

examine it more closely. *Power* can be defined as the ability or official capacity to exercise control or authority. That control may be over things or people; and in the case of a director, it should be over personnel, program, and facilities that constitute the full scope of administration. Power provides the director the capacity to influence and make changes within the scope of the assigned responsibilities. It usually is related to either possessing resources that others desire or having access to those resources. The greater a director's ability to satisfy the needs and desires of others, the more power he or she has. As mentioned earlier, the power may come from the position, or it may result from having a following. Ideally, the director has power from both sources.

Also noteworthy is that the director's influence downward is proportional to his or her influence upward. The more influence the director has with his or her superior, the more influence he or she will have with subordinates. This balance is always maintained. To illustrate, if a superior delegates only a small amount of authority to the director, the director does not have much influence downward, because he or she has not influenced the superior to the degree needed to gain more

power; also, if the director is originally delegated a large amount of power but cannot use that power effectively in influencing subordinates, then his or her influence on the superior proportionately diminishes, and the power may be withdrawn. Bob Hayes, former dean and president of Marshall University, stated that power and authority cannot be delegated, but the right to assume power and authority can be. In other words, it takes action on the part of a director to use the power available.

Ethics in Administration

Few would argue with the statement that leaders and organizations have a responsibility to behave ethically.

What is ethical behavior and how do managers insure that it is a hallmark of their organization or business? Ethics are principles of right and wrong in conduct. Ethics include duties, obligations, rights, and responsibilities. In making ethical decisions, a person uses words like *ought, should, fair, unfair.* The term *ethics* is usually applied to professional conduct, whereas *morality* is used to describe personal conduct.

Ethics are based on legal requirements, moral requirements, and social/cultural considerations. Each society, culture, and organization has traditions, mores, or expectations which determine if an action is ethical. In many cases, an action cannot be judged to be either ethical or unethical unless the societal or organizational climate is taken into consideration.

Why is it important to be ethical? Because people need to know what to expect when confronted with a specific set of factors, individuals, organizations, and societies must behave ethically to bring order and consistency to situations. It is also easier to live with oneself if one behaves ethically. It has been said that a good conscience is the softest pillow.

Why is it that we regularly read and hear of unethical and immoral behavior by officials, leaders, and sports figures? People who make unethical decisions are not necessarily bad people but often moral people who find themselves in an ambiguous situation. Situations can become ambiguous when an organization has no clearly defined standard of conduct or clearly stated expectations. Increasingly, organizations are developing codes of ethics which guide all activities carried out by employees. These codes range in detail and specificity but serve as a guide for employees' dealings with the public, other employees, and the organization.

The Northrop Corporation's Code of Ethics and Standards of Conduct statement could serve as a model for many organizations. It contains general principles as well as specific guidelines to help employees perform ethically. The statement, "At Northrop, every individual is responsible for both the integrity and the consequences of his or her actions," is a general principle. A specific guideline would be: "Employees will not use company information, property, or services for personal gain; the unauthorized removal of company materials, supplies, or equipment is prohibited." The document, which is only two pages long, serves as a guideline of conduct against which any action can be measured.

Every manager has a responsibility to ensure that his or her unit or organization displays the highest standards of conduct. These standards must be communicated clearly to all employees so that everyone knows what is expected of them in every situation. There are a number of ways to accomplish this: One method is via the written code of ethics; another is to develop a climate in the organization where ethical conduct is nurtured, even required. Although the development of an ethical organization may require considerable effort, it is always time well spent—even one occurrence of unethical activity can substantially damage an organization's reputation, one ill-conceived action by a manager or employee can negate years of hard work. Regardless of the method selected to ensure ethical conduct at all levels within an organization, the leader of the unit must serve as a model of integrity for the rest of the members to emulate. Ethical behavior starts at the top.

Resources over Which the Director Has Power

As mentioned earlier, a director has power because he or she possesses something, or has access to something, that others desire. A look at the resources a director controls should provide a better understanding of the statement.

Knowledge Knowledge is power, and the director is usually the first in a department to know what the future holds in regard to program budget, new positions or cutbacks, available funds for pay increases or new equipment, and the priorities of higher-level authorities. These normally are items of interest to every employee. The news that the director possesses may be good or bad, and properly sharing the information takes a certain degree of skill. For example, if funds are not available for pay increases for the following year, the director should not try to blame the misfortune on some specific person. Being quick to lay blame is an indication that the director may be insecure in his or her own position, and it serves no other purpose than to create a negative attitude in the minds of the other personnel. The director has an obligation to shape attitudes in a positive direction, and that may require highlighting the good things about the organization in hopes that they overshadow the negatives. Similarly, if the news is good, the director should share the information in such a way that subordinates believe they are responsible for the success.

Budget The allocation of department funds concerns every employee. The director controls the allocation and has a responsibility to share funds equitably. Salary increases, equipment purchases, funding for special-interest programs, and professional travel funds are four budget items that hold the interest of subordinates. Those affected (which includes everyone) should have input in establishing guidelines for resource allocation, but the final decision rests with the director. On the surface, the director may appear to have an easy way out: dividing equally the resources among the employees. The problem with this procedure is that the only ones who are pleased with it are those who know that they are not as deserving as others. For example, those who best represent the organization at professional meetings should get a larger slice of travel funds, and the innovative and productive staff member should get a larger raise than the one who just fulfills minimum requirements.

Task Assignments   Productive employees should be rewarded with prime assignments. The employee as well as the organization reaps the benefits when this occurs. On the other hand, non-preferred tasks should not be assigned in a vindictive spirit. The director must have the courage to inform the less productive or nonproductive staff person why assignments are made as they are, and to encourage the person to lift himself or herself up to a deserving position for the preferred assignments. A wise director can sometimes rid the department of a staff liability through the power of assignment.

Defense   The director is the defender of the organizational unit. He or she is the one who carries the message from the department to the upper levels of administration. With this power comes the responsibility to represent the consensus of the department members, and the wise director makes sure either the consensus or the position of the power people is supported. The director has the power to push for personal aspirations if these do not diverge far from those of the people being served. It is fair to state that a director is in

many cases in a position to know what is best for the department if he or she maintains an unselfish stance.

Communications   The director is responsible for communications to the outside world—newspapers, alumni, professional organizations, school and business leaders, and central administrators. By being the voice of the department or organization, the director is in a position to give advice, provide information, and influence the thoughts and opinions of important people.

Committee Appointments   In most instances, the director has the power to place people on important committees. Those who will represent the views of the director are usually put on these committees. Adversaries get the noninfluential assignments. Thus, a director can wield power through committee action.

In reviewing the influence that an administrator possesses, we can see that a director is not just another department or organization member who chairs meetings and carries the messages and votes forward. The director has influence, power, and the authority to control resources.

DIFFERENT STYLES OF LEADERSHIP AND MANAGEMENT

Leadership and management styles vary as much as personalities. Each individual in a leadership role has his or her own mode of operation, and each director's style has certain unique characteristics. Still, a small number of general styles can be identified, and each leader's method of operation is similar to one of these. Managerial styles have been classified as authoritarian, participatory, or anarchic.

AUTHORITARIAN   PARTICIPATORY   ANARCHIC

Managerial styles have been classified as: authoritarian, participatory, anarchic.

The Authoritarian Style of Management

The authoritarian style of leadership is often referred to as the autocratic style, and that is exactly what it is. Authoritarians have the initial and final voice in all decision-making situations. They are dictators with absolute authority and power, and their rule can be either oppressive or benevolent. Life under these two types of dictators is very different, even though the precepts guiding each are similar in many ways.

The Oppressive Dictator   This authoritarian leader rules with an iron fist. There is very little, if any, consultation by this type of dictator. Strict command and response is the order of the day. A very rigid chain of command exists, and those at every level are expected to do as they are told without objection or reason. Those who dare question or rebel against the command are eliminated or pushed into a corner of the organization where they are ineffective. The oppressive dictator surrounds himself or herself with a small circle of yea-sayers who are expected to acclaim the superiority of the leader. The opinions and the participation of the majority relative to rule or governance are neither sought nor tolerated. In Western society, this type of administrator or leader is rapidly disappearing from the scene because the courts take a strong position supporting

individual rights when unjust actions have been challenged. In the United States, this leadership style has always been less effective than the participatory style.

The Benevolent Dictator   Life under this style of autocratic rule can be quite enjoyable and sometimes productive. The benevolent dictator is similar to the oppressive dictator in that strict obedience to rules and policies is expected, and only the opinions of a very few are sought. The opinions of most of the members of the organization are treated as those of children. It is surprising how many people working in this democratic society prefer this style to the participatory style of governance. The one important difference between the benevolent dictator and the oppressive dictator is the sincere concern this parentlike leader has for the well-being of subordinates in the organizational unit.

Insight through Illustration

In a high school athletic department directed by a kind, fatherly gentleman, a recently hired young coach came to the director to suggest what he thought was a more effective way of operating the concession stands at the athletic contests. The athletic director listened to the suggestions, but in a fatherly manner closed the brief meeting with the comment, "Tom, I appreciate your concern for improving the operations of the department; however, I have found that young coaches get along much better if they observe how we do things for four or five years before trying to change them. If after that period you still think improvements are needed, come back and see me."

This example is very typical of the benevolent dictator's style of leadership. The athletic director was firmly convinced that his way was best, but he did not wish to be unkind to a member of his department family.

One of the major disadvantages of the authoritarian style is that it stifles initiative and creativity. Because the autocrat is uncomfortable with change, the danger of stagnation is ever-present. Unjust treatment of subordinates who do not fall in line is another major disadvantage. Other disadvantages include a lack of continuity, high turnover of employees, and a low level of morale. Although the disadvantages seem to greatly outweigh the advantages, some positive points can be made for dictatorships. Expediency and efficiency usually result from the methods, and if the leader communicates well, all members of the organization always know exactly where they stand and what to expect. A smooth, trouble-free operation results when everyone accepts the style.

The Participatory Style of Management

The participatory style is the American way. It is the form of governance most readily acceptable to those who believe in government of the people, by the people, and for the people. It is democratic in nature, but by that very fact requires more effort on the part of each individual in a group than any other form of administration. It is slower and more inefficient than any other style, and as the organization becomes larger, bureaucratic hindrances can be expected. Unlike other styles, it requires more effort from managers, as they must constantly be motivating their subordinates to fully participate by doing their homework before casting their input into the decision-making process.

The role of the democratic director is often misunderstood by other members of the organizational unit, and the director must make it clear that he or she is the decision maker of the unit. It is his or her responsibility to see that every member has an opportunity to participate in the process of making and revising policies, and it behooves any director to seek the involvement in decision making of each person who will be affected by the decision under consideration. Note that every member is given the opportunity to have input within a reasonable period of time. If unit members do not respond to the opportunity, they are in the same class as voters who have the opportunity to vote but, for whatever reason, fail to exercise their privilege. And although all members have the opportunity to take part in the decision-making process, the final decision still rests with the leader.

Whenever any administrator is appointed to the position of leadership, confidence and authority must accompany the responsibility of the position. The leader is the decision maker and must be trusted to receive input and feedback from every appropriate source and then make the best decision based on all the evidence. One reason why the final decision must rest on the shoulders of one person is that a group cannot be held accountable: If a decision is made by a vote of the majority and that decision goes wrong, finding those who will claim responsibility for the mistake will be difficult.

If the participatory style of management is so cumbersome and difficult, why is it recommended? The reasons are as follows:

Through the group process, students hone their skills in participatory management, a method of leadership most compatible with the American notion of freedom and democracy.

- The members of an organization more easily accept decisions and working conditions if they have an equitable role in establishing them.
- Creativity and initiative are enhanced when people know that their ideas have a chance of becoming reality.
- Program continuity is maintained even when the administrator is replaced or leaves.
- It is compatible with the freedom of living in America.

Good human relations are vital for any effective working effort. The considerate leader who is devoted to the welfare of the employees will have an effective group. The manager whose staff has been highly effective is much more likely to involve them in the decision-making process than one whose staff has been ineffective or hostile toward him or her as an administrator. For a staff to be productive, they must be challenged to establish worthy goals and then encouraged and assisted in meeting those goals.

Insight through Illustration

The writer recently attended a university-sponsored conference entitled Management of Quality. Representatives from IBM, Xerox, TRW, Hewlett-Packard, Federal Express, Pacific Bell, Lockheed, Cadillac, Westinghouse, American Eagle, California State University, Cal Poly University, and Oregon State University served as lecturers and session leaders. The theme from every corporate leader related to total quality management, a philosophy of management that has recently been adopted by highly successful industrial and educational organizations across the nation.

Edward Deming, pioneer of the movement, first introduced the managerial approach to industry forty years ago. The Japanese adopted the philosophy, but U.S. companies were unwilling to change until recently. It is assumed that the belated willingness to change was motivated by the reality that the Japanese were experiencing much greater success in productivity than their U.S. counterparts.

The conference theme communicated by every speaker was total customer satisfaction and employee participation and input in all company activities, including management. To illustrate what total quality management means, the words and statements repeated over and over during the conference are listed below:

- focus on the customer
- participation—the key to quality
- be ethical, inspiring, empowering, enabling, and open
- team interaction rather than individual competition
- lead by example
- respect the individual
- build on leadership and trust
- action without a vision is activity; action with a vision is productivity.

Effective administrators guide instead of dictate; coach instead of direct; lead instead of manage from a distance; empower instead of control; encourage rather than reprimand; and motivate rather than threaten.

The Anarchic Style of Management

Very little space will be devoted to discussing the anarchic style of management. Some consider it more a mode of operation than a style of management because it is characterized by leaderless actions. Anarchy, in a broad sense, means the absence of any form of authority, and it is typified by disorder and confusion. *Laissez-faire* is the term most often used in referring to the anarchic type of administration. Because it is impossible to imagine a leader who does not exercise some authority, managers who are pure anarchists do not

exist. Just to inform subordinates to do their own thing constitutes a decision-making effort. However, administrators do exist who more closely follow the precepts of this style than any other.

Some program directors and department heads say, "I just hire good people and then get out of their way and don't interfere." The statement sounds appealing and pleasant on the surface, and many would immediately respond that they would like to work under those conditions. But it does not take long to realize that coordinated effort by a group of people cannot occur without someone leading. When individuals are permitted to establish their own goals and do as they please in pursuing those goals, organizational chaos is not far behind. The unified effort never becomes a reality, and complacency takes over as the organization decays. This style of governance will not survive. History has taught us that a strong dictatorship will soon prevail over the unstable mode of operation. The total freedom precept is not recommended.

The most common styles of management found in the physical education and fitness departments in North America are eclectic in nature. This means that most are basically democratic with varying amounts of laissez-faire and authoritarian precepts existing. Each leader needs to find the style with which he or she and the staff are most comfortable and then work together toward being maximally productive. The key to such success depends on how effective the manager really is and how dedicated he or she is in striving for the well-being of the employees, the employer, and, most of all, the clientele being served.

GUIDES FOR MANAGERIAL DECISIONS AND ACTIONS

Guides for managerial decisions and actions are statements that offer the decision maker direction and are referred to throughout the text as *action guides*. These action guides are based on truths, facts, concepts, premises, or expert opinions; and, in most cases, they can be categorized as principles, policies, standards, benchmarks, procedures, or rules.

The difference between principles, policies, standards, benchmarks, procedures, and rules can often seem confusing. They are listed here in the proper order of stability.

Principles

Principles are generalizations or hypotheses that have been tested for accuracy and appear to be true in reflecting or explaining reality. In the absence of truths or facts, they are based on opinions of experts from the field to which they are being applied. They are quite stable and have value in predicting what will happen when similar circumstances prevail. They are not as stable and unchanging as laws, but they are more stable than policies, standards, procedures, and rules. They certainly can be used as reliable decision or action guides.

Example: Everyone affected by a decision should have an opportunity for involvement in making the decision.

Policies

Policies are statements that guide or channel thinking and action in decision making. They are based on hypotheses, principles, truths, facts, expert opinion. Sometimes, in the absence of these elements, they may be based on expediency. A policy is less stable and more likely to change than a principle. All principles can be policies, but not all policies can be principles.

Example: No employee shall accept any gift or money from a merchant or supplier at any time except for token gifts of nominal and minimal value.

Standards or Benchmarks

A standard can be defined as a requirement of some degree or level of excellence or attainment. As it applies to administration, a standard can be considered to be a normal or acceptable level of quality or performance, usually established by the organization. An administrative standard is less stable than a principle and is subject to frequent change.

Example: Applicants for the advertised position must have a bachelor's degree.

A benchmark is a term that has been coined by quality management experts from industry. Our use of the term is defined as: a requirement of some degree or level of excellence or attainment more specific than a standard.

Example: Applicants for the advertised position must have a bachelor's degree with a specialization in corporate fitness.

Procedures

Procedures are methods or techniques for conducting activities. They describe the exact manner in which a certain activity must be accomplished. As the administrator usually has total freedom in selecting procedures to carry out policy, procedures change often.

Example: When an application for an advertised position is received, a letter of acknowledgment is sent to the applicant.

Rules

A rule is an authoritative directive regarding conduct or procedure. Rules are established by the local enterprise or specific organizational unit. They are more subject to change than any of the other action guides listed.

Example: On the baseball field there will be no pepper games in front of the seating areas.

KEY WORDS AND PHRASES

Administration

Anarchic

Charismatic leaders

Leadership

Motivation to lead

Positional leaders

Principles

Authority

Policies

Benchmarks

Standards

Productivity

Action guides

Authoritarian

Participatory

Management

Power

Rules

QUESTIONS FOR REVIEW

1. Define the following terms:
   a. administration
   b. management
   c. leadership
   d. power
   e. authority

2. List four reasons why physical education majors should take a course in management of activity-based programs.

3. Explain the difference between power and authority.

4. Why is it important to be ethical in physical education and athletic organizations?

5. What is a manager's responsibility regarding ethics?

6. Identify the resources over which a director of an activity-based program has authority or power.

7. List four reasons why the participatory style of governance is preferred over the other traditional styles.

8. What is the difference between a policy and a principle? A standard and a benchmark? A rule and a procedure?

SELF-TEST

Corrected True-False

If the statement is true, mark it T. If the statement is false, mark it F and change it to a true statement by adding or deleting words.

_____ 1. Management and leadership are synonymous terms.

_____ 2. Leadership can occur without intent.

_____ 3. Management is classified as a social science rather than an exact science.

_____ 4. The participatory style of administration is slow, sloppy, and frustrating at times.

_____ 5. A desired result of taking an administration course is the value derived in managing one's own personal life.

_____ 6. Power and authority are tools of both charismatic and positional leaders.

_____ 7. The director's influence downward has very little relationship to his or her influence upward.

_____ 8. The ability or capacity to act or perform effectively and provide satisfaction is referred to as power.

Multiple Choice

_____ 9. The right to command, determine, judge, and enforce rules is referred to as:
   a. management
   b. leadership
   c. authority
   d. power

_____ 10. Which style of management is referred to as a dictatorship?
   a. anarchic
   b. autocratic
   c. authoritative
   d. either b or c

_____ 11. Which of the following action guides is less changing than the others?
   a. principle
   b. policy
   c. standard
   d. benchmark

_____ 12. Ethics are based on:
   a. legal requirements
   b. moral requirements
   c. social/cultural considerations
   d. all of the above

_____ 13. Which is most similar to a standard?
   a. a principle
   b. a policy
   c. a procedure
   d. a benchmark

_____ 14. The most effective leaders usually have which of the following?
   a. charisma
   b. authoritative position
   c. top salaries
   d. both a and b

_____ 15. This is not a reason to take a management course:
   a. to gain charisma
   b. to gain a theoretical base
   c. as preparation for managing one's personal life
   d. to be better able to serve in a participatory group situation

CASE 1.1 SHOULD THE MANAGEMENT COURSE REMAIN IN THE CORE?

The Health, Physical Education and Recreation faculty at Blackford State University were in the process of reviewing the physical education major requirements for their 1994–1996 catalog. The department had been adding classes to the major for the past few years without dropping required courses. Without exceeding the 124 semester units needed for the bachelor of science degree, the students were restricted to only three units of free electives. This was considered too restrictive, and the curriculum committee was asked to review the courses in the core requirements and bring a recommendation to the faculty as to whether two or three courses could be dropped from the core. When the next department meeting was held, Dr. Susan Pillar stood to present the committee recommendation. Susan stated that she and the other members had carefully considered each course in the core requirements as a candidate for change from a required course for all concentrations to an elective. She stated that all three members agreed that only one course— Management of Physical Education and Fitness Programs—should be eliminated as a core requirement. Dr. Joe Clay, another member of the committee, presented the following rationale for the recommendation:

1. None of the teaching-option graduates would be taking jobs as physical education or athletics directors. They would teach and coach, whereas the more experienced teachers would become administrators.

2. Some of the corporate fitness graduates would be appointed to first-level management positions, but the course was being taught from a textbook that addressed situations and problems only from a school setting. Also, they assumed that most corporations preferred to train their own managerial staff.

Dr. Chris Janes, the instructor of the administration course, was asked by the department head to respond to the committee report. Dr. Janes came to the meeting well prepared and was ready to state his position.

Your Response

1. What is the central issue?
2. What are the problems with the committee report?
3. What are some barriers or hurdles that may stand in the way of the best decision?
4. What should Dr. Janes' position be and what actions are needed?
5. What action guides can be used to oppose the committee recommendation?

BIBLIOGRAPHY

Bucher, Charles. *Administration of Health and Physical Education Programs Including Athletics.* St. Louis: Mosby, 1980.

Dougherty, Neil J., and Diane Bonanno. *Management Principles in Sport and Leisure Services.* Minneapolis: Burgess, 1985.

Drucker, Peter F. *The Effective Executive.* New York: Harper & Row, 1966.

———. *The Frontiers of Management.* New York: Harper & Row, 1987.

Eble, Kenneth E. *The Art of Administration.* San Francisco: Jossey-Bass, 1978.

Frost, Reubin B., and Stanley J. Marshall. *Administration of Physical Education and Athletics: Concepts and Practices*. Dubuque, IA: William C. Brown, 1981.

"Has the 'Fitness Boom' Gone Bust?" *Athletic Purchasing and Facilities* 7 (July 1983): 13–16.

Johnson, M. L. *Functional Administration in Physical and Health Education*. Boston: Houghton Mifflin, 1977.

Koontz, Harold, and Heinz Weihrich. *Essentials of Management*. 5th ed. New York: McGraw-Hill, 1989.

Resick, Matthew, Beverly Seidel, and James G. Mason. *Modern Administrative Practices in Physical Education and Athletics*. 3rd ed. New York: Random House, 1979.

Tucker, Allan. *Chairing the Academic Department: Leadership among Peers*. Washington, DC: American Council on Education, 1981.

VanderZwaag, Harold J. *Sport Management in Schools and Colleges*. New York: Wiley, 1984.

Ziegler, Earle F. *Decision-Making in Physical Education and Athletic Administration: A Case Method Approach*. Champaigne, IL: Stipes, 1982.

2

The Purpose and Scope of Managing Physical Education, Fitness, and Sports Programs

The future belongs to those who prepare for it.
Ralph Waldo Emerson

Chapter Objectives

After reading this chapter and completing the exercises, you should be able to:

1 Identify the purpose of management and for whom management exists

2 Explain what is meant by *scope of management* and identify the three areas of responsibility falling under the scope

3 List the two most important basic skills of management and explain why they are so important

4 Identify the qualities an office manager should possess

5 Explain the importance of developing an office management manual

6 Discuss the three most basic processes or functions of management

7 Define supervision and evaluation and explain how they relate to the controlling function

So far we have discussed what management is, which resources the director controls, and how he or she controls them. But what, exactly, does a manager do? We turn to that question now.

THE PURPOSE OF MANAGEMENT

The purpose of management is to get the right things done and to get things done right. Management's only reason for being is to make the program or the organization effective. Management exists for people; people do not exist for management. Administrators sometimes lose sight of these concepts, and when that occurs, the organization has greater difficulty in achieving its goals. When organizational goals become secondary to managerial goals, faculty or staff become displeased with what they see occurring, and their production level decreases.

THE SCOPE OF MANAGEMENT

The scope of managerial responsibilities encompasses three areas: personnel, program, and facilities. Every administrative duty falls under one of those three headings, as the following lists indicate.

Personnel Matters

In the area of personnel lie the responsibilities that consume most of a director's time. This is also where the most significant decisions are usually made. Personnel matters can include:

- recruiting and recommending appointments of staff
- assigning appropriate responsibilities to instructors, coaches, and other personnel

- observing and maintaining records of staff performance
- communicating performance ratings to employees
- monitoring and initiating actions to maintain or improve morale
- initiating recommendations for pay raises and promotions
- responding to staff performances that are not satisfactory
- initiating termination procedures
- promoting and encouraging participation of staff members in professional activities
- conducting in-service training programs for staff
- stimulating individuals toward research and publishing activities
- serving as a mediator and counselor to prevent conflict among staff members
- delegating appropriate responsibilities to individuals on committees
- encouraging unit members to make suggestions for improvement
- evaluating staff performance

Program Responsibilities

It is critical that a quality program be offered in any administrative situation. In the educational setting, a physically educated student is the product of a good program. In the public, private, and corporate fitness settings, the organization's existence depends upon providing a sound and satisfying program of activities. Activities relating to programming are:

- scheduling
- revising curricula, courses, and programs as needed

Scheduling employees' work time satisfactorily to both employer and employee is just one of the jobs of management.

- supervising in-house and extended programs
- recruiting and enrolling students or participants
- advising and counseling program participants
- communicating unit needs to the next administrative level
- maintaining and/or improving the program's image and reputation
- coordinating activities with other programs
- providing information about the program when requested by agencies and individuals
- preparing and proposing the department or program budget
- seeking funding and grants from other organizational sources
- controlling the department or program budget
- establishing priorities and approving travel funds for program members
- preparing year-end reports
- serving as the principal advocate for the department or program

- conducting meetings of the department or program
- establishing and using department committees
- developing and implementing long-range plans for programs

Facility Concerns

Even though facility concerns and problems are usually less perplexing, the administrative responsibilities relating to facilities require a significant amount of time of the director of an activity-based program. Some of these responsibilities follow.

- initiating recommendations for new and renovated facilities
- serving on and/or advising facility task forces
- working closely with the architect in planning new facilities
- supervising facility maintenance directly or indirectly
- maintaining a master schedule of facilities
- leading in establishing priorities for facility use
- purchasing or requesting needed equipment
- maintaining safe condition of facilities and equipment
- inventorying equipment and maintaining records

As this list of duties makes clear, the job of administration is complex and difficult, and those who can accept such a challenge and be effective are, indeed, unique.

The scope of management for the physical education, athletics, or fitness director is illustrated in Figure 2.1. Every administrative function falls within the scope of these three concerns.

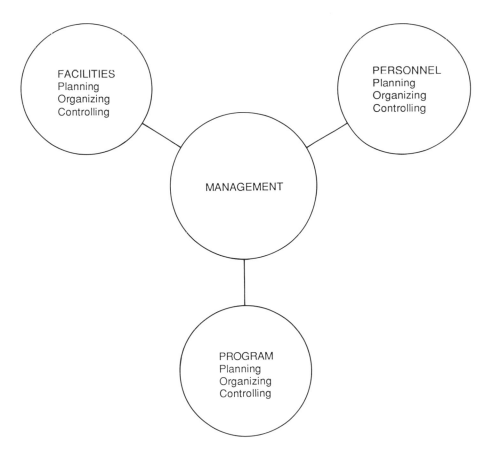

Figure 2.1 *The Scope of Management: Every Administrative Function Falls within These Three Concerns.*

MANAGING THE OFFICE

Sound office management can be attained through good leadership, a qualified staff, a well-planned environment in which to work, and the appropriate tools and equipment to get the job done right. Office procedures may vary from one department or fitness organization to another, but the objectives of each will show a marked similarity.

In most departments and fitness environments, the office management function is the re-sponsibility of the director, associate director, or a senior secretary who has been delegated that responsibility. He or she and his or her staff are expected to provide the administrative support needed for management decision making, formulation and implementation of plans, and efficient conduct of business. The office management staff is also looked to for ideas which will improve the service, membership sales, and/or overall operation of the unit.

Regardless of whether the office manager is the director, owner/manager, or senior secretary, there are certain qualities the person should have:

- knowledge of accounting
- knowledge of purchasing function
- ability to manage records, word processing, and dictation
- knowledge and ability to manage mailroom distribution
- ability to deal with personnel and provide direction over their assigned tasks.

Office Layout

The office manager obviously must consider the office space and environment in which people will work. Although the office manager may not have the responsibility for office layouts, he or she should play some part in their design, especially in the planning of a new facility or renovation of an old one. Important facets would include a plan for adequate lighting, the placing of work carrels, telephones, duplicating equipment, computers, terminals, word processors, and probably lateral filing cabinets or open shelves; even placement of the water cooler and the coffee maker and its supplies need planning.

Properly placed equipment results in an atmosphere conducive to efficient operation and will put every inch of prime office space to the most productive use. With the high cost for such space, office layout is always an important concern of management.

Office Management Manual

A policy and procedures manual is a comprehensive guide to control all operations under the direction of the office management function. The manual should follow a well-defined outline and be written in concise, direct language. Procedures should be outlined in detail and examples clearly defined.

The preparation of the manual begins with an outline made up of clear main headings and subheadings. The following example (Heyel and Menkus, 1986) may be expanded or reduced to meet the needs of a particular department or fitness center.

I. Introduction

The purpose of the manual

A brief philosophical statement about the office

The goals and policies for the department or entity

Directions

Directions for using the manual and for updating it to ensure its keeping pace with the unit's growth, changes in service, or accepted suggestions from the staff

II. The Department's or Unit's Organizational Plan

A copy of either an organization chart or chain-of-command statement

III. Unit Policies

Personnel

A description of employee responsibilities and benefits

Operating

General regulations

Purchasing

Limitation of purchases billed to department

Ordering procedures

Management of supplies and inventory control

IV. Records Management

General information and listings of subjects

V. Forms Control
    Responsibilities for creating and controlling

VI. Exhibits
    Reproductions of forms, rules for alphabetizing, established forms for letters or memos, samples of numerical sequences if applicable

VII. Title Page and Index
    When the manual is in its final form, you can prepare a title page, followed by the table of contents. As a final step, add a detailed index as a tool for locating any information offered in the manual.

Distribute the manual to all employees of the department or unit. A sound office management plan, well documented in the manual, will provide the foundation for better service and satisfaction among all who are being served.

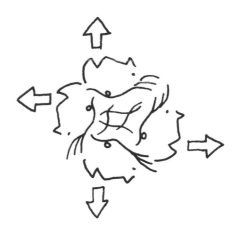

For effective communication, communicate continually in every direction—up, down, and sideways.

BASIC SKILLS AND FUNCTIONS OF MANAGEMENT

The most basic skills needed by a manager or director are communicating and decision making. The most basic processes or functions for which the manager is responsible are planning, organizing, and controlling. We will look only briefly at each of these skills and functions here, but later in the text an entire chapter is devoted to each.

Communicating

Communication is the cement that binds an organization together. The importance of effective communication cannot be overemphasized. A recent survey found that a majority of directors of fitness, athletics, and recreation selected communication over all other skills as being most important in their jobs. Many directors and managers fail to communicate well, even though all talk about the necessity for it. Ineffective communication is the leading cause of people problems. Effective communication has many prerequisites, but perhaps the most important one is to communicate continually in every direction—up, down, and sideways.

Decision Making

Making decisions is the primary concern of the administrator, and making effective decisions is the mark of an able administrator. Because an administrator is hired to make decisions, decision making is the one skill everyone expects him or her to do well. One of the qualities that sets the administrator apart is the willingness to face problems and take the responsibility to decide. The possession of this skill is the reason, more than any other, why the administrator receives a better salary, more prestige, and more power and authority than others in the organization. The administrator cannot avoid making decisions. Even choosing to do nothing is a decision. There is no magic ingredient in making wise decisions, but a good decision maker knows that the objectives of

MAYBE I'LL CUT THE GRASS...

OR SHOULD I WASH THE CAR?

HO-HUM... I'LL DECIDE TOMORROW...

Indecisive as this man appears, he has made a decision.

the organization must serve as the guide to success.

The final step in the decision-making process is to put the decision into action. If any enterprise is to succeed in reaching its goals, its leaders must be oriented toward action. The director's skill in decision making is wasted if plans and decisions are not put into action.

Planning   People do not plan to fail; they fail to plan. Planning is the administrative function that precedes all others. The administrator's ability to look ahead and lead the members of the organization in setting worthy goals and objectives for themselves as well as for the enterprise is an initial step toward succeeding. There are, basically, three prerequisites for being a good planner: good vision and perception, the ability to acquire and interpret information, and the ability to objectively set worthy goals and objectives. Risks, which always accompany decisions, are significantly minimized through a solid and ongoing planning effort.

Organizing   Organizing consists of identifying and grouping activities, assigning authority to directors and staff, and eliciting cooperation. Organization refers to an intentional structure of job

functions. People working together must occupy certain positions and be responsible for important tasks, and the activities that are intentionally planned for each individual must fit together so that the people can work efficiently, effectively, and successfully in groups. There is no single best way to organize. Such factors as the type of people involved, the people being served, the kind of service or product provided, and the technology involved may determine the pattern of organization implemented.

Controlling   Controlling is defined as regulating, directing, or exercising authority over something or someone. It is sometimes described as the function that highlights the flaws in the other functions. It ensures that the objectives of the organization are actually being achieved, and if deviations occur enroute to the objectives, it is the function exercised in making the necessary corrections. The direct route from planning to achieving organizational goals is marked by standards, and performance is measured against these standards. When a worker deviates from these standards, the administrator must exercise control by criticizing and correcting the worker. Understandably, controlling is not the most popular of the administrative functions. Two important parts of the control function are supervising and evaluating.

Supervision is the administrative function that is concerned with overseeing and assisting in the improvement of the situation within which personnel function. Good supervisors know when to intervene and advise and when to back off and leave the employee alone. The amount of supervision needed depends entirely upon the situation. Staff members who are responsible, dependable, and skilled need little or no interference. General directions and support from the supervisor may be the extent of supervision necessary for successfully attaining organizational objectives. Oversupervision may lead to discontent and resentment among the staff because of

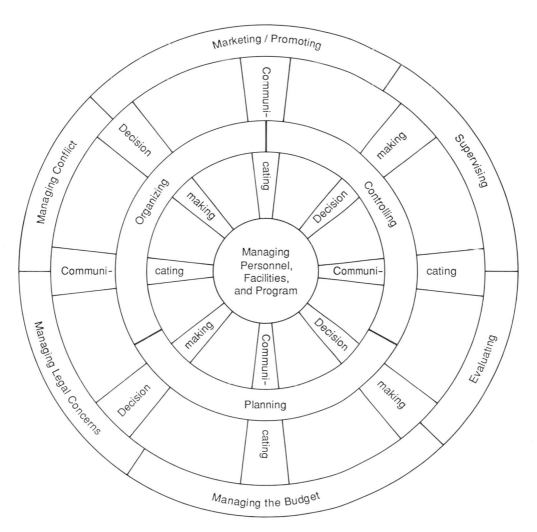

Figure 2.2 *Functions of Management*

the lack of freedom, and it may imply that the supervisor lacks confidence in the employee's ability. On the other hand, some employees may require close or constant supervision. Young and/or new employees, for example, are expected to need more supervision than tenured personnel.

To evaluate is to ascertain or determine the value or worth of something or someone. The program director evaluates personnel, program, and facilities—the entire scope of his or her responsibility. The purpose of evaluation is to determine the status of whatever or whoever is being evaluated so that a person's performance, a program's worth, or a facility's function or safety may be improved. Evaluation should be viewed by both the evaluator and the staff as a positive function, but, unfortunately, in the case of a personnel evaluation, it is too often viewed negatively. Criticism overshadows positive comments in more cases than the reverse. Evaluation should be a continual process, and it should be based upon both personal and organizational objectives.

The relationships among these basic functions of management are conceptualized in Figure 2.2, along with their relationships to the peripheral functions of managing conflict, budget, and legal concerns, and marketing. In the chapters that follow, each of these managerial functions will be covered in detail.

KEY WORDS AND PHRASES

Purpose of management

Manager's basic skills

Program concerns

Planning

Scope of management

Personnel concerns

Communication

Organizing

Basic processes

Facility concerns

Decision making

Controlling

QUESTIONS FOR REVIEW

1. What is the purpose of management?
2. What is the difference between scope of management and skills of management?
3. Explain how communication is the cement that holds an organization together.
4. List the five skills and functions that have been identified as most basic and make one significant statement about each.

5. In your opinion, what are the five most important managerial responsibilities in the area of personnel? In the area of facilities? In the area of program?
6. In your opinion, what are the two most important administrative functions? Support your response.

SELF-TEST

Corrected True-False

If the statement is true, mark it T. If the statement is false, mark it F and change it to a true statement by adding or deleting words.

_____ 1. The primary purpose of management is to administer programs and facilities.

_____ 2. The mark of an effective administrator is effective decision making.

_____ 3. Communication is identified most often as the critical skill that an effective administrator must possess.

_____ 4. The scope of administration includes the major areas of personnel, program, and scheduling.

_____ 5. It is important that the director does not delegate the office management function.

_____ 6. Effective office layout plans should even include the placement of the coffee maker.

_____ 7. Two important parts of the evaluation process are supervising and controlling.

Multiple Choice

_____ 8. These consume most of the director's time:
    a. personnel matters
    b. program concerns
    c. facility schedules
    d. office management

_____ 9. The product in educational/athletic activities is:
    a. wins/losses
    b. the coaches
    c. the student
    d. the equipment

_____ 10. The administrative function that precedes all others is:
    a. communication
    b. decision making
    c. planning
    d. organizing

_____ 11. Putting a decision into action is:
    a. the final step in decision making
    b. absolutely essential if a decision is to have worth
    c. an action to which leaders must be oriented
    d. all of the above

_____ 12. Worth is determined when this function is carried out:
    a. supervision
    b. organizing
    c. measuring
    d. evaluation

_____ 13. Which is most appropriately identified as a skill?
    a. communication
    b. planning
    c. organization
    d. controlling

_____ 14. The intentional structure of job functions is referred to as:
    a. planning
    b. organization
    c. controlling
    d. personnel options

_____ 15. Which statement is true?
    a. Supervision is part of the control process.
    b. Supervision is part of the evaluation process.
    c. Evaluation is basic process as is controlling.
    d. none of the statements is true

CASE 2.1 HOW AM I TO SUPERVISE THESE PEOPLE?

Joshua T. Hatchapy, in his new role as associate director of the corporate fitness program of Rally Sports Corporation for about three months, felt everything was going well as far as he could tell. One of his major assignments was to supervise the twelve employees working in his department. Three of the fitness specialists had been with the program for more than five years; five had been working at Rally for less than one year; and four were interns who had been on the job for less than six months.

Setting up a schedule that allowed him to visit, observe, take notes, and then meet one-on-one with each person regarding his observations, Joshua felt each employee was receiving an equitable amount of his time. The staff seemed to respond positively to his observations and appraisals, but he received a phone call from Jillian Rakel, the director, indicating that three of the staff members had come to her complaining about feeling uncomfortable with the frequency of his observation-appraisal sessions.

Since he had not been given directions as to how often he was expected to observe and meet with the fitness personnel, Joshua was not sure how to respond when he met with Jillian.

Your Response

1. What seems to be the issue here?
2. What is most likely to be the problem?
3. What barrier may stand in the way of the best solution?
4. What actions seem to be appropriate?
5. What are the action guides that prompted you to suggest the above actions?

CASE 2.2 WHERE ARE THE PRIORITIES?

Scott Shawner, a senior at Central High School, had been an active participant in the intramural sports program for the past three years. The intramural basketball program was conducted from 2:00–3:00 P.M., Monday through Thursday until the girls' interscholastic volleyball and basketball teams' practices were moved from the 5:00–6:00 P.M. time slot to the 2:00–3:00 P.M. time slot; the intramural supervisor was told to reschedule intramurals after 5:00 P.M. This was inconvenient for the majority of students since most rode school buses that did not transport students after 5:00 P.M.

Scott knew that during the noon hour nothing was scheduled in the gym, only that the faculty shot baskets and sometimes played three-on-three if enough showed up. The principal and athletic director were always on the floor at noon to shoot or play. Scott went to Mr. Bills, the principal, and asked if the intramural teams could have the gym from 12:00–1:00 P.M. for their league play rather than after school.

Without hesitation, Mr. Bills said, "Absolutely not! I have always felt that it is important to provide the faculty and staff with an opportunity to relax and recreate in the middle of the day."

Scott was disappointed and frustrated with the response and made an appointment with Miss Jankovitz to see if she would try to change Mr. Bills' decision.

Your Response

1. What is the issue in this case?

2. What are the problems?

3. What barriers/hurdles may stand in the way of the most appropriate decision?

4. What actions would you take if you were the principal?

5. What action guides prompted your actions?

BIBLIOGRAPHY

Bucher, Charles. *Management of Physical Education and Athletic Programs.* St. Louis: Time Mirror/Mosby, 1987.

Eble, Kenneth E. *The Art of Administration.* San Francisco: Jossey-Bass, 1978.

Heyel, Carl, and Belden Menkus. *Handbook of Management for the Growing Business.* New York: Van Nostrand Reinhold Company, 1986.

Koontz, Harold, and Heinz Weihrich. *Essentials of Management.* 5th ed. New York: McGraw-Hill, 1989.

3

The Effective Leader and Director

*The most important quality in a leader
is that of being acknowledged as such.*

André Maurois

Chapter Objectives

*After reading this chapter and completing the exercises,
you should be able to:*

1 Explain how effectiveness as a leader and director is determined

2 Describe the unique aspects of the program director's role

3 Explain why anyone would want to be the director of a physical education, fitness, or sports program

4 Discuss the price one must pay to be a leader and director

5 Categorize as natural, acquired, or learned the attributes and skills needed to be an effective director

6 Identify those qualities and/or actions that detract from a director's ability to be effective

7 Comment on the value of leadership and managerial training

In the opening chapter we took the position that leadership differs from administration. We also believe that leaders differ from directors.

Leaders are the heroes others wish to emulate, follow, and trust, those who command respect and loyalty from their followers. They often are considered to be larger than life; they attract people the way honey attracts bears. It is not difficult to identify leaders, because they are never alone. When you see a group of people, look for the one who has influence and power; among leaders and followers, there is always an imbalance of influence and power. Natural leaders have charisma, and that is the basis for their influence.

We could make similar statements about directors, but they gain their influence and power from a different source: their position. The director is best identified by looking on the organizational chart, since this leader's role results from an appointment rather than from charisma. It often occurs, however, that the appointed director is also the natural leader—a person with charisma. When the appointed manager also has the gift of charisma, the organization has a very powerful administrator.

Distinguishing the appointed director from the natural leader is relatively easy. It is more difficult to establish a set of traits or characteristics by which to judge an effective leader. Even an established model for predicting the effectiveness of a director is not as reliable as most employers would prefer. Still, the importance of finding an effective director for the activity-based program cannot be overemphasized.

THE IMPORTANCE OF LEADERSHIP AND MANAGERIAL EFFECTIVENESS

Directors are located on the lower rungs of the managerial ladder, but their competence and quality of performance is most vital to the success of an organization. Fitness center, sports clubs, and secondary schools with highly competent middle- and top-level administrators cannot succeed without competent directors or chairpersons. On the other hand, any of these enterprises with barely competent middle- and top-level administrators are usually successful if they have effective leadership in the program-level administrative positions. That reality is a strong indication of just how important directors, chairpersons, coaches, and instructors really are. Successful upper-level administrators are aware of that reality.

A 1985 survey of more than one hundred activity program employees and administrators found that a majority listed effective leadership as the most important factor in the success of sports and fitness programs. This finding is not surprising, despite the fact that many educational institutions seem to use the athletics director's position as a dumping site for coaches who can no longer win. The director or department head is considered by many experts to be the person in management most responsible for organization success or failure. It follows that organizations must be thorough in their search for directors who will be effective.

Declining resources have created a situation where those who direct programs or departments are having an even greater influence on the direction of their organizations. For institutions or businesses, private or public, to maintain quality, flexibility, and accountability, and respond to the ever-changing needs of the clientele being served, directors are being asked to take on more and more responsibility each year. In this circumstance it is certainly in the best interests of schools and profit-making entities to ensure that program directors become as knowledgeable as possible about the various leadership and administrative processes and functions.

DETERMINING LEADERSHIP EFFECTIVENESS

The effectiveness of a leader is determined by how well those who are being led achieve the goals of the unit or organization. A coach who has just completed a losing season, for example, will in most cases emphasize how well every team and individual objective, other than the goal to win, was met. Nothing is wrong with that type of reasoning and justification of success, if building character and producing better scholars and future leaders are important objectives of athletics. They certainly should be; but, unfortunately, few coaches are given credit or maintain their jobs because of their ability to lead team members in achieving those goals. Most coaches must win, or they are considered ineffective. In this society, success and effectiveness are very closely aligned with winning.

Aside from winning, productivity is the organizational objective that is most often used as a measuring device for effectiveness. Productivity for a privately owned health club is related to the number of dollars the general director can generate through memberships and the margin of profit that can be maintained from the gross income. If the director can show a sizable profit, he or she is considered an effective director. In a business enterprise, profit is the primary objective in practically every instance.

On the other hand, some organizations—and schools are a good example—often emphasize effectiveness in terms of organizational stability instead of optimum productivity. That stability is often measured by how well employees are motivated. During the late 1970s and early 1980s, physical education and athletics directors who could take charge of a department and smoothly bring about equity between the sexes were considered effective directors.

Whether winning, productivity, or organizational stability is the organization's goal, leadership effectiveness is measured in terms of how

Effectiveness is often measured by productivity.

well the goals are met. Consequently, the criteria for managerial effectiveness are established when the goals of an organization are clearly identified.

MANAGERIAL OPPORTUNITIES AND REQUIREMENTS

In considering effective leadership in physical education, fitness, and sports, we need to consider whether there is a shortage of qualified directors in the field. Although the gap is narrowing between supply and demand, there *is* a continuing shortage. Fitness centers and schools are appointing to leadership roles people who are without preparation and/or experience in either management or exercise science, or both. A supply of better-qualified potential directors probably exists, but the organizational officials responsible often are failing to find and appoint these better-qualified people. This failure may be due to an official's or committee's inability, or lack of courage, to identify the best from the list of applicants. It may be a result of the organization's failure to make the position desirable enough to attract better-qualified professionals. Positions for directors exist where the demands are many and the rewards are few. If an organization hopes to attract quality people who are best able to lead and direct others to successful achievements, then it needs to carefully consider what will draw these people to administrative positions.

The Unique Challenges of the Director's Role

The director, in most situations, serves under conditions that are not duplicated at any other level of leadership. The director is expected to lead; yet, restrictions of some kind are usually placed upon the amount of authority he or she is permitted to assume. The director has authority; yet, he or she often must work side by side with subordinates. The director is assigned the primary responsibility for establishing program goals and leading constituents to achieve those goals; yet, a unified effort on the part of those constituents can severely and adversely affect his or her ability to lead. The director is sometimes described as the first among equals and the one who is more responsible than anyone else for bringing about change; yet, to implement certain changes is an almost impossible task. Consider the following examples.

Insight through Illustration

A recently appointed athletics director, trying to control and maintain the direction of the football program toward the department goals, was convinced that certain changes had to be made. Although the present football staff led the team to a very impressive win-loss record of 28–2 over the past three years, other aspects of the football program were in a state of decay. The football staff, believing they had the support of the school administrators and public, refused to cooperate in making the needed changes. When the athletics director recommended changes to his superior without the support of the football staff, he was told that he should leave the football program alone or resign.

Similar circumstances can occur in any work setting.

Insight through Illustration

A fitness director of a corporation fired an aerobics instructor for a flagrant violation of policy. The director then experienced a tremendous amount of criticism from clientele and staff because the instructor had been popular with both participants and other fitness center employees.

Another unique circumstance that characterizes the director's role is the similarity of most sports-related and fitness-related units to the family. Universities have deans and vice presidents, high schools have principals and superintendents, sports clubs and YMCAs have general managers and executive directors, and all of these central- and upper-level administrators make decisions with which the director and his or her unit members must live. In many cases, the decisions are unpopular ones and may even create hardships for the staff members' families. Those administrators can make unpopular decisions and not have to face the affected employees. However, when directors make unpopular decisions, because of their physical location and the family type of relationship, they must live with the effects of the decisions every day.

The director has many things in common with unit members. They have had similar preparation; they belong to the same professional groups; they share the same professional values and creeds; and, in most cases, they live under the same roof during the workday. The director can be compared to the parent whose top priority is to set the course that will mutually benefit and be best for the total family. However, because of the uniqueness of the position, the director is a leader who is often led—sometimes the captain and sometimes the soldier; sometimes the counselor and sometimes the one needing counsel—but always in the position that can affect the success or failure of the organization more than any other.

Qualifying as a Director

If you hope to become an effective director of an activity-based program, what qualifications will you need?

Desire to Lead   The first requirement for being an effective director is the desire to serve in that capacity. Few people are forced to assume managerial positions against their will. Those who are not motivated to be a director are simply not considered because they do not express an interest.

Potential leaders often surprise their coworkers and superiors by showing no interest in a specific administrative role even when they seem to be the most logical candidates. However, those who show no interest in one managerial job may be motivated to seek a similar position at a different place or at a different time. Interest depends upon the specific circumstances surrounding each administrative role. It is not difficult to

understand that factors specific to the position such as rewards, predicted difficulties, and relations with others have a significant bearing on a candidate's interest. Because every job is unique and specific to the situation and circumstances surrounding it, the best-qualified leader simply may not be interested in every administrative position available in an organization.

Leadership Attributes and Skills   The next requirement for someone who desires to direct an activity-based program is the possession of recognized leadership attributes and skills. We will list these qualities later in the chapter.

Training and Experience   Because every job and every person must be considered individually, we cannot identify any specific program of study or exact number of years of experience required to qualify for a director's position. However, except in an exceptional circumstance, anyone in a managerial role should have a strong educational background in physical education or exercise science. At least one course in administration with an application to the sports and fitness field should also be a basic requirement.

Motivation to Lead

Many qualified leaders have no desire to seek a managerial position, and scores of successful directors, after serving for a period of time, decide to get out. Why?

After comparing the demands made upon the director or other first-line administrator to the demands made upon those in nonleadership roles, we can reasonably wonder why anyone would want to be an administrator. What factors inspire people to seek positions of leadership and remain in them until retirement? And what conditions are necessary for a good experience?

The Rewards   First, the economic advantage becomes obvious when we compare the salaries of

Leadership careers often begin on the courts and fields of sports.

directors to those of other employees. Directors earn a higher salary in practically every situation. Second, power is a form of reward for leadership that has nothing to do with financial gain. It provides the satisfaction of having control, not only of one's own destiny, but also of the fate of others. Contrary to what many claim, people like power, and most like power because they are in a position to facilitate satisfaction. The most gratifying reward can be realized by providing satisfaction for others.

A Supportive Staff   A few years ago a director of physical education and athletics at a small college was offered the opportunity to direct that department at a much larger university. He was aware that the new department head would be faced with a number of internal problems, and the first question he asked after receiving the offer was, "How much support will I have from the members of the department?" He was told that all members would not be supportive but that the large majority would be very supportive. He accepted the position and experienced a challenging and rewarding tenure for seven years. If he had not been assured of majority support, he should not have accepted the challenge, and if he had not been supported and accepted after his arrival, it would have been a mistake for him to remain in the leadership role.

It is important that the leader be supported and accepted by those being led. Salary and power seldom provide enough satisfaction to offset the professional aches, pains, and problems that a lack of support creates. One of the major reasons why people will not consider a leadership role is the fear of being rejected by their constituency.

A Chance of Succeeding   Directors of physical education, fitness, and athletics need to be realistic in analyzing and evaluating their chances for achieving the goals that are essential to organizational success. Potential candidates, after comparing the job expectations to the resources avail-

able and other job specifics, often decide not to seek administrative positions regardless of the salary and promise of support. They realize that failure to meet expected goals creates a void that cannot be filled by pay, power, or subordinate support. When the design of a leadership position causes the defeat of effective leaders, the organization has a responsibility to redesign the job so that effective leaders have at least a fair opportunity for succeeding.

THE COST OF LEADERSHIP

For those with the proper motivation, the beckoning call to leadership is persuasive. Few things are more professionally satisfying and fulfilling than being a fitness director, head trainer, head coach, director of athletics, or head of a physical education department. The challenges and satisfactions are tremendous. The feeling of knowing that you are the person most responsible for the success or failure of your particular team or department surpasses any description.

The experiences and rewards of the leadership role are priceless, and anyone who is strongly motivated to lead should go for it. The desire to lead creates a void that can never be satisfactorily filled with any experience other than that opportunity to lead.

But the leadership coin does have a second side, the high cost one must pay to be a leader or director. Administrators live in a very real world, and sacrifices are required of them.

Insight through Illustration

A college baseball coach left the best such job in the nation because of a burning desire to manage a major league club. Having played professional baseball, he approached the new challenge with excitement and a vision that was seemingly clear.

CONGRATULATIONS! YOU'VE DONE SUCH A GOOD JOB WORKING 9 TO 5 WE'RE MAKING YOU THE BOSS...

... STARTING MONDAY BE HERE BY 7:30, YOU CAN LEAVE WHEN YOU'RE FINISHED ... IF EVER...

The rewards of leadership and the responsibilities of leadership go hand in hand.

He knew the ups and downs of a manager's life, and after one year as a major league coach, he got the opportunity to manage an American League team. He did a super job and was challenging the league favorites for the divisional lead after only one year as manager, when his authority was questioned by a player who had been around for some time. This was not a unique problem—it happens quite often, and the manager knew exactly what decision was appropriate. After unsuccessfully trying to resolve the problem with the player, he went to his general manager with the only alternative that would not compromise his position as the field leader: Either he or the player had to go. In spite of the superb job he had done with average talent, he found out the hard way that major league decisions are not always reasonable and fair. In this case, a $50,000-per-year manager was more expendable than a $500,000-per-year ball player.

That shock was mild compared to his experience with another club three years later. With a young team that had been depleted of its superstars through the free-agent draft, the manager and his club were in first place in their division halfway through the season. The entire world would have thought that top management would be appreciative of that achievement—but not so. After constantly being criticized and harassed by his boss, he resigned in order to maintain his dignity and sanity. The story does not end here, since the man has had a very successful career serving in authority positions with other major league teams, but it does serve to illustrate how high the cost of leadership can be.

There are three realities that a person in a director's position must face. They constitute the price that must be paid for the higher salary, power, and prestige that go with the position. We should warn you against thinking that you can rise above paying the price by being highly successful. How well coaches know that the more you win, the more you are expected to win!

Responsibility

The first reality that directors must face is that they are totally responsible for the well-being and production of their organizational unit. When things go wrong, regardless of who in the unit is at fault, the director must accept the responsibility. Leaders only jeopardize their own credibility by shifting the blame to subordinates, even if the subordinates create the problems.

On the other hand, when everything goes well, directors cannot expect to be overly blessed with praise. The public, especially, will look for someone other than the leader to pay tribute to. When coaches win, the public says, "They had

WE'VE WON THE SERIES!

LAST PLACE... LOOKS LIKE WE
NEED A NEW MANAGER...

*A leader with tough decisions often
feels the pain of loneliness.*

outstanding players. Any fool could win with them." Directors should expect similar expressions when they lead their department or unit to some outstanding achievement. Administrators do not make good heroes; therefore, they should not be discouraged when others fail to give them credit for outstanding performances. They must gain their satisfaction from the other rewards that come from leading.

Besides, directors have much to gain by giving employees an opportunity to share the spotlight. Regardless of who says otherwise, everyone enjoys seeing his or her name on the marquee. The appreciation and gratitude that subordinates will extend to the director for sharing the glory will pay long-term dividends that will more than compensate for any recognition lost by the director.

And for a director to do otherwise only creates problems. One of the most demoralizing things that can happen to a staff person is to do a great job behind the scenes and then have the administrator take all the credit.

Loneliness

Another price the director must pay for the rewards of leadership is the emotional stress of being alone. This does not imply that the administrator is physically alone, because one of the realities of leading is that you lead people, and others are always physically present. The feeling of loneliness occurs at times when the director must make tough and unpopular decisions; and be assured, those times do occur.

The director sees, feels, hears, and even seems to be able to smell opposition to his taking action on decisions that adversely affect the lives of others. At times, it may be difficult for courageous administrators to even like themselves. For example, circumstances may dictate that a director must lay off a staff member. That sword may fall on the head of a young staff person with family responsibilities. The person's past performance may have been outstanding, but because of the principle of seniority, the director must make a decision that will affect that life as well as the lives of family members. Those circumstances, indeed, create a time of loneliness for the decision maker.

Criticism and Abuse

The last reality relating to the high cost of leadership is the unjustified criticism and abuse that is directed toward leaders and administrators. It happens to even the very best. When leaders make mistakes, they expect to be criticized, and the average mature adult is capable of accepting and adjusting to constructive criticism. However, it takes a special kind of understanding to gird up the professional loins and go on about business when criticism is unjustly leveled. The criticized person, of course, is expected to use reasonable means in defending himself or herself, and a mature response is needed. Our natural inclination is to fight back and try to hurt those who have been unfair to us. But although that response is natural, it is unacceptable. When we get caught up in vengeance, our day-to-day performance suffers, and responsible directors must rise above that kind of response.

ATTRIBUTES OF AN EFFECTIVE LEADER AND DIRECTOR

The American Council on Education has identified a number of characteristics to guide the evaluation of candidates for its administrative intern program (Eble, 1978). These characteristics are: resourcefulness and adaptability, integrity and honesty, courage and commitment, ability in interpersonal relations, professionalism, assertiveness and sense of direction, organizational and

analytical ability, poise and confidence, communication skills, vigor and capacity for work, judgment, imagination and initiative, and motivation and enthusiasm. Included also are: loyalty, perseverance, breadth of interests and curiosity, intelligence, cultural level, scholarship and teaching ability, common sense, sense of humor, candor and openness, sense of values, sensitivity for colleagues and community, dependability, patience, sense of perspective, maturity, decisiveness, and overall standing among peers.

Eble discusses some of these characteristics and adds the following attributes: tact, reputation for fairness and respect for the opinions and actions of others, tolerance and compassion, and being able to put up with petty annoyances. Although these characteristics are probably encompassed by those listed by the American Council on Education, their specific identification is worthwhile.

When we were compiling this chapter, we carefully considered the characteristics, attributes, and skills most often identified with successful administrators. First we listed them, and then we organized them into groups according to when they probably are acquired. For the sake of discussion, we group them here as natural gifts of leadership, acquired qualities of leadership, learned skills of leadership and administration, and specific skills related to being an effective director. These categories are only approximate and are based on subjective observations rather than objective investigation. Still, they provide a point of departure for discussion.

Natural Gifts of Leadership

The qualities grouped under this heading are thought to be those that are either genetically related or developed at a very early age; therefore, the descriptive term *natural* is not intended to refer exclusively to born traits. These qualities are considered basic, and all can be affected to some degree by the environment.

Intelligence   Most effective leaders have an IQ above normal but below the genius range: between 120 and 135 is thought to be most common. At this level the person is able to rationalize and conceptualize effectively and still maintain the patience to tolerate human error and relate well to other people. All three capabilities are essential.

Common Sense   This attribute is especially important for leaders in that they are often viewed as special people. A lack of common sense can create the image of a boob, when in fact the person may be extremely intelligent. Common sense is essential for a person to be able to put all the parts together into a meaningful whole when the directions are incomplete.

Creativity and Initiative   These two qualities, although somewhat different in definition, go together in a person's ability to originate or conceive, and then follow through in the planning of a new program.

Charisma   This is a rare quality of power and exceptional ability to attract followers and devotion. It is not an absolute essential for effective leadership, but it does provide an advantage for those who have it.

Acquired Qualities of Leadership

The characteristics and qualities in this category are acquired early in life—perhaps by the age of twelve. Most of these attributes depend on what we refer to as spiritual sensitivity. Spiritual sensitivity is related to the strongest feelings of concern for the welfare and well-being of others. It goes a sensitive step beyond the concept of humanism. It is a concern strong enough to make a person want to give without expecting anything in return.

Compassion   This characteristic refers to sensitivity to the thoughts and feelings of others and a strong sense of justice. It is not difficult to recognize a director who has a compassionate spirit. Unfortunately, some directors relate compassion to weakness and believe that too many people take advantage of compassionate leaders. Undoubtedly, some do; but the administrator who is more concerned about the one person he or she might treat unjustly than the few who will take advantage of compassionate actions is a stronger leader.

Respect for Others   Administrators can be more effective if they hold other human beings in high esteem. Positive outcomes result from positive feelings. Being respectful to subordinates, superiors, and co-workers causes them to treat the director with greater respect and be more productive.

Integrity and Honesty   These two terms do not mean exactly the same thing, but they are so closely related that we deal with them as one. They relate to a rigid adherence to a code of behavior characterized by unimpaired probity, truthfulness, and sincerity. Someone once stated, "If you always tell the truth you never have to worry about what you said yesterday." It is difficult to maintain high morale among department members if the director deceives them in the slightest manner.

Loyalty   Loyalty is established early if it is present in a person's environment and relationships, and the institutions of home, church, and school have the greatest bearing upon its establishment. A lack of loyalty on the part of the leader can undermine the very foundation of an organization. The director needs to uphold his or her employer, and the unit members need to uphold their director. If something disagreeable exists and criticism is in order, then it should be presented in a constructive form, and a change sought.

Ability to Instill Good Will The ability to instill good will relates in some way to every other attribute in this category and should result from strict adherence to the code of behavior of which each of the qualities are a part.

Commitment The theme of commitment is best exemplified by a quote from the late President John F. Kennedy's inaugural address: "Ask not what your country can do for you, but, rather, what you can do for your country." Without commitment from the administrators and other leaders, no organization can succeed. The leaders must believe in the purpose and goals of their institution or enterprise, and be willing to serve those goals. An effective leader asks periodically and often, Is there anything else I can do that will improve our product or service?

Administrative Mind This quality exists as a result of having a reasonably logical mind and some experience in decision making. Experience with case studies probably can help develop this quality. It is the ability to think like an administrator and is observable quite early in a person's life.

Decisiveness If anything can drive subordinates up the wall, it is a leader who wavers or sits on the fence when a firm decision is needed. Decisiveness is a quality a person must have before becoming an administrator. Decision making is the crux of administration, and a person does not learn to be decisive *after* accepting an administrative position.

Courage This is a basic ingredient of decision making, and both physical and moral courage are needed by the director and decision maker. At no time in history has our very existence been more threatened by wishy-washy attitudes of leaders

RIDING THE FENCE

*If anything can drive subordinates up the wall,
it is a leader who sits on the fence when
a firm decision is called for.*

than now. Moral problems must be recognized, and leaders must, in spite of criticism and threats from organizations that operate under the pretense of protecting individuals' rights, take a firm stand against those things that ruin careers and threaten lives. Professional and amateur sports organizations are finally taking severe actions against participants who have compromised the moral dignity of sports; still, the damage that already has been done to the youth of the nation by the immoral behavior modeled by large numbers of athletes, coaches, and administrators is irreparable. Courage by those in authoritative positions could have prevented the damage or, at least, could have diminished the magnitude of it.

Patience and Tolerance The effective director must be tolerant of the petty irritations that sometimes are created by well-meaning employees. The basic foundation for patience is acquired early in life, but improvement can surely be realized

A high level of physical fitness is a given for directors; otherwise there will be doubt about what they represent.

with practice. An impatient or intolerant director is doomed to failure or, at best, mediocrity. Patience is a virtue that can overcome adversity and turn a person who is a pain in the neck into a responsible and productive contributor to organizational goals.

Wisdom   Thoreau said, "It is a characteristic of wisdom not to do desperate things." Wisdom encompasses and expands upon knowledge, insights, and understanding of what is true, right, or lasting. It requires sagacity and good judgment and is a gift upon which experience can improve. In the Christian tradition, Jesus epitomizes the wisdom of the highest ideal.

Learned Skills of Leadership and Administration

The leadership abilities we have just discussed are basic to the management skills of an effective

director. Just as a proficient basketball player must first be an athlete, or the captain of a spacecraft must first be a pilot, a successful director must first be a leader.

A successful manager in one setting will not necessarily be effective in another, but there are general skills of management that all administrators need, regardless of the setting in which they serve. Without elaborating on each, we present the following list of skills important for the administrator of a physical education, sports, or fitness program to have:

- ability to make decisions
- good communications
- command of administrative techniques
- willingness to set the pace and example
- willingness to accept responsibility
- understanding of how to motivate
- tact

- support of staff
- maturity
- persuasiveness
- ability to innovate
- physical fitness
- wit and sense of humor.

Specific Skills of an Effective Director

As we move from the general and basic attributes of leadership to the more specific skills of the administrator, the less essential each individual skill becomes. In other words, it would be foolish to propose that every skill listed is essential for managerial success. We list here with a brief comment of justification the specific skills that contribute to a director's effectiveness.

Skill as an Educator The effective director of physical education, athletics, or fitness needs to constantly teach employees how to perform their tasks more efficiently.

Fund-raising Ability Most programs can be significantly improved with solicited funds; many rely entirely upon funds raised by the organization or unit; and only a few program situations require no effort in fund raising.

Writing and Editing Skills In communicating the position, goals, achievements, and needs of an organization, the director must be able to write well, or edit what a co-worker has written, to best represent the organization.

High Level of Fitness Unless directors personally practice the teachings of their programs, one must question whether they really believe in what they represent.

Knowledge of Fitness and Sports Managers in any field of endeavor can serve better if they have a thorough understanding of their product and/or service.

Traits to Avoid

Certain traits are detrimental to a director's effectiveness, and it is essential that both the director and those in a position to hire a director be aware of the more common ones.

- secretiveness
- aloofness
- insecurity in present position
- indecisiveness
- pomposity
- arrogance
- heaviness

LEADERSHIP AND MANAGERIAL TRAINING

Industry, government, the military, and education spend millions of dollars each year for the training of leaders and administrators. This training usually consists of seminars and conferences that last from one day to two weeks. Although the sum that organizations spend on training administrators is a testament to the primacy of their concern with effective leadership, whether such training is of value is not at all clear.

Fiedler and Chemers (1974) have studied extensively the effects of leadership training under various conditions. They have concluded that a step-by-step recipe that guarantees leadership success is not available. In fact, we can conclude that most people attending the short courses in leadership benefit very little from the effort unless the courses are directed toward learning technical skills specific to task performance.

Most evidence supports a belief that training for managerial effectiveness may be much more successful than training for leadership effectiveness. This substantiates the position that the administrator is made, but the leader is born. As we have stated, we believe that a high percentage of the attributes of a leader are established at a very young age, perhaps during the first twelve to fourteen years. We further believe that the skills or characteristics of an administrator can be learned at a later time, especially those that are specific to the job.

KEY WORDS AND PHRASES

Leadership effectiveness

Productivity

Stability

Motivation to lead

Rewards

Cost of leadership

Spiritual sensitivity

Natural gifts

Acquired qualities

Learned skills

QUESTIONS FOR REVIEW

1. Are leaders born or made? Explain.
2. Why is the director's role unique?
3. Discuss the differences among acquired qualities of leadership, natural gifts of leadership, and learned skills of leadership. Tell why you agree or disagree with this classification.
4. Identify seven qualities that you believe are most indispensable if a director is to be effective. Justify your answer.
5. Differentiate between wisdom and intelligence; decisiveness and good decision making; administrative mind and command of administrative techniques; and poise and maturity.
6. Describe the cost of leadership.
7. What factors would make you want to be the director of an activity-based program?
8. What skill or quality do you believe is most important for a director of an activity-based program to possess? Why?

SELF-TEST

Corrected True-False

If the statement is true, mark it T. If the statement is false, mark it F and change it to a true statement by adding or deleting words.

_____ 1. It is easy to establish a set of traits by which to judge an effective leader.

_____ 2. The effectiveness of a leader is determined by how well those who are being led achieve the goals of the organization.

_____ 3. Fitness and athletic directors have many things in common with those whom they direct.

_____ 4. The first requirement for being an effective director is appropriate education and training.

_____ 5. Because staff support can be won after accepting a position, lack of staff support should not affect a person's decision to accept or decline a director's position.

_____ 6. There is a relatively low cost for being a leader when compared to the rewards.

_____ 7. One of the costs of being a leader is loneliness, which means that the leader has little contact with others.

_____ 8. Both intelligence and common sense are listed as natural gifts of leadership.

_____ 9. Being truthful and honest in all matters is an essential quality for a leader if high morale is to be maintained.

_____ 10. Training for managerial effectiveness is probably more successful than training for leadership effectiveness.

Multiple Choice

_____ 11. Which of the following traits is out of place in this list?
   a. pomposity
   b. aloofness
   c. charisma
   d. arrogance

_____ 12. Which of the following is not part of the cost of leadership?
   a. power
   b. authority
   c. loneliness
   d. both a and b

_____ 13. The least essential quality for becoming an effective director of an activity-based program is:
   a. high intelligence
   b. respect for others
   c. patience
   d. decisiveness

_____ 14. A director's effectiveness may be measured by:
   a. meeting unit goals
   b. productivity
   c. program stability
   d. all of the above

_____ 15. The director is:
   a. always the captain
   b. first among equals
   c. paid less than workers
   d. always popular

CASE 3.1 WHO GETS THE DIRECTOR'S JOB?

Silicon Valley Computer Corporation has had an on-site recreation and fitness program for six years. The company invested $1.5 million in a fitness and recreational facility with a staff of five full-time and eight to ten part-time instructors and administrators plus two full-time secretaries/clerks. Bill Akers, program administrator for five years, resigned to accept a position at West Coast University. Upper and middle management were pleased with the job Bill had done in putting the recreation and fitness program together and stabilizing it. Bill was also very popular with the staff.

The vacancy was advertised nationally, and the screening committee eliminated all but two candidates for the administrative post. The two candidates, Gloria Peck and Sam Palmer, were invited for an on-site interview.

After each candidate spent a full day interviewing, the committee sat down together to decide what recommendation they would make. As each of the four committee members spoke, it became evident that the two candidates were comparable in many ways. Their experiences were similar, as were their educational backgrounds, letters of reference, health and physical fitness status, age, and vitality.

After two hours of discussion, the committee came up with the following comparisons:

- Gloria seemed to have a better vocabulary than Sam and generally seemed to be highly intelligent. She also seemed to be more creative. She made several excellent suggestions for improving the program. Two things bothered the committee. First, she seemed more concerned about redecorating the office than improving the program. Second, on three different occasions she made a point of how good "that martini" would taste after the interview was over.

- Sam seemed to have a better grasp of the overall situation of the recreation and fitness operation at the corporation. He was open and a better conversationalist with all the staff than Gloria. When discussing budget, facility, and office procedures he seemed to have a thorough knowledge of how to direct a program. Two things did cause the committee some concern. First, during the interview he stated that he would never make a decision that was opposite that of the majority of the staff. Second, he displayed distracting facial expressions and winked his left eye all during the interview for no apparent reason.

The committee began their deliberations and prepared to compose their recommendation to the manager of health and welfare of the corporation.

Your Response

1. What are the issues and problems in this case?

2. What barriers may stand in the way of the best solution?

3. What action do you think would be appropriate?

4. List the action guides that led you to your decision.

CASE 3.2 TO APPLY OR NOT TO APPLY

Bob Billings had taught physical education at Clay Webster High School since graduation from Victory University eight years earlier. When he came to Clay Webster he had two high priorities: He believed that every high school should have a good weight-training program and facility, and a quality athletic-training room and program. During his eight years he achieved these two goals, and his programs became prototypes for others in the state. Bob enjoyed teaching physical education and had not thought about doing anything else.

Next door to Bob lived Dr. William Astin, president of Creekside Community College; the two became friendly neighbors, frequently discussing their respective programs across the backyard fence. One day, Dr. Astin told Bob that the head of his physical education and athletics programs was leaving to accept a position in another state. He asked Bob if he ever thought of moving into administration. "If you are interested," Dr. Astin said, "I would like to see you apply for the position."

Bob said he was flattered by the invitation to apply but had not considered changing jobs. As they parted, he told Dr. Astin that he would give some thought to an administrative position; and the more he thought about it, the more interested he became.

Your Response

1. What is the issue in this case?
2. What are the problems?
3. What barriers may prevent the best solution?
4. If Bob asked you what you thought he should do, what would you say?
5. What action guides are basic to your advice?

BIBLIOGRAPHY

Adair, John. *Training for Leadership.* London: McDonald Press, 1968.

Bittel, Lester R. *Leadership: The Key to Management Success.* New York: Franklin Watts, 1984.

Burley-Allen, Madelyn. *Managing Assertively: How to Improve Your People Skills.* New York: Wiley, 1983.

Cohen, William A., and Nutrit Cohen. *Top Executive Performance: 11 Keys to Success and Power.* New York: Wiley, 1984.

Drucker, Peter F. *The Effective Executive.* New York: Harper & Row, 1966.

Dyer, William G., et al. *Challenge of Management.* San Diego: Harcourt Brace Jovanovich, 1990.

Eble, Kenneth E. *The Art of Administration.* San Francisco: Jossey-Bass, 1978.

Fiedler, Fred E., and Martin M. Chemers. *Leadership and Effective Management.* Glenview, IL: Scott Foresman, 1974.

Tucker, Allan. *Chairing the Academic Department: Leadership among Peers.* Washington, DC: American Council on Education, 1981.

4

Making Wise Decisions

*A man who has made a mistake and doesn't correct it
is making another mistake.*

Confucius

Chapter Objectives

*After reading this chapter and completing the exercises,
you should be able to:*

1 Define decision making and tell how it relates to
   management

2 List the factors that affect a decision

3 Describe the four approaches to decision making

4 Name the elements involved in decision making

5 Quote the principle of the limiting factor

6 Explain the need for alternatives, disagreement,
   and time in decision making

7 Realize that decisions necessitate change and
   change creates resistance

8 Observe improvement in your decision-making
   ability

9 List the seven steps one should follow in the standard problem-solving methods

Decision making in management is like the mechanism in a video game that controls the direction of the character by selecting among alternative paths around an obstacle course. If the wrong path is chosen, the objective is not fully achieved. In an organization, if a wrong decision is made, the goals of the enterprise become more difficult to attain. Because decision making is the primary source of control in taking an organization from planning to fulfilling objectives, it has been viewed by various scholars as the key to management.

In this chapter, we look at decision making as a managerial skill and an organizational process. In an organization managed through the participatory style of leadership, the sports director does not always make decisions in isolated privacy. Group decision making is also a factor. The director not only can influence the decisions of the group, but she or he can also be influenced by the group's decisions. Accordingly, although the discussion in this chapter is oriented toward individual decision making, information on group decision making is also included.

IT'S HARD TO DECIDE...
THEY EACH HAVE THEIR GOOD POINTS!

The ability of the director to make effective decisions can mean the difference between success and failure.

DECISION MAKING: THE KEY TO MANAGEMENT

Decision making is the act of making up one's own mind, reaching a conclusion, and passing a judgment on an issue of consideration when at least two alternatives are available. If two or more alternatives are not available, no decision is needed.

Administrators are known by the decisions they make. That statement is not an absolute truth, but it does imply that making decisions is the business of the administrator. Both superiors and subordinates expect the administrator to be a good decision maker. The ability of the director to make effective decisions can mean the difference between success and failure.

The salary, prestige, and power that managers can demand correlates highly with the significance of the decisions they make. Managerial personnel earn significantly more than other staff members who have similar experience and education. Administrators who have proven themselves effective as decision makers may earn twice the salary of their best-paid staff members. By the same token, because administrators are in a decision-making position and thus have power, prestige, and control over the lives of other people, they are more visible than others in an organization and get more attention from people seeking influence.

But although the director is the primary decision maker in an organization, we should not think that the major portion of the director's workday is spent making judgments related to a continuous flow of problems coming from the staff and those who are being served. This is not true; or at least, it should not be true. The effective director spends quality time in making decisions, but he or she does not spend nearly as much time on the function as most people think. The wise decision maker does not make a great many decisions but does make key decisions, slowly and with wisdom. Most issues can be resolved with a policy, procedure, standard practice, or rule; therefore, the director needs only to implement an existing action guide in making corrections. If a director is making separate decisions for every problem that arises, it probably means that he or she is either lazy, disorganized, or both. A well-planned and well-presented operating guide that has been created or revised in cooperation with staff members can remedy most concerns before they become serious problems. The director or decision maker is responsible for seeing that a current operating guide or policy manual is available.

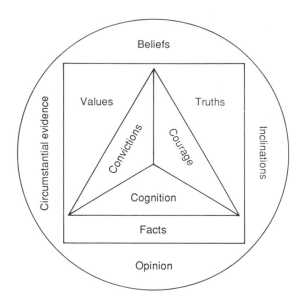

Figure 4.1 *Decision Ingredients*

FACTORS DETERMINING CHOICE

Many factors and forces come to bear upon the mind and emotions of the decision maker when he or she is faced with choosing between two or more alternatives. Figure 4.1 shows the ingredients that result in a decision. Cognition, convictions, and courage are in the center of the illustration because they have more influence than the other factors.

Cognition

Cognition is the gathering, analyzing, and interpreting of information. It is the process of intelligently separating information into either facts or circumstantial evidence, opinion, beliefs, and inclinations. As such, it is a rational process.

Convictions

Convictions also come to bear upon choice. A conviction is a strong belief reinforced by feelings such as fear, anger, hate, love, and sympathy. Regardless of how objective a director tries to be,

his or her convictions will significantly affect most of the tough decisions made.

Courage

Courage is the administrator's intestinal fortitude to move and to act even if it means that people whom he or she would prefer not to upset are offended. Some of the best decisions ever made have never been put in place because of an administrator's lack of courage. Values, facts, and truths also significantly affect the decision-making process, although not as much as the three factors just discussed.

Values

Values are principles, standards, or qualities considered worthwhile or desirable. Values affect choices more than most decision makers realize. Our response to any issue is affected by personal, political, educational, or moral values, often without our ever being aware of them. In fact, most of us have values of which we are not aware. Most underlying values are established at a very early age, with the home and family having the greatest influence, followed by religious teachings, formal education, and peer pressures.

Truths and Facts

Truths and facts have similar meanings and influences on the matter of choice. *Truths* are statements that conform to knowledge or logic. They also relate to honesty, sincerity, and integrity. *Facts* are statements that have been asserted as certain or objectively verified.

A search for truths and facts is always basic to the investigation that should occur in the early stages of the decision-making process. Contrary to the opinions of many, when solving a problem, one does not begin with the facts, because facts are not available at first. Only unsubstantiated information exists at the beginning, and it must be verified before facts are available.

Unsubstantiated Information

Opinions, circumstantial evidence, beliefs, and inclinations are also ingredients in the decision-making process. These are elements of information that have not been verified as facts or truths. Although ideally these factors should not influence an administrator's final choice, truths and facts are not always available, and thus opinion, circumstantial evidence, beliefs, and inclinations often do enter in.

FOUR APPROACHES TO DECISION MAKING

Basically, four approaches can be used in making decisions. The approach selected depends on the decision maker and the circumstances surrounding the problem or issue at hand. Different situations require different approaches. The four approaches are discussed in the paragraphs that follow.

The Immediate-Response Approach

This approach is based on an instinctive response to some given stimulus, and requires very little thought prior to the decision. It may be as automatic as the decision a skilled basketball player makes while dribbling if an opponent makes an unexpected move on him. He doesn't think—he just reacts. As another example of this approach, a basketball fan threw a package of breath mints that struck an official in the face. Without hesitation or consultation, and with very little time for thought, the athletics director went to the microphone and announced that any other similar act would result in a forfeiture of the game.

The Precedent Approach

The precedent approach is a traditional approach whereby the administrator makes judgments and decisions based upon how similar situations have been handled in the past. The classic example of this approach is the court judge's rendering of a judgment based upon a past case. In sports, an intramural player may be suspended for two weeks for a violation in the gym because one month earlier another player was suspended for two weeks for a similar violation. In many cases, this approach is appropriate and works well, but, unfortunately, it is used too often. What has proven successful in the past is not always right for the immediate situation.

The Logical Approach

The logical approach is based on reason and logic, and administrators use this approach quite often. In using this approach, they do not follow a

The Problem-Solving Approach

The problem-solving approach to decision making is more thorough than the others and is characterized by a prescribed routine that is thoughtfully and meticulously followed. It may be reserved only for the most significant and difficult decisions. The problem-solving method described later in the chapter is an example of this approach.

FUNDAMENTAL ELEMENTS OF GOOD DECISION MAKING

Each of us at some time must make vital decisions, decisions that although they may affect only the people close to us, mean the difference in someone's performance. When we hold a position of power and authority in an organization, our decisions are even more vital, for they affect the success, failure, or mediocrity of that organization. In summary, none of us can avoid making vital decisions. If we accept that statement, then it behooves each of us to improve our decision-making ability. Understanding what decision making is all about can help us in that improvement. Toward that end, we discuss five basic elements of good decision making.

Distinguishing Common from Unique Issues and Problems

One of the basic things that a decision maker must do is to recognize whether a problem is one that occurs universally under similar circumstances or whether it is confined to the immediate situation. If it is one that has occurred somewhere else under similar conditions, it is a common problem or issue. If it is one for which no precedent exists, it is unique (see Table 4.1). The approach to solving these types of problems is totally different.

An immediate response approach of a director can be as automatic as the decision of a skilled racquetball player if a competitor makes an unexpected move.

structured procedure nor a prescribed step-by-step routine, but simply mentally arrange all the known elements or circumstances pertaining to the situation and then make a decision. Reasons are then listed justifying the decision and subsequent action. Athletics directors often use this approach in recommending merit salary increases where no salary schedule exists. A coach who wins often and who may be sought by another school to head up its program may be offered an unusually high salary to persuade her or him to stay. Reason, common sense, and logic can produce supporting arguments justifying the decision. Seldom are directors criticized for using this approach.

Table 4.1 *Examples of Common and Unique Managerial Problems*

Common Problems	Unique Problems
Food and drink in the gym	Middle-of-year budget reduction
Outdoor activities and rain	Accusations/staff misconduct
Pool being left unlocked	Staff permits unauthorized entry
Poor quality educational film	Film shown: Porno or educational?
Hiring best qualified applicant	Grievance of hiring practice
Teacher/Maternity leave in March	High School football coach wants to accept college job March 1

Common Problems Common problems can be handled according to decision or action guides. These guides may be principles, policies, standards, procedures, or rules, and they should appear in the operating manual of the organization or department. After a problem occurs more than once or twice, it should no longer be considered exceptional or unique. It should be considered a common problem, and the director should establish an action guide that specifically states what will happen if the problem recurs.

The malfunction of some plumbing device in the restroom is an example of a common problem, and a standard operating procedure should direct the action that is appropriate. Usually, a plumbing malfunction is reported to a secretary, who calls the plumber. A problem this simple and common should never be brought to the attention of the director, but there always seem to be one or two people who think that plumbing problems fall within the realm of administrative responsibilities that need the director's attention. The administrator does not have time for such trivial occurrences.

A more borderline example of a common problem would be an instructor's intercepting a package of completed student evaluations and making changes to five of them. This still is not a unique problem because it does occur universally. This problem should also be resolved by a policy or standard operating procedure. In other words, in

this case the director's responsibility is to administer an existing action guide rather than to make a unique or one-time decision.

Staff members are much more involved in decisions relating to common and generic problems than to unique situations. Action guides appearing in the operating manual are established by the faculty in a school setting or by the staff in a public or private fitness or recreation center. This is primarily how employees are involved in decision making in an organization that follows the democratic style of management.

Unique Problems Problems that cannot be handled with an established policy, standard practice, or rule are considered to be unique, and the administrator must be the central figure in resolving them. Deciding how to resolve these problems requires research, time, thought, argumentation, meditation, and, for some administrators, prayer. When dealing with serious and exceptional circumstances, the administrator is the lonely decision maker.

One unique problem that a physical education, athletics, or fitness director faces is related to the employee whose performance is only mediocre. Does the director fire, conditionally rehire, or reduce the salary of this employee, or choose some other alternative? Help may come from a personnel committee, but the committee can only provide evidence and make a recommendation. The

COME OVER AND MEET YOUR NEW COACH !

Decisions must satisfy peripheral conditions.

final decision is the responsibility of the administrator.

Satisfying Peripheral Conditions

A second element of good decision making is seeking to satisfy not only the primary purpose of a decision, but also the conditions surrounding it—the peripheral conditions. For a better understanding of this element, consider a situation that occurred a few years ago.

Insight through Illustration

The facilities at a state university included two physical education buildings. On the second floor of the main gym, two classrooms and faculty offices were located across the hallway from a space that had been used as a wrestling and mat room since the building was occupied fifteen years earlier. Most physical education, athletics, and recreation activities requiring a matted area were scheduled in this facility. Since it had been used for this purpose since the building was new, no one seemed to seriously question the arrangement. The room was a nice facility for classes, the

wrestling team, and the martial arts clubs. But although the primary purpose for originally scheduling activities in that particular space was being satisfied, the peripheral conditions were not. Noise from the activities was a real hindrance for both the classes meeting across the hallway and the faculty and staff occupying the nearby offices.

Because all conditions were not being satisfied and because the department desperately needed space for a motor learning and biomechanics lab, the department head appointed a committee to study the possibility of moving wrestling and martial arts activities to some other area. After a thorough investigation, the committee recommended that the mat activities be moved to the older gymnasium in the other physical education building. That area, which was slightly larger, would become a semipermanent gymnastics, wrestling, martial arts, and aerobics exercise gymnasium. The decision would also necessitate moving some social, folk, and jazz dance classes and activities to a smaller dance studio.

This decision satisfied the purpose of gaining a space for the motor learning and biomechanics lab, and it also satisfied a peripheral condition by removing the noisy activities to a more isolated location. Other peripheral conditions also had to be satisfied to make the decision an effective one. The gymnastics and wrestling teams needed adequate practice conditions, and adequate space for apparatus and activities using them was needed. Adequate provisions also needed to be made for the displaced dance classes and recreational activities. When the department head was confident that these peripheral conditions had been satisfied, the decision was made and implemented.

Any time a key organizational decision is made, there are winners and losers. It is important to try to satisfy those who were opposed to the decision, for making unpopular decisions acceptable strengthens the position of the director.

Allowing Acceptable Compromise

One of the realities of decision making is that compromise plays a very important role. Compromise is often conceptualized as an indication of weakness, and it is in some situations; but when providing satisfaction for all people concerned is important, compromise can be a valuable tool. Values, truths, and principles should not be compromised, but concessions in the decision process can be made without compromise in these areas.

An effective decision satisfies both the central purpose and the peripheral conditions without requiring any unacceptable compromises. In the example related earlier, it was possible to satisfy all those conditions in the decision to move the mat activities to the other gym, even though some of the staff coaching the activities would have been happier if the move had not been made. On the other hand, an example of an ineffective decision that does not satisfy all of the conditions is one seen often in coaching and teaching situations when the teacher-coach is assigned more responsibilities than one person can perform effectively. Consequently, at least one of the responsibilities receives inadequate attention, and mediocrity results from this compromise.

Insight through Illustration

A top-level administrator recently made a decision against the advice of the athletics director, the physical education director, and the coach to keep a baseball field in its same location even though a new classroom facility that was being built occupied a sizable chunk of the existing baseball field and reduced the right and right-center field to unacceptable limits. After one week of practice, the team had to move to the city stadium. This decision did not satisfy the surrounding, or peripheral, conditions, and required an unacceptable compromise.

Putting Decisions into Action

We've already stated that the best decisions can be totally useless unless they are put into action. Putting decisions to work may not be as difficult as making sure a decision satisfies the central purpose and the peripheral conditions, but it is likely to require more time. Execution requires not only that the director identify what needs to be done, who will do it, and how it will be done, but also that he or she communicate the decision through the proper channels to the person or people who actually will implement the directive.

Insight through Illustration

A school reached an agreement with a local health club to trade swimming pool use for racquetball court time. The arrangement would provide the club members an activity that otherwise would not be available and would provide physical education students an opportunity to play racquetball on quality courts. Everything seemed to go smoothly except at the beginning of each term, when the students found that no court time had been reserved for them. The reservation clerks scheduled the courts one week in advance, and the club's fitness director was failing to give the clerks enough advance notice to block out six courts for two hours each day for the physical education class. Consequently, a good decision was losing some value due to a breakdown in communication.

Getting Feedback

After a decision is made and put into action, the director must build in a system of feedback that will continually test the relevancy of the decision. Peter Drucker (1966:139) has stated, "Decisions are made by men. Men are fallible; at best, their works do not last long. Even the best decision has a high probability of being wrong. Even the most effective one becomes obsolete."

Insight through Illustration

Many schools in California experienced personnel cutbacks in 1980 due to Proposition 13, and administrators scrambled to make adjustments that would be least detrimental to their programs. One sports director decided to replace a part-time tennis coach with a full-time faculty member, who also functioned as an assistant football coach, to avoid laying off the full-time faculty member. The football coach's job description was revised to include the tennis coaching responsibility. The coach was marginally qualified to assume the responsibility and said he wanted the additional work (maybe to save his job). The head football coach reluctantly agreed to cooperate with the new arrangement so that he would not totally lose an assistant. The situation was closely monitored to test the wisdom of the decision, and it did not take a full season for the feedback to indicate that the new arrangement was not working. The coach seemed to have an interest in doing well, but his temperament and the coaching methods that worked well for football were not effective for tennis. Other problems seemed to surface, and after a year the plan was abandoned. This decision was not right from the beginning, and the feedback showed it.

An effective feedback system also serves to monitor decisions that seem right when put into action but that later may become obsolete and ineffective.

Insight through Illustration

A swimming pool maintenance policy at a sports facility stated that the temperature of the pools would be maintained at eighty degrees Fahrenheit. The temperature seemed to be satisfactory for the various users, who included members of instructional classes, competitive teams, and various recreational swimming groups. Feedback on the total pool operation was routinely reported to the department head, and adjustments were made as necessary.

Then a large federal grant was awarded for an aquatics program for victims of arthritis. All competitive swimming was moved from the indoor pool to the outdoor pool. Classes and recreational periods were scheduled at both pools, so the users had a choice of two pools they could use. Since the arthritis group was composed of people from fifty-five to ninety years of age, it was essential that the water temperature be increased by three to four degrees.

The director of plant operations was very much opposed to raising the water temperature because of the increased cost of heating the water. He finally was convinced that the arthritic group was not going to participate in the federally funded program unless they were comfortable in the water. The additional cost for heating the water was more than offset by the grant money, and the school could provide a much-needed service to a group of citizens whose health could be improved by the activity program. In this case, although a decision to maintain the pool temperature at eighty degrees had been a good decision for many years, it became obsolete and needed to be changed because of changing conditions.

PRINCIPLES RELATING TO WISE DECISIONS

In Chapter 1 we defined principles as generalizations that appear to be true in reflecting or explaining reality. Principles are reliable guides to action. The following principles can be followed to produce wise decisions.

Decisions Require Alternatives

A decision is a choice and requires the decision maker to choose from two or more alternatives. Developing alternatives is the first step in decision making. Without alternatives the course of action is fixed and determined. If our thought produces only one possible course of action, then we have not spent enough time in thought.

Peter Drucker (1966:143) has stated that a decision "is rarely a choice between right or wrong. It is at best a choice between almost right and probably wrong—but much more often a choice between two courses of action neither of which is probably more nearly right than the other." This quote implies that although the person selecting one alternative over another is taking a risk, the risk is not great since the viable alternatives are usually similar. A director needs to avoid playing it so safe in making a decision that an unacceptable compromise results.

Developing alternatives may be as important as making the best choice between or among them. Creative thought, research, common sense, and rationality usually produce so many possible courses of action that adequately appraising each one becomes difficult. In an organization, the wise administrator seeks help in developing alternatives. Committees that have been properly oriented and motivated can provide valuable assistance in creating and analyzing a list of reasonable alternatives.

Alternatives may be restricted by certain *limiting factors,* defined as anything that stands in the way of achieving a desired goal. The *principle of the limiting factor* is that only when we recognize and deal with those factors that stand critically in the way of our achieving our goal are we able to select the best course of action.

To understand this principle, put yourself in the position of a fitness director in a corporate setting. The weight-training facility is small and the equipment consists of incomplete sets of bars and weights. The director's goal is to provide a quality program, knowing the fitness benefits that can be gained from a top program of resistance exercise and realizing the attractiveness of a well-planned and well-equipped weight-training facility. His research is leading him to consider buying isokinetic equipment; however, the limiting factors are two: (1) The equipment budget was planned only for conventional bars and weights and is inadequate for the more expensive machines; and (2) the present weight-training area is too small for the desired equipment. For the director to consider the alternative of buying isokinetic equipment as viable, the two limiting factors must be overcome. If they cannot be overcome, then the alternative must be eliminated.

Wise Decisions Result from Disagreement

Not only do wise decisions result from disagreement; no decision is necessary if there is no disagreement. In a fascist state, fear may prevent disagreement from being voiced. Nazi Germany had some of the most brilliant military minds in the world, but for the generals to disagree with Hitler and staunchly argue for their position meant risking disgrace and possibly death. Because the generals were not given the opportunity to change the mind of the decision maker, Germany made many strategic blunders during World War II.

It often has been stated that the key to a healthy discussion or debate is to disagree without being disagreeable. This statement could not be more true of organizational decisions. Emotions must be controlled and criticism must be properly handled if the leader is to fully benefit from the wisdom of those who can offer assistance. The decision maker should even argue

In administration as in sports, you must either decide to play it safe or take risks.

against herself or himself and should give those who disagree with her or his point of view full consideration.

Drucker (1966:149–52) lists three main reasons for insisting on disagreement: (1) It is the only safeguard against the decision maker's becoming a prisoner of the organization; (2) it alone can provide alternatives; and (3) most important, it is needed to stimulate imagination.

Critical Decisions Require Time

One of the worst mistakes an administrator can make in decision making is to rush the process. This is not to imply that the process should be slowed down intentionally. It means that the de-

cision maker needs to recognize that critical decisions are not made hurriedly nor without full thought and deliberation. Most critical decisions are related directly or indirectly to personnel, and a rule of thumb is that an administrator when making personnel decisions should delay as long as possible without procrastinating. The director is procrastinating when the program or the people in the program suffer from a delayed decision, and the director must possess enough wisdom to know when that occurs and avoid it.

One successful director uses the following simple routine for making critical decisions:

1. After all information is in, she gives full consideration to the evidence.

2. She then makes a decision and writes it down, including every detail.

3. She goes through this process on each of the two following days, and each day thereafter as long as there is any variation from the original decision.

4. When her decision has been exactly the same for three days in a row, she puts the decision into action.

This routine may be slower than most directors prefer, but it does tend to prevent hasty and premature decisions.

Decisions Necessitate Change

When decisions are made, changes are going to occur. Just how critical and far-reaching these changes become depends upon the magnitude of the decision. A decision to convert three part-time positions into one full-time position will create certain critical changes, especially in the lives of those who have been holding the three part-time positions and the one selected for the full-time job. Compare that decision to one that will bring about a total reorganization of a school, business, or department, and the changes in the former case do not appear to be that critical.

Change creates resistance. Human nature is predictable enough for us to realize that when a situation changes due to some other person's decision, resistance will follow. How well the administrator who makes the decision that causes the changes can relate to the resistance and to those resisting will determine the probability of his or her success. In a decision to reorganize, if the people presently holding leadership roles cannot adjust to the changes, they may need to resign or be removed by some other means. Resignations, retirements, and firings are not unusual in a major reorganization decision.

IMPROVING DECISION-MAKING SKILLS

Physical education, fitness, and sports administrators and leaders have a responsibility to make effective decisions, and decision-making skills can be improved through concentrated effort and practice. A very simple method for improving as a decision maker is to practice on the simple and routine decisions you make each day. Use the problem-solving steps we present in deciding which foods you will buy at the supermarket or the type and amount of exercise you will do each day of a given week. You may find after a short while that using this organized step-by-step approach results in wiser decisions for these simple daily problems. The decision-making skill you gain through this kind of practice will carry over to solving the more complex problems you encounter.

A Standard Problem-Solving Method

The steps that follow are specifically intended for a problem-solving committee to use in preparing a list of viable alternatives for the director or administrator to choose from. However, with the exception of step 5—brainstorming—an individual can use the routine for solving problems and issues quite effectively.

Step 1 Define and clarify the problem. This first step is probably the most important. The ultimate, or underlying, problem may be hidden behind some superficial issues and symptoms. When the ultimate problem is identified and corrected, the superficial problems and symptoms will disappear. Unfortunately, the reverse is not true; therefore, thoroughness at this step is critical.

Step 2 Identify the decision objectives. To identify the decision objectives, answer the question, What do I hope to accomplish by solving the problem? Objectives offer direction for proceeding toward the selection of the best alternative.

Step 3 *Identify the hurdles that may hinder the solution.* These hurdles may be physical (such as lack of skill), social (such as community mores), emotional (such as fear), or intellectual (such as expectations). A smoother path toward solution will result from identifying and removing the blocks.

Step 4 *List, analyze, and categorize all relevant information.* After information has been gathered, it should be organized and evaluated.

Step 5 *Brainstorm for alternatives.* There are a few simple rules for holding an effective brainstorming session: (a) Select a group leader who understands the technique; (b) work in groups of five to seven people; (c) select an isolated meeting place that will be free from interruptions; (d) use a tape recorder; (e) to get the group members in a responsive mood, use a warm-up question, such as, what are some ways that adhesive tape may be used?; (f) encourage members to say the first thing

that comes to mind without evaluating the response; (g) do not permit criticism of any response; and (h) prevent time lags and end the response period at an agreed-upon time. Make a list of the responses. Keep only those alternatives that are reasonably valid.

Step 6 *Analyze the list of alternatives, retaining only those that are viable, and present to the decision maker.* After thoroughly studying and testing the alternatives against the limiting factors, narrow the list to three to five viable alternatives from which the director may choose.

Step 7 *Make the decision and put it into action.* The decision maker studies the alternatives, taking full advantage of the committee's effort, makes her or his choice, and implements the decision.

A Final Note

Count yourself fortunate when faced with problems. Only when we come face to face with trying problems and solve them can we grow. Those without problems are either in a cemetery or an institution.

KEY WORDS AND PHRASES

Decision	Disagreement	Compromise
Common problems	Problem-solving technique	Alternatives
Unique problems	Ingredients of choice	Resistance to change
Feedback	Decision-making approaches	

QUESTIONS FOR REVIEW

1. List five factors that affect most decisions.

2. Explain the principle of the limiting factor.

3. Make at least one statement about each of the five elements of good decision making.

4. Instinct is one approach to making a decision. What are three other approaches to decision making?

5. Discuss the statement, "In making a decision, sometimes courage is more critical than judgment."

6. What are the steps in an organized problem-solving technique?

7. How do the following contribute toward more effective decisions?
   a. Alternatives
   b. Disagreement
   c. Asking the question, "Why is this decision needed?"

8. What is the rationale for delaying as long as possible without procrastinating in making a tough decision?

SELF-TEST

Corrected True-False

If the statement is true, mark it T. If the statement is false, mark it F and change it to a true statement by adding or deleting words.

_____ 1. A decision is totally useless without action.

_____ 2. Effective directors make many decisions.

_____ 3. Generic problems should be answered by a rule, policy, principle, or standard.

_____ 4. A director's initial position when making a decision should be based on what is acceptable rather than what is absolutely right.

_____ 5. There is no one formula for making a tough decision.

_____ 6. Convictions or feelings have an insignificant effect on most big decisions made by effective managers.

_____ 7. A decision is rarely a choice between right or wrong; it is a choice between alternatives.

_____ 8. In making a decision the director needs to start with facts rather than opinions.

_____ 9. The first rule in decision making is that one does not make a decision unless there is disagreement.

_____ 10. There usually is only one alternative that is not acceptable, and that is to do nothing.

Multiple Choice

_____ 11. Administrators and directors are known by the:
  a. decisions they make
  b. toughness they show
  c. charisma they have
  d. all the above

_____ 12. Decisions cause change, and change creates:
  a. turmoil
  b. alternatives
  c. resistance
  d. a step backwards

_____ 13. Getting feedback into the decision-making process:
  a. assures the right choice
  b. is secondary to action
  c. causes procrastination
  d. tests decision relevancy

_____ 14. One of the following is not an ingredient of choice:
  a. courage
  b. character
  c. conviction
  d. cognition

_____ 15. These problems are more difficult for the director than common problems:
  a. generic
  b. unique
  c. past
  d. personnel

CASE 4.1 TRAMPOLINES—YES OR NO?

During the 1960s, many trampoline centers sprang up throughout the nation. Because of the exhilaration people felt in flying through the air while executing flips, rolls, and layouts, entrepreneurs were doing quite well by charging a fee for a few minutes on the trampolines. Most trampolines were at ground level and appeared safe. The businesses prospered until some very severe accidents and injuries began to occur. Then lawsuits began to take their toll.

Insurance became so costly that the businesses were forced to close. Shortly after this craze subsided, there were isolated incidents of critical injuries to other trampolinists, including an Olympic champion. The news media gave the trampoline the reputation of being a killer. Professional orga-

nizations were asked for position statements regarding the activity.

The American Medical Association and its affiliates came out very strongly against trampolines being used anywhere. Professional physical education organizations strongly advised that rigid safety precautions be taken, emphasizing the need for adequate and properly trained "spotters" and qualified supervisors. Because of the high cost of insurance, position statements of professional organizations, and the threat of legal actions, many schools removed all trampolines from school premises.

John Low came to State University as department head of physical education in 1982 and discovered that trampolining was a very popular activity in both the physical education classes and the recreational program. Dr. Low consulted the gymnastics coach regarding the wisdom of continuing to teach trampolining and allowing the gymnastics club to work out on the tramps. Coach Mann believed that trampolining could be a very worthwhile activity if properly taught and supervised. He wondered why the public was so negative toward trampolining when many more injuries per capita occurred in football and certain other sports. He commented, "If every activity that involves risk is eliminated, there will be nothing left to teach in physical education."

After discussing trampolining with other faculty members, Dr. Low proposed to the faculty that the word *trampoline* be removed from the title of the only course that specifically listed trampolining as part of the activity. This proposal was accepted, but instructors were permitted to continue teaching trampoline in the tumbling classes if they felt competent to safely teach it.

Trampolining also had been a traditional activity of the gymnastics club, and Coach Mann was the faculty advisor for that club. The trampolines continued to be chained and locked in the gymnastics room, and Coach Mann, the club president, and the equipment attendants were the only people with the combinations to the locks. The club continued to use the trampolines during its workout sessions in the evenings, even when Coach Mann was not present. Two club members, including the president, were considered by Coach Mann as being excellent trampolinists and qualified supervisors of the activity.

No accidents on the trampoline had occurred since Dr. Low arrived, but an air of uneasiness hung over his head regarding the club's use of the equipment. He permitted continued use of the trampolines until March 1983, when it was brought to his attention that the trampolines were found unlocked twice after the club's evening workouts. He immediately placed a moratorium

on the use of the trampolines by the gymnastics club until further notice.

The club president and the club advisor came to Dr. Low to request that the trampolines be allowed in their activities. It was especially important for them to use the tramps since they had planned a performance for the upcoming health fair that was scheduled for March 25. Dr. Low refused to lift the moratorium without some evidence of more club responsibility and supporting statements from the academic and student administrators. He informed the club officers that it was their responsibility to get the supporting statements in writing to him with some assurance that more responsibility for securing the trampolines would be taken.

As a result of the students' visit to the office of the dean of students, the business manager wrote a letter to Dr. Low supporting the use of the trampolines on the basis that the associated students organization carried an unusually large amount of insurance for students participating in club activities. The dean of students also wrote a letter strongly supporting the club's use of the equipment. After the combination locks were removed and replaced with heavy key locks, the students were told they could use the trampolines, at least until after the health fair, by checking out the key from the equipment attendant each day and returning it to her before 8:00 A.M. the following morning.

Prior to lifting the moratorium, Dr. Low had called a legal advisor regarding the moratorium decision, and although the legal advisor was hesitant to condemn the activity, he did express his opinion that the moratorium was a wise move. On April 15 the head of all state university physical education departments held their annual meeting, and Dr. Low asked if any of them permitted the gymnastics club to use the tramps without a certified faculty member present. All who responded said they did not permit trampoline use without a certified instructor present. Coach Mann, upon being informed of their position, stated that he had observed unlocked trampolines standing open in two of the gyms at state universities with unsupervised individuals bouncing on them. When some of the department heads did not respond, Dr. Low suspected that they did not want to admit leaving their trampolines unlocked and unsupervised.

The health fair is now history, and the department head is faced with the decision of permitting the club to continue to use the trampolines, restricting their use to classes only, removing all trampolines from the physical education facilities, or finding another alternative.

Your Response

1. What are the issues and problems in this case?
2. What barriers may stand in the way of the best decision?
3. What action do you think would be appropriate?
4. List the decision and action guides that led you to your decision.

CASE 4.2   WAS A WELLNESS PROGRAM NEEDED?

Sam Wellington was, in the true sense of the word, a self-made man. After being discharged from the U.S. Navy in 1955, he took advantage of the GI Bill and went to college at State University in Silicon Valley. He had served as an electronics technician while in the Navy, and because of the excellent electronics schooling he received, the three years experience, and his special ability to understand the technical concepts relating to the electronics field, he was considered the electronic whiz kid of the naval air station.

At the university he majored in business administration and after graduation planned to open his own manufacturing enterprise. He knew that if the military's present radar systems had an added electronic device that he referred to as the "seeker," the technology in that area would be advanced by twenty years.

His dream became a reality when he was able to convince a wealthy friend to financially back him in his industrial venture. He worked hard, long hours getting the business going and gained the reputation of being a tough, hard-working, dictatorial, but fair, industrialist.

Bob was Sam's only son and, being an outstanding basketball player, chose to attend Cal Poly University as an athlete and physical education major. Upon Bob's graduation, he accepted Sam's offer to come into the business as a junior executive in charge of personnel development. The business had grown and now employed more than fifteen hundred men and women. Although Sam cut back on his own demanding work schedule and began to shift more responsibility onto Bob's shoulders, there was no question that he was still the boss and decision maker on the important issues.

Bob attended a meeting in Chicago in early January with about twenty-five hundred other corporate executives. The theme of the conference, "Shaping Up Your Business," stressed the central message that companies could do themselves a tremendous favor by adding a wellness and fitness department to their operations. Numerous executives, from both large and small businesses, gave testimony to their increased production since initiating sound programs of wellness and fitness.

When Bob returned to Silicon Valley, especially since physical fitness and education had been his interest while in college, he was pumped up to add a wellness program to his father's corporation. His enthusiasm received a jolt, however, when he presented to Sam his hopes for investing a million dollars into the program. Sam's response was that he felt they were already doing enough for the employees' well-being—they sponsored teams in basketball, softball, volleyball, and soccer. He could not understand how more of that type of investment would increase production, nor when time could be devoted for fitness activities. He believed in hard work, dedication, and loyalty as the keys to his past success and was not excited about investing a million dollars into what he called "play activities."

Your Response

1. What is the central issue in this case?
2. List the major problems with which Bob is confronted.
3. What barriers or hurdles can prevent the best decision from being made?
4. What actions would you take if you were Bob?
5. List the action guides that would direct your actions.

BIBLIOGRAPHY

Cohen, William A., and Nutrit Cohen. *Top Executive Performance: 11 Keys to Success and Power*. New York: Wiley, 1984.

Dougherty, Neil J., and Diane Bonanno. *Management Principles in Sport and Leisure Services*. Minneapolis: Burgess, 1985.

Drucker, Peter F. *The Effective Executive*. New York: Harper & Row, 1966.

Dyer, William G., et al. *Challenge of Management*. San Diego: Harcourt Brace Jovanovich, 1990.

Eble, Kenneth E. *The Art of Administration*. San Francisco: Jossey-Bass, 1978.

Koontz, Harold, and Heinz Weihrich. *Essentials of Management*. 5th ed. New York: McGraw-Hill, 1989.

Tucker, Allan. *Chairing the Academic Department: Leadership among Peers*. Washington, DC: American Council on Education, 1981.

Ziegler, Earle F. *Decision-Making in Physical Education and Athletic Administration: A Case Method Approach*. Champaigne, IL: Stipes, 1982.

5

Communicating Effectively

A soft answer turns away wrath,
but flagrant words stir up anger.

Proverbs 15:1

Chapter Objectives

After reading this chapter and completing the exercises,
you should be able to:

1 Define communication

2 Outline the purpose of communication

3 Discuss the importance of effective communication

4 Diagram the communication process

5 Name two types of communication

6 List five barriers to communication

7 Name at least three ways to facilitate upward communication

8 Outline the steps in preparing for meetings and presentations

9 List five guidelines when using audiovisuals in a presentation

10 Describe how to make the best impact in televised presentations

Administrators talk about the value of communication, but many still do very little to change the quality of it. In leadership, communication is essential to effectiveness. People in leadership roles realize the importance of and the need for communicating, yet many of those same leaders fail simply because they do not practice good communication skills. A leader cannot take for granted this important aspect of administration. This chapter will examine the art of communication, present methods to improve your communication skills, and help you understand the value of effective communication in an organization.

WHAT IS COMMUNICATION?

Communication has been defined in a variety of ways. Literally, *communicate* means to share or to make common. Communication is also a transmitting—a giving and receiving—of information or the search for all available means of persuasion. The primary concern of communication is to take an idea; find symbols for it such as words, voice tones, posture, and gestures; and express that idea to others in such a way that is easily and readily understood.

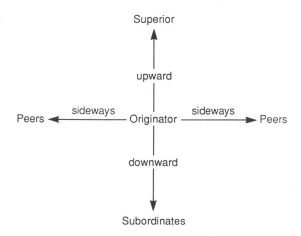

Figure 5.1 *Levels of Communication*

Communication can be broken down into three parts. There is the information to be transmitted (the message), a sender to give the message, and a receiver to receive it. As the core of effective leadership, communication occurs at all levels. Upward communication happens between a person and his or her superiors. Downward communication occurs between a leader and his or her subordinates. And sideways communication, also known as teamwork, occurs among peers at the same level. These different levels of communication are diagrammed in Figure 5.1.

WHO NEEDS COMMUNICATION SKILLS?

Leaders in physical education, fitness, and sports need good communication skills as much as any manager or administrator in business, education, or politics. In fact, activity leaders may need to concentrate on communication skills more than leaders in other fields, for two reasons.

First, those being led in sports and fitness activities are competitive action people who are ready to move on first cue even before receiving full instruction. Action without complete direction or without full appraisal of the results of such action may be disastrous. For example, a coach who is hired with a clear understanding that winning is important may cause irreparable damage and embarrassment to the institution and himself if he charges toward the goal of winning without fully communicating to his assistants and alumni the necessity of full compliance with recruiting regulations. As another example, a fitness director who assigns a lab assistant the responsibility of assessing the fitness levels of a group of seniors must be sure that the assistant fully understands the safety precautions necessary in testing older people who may be at higher cardiac risk.

The second reason why it may be more imperative for activity leaders to concentrate on communication skills relates to the ego involvement of their peers. Many former superstar athletes remain in the field as instructors, coaches, or directors, and these people often have abundant self-confidence. Self-confidence is an admirable trait in leaders, but if it erodes into cockiness or a pompous attitude, it can be destructive. There is a lot of truth to the saying, "The older we get, the better we were." Communicating with an overconfident staff person is more difficult than with young, anxious neophytes who recognize that they do not have all the answers.

THE PURPOSE OF COMMUNICATION

We generally communicate to bring about change. Communication is the means by which any organization strives to achieve certain goals. Through written and oral interaction, activity program instructors, coaches, maintenance staff, and the director work together toward common results. Cooperation and coordination are impossible without communication, and without a cooperative and coordinated effort of the people in a group, change will not occur.

For example, the director of a corporate fitness program must gather information about all participants in the program including age, health history, body composition, and present fitness level, as well as their daily schedules. This knowledge becomes the basis for decisions affecting individualized workout prescriptions, facility schedules, and number of fitness employees needed to meet the health and fitness needs of that company. The organizing and assimilating of that information and acting in response to it become more difficult where several hundred people are involved. In a like manner, a high school athletics director, when staging a contest, must know the attitude of the spectators, the degree of rivalry

between the two schools, the amount of control both coaches have over their teams, as well as the number of spectators who will attend. When he or she has gathered and appraised this information, then plans for security, concessions, and traffic control can be made in order to assure a safe and controlled event. In both of these examples, communication needs to take place for information to be gathered and planning to occur.

Communication is absolutely essential if the various aspects and functions of an activity-based program are to be integrated into a smooth operational unit. No other function of the administrative process is more vital to the success of an organization than the communication function. Through communication, objectives are established and disseminated, plans are developed in order to achieve the objectives, resources are organized, and every aspect of the operation may be controlled.

TYPES OF COMMUNICATION

There are basically two types of communication: one-way and two-way. Each type has its uses and its drawbacks for leaders.

One-Way Communication

One-way, or unidirectional, communication is useful in circumstances where information must be transmitted to a large number of people, and one-on-one contact is impossible or unnecessary. Newsletters, handbooks, memos, bulletins, bulletin boards, pamphlets, and public addresses are examples of common unidirectional forms of communication.

In unidirectional communication, it is important to present information clearly and simply. The common rule of speaking—Speak at the lowest level of understanding in the group—also per-

I WANT YOU TO DO IT THIS WAY.

It is important in one-way communication to present information clearly and simply.

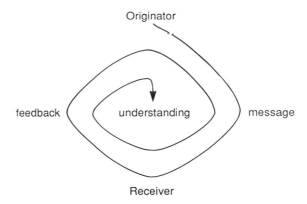

Figure 5.2 *Bidirectional communication*

tains to written communication. Brevity is also important, and the message must be pertinent and easily interpreted.

Although these guidelines can help to make unidirectional communication more effective, they can also create hazards to communication. Keeping information brief and easy to understand may water it down so much that the message is weakened. Perhaps the biggest drawback to unidirectional communication is that the administrator cannot tell whether the message is getting through and being understood clearly. Therefore, effective communication is impossible if it only incorporates unidirectional methods.

Two-Way Communication

Two-way, or bidirectional, communication is preferred for administrators and leaders because it allows immediate feedback after a message is conveyed. Bidirectional communication can be thought of as a spiral with the message originating with the sender, going through the receiver, and returning to the sender along with pertinent responses (feedback). The sender can then expound upon, modify, or change the message in response to the feedback received. (See Figure 5.2.) This process continues until mutual understanding is reached. Another advantage of bidi-

rectional communication is that the idea and the method of presentation can be tailored to fit the recipient.

Still, in bidirectional communication, misunderstanding is inevitable. The leader must be alert to recognize and quickly clarify it. Testing understanding and clarity can be accomplished by paraphrasing a message and returning it to the sender. If any discrepancies are found, they can be cleared up on the spot.

Asking subordinates what their idea of their responsibilities is might surprise a leader. Some will have an inflated view of their role, whereas others may feel less important than they actually are. Using this method, the leader can determine staff members' attitudes, and if major differences exist between a person's image of a job and its actual description, they can be cleared up diplomatically.

ACTIVE LISTENING

Effective verbal communication is a two-way process. The leader should always be cognizant of what people are saying, how they are acting, and how they are reacting to what he or she is saying.

Since listening is vital to open communication, an effective leader will make a conscious effort to become a skilled listener.

Active listening involves considering both the words and feelings of the speaker along with paraphrasing and devoting physical and mental attention to the speaker. Paraphrasing is a key way for a listener to assure that he or she is hearing what is intended. Repeating important messages and key statements will reinforce the message being delivered for both parties.

The first step in effective listening is to want to listen, to eliminate distractions, and to put aside expectations, first impressions, and premature judgments. Listening with an open mind allows us to be open to new opinions and change. Even though this is a difficult thing to do, it is essential in effective communication and decision making.

Listening is often thought of as being passive, but in fact it has both passive and active components. The passive part is to actually listen. This involves not talking and not mentally arguing. Free your mind to take in all the information that is being delivered, nonverbally as well as verbally. At first you may need to act like a good listener before you actually perfect the skills. Acting like a good listener includes maintaining eye contact, not talking, and not preparing your response before all the facts are delivered. Keep your mouth shut. If a person is talking to you and you keep trying to interject, you are a poor listener. Also keep your hands unoccupied. Some people may find that jotting down notes and key points is essential to remembering, but if the pen becomes a distraction or you tend to doodle, then taking notes hinders your listening ability.

The main components of active listening are concentration and understanding. Concentration requires effort; it does not just happen. Concentration is aided by maintaining eye contact and thinking about what is said as it is being said. Do not let things go in one ear and out the other. Aim to be an empathetic listener—one who not only hears the words but understands the feelings and emotions behind the words.

Understanding what is said involves both thinking about the content and offering verbal reinforcement. Paraphrasing the speaker's words, using terms such as I feel and I think, allows you to check your understanding. Be aware of words with multiple meanings and clarify these whenever they occur in a conversation.

In summary, good listeners not only keep their mouths closed and minds open while a speaker is delivering a message, but they also know when to break silence to clarify the speaker's key points.

WHY COMMUNICATIONS GO WRONG

For communication to work, everyone involved must be committed to making it work. A lack of commitment at any point in a communication network will result in a breakdown of communication. Just as a chain is only as strong as its weakest link, the chain of communication can be broken by an ineffective sender, a distorted or unclear message, or poor reception of the message. Some weak links or barriers to effective communication are discussed in the following paragraphs.

Failure to Consider the Receiver

When you fail to consider the person or persons for whom your communication is intended, you risk being misunderstood. This is a common pitfall. Awareness of others' feelings and past experiences is necessary for understanding. To be a good communicator, never assume that others have the same basis of understanding or have had the same experiences as you. Consider whom you are communicating with and then modify the message to fit the recipient. If you can phrase requests so that they clearly relate to the receiver's interests, you will find it easier to gain support from others.

There are a variety of theories why communications go awry, involving differences in style and even differences between the sexes. Although this text does not attempt to discuss all theories, we will briefly review two of these theories. Awareness of others is useful in all forms of communication. Even unidirectional communication is improved if the sender considers for whom the message is intended.

Social styles attempt to categorize people by the manner in which they are perceived by others. The theory of social styles purports that all people are creatures of habit and will usually act and react for specific motivations and within their own comfort zone. This theory is the basis of management training by Wilson Learning Corporation of Eden Prairie, MN. Social styles categorize people in one of four main styles: Analytical, Driver, Amiable, and Expressive. Within each style are subcategories to further define people's behavior.

Analytical   The analytical style is motivated by the desire to be an expert on the subject at hand and to observe correct procedure at all times. When learning about a topic, the analytical will not only read the information provided but conduct his or her own research to augment that received by others. This person is characterized by conservative dress and mannerisms, and slow, deliberate speech. When communicating with an analytical, a person is wise to be well-informed on all details of a subject and to provide as many details as possible to the listener. If a decision is needed, it is better not to pressure the analytical but to allow him or her ample time to research and formulate an opinion.

Driver   A person who possesses the style of driver is motivated by the desire for control and

power. This person is characterized by fast talking and quick actions. These are the movers and shakers of an organization. Because of the desire for quick decisions, it is better to give key points rather than many details to a driver. Memos in bullet-point format characterize this person's written communication. In school, the driver is a person who reads the abstracts or Cliff notes of an assignment and gleans only that information deemed important. They follow this same style of research in business. Because a driver likes to feel in control of a situation, it is best not to order or assign but to pose requests in such a way that drivers can feel as if they have made their own decision how best to proceed.

Amiable   The amiable is often the pleasant person in the group who gets along well with everyone, even the jerks. Amiables are motivated primarily by achieving a calm environment and cohesive team; they enjoy building relationships with others. Where a driver thrives in the midst of excitement and turmoil, the amiable feels extremely uncomfortable and will attempt to restore order and peace to the surroundings. Networking is very important to this person, and decisions are often made by committee or group consensus. When communicating with an amiable, take a few minutes to ask about his or her family or otherwise make a personal connection before moving into the business discussion. If a decision is required, it is best to allow this person time to gather input from others who may be affected by the decision, whether it is family or co-workers.

Expressive   The expressive, as the name implies, communicates with much facial expression and gesticulation and often dresses to communicate a fun-loving approach to life. As with the amiable, expressives are people oriented. However, where the amiable is content being one of the team, the expressive strives for approval and status within the group. An expressive person is a fast talker and often makes quick decisions based more on gut reaction than on facts. When presenting information, do not dwell on details but give an overview of the information. In meetings, the challenge is to rein in the enthusiasm of the expressive and allow others to participate fully.

No matter the social style of the person, when you are communicating, attempting to mesh with the person's style will help you gain acceptance and trust. If the person is slow and deliberate of speech, matching your pace and volume to his or hers is wise. If the person talks fast and varies the volume, avoid the tendency to match them, or you both may end up in a loud oral competition. When dealing with amiables or expressives, disclosure of personal information may gain trust. Maintaining diplomatic relations with others is important in management. Better understanding the recipient will help convey the message.

Sexual Differences in Communication

In her book, *You Just Don't Understand: Women and Men in Conversation,* Deborah Tannen claims that men and women converse so differently that it is akin to people of different cultures attempting to communicate. Dr. Tannen purports that women communicate to establish connection and intimacy with others; men communicate to gain status and independence. In arguing and persuasion, women will use more personal anecdotes, whereas men will make more categorical statements of right and wrong. This theory of sexual differences in communication is illustrated by the following observations from a corporate lunchroom. In unguided discussion, men talked about work, and women talked about other people such as friends and family. When given the topic of food, men focused on what they were eating and different restaurants, but women talked on a more personal level about diet and health. On the subject of recreation, men discussed sports and vacations while women talked about exercise. In discussing housing, external issues such as loca-

tion, commuting times, and property values were important to the men. Women focused more on internal issues such as decor, family activities, and household duties.

The above illustrates that men and women focus on different aspects of the same subject, but another example shows that even words can be interpreted differently. The phrase, "I'm sorry," is perceived by a man as putting him in a subordinate role, as apologizing for an action. To a woman, "I'm sorry" may mean an apology or simply, "I'm sorry to hear that." Try to frame words in the language of the receiver and converse on his or her terms to enhance understanding.

The same recommendation applies to participating as an active listener. Women tend to relate better with listening responses such as "I see," "Uh huh," or nodding and laughter. Men, on the other hand, tend to make fewer responses and may view running verbal feedback as talking instead of listening. Women may view the male tendency to silence as inattentiveness. In discussion, women may agree more than challenge, whereas men do just the opposite. It is important to consider the other party in all conversation whether one plays the role of listener or talker.

Poor Planning

Lack of planning or poor planning will result in inadequate communication. By now, you should realize that effective communication does not just happen; it must be practiced. As in attaining any other goal, a game plan must be devised and implemented. Planning lets the leader as well as those led know what is expected. Planning provides a rational and efficient approach to the goal of effective communication. We discuss planning in depth in Chapter 7; therefore, for the present, we will limit our discussion to planning for effective communication.

Awareness of problems and opportunities in communication is essential in formulating a plan.

If an organization has a communication problem, defining the problem is the first step in solving it. The leader should also be conscious of the environment in which communication takes place. What channels of communication are available to her or him? Are group meetings feasible or will one-on-one meetings serve the purpose better? Can unidirectional communication such as newsletters or memos be used to disseminate information to a large number of people? If a computer network is available, can it be used as a channel to conduct conversations?

With the technology of conference calling and video or television teleconferences, the need for lengthy travel and face-to-face meetings may be replaced, in some cases, by an hour or two on the telephone. If an organization has members in a variety of locations, teleconferences can bring together local groups and facilitate dialogue among participants in several locations. One example of the effective use of teleconferencing is by the American Medical Association. When new information is available for physicians, a teleconference can bring together specialists in numerous cities and allow them, via satellite television, to hear about the new treatment from a panel of experts. Telephone hook-ups can allow participants to call in to the panel and ask questions. This allows new medical technology to reach the field in a much more efficient and timely manner than would be available via annual conventions or published updates.

Knowing the opportunities and limitations enables formulation of realistic objectives and the means to obtain them. Once the short- and long-range objectives relating to improved communication are established and the channels examined, various alternatives can be developed for improving communication. Involving a greater number of employees in planning will allow more variety in alternative ideas. It is the administrator's duty to examine the alternatives and choose the best approach to attaining the goal.

The final step in planning is implementing the program or method to attain effective communication. This involves all types of support, including monetary, personnel, and equipment. It is important to realize that only with commitment and support from all levels of administration and staff can the chain of communication bear its burden.

Poor Message Retention

Poor retention of the message is another communication barrier, one for which no one to date has come up with a good cure. People generally remember only 10 percent of what they hear, 30 percent of what they see, and a mere 50 percent of what they do. For this reason, repetition by the sender is necessary. This does not mean that a leader should state the same facts over and over. What it does mean is that important points and key phrases should be subtly reworded and reiterated so that they will be included in that 10 percent that the listener recalls.

Key phrases can be catchy sentences or mnemonic devices. For example, we knew a two-year-old who kept repeating a commercial with a message, "Milk! It does a body good." This catchy phrase had made a lasting impression on him and undoubtedly on many others.

The echo is another device that can be effectively used to boost listeners' retention. The echo states a point or phrase, illustrates it, then restates the opening point, to give overall unity.

Providing visual and tangible reinforcement can also help staff members retain important information. Using this approach in training sales representatives, for example, can be beneficial. If a fitness center prides itself on its state-of-the-art fitness evaluation equipment, yet the sales staff does not fully understand what procedures are involved, how can they use this as a promotional tool? If the sales staff is told about and shown the various procedures for evaluating the fitness level of clients, they will begin to understand and remember this aspect of the facility. Better yet, involving the staff by conducting a complete fitness

Lines of communication.

evaluation on each individual will encourage further understanding. When staff members have had personal experience with a hydrostatic weighing tank and calipers, they will be better able to serve and relate to clients whose percentage of body fat they are measuring. This personal reinforcement will also emphasize the importance of the testing equipment to people not directly involved with its use.

Other Obstacles

Other obstacles to communication, more easily overcome, include an unsuitable environment full of distractions such as noise, people passing through, and temperature extremes. Discussions are best conducted in a comfortable, quiet area free from these distractions. Comfort in a discussion also stems from attitudes. Hostility, displays of status and power, anxiety, fear, condescension, or false deference are detrimental to clear communication. Language barriers can also exist between people. Ambiguous words and phrases should be avoided. Technical terms should only be used when they will facilitate understanding between people who possess technical knowledge. They should not be used to impress or intimidate others.

Although it is not always easy to put personal feelings aside, it is important to enter into any discussion with an open mind free of preconceived notions. This allows a manager to practice effective listening as discussed earlier.

IMPROVING COMMUNICATION

Too often, downward communication is the primary mode of communication for managers and directors. In a survey of five thousand American workers, 90 percent felt that their companies foster downward communication, while only 40 percent reported adequate upward communication. In addition to these numbers, of those who believed their company solicited ideas, only 29 percent felt these ideas are acted upon (Wyatt Company, New York, NY, 1990). There are a variety of ways to foster upward communication, including questionnaires, face-to-face or group meetings, and maintaining an open-door policy. These are discussed in greater detail throughout the following pages. One method employed successfully by many managers is MBWA—management by walking around. This entails unscheduled visits to all areas of an organization, along with informal discussions with workers at all levels of the organization. This visibility helps the top managers to be more accessible and observe, firsthand, the daily functioning of his or her organization.

One's style of communication is dependent upon one's self-concept. Whereas one leader may be effective by taking a hard-line stand, another may be just as effective using humor. It all depends upon the individual's beliefs, perceptions, and emotions. Regardless of one's personal style, communication can be improved by cultivating certain attitudes and sensitivities to those he or she manages. As discussed in the previous section, this sensitivity will aid a manager in communicating.

Many believe that the most effective leader is one who, despite her or his style of communication, focuses on what he or she can contribute to an organization or other individuals. This attitude carries over into communication through self-disclosure, empathetic listening, using feedback, and awareness of feelings and emotions. Good human relations lead to improved channels of communication, and good human relations are developed not by asking, What can that person do for me or the company? but What can I do to help that person be more effective? Improved performance results from focusing on the contribution one can make. Consider the following story.

Insight through Illustration

During a meeting of a campus club, members discussed individual merits of the candidates for new membership. As one name was brought up, members discussed the woman's prior achievements and potential contribution to the organization. This shy woman had not really set the world on fire, and many in the group felt she would contribute little to the club. After lengthy discussion and deliberation, the point was raised that maybe this shy woman had not proven herself yet and membership in this organization could be the outlet for all of her untapped potential. By asking not what she could do for them, but what they could do for her, the group gained a valuable member who not only blossomed into a hard-working member of many committees but eventually held one of the top leadership roles of the club.

Improved communication also results from realizing that words are only a small part of the communication process. Words can be presented in written or oral form, and they can be accompanied by pictures and other nonverbal cues—such as facial expression, handshake, clothing, body language, and even breathing—that give clues to the true meaning behind the words. Table 5.1 shows

Table 5.1 *The Importance of Words in Verbal Communication*

	Face-to-Face	*On Telephone*
Body Language	55%	———
Tone of Voice	38%	85%
Words	7%	15%

Adapted from Wilson Learning Seminar: "Selling Strategies with Social Styles," November 26–30, 1990, Atlanta, GA.

the weight that body language, tone of voice, and words play in delivery of a message. As one can see by this information, in verbal communication, words can play much less a role than a pleasant voice, a smiling face, and a comfortable posture. Take a moment and say the sentence, "I'm really happy to be here." This one sentence can be said in an excited, apprehensive, or facetiously angry manner, all by changing the tone of voice and facial expression.

Think, for example, of a person getting ready to take a graded exercise test in a fitness laboratory. Even though she is dressed in exercise gear, has a smile on her face, and says she is excited and ready to get the test going, a perceptive test technician might detect the sweaty palms and rapid breathing that indicate she is actually anxious and nervous about the pending test. To alleviate her fears, the technician might take time to sit her down and explain fully what the testing procedure is and what is expected of her. Clearing up uncertainty usually puts an end to unwarranted fears. This simple act of communicating will probably lead to better test results and a more confident client.

Giving and receiving feedback, both positive and negative, is also an essential part of communication, and an area where improvement can be made. A supportive, nonthreatening attitude will allow honest feedback to come out. The leader does not have to mimic former Mayor Koch of New York City by asking everyone, "How am I doing?" Conveying an open, interested attitude allows others to express their opinions without fear of retribution.

In summary, improving communication involves overcoming the barriers mentioned previously, being an active listener, and maintaining sensitivity to the receiver by using simple and direct language, being empathetic to the individual's feelings and personality, and being open to feedback.

DELIVERING AN ORAL MESSAGE

The oral message is the most common form of communication used in business. Verbal messages involve formal presentations, meetings, hallway chitchat, and individual or group discussions. Actually, an administrator is always communicating. Whatever he or she says or does communicates feelings and beliefs.

Holding a Private Meeting

The first step in delivering an oral message is preparing the message itself. It is important to know what information needs to be conveyed and the action desired by imparting this information. A discussion should never be launched into without preparation, or the message will be confusing not only to the listener but eventually to the sender as well. Preparation for a one-to-one meeting should be no less diligent than for a large group presentation, or the time spent in the meeting may be wasted in unimportant chatter. Doing the pre-meeting preparation involves focusing in on the key points of the message, then gathering as much information as necessary to support these opinions or persuade the listener to the desired action.

Another aspect of preparation is arranging the time and location for the meeting. Avoid popping in unannounced for important discussions. Allow the other party to be prepared for the discussion as well. Choose a private location where interruptions are kept to a minimum. What atmosphere is desired in the meeting? If a formal atmosphere or position of authority is desired, having the other party meet at the office or desk of the superior may be best. If a more relaxed atmosphere is needed, choose a location where both parties are on equal footing, such as side by side chairs or a small round table in a neutral area. Traditionally, individual meetings are held in offices or over a power lunch, but in some situations a nontraditional location may better serve the needs of the participants of the meeting. If both parties are pressed for time and enjoy exercise, meetings can be held in gyms, on racquetball or tennis courts, golf courses, or even while both parties are jogging. If a less active meeting is called for, there are private areas outside the traditional office setting. If one or both parties are traveling to meet the other, many hotels and airlines provide executive lounges with meeting areas, telephones, facsimile machines, and copiers, allowing business to be conducted in a private, business-like surrounding without the headaches of cross-town travel. A weight management company, with employees across three continents, regularly encourages executive meetings which combine relaxation and business. Recently, this company's meeting of senior managers was held on board an antique train traveling through the Colorado Rockies. This setting encouraged not only the discussion of business but a closer feeling of camaraderie among the managers.

When the meeting begins, the listener should be put at ease with small talk unrelated to business. Then the agenda should be outlined, covering what contribution is expected of the listener. In a private meeting the agenda is usually covered orally as opposed to in written form. If possible, the topic at hand should be related to the listener's past experiences or performance. For example, a director needs a report on new weight-training equipment, and she wants Tom Hardy to do the legwork in finding out what is available, the cost, and the feasibility of purchasing it. Tom will better understand what is required of him if the director tells him: "Find out the information on weight-training equipment, the same as you did for our purchase of the treadmills last year."

After the basic topics have been covered and the listener knows what is expected, then the particulars should be discussed. In the preceding example, the director would present topics such as budget range, limitations, and restrictions at this stage of the oral message. In summing up the presentation, the main topic, purpose, and whatever specifics need to be emphasized should be reviewed.

When the initial proposal has been presented, the receiver should be asked for his or her opinions and any pertinent feedback. At this stage of the discussion, any questions the receiver has can be clarified. This feedback stage can be very lengthy if the receiver has many questions. This stage should also give the receiver an opportunity to express his or her opinions in a relaxed and receptive atmosphere. It is important for both parties to maintain an attentive attitude by echoing important points and avoiding distractions such as doodling or paper shuffling.

Avoiding judgmental language is also important. If discussing an emotional topic such as performance or a reprimand, avoid phrases which depict the listener as a bad person. Focus instead on the behavior and the result. For example, "You are such a messy person. Straighten up your work area," could be better phrased by focusing not on the personality but on the action: "Suzanne, when you leave papers and files lying around, it makes it difficult for others to locate material they need. It also presents a poor image to customers who come into this area. Please refile all information as soon as you have finished using it."

After all details and feedback have been discussed, conclude the meeting with a specific call to action and plan for follow-up. Many administrators may feel that the delivery of the message

is complete with the initial meeting. But this is incorrect. The final, and often overlooked, stage in delivery of a message is the follow-through. Follow-through is just as important to communication as it is to a golf swing. This is the step where words become actions and reinforcement is required. By monitoring the actions initiated by the original conversation, the administrator retains control of the situation. Correcting mistakes and complimenting positive progress are equally important. In some circumstances, a follow-up letter may be in order. Often in business, especially in customer service and interviewing, follow-up letters do little more than thank listeners for their time and attentiveness. A more dynamic follow-up note may be handwritten and should include not only the courtesy thank you but a review of key points, the call to action, and plans for follow-up. This provides a mechanism for politeness as well as a written record of the discussion.

Leading a Group Meeting

Leading a group meeting is similar to holding a private meeting in that the topic must be decided upon and the information gathered before the meeting begins. An agenda or outline of topics to be covered should be prepared. This will include a statement of objectives, background of the problem, general information pertinent to the topic of discussion, and proposed questions or areas to be covered. The purpose of the agenda is to give structure to the meeting. Without structure, the meeting can become chaotic, and for this reason, it is important to discuss strictly what is on the agenda and not allow conversation to turn to other topics.

As in a private meeting, the group meeting location is important to the productivity of the time invested by all participants. There are a variety of seating arrangement options that act to encourage or discourage interaction among participants. Figure 5.3 shows a few of these options.

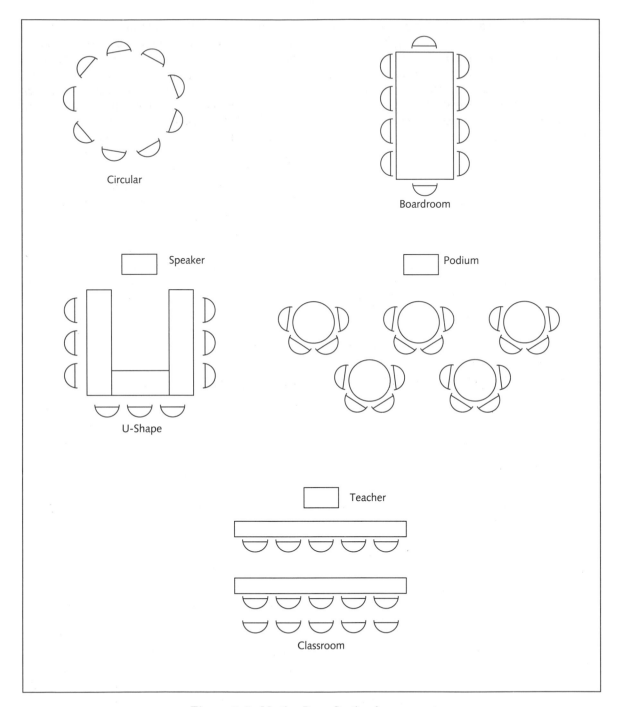

Figure 5.3 *Meeting Room Seating Arrangements*

Classroom style seating is the least conducive to interaction, whereas round tables or circular seating groups give all participants equal opportunity to be visible and to contribute. The boardroom table offers a position of authority to the person seated at the head of the table. If smaller group discussions are desired as part of the larger meeting, seating people at several round tables allows easy transition from large group to small discussion groups.

Getting everyone involved in the discussion can often be difficult, especially if some participants try to dominate the discussion. Facilitation can be achieved by asking direct questions of less assertive participants and clarifying and summarizing comments of those who tend to ramble on. This should be done in a friendly and impartial manner and not used to humiliate or criticize participants. Adults are less willing to make mistakes in public than are children. In meetings of peers, it is important to foster a spirit of trust. Complimenting new ideas is important to fostering a comfortable and receptive environment and will encourage everyone to feel free to express ideas. Even if an idea is presented that is not pertinent, criticism should be avoided and the person should be complimented for her or his contribution. The facilitator of the meeting should allow participants to pace themselves and use suggestions and summarization to guide members onto new subjects.

Creativity generated in the meeting process will aid creativity among participants. Seating arrangements, as discussed above, will facilitate or control dialogue among participants. Other activities can aid the creative process, too. One method used to make everyone feel more equal is to encourage participants to put on thinking caps, which can be a variety of funny hats and headgear. This helps people overcome inhibitions by making everyone share a little laughter. It is difficult to be critical of another person's idea when everyone has a silly hat on. Encourage participants to relate an issue to something completely outside the area of business. When people deal with an area of fa-

In meetings of peers, it is important to foster a spirit of trust.

miliarity, they think within their paradigms, or limits. By stepping into unfamiliar territory, people are free to think creatively because they do not know what is right or acceptable. It is interesting to note that when the idea of quartz watch movements was introduced to Swiss watchmakers, they deemed the idea ridiculous. However, Japanese watchmakers were willing to explore new ideas and embraced the idea of quartz movements. In a very short time, Japan took over the world watch market from the Swiss.

In group meetings, all ideas and decisions should be recorded during the discussion. A secretary or other staff person who is able to take shorthand or write fast should be involved to record all ideas as they are brought up. Sometimes, using flipcharts or write-on boards facilitates this recording.

At the conclusion of the meeting, a call to action is needed to determine what happens with the information and decisions developed during the course of the gathering. Assignments can be made by the facilitator, volunteers can be requested, or each participant may complete an action contract outlining what action they will take as a result of the meeting.

After the meeting, decisions that have been made and alternatives selected should be typed and distributed to all participants. This should be followed by monitoring of actions as described earlier.

Making a Personal Presentation

Preparation for a presentation does not differ greatly from preparation for other types of meetings. Know your subject matter thoroughly and know what your goal of the presentation will be. Is the goal to inform, excite, change opinion, or create buy-in to an idea or purchase of a product? Build the agenda of the presentation to elicit that goal. In a presentation, one must be cognizant of the interests of the audience—what the speaker feels is important may not be important to the audience. Researching the interests of the listeners will make for a more animated and useful presentation.

The location of a presentation may be out of the control of the speaker. Knowing the seating configuration of all participants, including key decision makers, may assist the presenter in structuring any use of visual aids. Audio and visual aids are discussed in greater detail in the following section. If appearing on a panel, request to be the first presentation on the agenda if possible. Time limitations are very important. If a meeting starts late, or other speakers run long, the last speaker may not have the same amount of time as the first. Also, at the beginning of a meeting, the audience is fresh and attentive. Later on, fatigue, hunger, and restlessness may cause the message to fall on deaf ears.

Time limitations are also important. The presenter should know how much time is allotted for the talk and practice to make sure the speech or presentation does not go beyond that time. If during practice the presenter finds he or she cannot conduct the entire presentation within the allotted

Presentations should be employed to enthuse, not bore.

time, then less important aspects should be weeded out to conform to time restrictions. Practicing the presentation will make the speaker comfortable with his or her topic. There are a variety of opportunities for practice: in the shower, in bed, while eating, while shaving or applying makeup, and even while driving to work. The more the presentation is practiced, the more at ease the speaker will be when he or she stands in front of a crowd to give the presentation. It is important, though, not to memorize the speech. If the presentation is committed to memory, and the speaker gets off track or loses his or her place, panic may set in until he or she regains composure. Anyone who has ever acted on a stage knows that momentary panic that occurs when a line is forgotten. If not for prompting, many scenes would be ruined.

Knowledge of the subject area for an oral presentation is crucial. Not only will the presenter be informing others about the topic, but often, the audience will ask questions and expect the presenter to answer knowledgeably. Structure for the presentation is necessary to keep on track and prevent rambling and wandering away from the issue. Many people use note cards to outline their presentation, and this helps them return to the topic if a question draws them away from the agenda.

As in any oral communication, nonverbal cues will add to or detract from the message. In large group presentations, long unexpected pauses and extended eye contact with audience members add impact and draw attention to the words spoken. Amplified body language, which adds visual interest, is achieved by holding arms out from the sides, hands on hips, or moving around on stage or into the audience. In smaller group settings, triangling hands with thumbs as base of the triangle shows confidence, power. If palms are shown to the listeners, it indicates asking or pleading, thereby placing the speaker in a subordinate role. Remain conscious of, and eliminate, nervous habits such as buttoning and unbuttoning suit jacket, playing with a pen, touching face or hair, or foot tapping. As the deodorant commercial says, never let them see you sweat. A confident speaker invites confidence and belief in the message being delivered.

The presentation should be started with a statement of purpose and some attention-getting device such as a joke or thought-provoking comment. Many speakers successfully use humor to ease into the body of the text. In a presentation on fad diets and weight-loss gimmicks, one speaker opened by emphatically reading advertisement headlines, including "Lose Twenty Pounds in Two Days!" and "I Lost Seventy-Five Pounds without Giving Up Chocolate!" These lines were absurd, but they served to amuse, inform, and intrigue the audience, who eagerly awaited the reading of the next headline to see if it would be more amusing.

A strong and definite conclusion is as important as an attention-grabbing opening statement. If the presentation calls for action, this can be stated in the conclusion along with an encouragement to take action. If the presentation is a controversial one, then posing thought-provoking questions or echoing the questions posed in the opening statement creates a good ending. Summarizing key points and statements is another way of tying up the loose ends of a presentation.

Using Audio and Visual Aids

The use of information packets, slides, overhead transparencies, and videos can add great impact to a presentation or meeting. Whenever visual aids are employed, they need to be the highest quality affordable. With the wide availability of computer graphics, there is little excuse for poorly drawn graphs or charts. However, even visuals can become a detraction from the message if not employed properly.

If distributing a packet of information, it may be wise to hand it out at the end of the presentation. If the packet contains a lot of information regarding the topic, the audience may spend their time thumbing through the pages rather than paying attention to the speaker. Make material in packets as professional, colorful, and interesting as that which is used on slides or overheads. Photos, graphics, and charts add impact to the written word.

When using slides or overheads, leave a few lights on. Keeping the audience's attention can sometimes be difficult in a darkened, quiet room. One college professor used many slides during his lectures. To keep the attention of his students he would slip in unexpected images or throw in a cartoon slide and humorous comment. This was an effective tool for keeping the attention of the class. Slides or overhead transparencies should contain a mixture of pictures, graphics, and words. Do not try to put too much information on one frame. Visuals augment the speaker's words, they don't replace them. One sure way of boring an audience is to place all information on slides and then read that information to the audience. Use visuals to add impact. Think of strong visual images that will emphasize key points. The success of Marlboro cigarettes and Benetton clothing advertising employ the tactic of strong visual images. The focus of their print and television ads is not on the products being sold but on the way these products will enhance or influence the user's life. With Marlboro the image is that of rugged outdoorsmanship. With Benetton, the image is that of politically correct people of diverse backgrounds and races living in harmony. Using this type of creativity in presentations will add sizzle. Think of an analogy to the information being presented and employ that. Make a graph of membership growth in a fitness center look like a growing plant.

Insight through Illustration

In a meeting of hospital managers, each manager was asked to present quarterly financial performance data. The manager of the obesity treatment center drew her division's profits in terms of an obese figure and the expenses in terms of a thin figure. Net profits were represented by another rotund figure. Few people in the meeting remembered the actual dollar amounts, but everyone remembered the slogan she employed—"The only bottom getting bigger in our division is the bottom line." Sure, it was corny, but corny is okay if it helps make a point.

When using a screen or board, it is important for the speaker to face the audience and not the screen. When using many visuals, try to mingle photos and charts to hold interest. If numbers are to be presented, using pie, line, and bar graphs makes figures easier to understand. If possible, mix in multiple media such as slides, overheads, and videos. Following are seven of the most common pitfalls and ways to avoid them when using AV equipment.

- Squeezing too much information on one slide: List only key points. Keep written slides to seven or less items.
- Looking at screen: Face the audience and use note cards to prompt.
- Audience cannot see visuals: Make sure that seating facilitates clear vision and the speaker does not block the screen or board. Control lighting and window shades at a level which facilitates viewing and note taking.
- Losing audience interest: Allow screen to go blank. Use dramatic pauses. Move around on stage.
- Long, boring video: Play only the section of a video which is pertinent and do not show unrelated information.
- Distractions on overhead transparencies: Use a laser pointer or point to the acetate. Do not run back and forth from screen to projector.
- Audience cannot read speaker's writing on board: If writing is not legible, prepare typed overheads, or ask for a volunteer with good penmanship to assist in recording information on flipcharts or boards.

Making a Televised Presentation

The emergence of videos and television as a business teaching and communication tool means that many managers may find themselves facing the red light of a camera rather than an audience. Public relations can be greatly helped or hindered by a televised statement or interview. Making the right impression on screen is different from in-person presentations, and if the speaker wishes the message to be received favorably, there are guidelines to follow.

The object of the televised presentation is for the audience to see the speaker and focus on his or her message, not to be distracted by gestures or clothing. The idea of appearing on screen is intimidating to some, so it is best to dress in a way that makes you feel comfortable but also projects a clear, professional image. In clothing, avoid extreme colors, such as black, white, or red, as these tend to be unstable when viewed on screen. Complicated patterns such as stripes or houndstooth may vibrate and be difficult for viewers to focus on. Choosing solid colors which complement the speaker's features is the best choice. Grays, blues, burgundy, and rose are good choices for the small screen. Choose a matte finish for all fabrics and makeup. As with clothing, makeup should be applied with muted colors and a light touch. There is no need for heavy stage makeup in television or video presentations. Avoid busy accessories such as earrings, ruffles, necklaces, or patterned scarves and ties. If the speaker wears glasses, avoid the glare of stage or natural lights by tilting the lenses slightly downward and into cheeks. Lenses can also be dusted with a light face powder to cut glare. Avoid tinted lenses. Seeing a speaker's eyes is important in gaining the audience's trust and attention.

Viewers will judge a speaker by his or her apparel and by the body language employed to emphasize points. A speaker may know he or she is communicating with many people via the screen, but gestures should be used as in an individual conversation. Keep gestures in line with the rectangular screen on which the interview or presentation will be viewed. Do not cross arms, but hold elbows close to the body. Hands should remain between chin and chest when gesturing. Flailing hands can be very distracting, and movements are magnified on the small screen. As with most presentations, avoid touching the face or hair. One notable exception is the removal of eyeglasses to emphasize a point. Practice in a mirror to hone expressions that elicit the desired response. Is the desire to look stern or pleasant? A half smile is all that is needed so as not to look like a grinning idiot. Lift brows and shift gaze upward for emphasis. Keep posture erect and elongated; it not only looks better on screen but makes the voice deeper and more resonant to the listener. With the right preparation, a televised presentation will be effective and comfortable for the speaker and the audience.

SENDING A WRITTEN MESSAGE

Writing a message does not differ much from delivering it orally, except that immediate feedback is not available to the sender. As in any presentation, an outline is necessary. The communication needs to have a structure which draws the reader's attention into the document, leads him or her through the material, and states a conclusion or presents a call to action. One example of an effective written message is an advertisement brochure for a product. A headline or attention-grabbing visual device draws the reader's attention, then pertinent facts are presented. These may include a description of the product, the use of the product, the benefit to the user, and pricing information. The conclusion in advertising is usually a call to action, such as "Call today for a free sample," or "Send $19.95 TODAY to order yours." As with the oral message, the writer needs to relate to the reader and her or his interests, use an attention-getting introduction, and close with a summary of key statements.

Awareness of the reader's level of understanding is extremely crucial in a written communication. Unlike a face-to-face communication, the receiver cannot immediately ask questions to clarify a misunderstanding. Writing above the level of understanding will often result in confusion and failure to act. Finally, the document should be proofread. It must have proper punctuation, correct spelling, and neat form so that it looks visually appealing. The visual appeal of a written document is as important as the appropriate appearance of a speaker. In the same way that a business person puts on a suit or other appropriate attire for a meeting, the appearance of the document will influence its credibility.

If one or two brief, key messages are to be delivered, do not hide them in a lengthy letter. When lengthy descriptions or details are necessary, break information into short paragraphs or columns, with white space between. This makes the information appear less overwhelming to the reader and will improve the chances that it will be read completely. Another device is to divide information into sections with small headings or teasers at the start of each. Many readers will skim information looking for a topic of immediate interest. Once they find an interesting topic, they are likely to read back or forward in the document for details and further explanations.

As in oral communication, written messages can benefit and be clarified by the use of visual aids. The authors of this text chose to include cartoons, photos, diagrams, and drawings to capture interest and illustrate key points. Often important messages go undelivered because the receiver does not read a message. The use of attractive stationery, pictures, or varying size type will draw the reader's eye into the document. Creativity in written messages interests the reader and improves the chances of the message being received as intended.

KEY WORDS AND PHRASES

Communicate

Key statements

Bidirectional communication

Feedback

Unidirectional communication

Message retention

Audiovisual aids

Social styles

Repetition

Barriers to communication

Oral communication

Agenda

Active listening

Written communication

Seating arrangements

Call to action

QUESTIONS FOR REVIEW

1. Most administrators understand how important good communication is to effective management. Why, then, in your opinion, do most experience many failures in this area?

2. In what ways do we communicate?

3. Why is it important for a speaker to observe body language, facial expressions, and other nonverbal cues, in addition to the spoken or written word?

4. What are three pitfalls of using audiovisual aids and how can a speaker avoid these?

5. As a communicator, how can you facilitate communication at a group meeting?

6. List four barriers to effective communication and explain how these can be overcome.

7. Why should you reread an important written message before sending it?

8. Why is the closing statement in a speech so important?

9. Which is more important in management: upward, downward, or sideways communication? Why?

10. List five guidelines you would follow if you were to make a video presentation.

SELF-TEST

Corrected True-False

If the statement is true, mark it T. If the statement is false, mark it F and change it to a true statement by adding or deleting words.

_____ 1. Basically, we communicate to influence people.

_____ 2. It is important when you deliver a message to different groups that you say the same thing in the same way to all.

_____ 3. When a verbal message is delivered, only about 40 percent of the message is retained by the receiver.

_____ 4. One way to improve two-way communication is to recognize that misunderstanding is inevitable.

_____ 5. Success in two-way communication depends largely upon your interpretation of how the process works.

_____ 6. When appearing on television, you should wear the outfit in which you feel most comfortable.

_____ 7. A face-to-face meeting in an office is the most effective forum for a business meeting.

_____ 8. Before delivering a speech, it is a good idea for speakers to mentally visualize their presentation from before they walk to the podium until they sit down.

_____ 9. One cannot keep from communicating.

_____ 10. Since a picture is worth a thousand words, pictures should be the director's primary means of communicating.

Multiple Choice

_____ 11. Communication becomes a reality when the message is:
   a. delivered
   b. acknowledged
   c. delivered and received
   d. none of the above

_____ 12. Listening may be as important to the director as sending messages:
   a. when it is active
   b. when it is passive
   c. either a or b
   d. only when it is bidirectional

_____ 13. Most directors prefer this type of communication because it allows immediate feedback:
   a. two-way
   b. bidirectional
   c. both a and b
   d. neither a nor b

_____ 14. When considering the importance of communication along with other managerial functions and skills, communication is:
   a. second to none
   b. second after decision making
   c. next after planning
   d. not a function or skill

_____ 15. When presenting as a member of the panel, it is best to be:
   a. first on the agenda
   b. second on the agenda
   c. last on the agenda
   d. brief and to the point

CASE 5.1 WHY IS COMMUNICATION FAILING?

At the end of his first six months as executive director of Techtronics Employees Recreation and Fitness Association (TERFA), Troy Edwards called in his three activity directors—Luci Barrett (director of recreation), Wally Walker (director of fitness), and Marlene Dobbs (director of health and wellness)—and the office manager, Helen Ferguson. He began: "I've asked you to come here hoping that you can shed some light on a very frustrating and serious problem. When I came to TERFA, I was aware that for whatever reason, I've had problems in the past with communicating with those who work under my supervision. For that reason, I was adamant that I would initiate a sound communication network on this job, but apparently I haven't."

Troy continued to explain that he had just received copies (thirty total) of the evaluation forms completed by the association personnel, and at least twenty listed lack of communication as a serious problem. Overall, he had received very strong support in all other categories of the evaluation from twenty-eight of the thirty who completed the form. As he reviewed the efforts he had made—a weekly director's info memo, current information posted on neatly kept bulletin boards, biweekly staff meetings, and daily directives sent to individuals as applicable—his four lieutenants agreed that they had noticed his extended effort and complimented him for it. They expressed their opinions that they did not feel they personally had a problem with his communication, but they had a feeling that the other employees felt the problems.

The directors were pleased with Troy's performance and wanted to help him. Finally, Luci suggested that the four of them talk with their respective staff members and solicit suggestions as to how communications could be improved. They were to open their conversations with, "Mr. Edwards recognizes the importance of good communication and would like your input for improving it."

Your Response

1. What are the issues and problems in this case?
2. What do you think should be done about the problem(s)?
3. What action guides surface in this situation?

CASE 5.2 COMMUNICATION BREAKDOWN

Kathleen O'Hale, athletic trainer at Johnstown College, was called to the head football coach's office at 8 A.M. on Monday. As she walked across campus to Scott Yukio's office, she knew the purpose would be to discuss the incident involving herself and an injured defensive lineman, Tank McLame.

As she entered the office, she greeted Tank and Scott and then took a seat across the desk from the coach. Scott said, "I'd like to get right to the point. I'm very disappointed in the display I observed last Saturday after the game. I expect all members of this team to work together and not argue and fight like children. Now, Kathleen, I'd like to hear your version of what happened, then yours, Tank."

Kathleen said, "Coach, Tank complains about the treatments I administer. Whether it's an ankle taping, ultrasound, or ice therapy, he always says it's too cold, too loose, not enough. He's just never satisfied. On Saturday, after he blew out his ankle, he tried to blame me for it! It wasn't my fault, it was that 270-pound guard who fell on him. I guess I had just taken his abuse as long as I could. I lost my cool."

Tank launched in. "Coach, it *was* partly her fault I'm on crutches now. She didn't tape me up tight enough! She even admitted it after I came off the field."

"I DID NOT!"

"You said you were sorry."

"That wasn't an apology. That was compassion!"

"Admit it, you're a lousy trainer. You never even listen to us when we have a complaint. Why don't you go work with some powder puff league and leave football to the men."

As the two continued to argue, Scott wondered if he had been wrong to hire a female trainer at this conservative school. He believed in Kathleen's abilities, but this was not the first time a clash had occurred between her and a player. Finally, he interrupted the two. "Stop this right now. Something has got to change. . . ."

Your Response

1. How did communication go wrong in this scenario?

2. What could have been done to prevent this?

3. What action guides do you recommend for Scott Yukio?

BIBLIOGRAPHY

Brooks, B. "Making Every Byte Count." *Public Relations Journal* 42 (1986):4.

Curtis, J. D., and R. A. Detert. *How to Relax: A Holistic Approach to Stress Management.* Palo Alto, CA: Mayfield, 1981.

Drucker, Peter F. *The Effective Executive.* New York: Harper & Row, 1966.

How to Do It Series #3: Communication with Groups. Centre for International Sports Management, Canada.

Introduction to Social Styles. Eden Prairie, MN: Wilson Learning Corporation, 1982.

Schuller, Robert. *Tough-Minded Faith for Tender-Hearted People.* New York: Bantam Books, 1983.

Tannen, D. *You Just Don't Understand: Women And Men in Conversation.* New York: William Morrow & Co., 1990.

Zeigler, Earle, and G. W. Bowie. *Management Competency Development in Sport and Physical Education.* Philadelphia: Lea & Febiger, 1983.

6

Managing Time and Setting Priorities

Time is the most valuable thing a man can spend.

Diogenes

Chapter Objectives

After reading this chapter and completing the exercises, you should be able to:

1 List and discuss the practical steps in managing time

2 Explain the value of keeping a time log and list several methods for doing so

3 Describe how to use an activity list in time planning

4 Delineate at least three ways the director can respond to requests for her or his time

5 List several time wasters and suggest how to avoid them

6 Explain the relationship between prioritizing, managing time, and achieving goals

7 Discuss the importance of keeping a written daily schedule

8 Describe several tactics to overcome fear of failure and procrastination

9 Describe how to manage employees who waste time

When I get some free time. . . . As soon as I get organized. . . . Just as soon as I finish this project. . . . How many times have you used excuses such as these for avoiding or postponing tasks? A few years ago, a popular novelty gift for bosses was an object labeled *round tuit*. The round tuit could be placed on the boss's desk to remind him or her of the age-old excuse, Just as soon as I get around to it. The phrase, My time is your time, was never truer than when spoken by a director of physical education, fitness, or athletics. Too often directors feel they have no time to call their own. That problem can be solved through effective time use, a skill that can be acquired.

The secret to effective time management is to use time more efficiently. A person cannot create more time. There are only twenty-four hours in a day, and when those hours are gone, they cannot be recovered. An effective director is one who manages himself or herself and others so both the organization and the people being managed profit from his or her presence. Even though time is often a manager's most precious asset, it is also the most easily squandered. A manager who earns $40,000 per year costs a company $5,000 each year by wasting as little as one hour per day. For a manager to be effective and use time wisely, he or she must not only select the important tasks to do but do those tasks in the most efficient manner. This chapter discusses how these skills can be developed.

STEPS IN MANAGING TIME

Time management is a step-by-step process consisting of recording time use, controlling time use, and using time efficiently. By examining each step, we can discover the essential characteristics of time and its effective use.

Recording Time Use

Time recording is often done in industry at the production level, but rarely do directors or other decision makers record how their time is used. Surely the time required to sew one seam of a football or produce a piece of weight-training equipment on an assembly line is no more important than the time required to make decisions about marketing or distributing those items.

There is no best way for recording how time is spent. Some time management experts recommend keeping a daily log to truly understand if time is spent effectively. Keeping a log involves writing down everything done during the day and how long it takes. A log of a sports director's typical day could resemble the one shown in Figure 6.1.

This kind of record keeping can be laborious and time-consuming, but it will produce a clear and precise log of how each minute is spent.

Another effective method of recording time use is to track only selected time-consuming activities. If it seems that a particular employee monopolizes the director's time with unnecessary interruptions, it would be wise for her or him to record and analyze the actual amount of time spent and the results of the effort. If it turns out that this person is causing continual interruptions, the director should schedule a weekly or biweekly meeting with the person and confine all but emergency discussions to those scheduled meetings.

In any method of time recording, time should be recorded as it is spent and not a day or a week later. Time recording is an excellent starting point for managing time and can also be valuable for keeping on a schedule once established.

Controlling Time Use

Taking control of one's time does not mean becoming enslaved to a clock or being forced to abide by a strict schedule. Controlling time allows managers to free themselves from external

```
MORNING  8:00—8:20     Talking in hall with Mr. Taft

         8:20—8:45     Reviewing notes for 9:00 meeting

         8:45—8:55     Gathering materials for meeting

         8:55—10:00    Staff meeting

        10:00—10:30    Socializing with staff

        10:30—10:45    Opening mail

        10:45—10:55    Phone conversation with spouse

        10:55—12:00    Appointments with unit coordinators
```

Figure 6.1 *Sample Time Log of Morning Activities*

restraints and judge for themselves how best to use their time.

Control begins with planning, which we discuss intensively in Chapter 7. In reference to time planning, we should realize that everyone plans his or her time. Every morning or at the start of each week, we mentally list what we wish to accomplish during that day or week. Some may even map out a plan of attack to attain those goals. The difference between effective and ineffective time planners is perseverance.

Perseverance is evidenced in all sports endeavors. As an aspiring runner begins learning the skill of hurdling, she may trip, fall, and stumble a number of times. Although many runners may turn to relays or other events where fewer skinned knees occur, the persistent runner will learn from her mistakes. By lengthening or shortening strides, raising the trail leg a half inch, keeping the lead leg high, and lowering the head a little more, eventually the runner will become a hurdler, and with persistence, may even become a champion. So it is with time management: Effective time planners plan and persist in accomplishing their goals. If they fail on a first attempt to accomplish a goal, they overcome discouragement by learning from their mistakes. They revise plans and make new efforts until they achieve success.

With the need for persistence established, one may ask, "How do I plan?" Planning, like exercise, should be scheduled into the manager's day on a regular basis. The choice of when to plan is as individual as deciding when is the best time to jog, cycle, or lift weights. Some managers find they are most productive in the early morning when they are fresh and their minds are uncluttered, allowing thoughts to flow freely. Others may prefer to leave planning for the end of the day. Some directors will not leave the office until they have planned the following day's schedule. In public education, teachers are allowed one free class period as a time to plan. Regardless of whether a person prefers to plan at 5:00 A.M., 1:00 P.M., or 4:30 P.M., it is important that the daily plan be done before the normal workday begins. Busy sports directors must make planning a habit.

Planning begins by listing and prioritizing activities to be accomplished. This daily listing is cru-

Time managers, like this athlete, become more skilled through practice and perseverance.

cial to carrying out any time plan. One individual who worked as an office manager in a health care setting found that by using a Day-at-a-Glance calendar, she could list each activity, phone call, and appointment for the day. This was also useful for advance planning. If a job or order had a specific deadline, she could flip forward to key dates and make notations to help her accomplish those goals.

There are a variety of methods for listing activities. Some people need to list every daily activity from going out for coffee to their daily workout to meeting with the president. Others may choose to record only uncommon events and leave routine tasks such as regular bank deposits and weekly staff meetings off the list. A third type of listing includes not only what must be accomplished during the day but also an administrator's wish list of hopes and dreams that would be nice to attain, but not absolutely essential.

Making a list is just the beginning. Prioritizing the activities on the list forms them into the be-

ginning of a plan. A manager should ask himself or herself, "How much is this task worth to my company?" A $5 task should be assigned a lower priority than a $1,000 task. Certainly there are other considerations than financial when prioritizing. The wise time manager is one who can honestly prioritize for not only the short term, but the long term as well. Doodlers may prefer to assign single, double, and triple stars to activities to indicate their importance. Others may prefer to number or letter items in order of importance. Then efforts can be concentrated on top-priority items. It is better to accomplish one or two top-priority items than to handle everything on the list in order. If small chunks of time become available, but are not large enough to get top-priority items accomplished, the director can often use these times to get several of the lower-priority activities completed.

Weeding out low-priority items allows a busy director to concentrate on higher priorities. Eliminating low-priority items can be done by delegating. One of the worst pitfalls any manager can fall into is the mindset of "If I want it done right, I'll do it myself." If a manager finds that all his or her time is spent in daily operations of an organization, he or she should step back and re-examine the job description. A director should be the person in the organization who is planning for the future, not necessarily running all daily operations. A wise manager is one who establishes an environment which solves problems quickly and well, avoiding personal involvement of every solution. Instead of thinking, "I'll do it right," a manager should ask, "Who can do this well enough or who can be trained to do this task?" Knowing when to step in and when to step back is the art of effective delegation. For delegated responsibilities and recurring problems, the director can compose step-by-step procedures so that anyone at any level of authority can handle the tasks and problems in a uniform and consistent manner.

Overstaffing can result in a variety of time-wasting activities. If there are too many people

and there is not enough work to keep them busy, excessive time will be spent socializing. Too much socializing often turns into gossip sessions, and the gossip sessions can create conflict. These conflicts usually require intervention by superiors.

The manager can also waste time that belongs to others. Asking employees "What do I do that wastes your time?" can be an eye-opening experience. The director must have the courage to ask, listen, and act on suggestions if he or she is wasting others' time and hopes to stop it. Many administrative techniques can be improved by listening to staff members.

Using Time Efficiently

External forces sometimes dictate how we must spend our time, but in most instances, we are free to choose. Imagine for a moment that you, as an administrator, are planning a schedule for using your school's gymnasium. When scheduling various classes, teams, clubs, and intramural sports in the gym, you have the freedom of choosing who gets to use the facility at any given hour. Consider another circumstance. The light system goes out and must be repaired immediately. If the electricians can only come for repairs on Thursday from 9:00 to 11:00 A.M., then that is an external factor that will govern how the gymnasium will be used for that particular day. And so it is with administrators' time. Each block of time is theirs

to use as they see best. They should not allow themselves to believe that others always control their time, although it does occasionally happen.

There are four ways a manager can handle requests when several people desire a portion of her or his time. Let us examine them individually.

1. *Accept the request and give time to it.* This can be considered as agreeing to the demands of others. It is an acceptable option if the outcome of the director's time investment is satisfactory to him or her and the other parties. In many cases, however, people will request more of the director's time than is advantageous to give. In this situation, any of the following options should be considered.

2. *Say NO!* If the request for time is not in the director's best interest or if it involves a task for which he or she may be unqualified, the director will do everyone a favor by saying no from the outset. It is far better to refuse to tackle a project than to do a poor job or back out before its completion. If a manager sorts through his or her nice-to-do basket and discovers a task which has been left undone for a week or month, chances are the organization will survive without the completion of this task. If a manager's daily schedule is interrupted by a request, that manager should ask "Is this task more important than what I had planned to do at this time?" If not, refuse the request or delay it.

   Saying maybe is a poor substitute for a No. Allowing another party to rely on us for a task and then pulling out not only makes us look bad but forces the other person to scramble for someone else on short notice. Saying no at the outset shows that the director has control of his or her time and allows the task to be given to someone who is more highly motivated and qualified to do a better job.

3. *Make a compromise to satisfy all parties in-*

Eliminating time-wasting activities is particularly essential for managers.

volved. To help determine if a compromise is acceptable, the director can discuss goals and priorities with the people making the request. Can they be satisfied with a shortcut? An example would be to outline key points rather than write a formal proposal for a large purchase. Another example of a compromise is a trade-off. The director can agree to lend expertise and time to someone if that person will help the director on a project he or she has been struggling with.

4. *Share time.* If more than two people require the director's undivided attention during the same time period, it will be impossible to fully honor all requests. When faced with this situation, the director must prioritize the requests and explain the conflict to each party. The director can agree to give full concentration to each request but for a shorter period of time for each person. This appears to be an easy solution to time conflicts, but it is often difficult

to fairly juggle all requests. It requires great effort from the manager and understanding by all other parties.

In addition to requests by others, there are time requests that managers make of themselves. Essential activities such as opening mail, reviewing routine updates, and observing exercise instructors at a health club usually require little thought on the manager's part.

There are ways to read or answer mail efficiently. For example, to save time in reading newsletters and periodicals, the director can scan the table of contents or headlines. Article and reports that are of interest can be read or marked for reading at a later time. Mail can be sorted into three stacks: Letters, urgent reports, and requests can be placed in the action stack, which requires immediate attention. Information sources such as quarterly reports and minutes of yesterday's meeting can be put in a folder and carried in a briefcase for perusal at a later date when a few moments are available. Periodicals can be placed in a basket or drawer and saved for reading or reference after dispensing with the higher-priority items.

Answering correspondence can be done quickly by jotting down the response on the original letter and turning it over to a secretary for typing, or even sending the letter back as is. Most people will appreciate a quick, informal response rather than a formal letter which takes several days to arrive. Copies of the original letter and the reply should be saved for later reference if needed.

Previously wasted time can be made more valuable. If a manager commutes by bus, train, subway, or carpool, he or she can use that travel time for reading or writing brief reports and answering letters. If a busy person must drive to work or travel during the workday, a tape recorder/player can turn a car into an extension of the office. Reports or correspondence can be dictated for the secretary. Many people find that driving, especially on long trips, is conducive to brainstorming and problem solving. A nearby tape recorder can serve to record these thoughts and inspirations. What about using a car's tape deck for learning purposes? For example, foreign language cassette tapes are available. The affordability of cellular phones, either car mounted or hand-held can turn any location into a mini office. A good time-saving device for returning phone calls is to jot down all calls in one log book or organizer. If a person finds himself or herself with fifteen spare minutes while sitting in traffic or waiting for the plane, these calls can be returned, freeing up time in the office or at home for more productive tasks. Another advantage of using cellular phones or pay phones to return calls is that most people are aware of the relatively high cost incurred and will not waste time in chitchat but will get down to business quickly. This also provides the caller with an easy exit when the business is completed.

Who could refuse this statement: "I've got to run, my plane is boarding."?

Another time waster is the great American tradition called the coffee break. True, it is wise to allow a time for relaxation during the long workday, but fifteen-minute breaks too often turn into sixty-minute bull sessions. The director must keep control of that discretionary time. If he or she is in a high-stress job, using the coffee break to do progressive relaxation or some other stress-reducing technique is much better than tanking up on caffeine and sugar.

The same can be said of the lunch hour. Rarely does anyone require sixty minutes to consume a well-balanced meal. Carrying a brown bag not only saves money, but it allows the manager to go to some private place and think while eating. In fact, we wrote a major portion of this chapter during our lunch breaks. Some people prefer to use the lunch period to exercise or run errands. Midday exercise is an excellent stress reliever, allowing the mind to function more clearly for the remainder of the day. A very annoying time waster is waiting for appointments, meetings, and interviews. Taking along periodicals or other reading materials can turn an annoying period into a productive learning session.

What about sleeping time? Everyone needs it to survive and function at an optimum level. Can that seven or eight hours be used for production? Some people find that by posing a question to themselves just before going to sleep, their subconscious minds work on it, providing a solution to the problem upon awakening. This technique has worked for many, but for others, it only serves to keep them awake or yield unrestful sleep. The individual must determine which techniques work best for her or him.

In summary, the director can use time efficiently by examining her or his present use of it. If he or she is doing something out of habit, without a conscious decision, it may be an unnecessary task, and that block of time can probably be used better. If something can go undone or be done by someone else as efficiently, the task should be delegated or left undone.

LINKING GOALS TO PRIORITIES

We've referred to top-priority tasks and efforts. How can a manager determine what tasks should take precedence over others? The answer lies in setting personal and professional goals. If we asked thirty managers and administrators to list their goals, we would likely get thirty different answers. Ask yourself what your goals are for the next five years. How about for the next year? What would you like to accomplish this week? It is easy to think of a variety of answers to these questions. Some goals may involve marriage and family; others may involve education and work. To plan how to attain goals, it is necessary first to prioritize them.

How to Set Goals

Initiate goal setting by developing a list of the things you would like to accomplish. Allow your brain to go uninhibited and record any possibility that appeals to you. You want to travel in space? Write it down. You want to start a family? Whatever fantasies you dream up should be included on the list. The key here is not to think about whether or not you can afford to do them or how realistic they are but whether or not they appeal to you. Put them down on paper. Forgetting is common, and paper and ink make great reminders. Also, when setting goals, writing will help you control the tendency to day-dream.

Once your imagination has created a list of common, uncommon, attainable, and impossible dreams, then reality will help sort out the good and not-so-good ideas. This stage is called prioritizing. Just as we mentioned in the discussion about making a daily list, a person must decide which goals are most important to do first.

Long-term and short-term goals sometimes conflict. This situation can only be resolved through careful consideration and weighing of consequences. For example, assume that you are the director of the local YMCA, and the floor of your basketball court desperately needs to be refinished. Members are complaining about the nuisance of playing on such a lousy surface. A few loose boards could even be considered a safety hazard. There is obviously a need to repair the facility, but on the other hand, construction will soon begin on the new YMCA facility that is to be completed in two years. A conflict then arises between tackling the short-term goal of refinishing the floor of the current basketball court, or targeting that money toward improving the new facility that is under way.

Each goal must be analyzed thoroughly before being accepted or discarded. Again, writing down and expanding upon a goal allows the mind to more fully concentrate and weigh the options. More than just one person is often involved when setting goals, so writing down the goals is necessary for mutual understanding.

Prioritizing Goals

When prioritizing, always look toward the opportunity that an action may create. Never be afraid to challenge old ways or diverge from a previous course. Without the courage to take risks, Columbus and the Wright brothers would not have left their marks on history. On a more personal level, risk is always involved in a life change—taking a new job or giving up a job to go back to graduate from school are two examples with which many of us are familiar. You must have the courage to look past the present and into the future, where the challenges and greater rewards lie.

Prioritizing and listing goals should be ongoing. As changes occur in one's life, goals and activities may take higher or lower priority. Following an old pattern out of habit is self-defeating and wasteful. Constant updating of priorities is necessary. Servicing the lifecycle in a cardiac rehab center may be low on the priority list, but when it breaks down, repairing it becomes one of the top-priority items for keeping clients satisfied.

Sometimes it is necessary to reprioritize. A manager may have set aside the first three hours on Friday morning for developing a new marketing strategy, but her creative ability has taken a brief vacation. By reprioritizing, she can use that block of time for some other purpose. By early afternoon, her creative vibes may have returned, and she may be able to work on the new marketing strategy she had planned to do earlier that day.

Once completed, the list of goals and priorities may resemble a small book. The means for attaining some goals may be obvious, while other goals may be less definable. If the goal is reorganizing a haphazard personal filing system, deciding upon the steps to accomplish that task is relatively simple. However, a goal such as increasing one's vocabulary will probably need further clarification.

When a goal is idealistic and appears overwhelming, it is best to break it down into smaller, easily accomplished activities. Remember, you cannot *do* a goal, but you can do an activity. If your goal is to get a master's degree in exercise physiology, you can break that goal down into specific activities or steps:

1. Get a graduate catalog from a local university.
2. Apply for admission to begin in September.
3. Register for two night classes during fall semester.

Once you have listed the activities for achieving a goal, then prioritize them (notice how those two words—*list* and *prioritize*—keep showing up). Top-priority goals should receive your immediate attention as you begin converting priorities into action.

USING A SCHEDULE TO CONVERT PRIORITIES INTO ACTION

An old adage states: "The best intention is not as important as the smallest deed." To transform intent into action, we must work goal-attaining activities into a daily schedule. Keeping a daily schedule is important, but enough flexibility must be allowed to handle such things as unexpected emergencies or delays caused by meetings that extend beyond the scheduled time. Reserving one or two hours each day with no appointments or commitments will allow time for the manager to get back on schedule after interruptions. If interruptions do not occur, goals of lower priority that do not require large blocks of time can be achieved.

Adherence to a schedule should be neither too strict nor too relaxed. Being inflexible is unwise because life often throws in disrupting surprises. The good time manager is flexible enough to handle these as they arise. Even though most people who interrupt feel that their need is an emergency, rarely does a situation arise that cannot wait an hour or two until time can be freed to handle it.

When scheduling the workday, the manager should schedule blocks of time for phone calls, appointments, reading significant articles and professional journals, and for meetings. Large blocks should also be scheduled for private, uninterrupted work. Time-management experts agree that large blocks of time are necessary for productivity. Just as a schedule should provide time for planning, it should also include time for implementing those plans. The large blocks of time should be set aside when the manager is at an op-

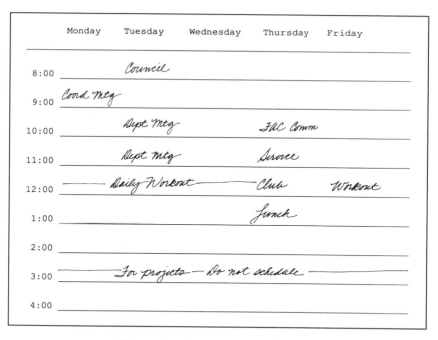

Figure 6.2 *Director's Weekly Schedule*

timum level of creativity and energy. The manager should examine current habits to determine when her or his prime production time is and schedule that time for work on top-priority activities. Another aid in determining what time of day is best for uninterrupted work is to track at what time of day most disruptions occur. Is it just as everyone arrives at the office, or is it prior to lunch? Saving this time as unscheduled allows the manager to complete those short tasks which do not require such strict concentration.

An often overlooked part of the schedule is personal time. As business gets more competitive, managers find their work days creeping into personal time, leading to an imbalance in their lives. By blocking out time for family, letter writing, recreational reading, the effective time manager can be assured of greater balance and energy for business tasks.

Posting a written schedule helps both the manager and those he or she interacts with. Private time for uninterrupted concentration should be identified with a large "X" on the manager's daily schedule. A well-planned schedule can also be color-coded with a red line around private time, a blue line around the time available for meetings, a yellow line around unscheduled catch-up time, and other colors outlining other time blocks as the specific job dictates. A director's weekly schedule may look like the one shown in Figure 6.2. Anyone can see with a quick glance the times that are open for meetings and appointments and the times that are reserved for other necessary activities.

To avoid interruptions during prime production time, the director should have the secretary hold all calls or refer them to someone else. In the absence of a secretary, a telephone answering machine can screen calls for the director, leaving her or him the option of answering or returning the call later. A well-known researcher and inventor who owns and operates his own sports research center refuses all calls except those from his business partner and his attorney. When he goes into his laboratory, everyone knows that he is not to be disturbed. If no one is available to screen his calls, he simply places all phone lines on hold during his creative time. That system may not work for everyone, but when a person reaches a high station in life, he or she cannot afford to devote time to everyone who wants a word or interview with him or her. Ideas are this man's business; therefore, he must schedule the time to create.

As a manager sits down to begin a period of intense concentration, it may be useful to warm up the brain for mental exertion, just as he or she warms up the muscles for exercise. This can be accomplished by reviewing short notes or memos or completing light paperwork related to the task at hand. Easing into brain work can make the task much more pleasant. For many people the ability to focus for long periods of time on one topic is difficult. Biofeedback, yoga, meditation, and even general exercise will assist a person in developing this skill. At work, centering the mind on the task at hand involves the same skills as performance of the above activities. As with these other abilities, developing forced concentration requires practice. A person who finds concentration to be difficult can start by forcing the mind to concentrate on one subject for ten minutes. If thoughts wander, pull them back to the chosen topic. Once a person has mastered this ability to center, begin extending the length of time spent in concentration. Eventually, this talent will be as easy to perform as tying one's shoes.

What should a person do if the creative juices start flowing at a time other than that scheduled for that purpose? If possible, go with it! It is frustrating to lie in bed with your mind racing, so, if possible, get out of bed, or even lie in bed and jot down a few notes or ideas as they pop up. For many people, nighttime has the effect of enhancing thinking and concentration. If creative genius strikes in the middle of the workday, can other tasks or meetings be rescheduled to allow completion of the task? This is a time where flexibility will well serve the manager's schedule as it is often difficult to recapture that intense concentration or creativity at a later time.

When someone requests a minute of a manager's time, it rarely ends after sixty seconds; therefore, the manager must force herself or himself at times to say no. A particular kind of courage is required to do this when one has a strong desire to provide satisfaction for people. If the director's office is not arranged so that the door can be closed for private time, then he or she may be wise to go to some other location such as a library or a meeting room that offers quiet space for thinking. One manager was having a problem meeting with her assistant without disturbances, and she began scheduling their weekly meetings in a nearby city park. The setting was perfect, and they spent several productive hours sitting under a tree in the park.

Prime contact time is a second type of prime time. Phone calls and meeting should be scheduled when it is likely that the targeted persons can be contacted on the first attempt. For example, if you are on the West Coast and wish to make phone contact with someone on the East Coast, be aware of the time difference and place your call when he or she is likely to be in the office. Also, when planning to meet with someone, be aware of his or her schedule and try to find compatible times for both of you.

Another consideration is span of concentration. A director who is aware that her or his concentration span is one hour should not schedule meetings for longer periods. After fifty minutes, the person being met with should be asked to summarize. The meeting should be ended within the hour and another one scheduled if the hour did not allow enough time to provide the satisfaction required. If people are too tenacious to gracefully honor the director's request, the director may need to get up and walk out on them. When they realize they are sitting in the office by themselves, they will soon get the message.

DEALING WITH FEAR AND PROCRASTINATION

With all these available tools for managing time, why is it that so many administrators still do not work as efficiently as they are capable of? There are a variety of reasons. Perfectionism is one obstacle for those who feel they must perform flawlessly or not at all. Initial attempts at controlling time may falter and even fail, but persistence will turn those mistakes into lessons and eventually into success. At Vic Braden's Tennis College in southern California, the motto Laugh and Win emphasizes the point that when you make a mistake, you laugh at it but then eliminate it from your game. A similar approach can be used when learning and practicing the art of time management. If a day, or week, gets off the charted course, examine the reasons why this occurred and use the new knowledge to get back on track with your schedule and priorities.

Two particularly tough but common obstacles to effective time management are fear and procrastination. But even these obstacles can be surmounted by using the tactics that we will describe.

Fighting Fear

The fear of failure often prevents a manager from confronting problems and controlling them. Another word for this is procrastination. Procrastination is the cause of failure for many potentially good administrators. When given a list of activities, many managers will spend time working on the smaller, lower-priority tasks instead of tackling the tougher but far more important tasks. Why bother prioritizing if the top priorities are pushed aside because they are difficult?

There are many ways to handle fear. One is to ignore fear, push it aside, and go forward with plans to achieve a goal. This is more easily done if the fears are minor and the reward for action is satisfying. The fear of face-to-face selling for

SHOULD I? WHAT IF SHE SAYS NO?
OH WELL... MAYBE I'LL ASK HER TOMORROW...

most can easily be pushed aside if the potential monetary reward is adequately satisfying.

A second approach, containment of fear, requires that fear be recognized, expressed, and attacked. Most support groups use this approach to conquer fear. A good analogy is found in fire fighting. To deny that fires during a hot, dry summer are a problem would be irresponsible and disastrous. Fires must be attacked and overcome, and one technique often used in battling a raging grass fire is to set a controlled backfire. Overcoming some fearsome managerial problem often requires setting an administrative backfire. For example, if a layoff at a fitness center is imminent due to seasonal cutbacks, a director may fear being forced to lay off a dedicated staff member with lack of seniority. To set a backfire, well before the layoff, the director can meet with employees to discuss the probability of seasonal cutbacks while emphasizing the necessity of recognizing the importance of seniority.

Many fears stem from a lack of knowledge about a particular subject. For example, some administrators may avoid purchasing personal computers, or adequately using them after the purchase, because they know nothing about them. This kind of fear can readily be overcome by talking with friends and associates who use computers in administration, self-study, and/or formal course work.

A fourth method of overcoming fear can be used when the other three methods fail. This technique involves an intentional effort to let your fears run wild, blow them so out of proportion that you see how ridiculous they are, and then laugh at them. Suppose, for example, you have this idea to build an indoor tennis facility four miles from the city limits on a four-acre plot that is now a chicken farm. You feel that the board of a local lending institution will think you are stupid when you ask for a $300,000 loan for such a wild venture. Let your fears run wild! They will call you incompetent and laugh at you. Worse yet, they will call your boss and get you fired from your present position for having such a dumb dream. You will be out of work for months; you will lose your home; your spouse will leave you; even your dog will hate you. Get the picture? That scenario is so unreal that it allows you to deal with fear in a positive way after having a good laugh about the thoughts that originally bothered you.

Fear can be a useful emotion for better preparing yourself for taking action and accomplishing tasks. A controlled fear can serve as a motivator. Most highly skilled athletes can relate how apprehensive they become before a meaningful competition. They probably have dreadful thoughts of embarrassing themselves with a poor performance, so they practice diligently to prevent such a thing from happening. In the same way, a little fear can be a good motivator when one is preparing for an important interview or a question-and-answer period before a board or audience.

Defeating the Tendency to Procrastinate

Other than fear, something distasteful about doing the task at hand is usually the reason for procrastinating. All of us often must force ourselves to get started on a big project such as writing a textbook or even a simple, easily performed task such as writing a letter.

Placing an object in sight that will be a constant reminder is often an effective way to overcome the tendency to procrastinate. Placing a letter that needs to be answered in the middle of one's desk or on top of one's briefcase, for example, may be the answer. Every time another task is begun, the procrastinator must first get past the constant reminder of the letter.

Another method for preventing procrastination is to remove distractions. If work is done in an office, either at home or at the place of business, it is important that the area is one that is conducive to productivity and supports concentration. Have on hand all office supplies needed for completion of the task. If a person has to get up from her desk, go downstairs and rummage through the kitchen junk drawer to find a pair of scissors or tape, this may result in her stopping to wash a couple of dishes or fix a bite to eat. It may take fifteen to thirty minutes to return to the office and begin work. In a large business, one of the most frequent wastes of time is the trip to the copier room. Not only does it take time to walk down the hall, but often hallway conversations turn a short trip into a long excursion. If a copier is not available at the immediate workspace, placing all items to be photocopied in one file and making one or two trips a day will save time in travel and visitation.

Another useful tool is to remove all other distractions from the work area so undivided attention can be given to top-priority tasks. Even when a task is so overwhelming that beginning is difficult, there are ways to force yourself into action. If you can commit ten minutes to scheduling appointments, gathering information, or listing activities related to the task, this initial kick in the pants often is all that is needed to generate enthusiasm for a project.

If enthusiasm just cannot be mustered, when all else fails, fake it. Faking enthusiasm will usually snowball. For example, if a manager goes to

*Focus on the positive and the work experience
will be more satisfying.*

work with a bad case of Monday morning blahs, should everyone in the department be subjected to whining and complaining? No! Responding to questions of "How are you?" by stating "Great! How about you?" can make others feel good about the day, and may even cheer up the manager. This approach can work the same on a difficult project. If you repeatedly tell those around you how much you enjoy working on the project, even though you're getting sick of it, it reminds you why the project is so rewarding. Focusing on the positive aspects and minimizing the negative will create a more productive work experience.

Managing Others Who Waste Time

We previously addressed the fact that some managers may waste the time of their employees by unnecessary or poorly planned meetings, and Chapter 7 addresses meeting planning in detail. But what about the employee who causes co-workers to delay completion of a task because of his or her poor time-management skills? Then it

is time for the director to step in and help the poor time manager to improve.

If the manager is the target of the time waster's interruptions, there are several tactics to thwart the offender. Asking "What can I do for you?" indicates a person's need to get straight to the point and eliminates pleasantries. If an employee or peer drops into the manager's office unannounced, the manager can stand up when the other person enters the office. This will speed up conversation by discouraging the visitor from sitting down. Removing side chairs from the office, or keeping boxes or stacks of papers on them, will serve the same purpose. If a particular employee is a repeat offender at dropping in unscheduled, keep a file of small tasks on hand. Each time the person drops in unexpectedly, give him or her a task to do. This will curtail the visits quickly. If a person asks for a meeting, offer to go to his or her office. It is easier to leave someone else's office than to ask a visitor to leave yours. Some professionals prefer breakfast meetings to lunch meetings. People are fresher and ready to get down to business. Meetings held prior to regular business hours, just before lunch, or at the end of the workday will usually finish as scheduled because of the built-in deadline.

When managing a group or committee, choose quality members over quantity. Staff can always be added, but it is difficult to remove someone from a committee without risking insult. In group projects, there are usually three types of time wasters that need to be managed: the task hopper; the procrastinator; and the person who neglects detail work. As in any other aspect of personnel management, aiding employees in time management will not only produce better work from a manager's division but will contribute to the professional development of staff.

The procrastinator is often the most difficult to manage because they claim they work better under pressure. Reviewing and implementing some of the steps discussed previously can aid this employee to complete tasks on time. Sit with this person and assist him or her to develop intermediate goals with specific deadlines. Monitor and reinforce progress, letting him or her know that others depend on this information and appreciate its timely completion. Even if a manager is accomplished at scheduling and completing tasks, if an employee completes tasks on time and with

quality products, accepting the last minute flurry of activity may be the best recourse.

The task hopper usually has trouble concentrating on one task for any length of time. To aid him or her in keeping on track, limit assignments to two or three at any one time. Encourage and assist in the formulation of a schedule which will allow transition between projects. If task hopping continues, request that any new assignments be cleared through the supervisor prior to any work being done.

People who neglect details can often cause problems which reverberate throughout a project team. Formulation of a step-by-step schedule or checklists for projects and assignments will help to ensure that details are not overlooked. Encourage the detail skipper to create expandable files for each project, and as anything pertinent to the project comes up, throw that note into the file. Frequent perusal of this file will act as a tickler file to keep details fresh. The best alternative, if budget and personnel allow, is to assign a detail oriented person to work closely with, or in a support capacity to, the detail skipper.

By employing these time management tactics, a manager will be able to increase productivity personally and within his or her organization.

KEY WORDS AND PHRASES

Time log	Setting goals	Daily schedule
Perseverance	Prioritizing	Procrastination
Time planning	Reprioritizing	Fear of failure
Efficient time use	Time wasters	Perfectionism
Concentration	Creativity	

QUESTIONS FOR REVIEW

1. Discuss the importance of achieving goals through prioritizing and managing time.

2. Briefly explain one method for recording time use, listing its advantages and disadvantages.

3. What are three steps in effective time management?

4. Based on your current schedule, explain how you would create a large block of time to complete an important project.

5. Identify three wasters of your time and how you might better control them.

6. Name five actions that a director can take to create large blocks of uninterrupted time.

7. Why is it necessary for a director to delegate daily operations to a senior staffer?

8. List four options for handling a time request. Which do you most often utilize and why?

9. Briefly explain how goal setting is accomplished and how goals are prioritized.

10. What are three ways to manage staffers who waste time?

SELF-TEST

Corrected True-False

If the statement is true, mark it T. If the statement is false, mark it F and change it to a true statement by adding or deleting words.

_____ 1. The first step in managing time is to determine where your time goes.

_____ 2. At the beginning of each workday, a manager should list the tasks he or she wishes to accomplish that day.

_____ 3. Recording every minute of the day is the best way of tracking time.

_____ 4. People who are effective time managers possess a natural talent and usually don't have to practice the skills.

_____ 5. The best way to develop concentration skills is to sit and meditate for long periods of time.

_____ 6. Time is a manager's most precious asset.

_____ 7. Delegation is the key to successful time management.

_____ 8. A manager should always delegate low-priority tasks and keep those duties which are interesting and fun to complete.

_____ 9. Once a list of daily activities is made, all tasks should be completed in order of priority.

_____ 10. Sorting mail into piles is the same as listing activities to complete.

Multiple Choice

_____ 11. Which of the following is a true statement?
   a. The best time to read periodicals is while commuting.
   b. Correspondence should always be in typewritten form.
   c. An excellent time for uninterrupted work is early morning.
   d. none of the above

_____ 12. Which of the following is not a time waster?
   a. coffee breaks
   b. midday exercise
   c. overstaffing
   d. phone conversations

_____ 13. Which is not appropriate for responding to requests?
   a. say no
   b. share time with requesters
   c. make a compromise
   d. postpone indefinitely

_____ 14. The reason for procrastinating is usually related to:
   a. fear
   b. distasteful nature of task
   c. either a or b
   d. neither a nor b

_____ 15. This is an acceptable way to overcome the tendency to procrastinate:
   a. fake enthusiasm
   b. do several tasks at same time
   c. remove all reminders
   d. none of the above

CASE 6.1 WHERE DOES THE TIME GO?

Mary Jo Domes had served as the assistant director of fitness at the Pentathlon Club for two years when Larry Short, general manager of the large private health club, called her to his office. During the past four months, Larry had led an effort directed toward club reorganization because he believed more effectiveness could be achieved. When Mary Jo entered his office, he said, "Mary Jo, I would like to promote you to a new position as director of athletics and fitness. Even though you are only two years out of college, I am inclined to believe you have the leadership ability to get better things accomplished in those areas. Your evaluations indicate that you are a tireless worker, popular with the clientele and staff, and most important, an achiever. If you accept, I want you to know my counsel is always available."

Mary Jo, of course, accepted the position because it was a professional achievement that came much sooner than anticipated, and it also carried a significant pay increase. During the first two months in the new position, Mary Jo enjoyed the challenge and spent many hours above the normal forty-hour week making things happen to the satisfaction of the staff, members, and her boss. She maintained an open-door policy from 8:00 A.M. to 5:00 P.M. for all who had problems or wished to chat for a few minutes. Her day consisted of seeing people and talking on the phone as well as closely supervising and observing the various activity instructors and special events coordinators. Her staff really enjoyed the close-knit feeling, and their morale seemed to be running higher than usual.

Each evening when Mary Jo left for home, her briefcase seemed to have more and more take-home work, such as budgets to devise and evaluation forms to complete. Her social life was practically nonexistent, and she was often late in meeting deadlines. This continued for two months before she decided to discuss the problem with

the general manager. She was becoming exhausted from the fourteen-hour day her job was demanding, and she was so frustrated that she wondered if she was administrative material. When she presented the details of her frustration to Larry, he smiled slightly and said, "I am glad that you came in, and I'm sure that I can help you."

Your Response

1. What are the issues and problems in this case?
2. What actions or advice do you believe Harry will offer?
3. What administrative action guides has Mary Jo been violating?

CASE 6.2 WHAT'S WRONG WITH THIS TEAM?

Carlos Shawner was the chair of the committee to develop new membership for the Center for Health Enhancement. He worked with three other department managers—Julie Kriston, Gail Storm, and Scott Husker. In two months of committee meetings, many good ideas were developed, but so far, no new membership promotions had been completed. Carlos was concerned and felt the need to show some fruits of the labor of the committee. As the meeting commenced, Carlos addressed his co-workers: "We need to have two new membership development plans in place by May 15. Now, which two do you think will be the easiest to complete by then?" Scott said, "I'm not sure I have the time to work on something this intense right now. I have two other important

projects, and of course, the daily fires need to be put out." Julie and Gail agreed that they should be able to make the time but would need Scott's knowledge of marketing tactics. As Carlos thought about the diverse talents of the group, he realized that all four members were big-picture managers, and the details would be difficult to manage on such a limited time schedule.

Your Response

1. What are the issues and problems in this case?
2. What action guides do you recommend for this committee?
3. What guides for time management have the members of this committee failed to follow?

BIBLIOGRAPHY

Blanchard, Kenneth, and Spencer Johnson. *The One-Minute Manager.* New York: Berkley Books, 1981.

Curtis, John D., and R. A. Detert. *How to Relax: A Holistic Approach to Stress Management.* Palo Alto, CA: Mayfield, 1981.

Drucker, Peter F. *The Effective Executive.* New York: Harper & Row, 1966.

Lakein, Alan. *How to Get Control of Your Time and Your Life.* Bergenfield, NJ: New American Library, 1973.

7

Planning for the Activity-Based Program

*Thinking always ahead, thinking always of trying
to do more, brings a state of mind in which
nothing seems impossible.*

Henry Ford

Chapter Objectives

*After reading this chapter and completing the exercises,
you should be able to:*

1 Write a descriptive definition for the term *planning*
2 List four reasons why planning is important
3 Describe the relationship between short- and long-range planning
4 Name the different types of plans
5 Identify the general steps a director should follow in the planning process
6 List six principles for effective planning
7 Discuss the importance of flexibility in planning
8 Explain how a director maintains the plan
9 Identify six reasons why planning sometimes fails

The most fundamental of all the administrative functions is planning. It is critical for everyone in an organization to understand the aim, purposes, and objectives of that organization if optimal effectiveness is to be achieved. It probably is even more essential that they understand what they are expected to do to attain the objectives. That is the function of planning. Koontz and Weihrich (1989) make this summation:

Planning is deciding in advance *what* to do, *how* to do it, *when* to do it, and *who* is to do it. Planning bridges the gap from where we are to where we want to go. It makes it possible for things to occur which would not otherwise happen. Although we can seldom predict the exact future and though factors beyond our control may interfere with the best-laid plans, unless we plan, we are leaving events to chance. Planning is an intellectually demanding process; it requires that we consciously determine courses of action and base our decisions on purpose, knowledge, and considered estimates. Simply stated, planning is *making arrangements in advance*.

WHY IS PLANNING IMPORTANT?

Imagine, if you will, that you are the coach of a high school baseball team which is playing in the state finals on the UCLA campus. You are traveling 200 miles for the game. You know how to get to Los Angeles, but when you arrive at the edge of the city, you realize that you have no city map and have no idea where the UCLA field is. It is an easy place to find if you have a map, but you failed to adequately plan. You knew *what* to do—to play a game at UCLA's field; you knew *when* to do it—the date and time were on the itinerary; you knew *who* was to do it—you and your baseball team; however, you did not plan well enough to know *how* to do it—to get from where you started to your objective.

You can still get to the campus. You might stop and ask directions, but what if there is road con-

struction on the suggested route and you must take a detour? You must stop, again, and ask directions, causing further delay. You have not allowed for the delays, and you arrive at the ball park one hour after the scheduled starting time. Frustrating? You bet it is!

Plans have been described as being similar to a road map. They indicate how to get from where you are to where you want to go, your objective. If your original plan of procedure runs into difficulty, like the road construction on the way to the ball game, and you must abort that plan, you need to establish alternatives to get to where you need to go. The planning process takes time, but the time is well spent. A careful plan will enable you to proceed directly to your goal, and if conditions change and a detour is necessary, you will be able to adjust by going with another alternative.

Insight through Illustration

If you have participated in organized sports, you know that some coaches plan thoroughly, while the plans of others fall short. For example, the head coach of a university football program was considered to be a master tactician. He lived up to this reputation as long as his team was even with or ahead of the other team. He had a game plan and fully used his assistants in their respective roles during a game, just as they had planned and prepared for during the entire preceding week. But if the opposition got a couple of breaks early in the game, such as recovered fumbles or intercepted passes, and was able to convert those breaks into touchdowns, the coach's game plan was never adequately thorough for adjusting to the unexpected situation. The assistant coaches might just as well go home for all the good they could do at that point because the head coach would take over the entire coaching responsibilities, aborting the original plan without an adequate alternative. He would react to events as they occurred, and because he had not planned

Planning gives purpose to action.

for the unexpected, he made some very poor choices. His teams seldom were able to come back and win after being down early.

Planning is an important process for several reasons. We will list four of these reasons here. First, *a plan is useful in determining and documenting the resources needed to accomplish the target project.* The resources needed to carry out a significant project seldom are just waiting for the director to use. In an organization, justification is needed before such vital resources as funds, personnel, and time will be released. A plan must have merit and must be justified. Documentation can be very convincing to a superior in an organization or to a banker if the need is for funds.

Second, once the necessary resources have been obtained *a plan assists in better using those resources in reaching the established goals.* A good plan stimulates and motivates thought, and when the director and staff have a well-conceived, step-by-step plan that leads from the starting point to the desired outcomes, they can proceed and progress with confidence. It is a pleasure to go to work when you can relate what you are doing to a quality product or worthwhile service and can realize the importance of your contribution.

A third reason why planning is such an important and indispensable function relates to the controlling function in administration. Planning and controlling have been referred to as the Siamese twins of administration, and that means that each of these functions significantly affects the other. Once a venture or project is under way, it is certain that everything is not going to proceed exactly as hoped. Things will go wrong, but *a plan assists in foreseeing some of the difficulties that are likely to occur.* In planning, alternatives to the original route can be conceived, thought through, and made ready to put in place with minimal interruption to the productive effort, thus saving hours, weeks, or months of valuable time. The project manager or program director, in fulfilling the control function, is constantly checking the

A good plan justifies resource allocations.

activities occurring against the goals and objectives to ensure outcome satisfaction, and when the activities deviate from the goal, a planned alternative can be put in place.

A fourth important reason for planning is that *a plan can keep other people informed and updated if they join the organization after a program, project, or venture is under way.* Personnel turnover is a reality of life. People leave an organization for various reasons—for other jobs, retirement, and death—before important projects are completed, and they must be replaced. With an effective plan, a few minutes of briefing may be adequate to enable the new employee to move into a contributing role in a short period of time. Coordination and cooperation in progress toward the objectives are assured.

THE PLANNING PERIOD

In terms of time, there are two kinds of plans: short-range and long-range. In differentiating between the two, no one seems to agree on the time span a plan must cover to be referred to as long-range. Since the determination is arbitrary, for the purpose of establishing a basis for understanding we will consider plans covering three years or more to be long-range.

Koontz and Weihrich (1989) make the following observations regarding the planning period:

- The key to choosing the right planning period seems to lie in the *commitment principle,* which states that logical planning encompasses a future period of time necessary to fulfill, through a series of actions, the commitments involved in decisions made today.

- Because of the cost involved in planning, an organization should not plan for a longer period than is economically feasible.

- Long-range planning is planning for the impact of today's decisions rather than planning for future decisions.

The most important factor to remember is the relationship between short-range and long-range plans. The planning may be done separately, but it is critical that the planners keep in mind that short-range plans must be developed so that they are compatible with the long-range plans and goals of the organization. If this principle of compatibility is not followed in short-range planning, resources are likely to be wasted, and long-term goals will become more difficult to achieve. For example, if a long-range plan calls for the construction of a new $15,000,000 activity center to begin six years in the future, it would be very unwise to plan to spend $750,000 on an interim facility to meet the immediate needs of the program, unless it could be incorporated into meeting the facility objectives of the long-range plan.

Anything called for in a short-range plan that is not compatible with long-range plans is considered a band-aid solution for meeting immediate needs. Using the band-aid approach to meet some needs is inevitable in activity-based programs, but overusing this kind of remedy leads to wasted resources.

SCOPE AND TYPES OF PLANNING

Plans for any physical education, fitness, or sports enterprise relate either to personnel, program, or facility. Recall that the scope of administration encompasses these three areas. It is essential that the director relate the objectives and planning activities in each of these three areas to the objectives and planning activities of the other two and to the ultimate purpose or mission of the organization.

The failure of some directors of exercise and sports to recognize that there are a number of different types of plans has often caused difficulty in making planning effective. It is easy to see that a major program, such as one to build a new fitness center or gymnasium, is a plan. But a number of other courses of future action are also plans.

Figure 7.1 *The Hierarchy of Plans*

Keeping in mind that a plan encompasses any course of future action, we can see that plans are varied. They are classified here as (1) mission, purpose, and objectives, (2) strategies and tactics, (3) action guides: policies, procedures, and rules, (4) budgets, (5) programs: major, minor, or supporting. To some extent, they are a hierarchy, as illustrated in Figure 7.1.

Mission, Purpose, and Objectives

In planning a facility, project, or business, determining the mission and objectives is basic to any further planning. The mission of an organization is its purpose or reason for being. An organization's objectives or goals are the ends toward which all other planning and activity—including staffing, organizing, controlling, supervising, and evaluating—are directed. Objectives serve as the basic plan of an organization, and every division or department may plan its own objectives, but they must be compatible with and contribute toward the general goals of the organization.

Strategies and Tactics

Strategic planning is the step of deciding upon the general action needed to attain the comprehensive objectives. A strategy describes the overall approach in reaching the objectives but leaves the specific details of how the organization or department is to accomplish the objectives to subunits of the organization. Strategies, however, do furnish the framework for guiding thought and action. Strategic planning has competitive implications, and in a business situation, strategies are definitely competitively oriented. For example, an aquatics center may select a strategy to capture the senior citizen market by catering to the needs and interests of the older populace.

As strategic planning is concerned with developing general programs of action for attaining comprehensive objectives, *tactical and activities planning is concerned with establishing specific and detailed programs of action for attaining specific organizational objectives.* Tactics are the specific action plans through which strategies are executed. For example, if the general goal of coaches at a particular high school is to improve the functional strength of the high school athletes, the strategy may be to acquire a sophisticated set of isokinetic resistance exercise machines, and the detailed tactics and activities may include both a fundraising program to purchase the equipment and individualized exercise programs designed to increase athletes' strength and flexibility. As another example, the aquatic center whose strategy is to capture the senior citizen market by catering to their needs and interests may plan the tactics of establishing a relaxing aqua-calisthenics and stretching class for seniors and implementing a transportation service that would pick the customers up and return them to their homes.

Policies and Action Guides

Policies and other action guides are plans in that they are developed in response to forecasting what is likely to happen. In essence, they are the answer to generic problems made in advance of the occurrence of the problem. They prevent the administrator from having to make unique decisions for recurring or common problems. Fortune-telling talent is not necessary for such forecasting; judgments and decisions can be made based on past experience.

To review our discussion of action guides in Chapter 1, *policies* are general statements that guide or channel thinking and action in making a decision from a list of alternatives. They are flexible enough to allow decision makers some discretion in their implementation. *Procedures* specify particular means of carrying out the policies and are relatively inflexible. *Rules* are inflexible guides for action that permit no discretion at all. For example, planners for an aquatic center may develop the following policy, procedure, and rule:

Policy: Health and safety procedures as they relate to the operation of the pool shall be developed and communicated to all employees.

Procedure: Lifeguards shall test the pH factor and chlorine content of the water when the pool is opened and in the middle of the afternoon each day.

Rule: All swimmers must shower before entering the pool.

Budget and Resource Allocation

Projects, programs, and businesses require resources such as time, money, and personnel. The budget is a comprehensive statement of, and plan for, expected outcomes expressed in numerical form and encompassing money, time, and personnel. Budget planning is a continuous process and requires the constant attention of the director for maintaining balance, and in the case of business, a profit. Details of the budget are discussed in Chapter 11.

Programs

Programs are complexes of objectives, procedures, rules, task assignments, steps to be taken,

Rules are inflexible guides for action that permit no discretion.

resources to be employed, and other elements necessary to carry out a given course of action, including budgets. Programs may be as major as a school's plan to build a $12 million physical education and recreation center or a corporation's program to develop a corporate fitness program for its two thousand employees. Or they may be as minor as a weight-training program by the football team.

A primary program may call for many supporting programs. In reference to a corporation's development of an employees' fitness program, plans must be designed for building and equipment maintenance. A program for insurance and health maintenance care must be a consideration, as well as a program for the professional development of the staff. These and other programs must be devised and implemented before employees actually begin their daily fitness activities.

Consequently, a program of any importance seldom stands by itself. It is usually one part of a complex system of programs, depending upon some and affecting others. The interdependence makes planning quite difficult. The results of poor or inadequate planning are seldom isolated, for a plan is only as strong as its weakest link. Coordinated planning requires extraordinary managerial skill.

STEPS FOR PROGRAM PLANNING

The steps presented here are in connection with a major project such as the development of a junior high physical education program or the creation of a new corporate fitness program for a large organization. However, a director would follow essentially the same steps in any thorough planning endeavor. As minor plans are usually simpler, certain steps are more easily accomplished or even omitted. For example, for a minor supportive program, the first step—being aware

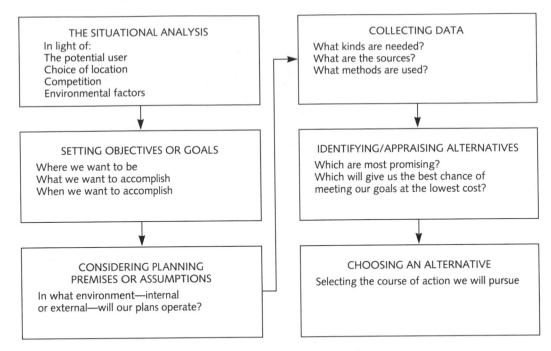

Figure 7.2 *The Steps in Planning*

of the opportunity—may be so obvious that to do a situational analysis would be redundant.

Regardless of the type of planning—objective, strategic, program, policy, or budget—a director is doing, he or she should follow these six steps: (1) Be aware of opportunities (situational analysis); (2) establish objectives; (3) consider planning premises or assumptions; (4) collect data; (5) identify and appraise alternatives; and (6) choose an alternative. These steps are diagrammed in Figure 7.2.

Step 1 Situational Analysis—Being Aware of Opportunities The situational analysis is the first step in any new planning endeavor and actually precedes the planning process in its strictest sense. However, being aware of opportunities is so critical to following with the other steps, we list it as the initial step. This analysis is a detailed consideration of the various factors that will affect the success or failure of a plan, and these factors include potential users, the choice of location, the competition, and various environmental factors. If the situational analysis indicates the probability that an adequate number of people would avail themselves of the services to be offered, then the venture has possibilities for success. If, however, the analysis reveals little or no chance of success, the process ends and the other steps are not taken.

Profile of the Potential User: Before selecting a location, the typical user must be profiled. Research must be undertaken to determine what type of customer would use the proposed facilities. Age, income range, education, exercise habits, and employment of potential users are usually included in the profile. Libraries, small-business organizations, related professional organizations, and university departments may be consulted in the search for information.

Choice of Location: After the characteristics of the potential clientele are identified, a location accessible to a large number of potential users is chosen. Such factors as weather conditions determine whether the facility should be outdoors, indoors, or a combination of both. Adequate space for parking and isolation from environmental disturbances, such as loud noises and industrial air pollutants, are also factors that are important in the choice of a good location.

Competition: Thorough knowledge and understanding of the competition is a critical factor for planning a business. It is not difficult to determine how many similar facilities are near enough to the customers to offer competition. Not only is it important to survey competing privately owned businesses, but also city, county, and school facilities must be analyzed and considered as competitors.

Environmental Factors: Other considerations that cannot be overlooked in the situational analysis are the environmental factors. Might building codes or legal restrictions present hurdles to overcome? Is the environment

OKAY STUDENTS, LET'S VACUUM THE PINE NEEDLES OUT OF THE POOL AGAIN ... CLASS STARTS IN TEN MINUTES ...

Environmental factors must be considered in a situational analysis.

conducive to the proposed activity?

Insight through Illustration

Two recent college graduates and a third partner with four years of experience in directing an employees' fitness program at a university decided to open an entrepreneurial service for fitness testing and follow-up programming. They were not short on the necessary energy and knowledge to develop a successful business, but they were short on opportunity and an adequate plan to identify the limits of the market. They found out after starting the business that the city was not large enough to support another fitness enterprise. Their competition included university, YMCA, and city recreation programs, as well as other small businesses offering similar services. They found out the hard way that it is especially tough for a new business to compete against government and nonprofit organizations. In this particular circumstance, the opportunity just was not there for them.

Step 2 Establishing Objectives The next step in planning is to develop, define, and clearly state the distinct objectives of the organization, unit, program, or special project. The objectives of the plan must be compatible with the objectives of any broader plan already in effect. For example, if a facility committee is planning a new gymnasium for a university, the objectives for the gymnasium must be compatible with the objectives of the departments it will serve. If a new department is being planned, the departmental objectives must be compatible with the school's and university's objectives.

Objectives specify the expected results and point to the outcomes to be achieved. They also indicate where the primary emphasis is to be placed and what is to be accomplished by the strategies, policies, and procedures.

Step 3 Consider Planning Assumptions Establishing and agreeing to use certain common planning assumptions is the second step in planning. A coordinated planning effort requires that those who are primarily responsible understand and agree to use a consistent set of planning assumptions. An assumption is anything that is taken for granted or accepted as true without proof.

Forecasting is an essential mental activity in planning and is important at this step. In planning a racquetball facility for completion four years in the future, a university department planner or committee must assume that racquetball is not a fad and will continue to be an activity in high

demand. The director at a private health and athletics club, in making plans to expand the program, facilities, and staff, must assume that the smaller corporations in the vicinity will continue to pay the membership fees for the corporation executives who patronize the club. A small group of business people who are planning to open a new aquatics center one-half mile from the city limits must assume that the growth of the economy will continue, and building will expand to eventually encircle the center. These are examples of key planning decisions that must rely on assumptions rather than facts.

In a small operation, the number of people who must agree to the planning assumptions may be limited to two or three, but in a larger enterprise, the number may include the top executives and several subordinate managers and leaders at various levels. If planning is to begin at the department level, it is imperative that the top-level administrators provide general policies and action guides to prevent the development of a complex of inconsistent plans.

Step 4 Collecting Data Data and estimates must be collected in the planning process, and sources for the information include those both within and outside the company or institution. Agencies or other departments and offices may have the needed information in their files. Organizations such as schools or corporations often have most of the needed information in their own libraries or collections.

The researcher begins by making a list of all the factors that must be researched to accurately describe the planning situation. If, for instance, the physical education department is planning an outdoor

Planning and research are essential.

fitness facility for the physically handicapped, such information would include the number of handicapped students, the number of handicapped individuals other than students who could benefit from the facility, possible sites on campus for the facility, supervision considerations, possible funding sources, the attitudes of the various people affected, other community facilities of this nature, benefits for students other than the handicapped, time needed for construction, and legal considerations.

After developing the list of every bit of information needed, the researcher indicates in a column opposite the factor the various sources where the information may be obtained. As the facts are obtained, each item is checked off.

Step 5 Identifying and Appraising Alternatives At this step, the planner generates and analyzes a list of alternatives in much the same way as a decision maker does in using the standard problem-solving method we presented in Chapter 4. Focusing on the planning objective, the planner should list and thoroughly consider the alternative methods of achieving it. Every alternative or possible course of action will have its advantages and disadvantages, which should be listed. For example, one alternative site for a facility may offer advantages in accessibility and supervision, but the location may be less permanent.

Having sought out alternative courses and examined the strong and weak points, the planner then appraises them in light of the planning objective.

Step 6 Choosing from the Alternatives The vital point of decision making in developing a plan is the selection of the course of action from the viable alternatives. This is the point at which the plan is adopted. Numerous variables and limitations must be considered in appraising the alternatives; therefore, choosing the best course of action may be quite difficult. Two or three alternatives may serve the situation equally well. In choosing from the alternatives, the decision maker should be receptive not only to recommendations from the planning committee but also to input from employees who may have some thoughts regarding the plan.

KEY PRINCIPLES FOR EFFECTIVE PLANNING

Planning can be done more effectively if the administrator keeps certain key principles in mind.

Principle of Flexible Planning

Because change is inevitable, plans should be created with change in mind. Indeed, many directors consider flexibility to be the most essential characteristic of a plan. Forecasting what the needs and desires of a clientele will be in five to ten years is a risky effort under any conditions, but it is especially risky if large investments are committed to a product, service, or facility. The value of being able to change a plan without undue risk and cost cannot be overemphasized. When for some unforeseen reason a plan must be changed, it is important to keep moving toward accomplishment of the original goal. In the profit-making world, drastic changes are expected and are important factors in initial planning.

Insight through Illustration

Recently, when a professional basketball team decided to move from one city to another, a large shell of a facility was constructed so that the team could make an early move and play there until a permanent building designed for basketball could be erected. The temporary arena will be converted to a large storage facility after the team moves to the permanent facility.

Another example of planning flexibility occurs every year when the very successful California Physical Education and Coaching Workshops are planned. The workshops normally attract approximately fifteen hundred teachers and coaches during a five-week summer period. The number of participants may vary by as many as three hundred, and that difference is not easy to predict because preregistration is not required. To accommodate last-minute changes in numbers, the workshop coordinator releases a conservative dollar figure to the directors for hiring instructors and consultants to facilitate a sound basic program. Four or five instructors who will be in attendance anyway stand by, ready to take a class in their area of specialization should added sections become necessary due to a large number of walk-in participants. The plan works quite well. There is no additional cost for building in this feature, because the instructors are already at the conference assisting in the staging of the program. The only cost occurs if the sections are

added, and the additional registration fees from the unexpected walk-ins more than pay for the instructors' stipends.

The principle that applies to building adaptability into plans can be summarized in two parts. First, the more flexibility that can be built into the original plans, the less is the risk of financial loss and disruption should unexpected events occur. Second, if there is a cost for building in flexibility, that cost must be weighed against the potential benefits of making future commitments.

Principle of Review and Change

Because even the most flexible plan cannot anticipate every possible development, another principle important to planning implementation is the principle of review and change. *Planning reviews should be conducted frequently to assure that the goals of the course of action do not change; and changes should be made in the course of action if expectations are not being met.*

Principle of Planning Commitment

Just as anything worth having requires a commitment to obtain, so does an effective plan. The principle of planning commitment states that *since planning involves forecasting and forecasting involves risks, the commitment of resources to planning objectives should be realistic and logical.* This principle implies that funds, time, and staff should not be either undercommitted or overcommitted. Anything other than the exact recipe for the proper commitment may result in something less than efficient and effective planning. For example, if there is an undercommitment of funds, the search for truths and facts in the situational analysis may fall short, leaving the decision maker with less than adequate information. If there is an overcommitment in terms of time, there may be a very costly delay in gaining returns for the investment.

Other Principles

Other principles for effective planning are the following:

- Planning requires a concentrated effort on the part of everyone involved, especially administrators.
- Planning should start at the top. Without a commitment from the chief executive, few projects or programs have a chance of surviving. Responsibility for the plan itself lies with the director.
- Planning must be organized. Operating codes and assignment of responsibilities must be precise and free of gaps.
- Planning must be clear and definite. Everyone involved must have a valid perception of what others are doing.
- Goals, premises, and strategies must be communicated clearly.
- Long-range and short-range planning must be integrated and must complement one another.

MAINTAINING THE PLAN

Maintaining the plan is a critical concern of the director, facilitated by these hints on how to stay on track:

- Do not panic because of current or short-term pressures.
- Maintain an emphasis on the basic objectives of the program.

People generally resist change.

- Fix the responsibility for the preparation and execution of each planning area or section.
- Coordinate all types of planning required to support the program.
- Review results periodically and make appropriate revisions.

WHY PLANNING FAILS

Successful planning requires demanding and concentrated effort on the part of all participants in the planning process. Success does not occur without careful planning. For that reason, project directors need to be aware that there are many reasons why planning sometimes fails. Ten of the more common reasons are listed below:

- lack of meaningful and purposeful goals
- lack of commitment in seeing the project through to the end
- lack of top-management support
- failure of planners to see the full scope of the plan
- planners relying too heavily on their experience
- mistaking planning studies for the overall plan
- lack of clear delegation and authority

- failure to develop and follow through with sound strategies
- people's resistance to change

- lack of a strong communicating and coordinating effort

KEY WORDS AND PHRASES

Short-range plans	Situational analysis	Resource allocation
Levels of planning	Review and change	Planning assumptions
Flexible planning	Long-range plans	Program strategy
Mission and objectives	Program tactics	Planning commitment

QUESTIONS FOR REVIEW

1. Discuss the meaning of the term *planning*.
2. What, how, and when should the director of an activity-based program plan?
3. What steps are involved in effective planning?
4. Discuss the principle of planning commitment.
5. What is the relationship of short-range plans to long-range plans?
6. Why does planning fail?
7. Discuss the role of strategies and policies in planning.
8. Be prepared to expand on any of the principles for effective planning as listed in the text.
9. List the steps in planning and make a significant statement about each.

SELF-TEST

Corrected True-False

If the statement is true, mark it T. If the statement is false, mark it F and change it to a true statement by adding or deleting words.

_____ 1. A plan basically means making arrangements in advance.

_____ 2. When focusing on your objective, you should have a means of delaying it.

_____ 3. The first crucial phase of the planning process is to establish the premises.

_____ 4. Planning involves selecting from alternative future courses of action for the program or some aspect within it.

_____ 5. Strategies are general programs of action toward the attainment of comprehensive objectives.

_____ 6. Procedures guide our thinking in decision making.

_____ 7. Tactics are plans that establish a required method of handling future activities.

_____ 8. Innovation refers to the ability and power to develop new ideas.

Multiple Choice

_____ 9. This built into plans reduces the danger of losses that may occur due to unexpected events:
   a. change
   b. strategy
   c. flexibility
   d. creativity

_____ 10. One of the following is not a value of planning:
   a. documenting resources
   b. updating new employees
   c. better use of resources
   d. delegating tasks

_____ 11. The last step in planning is to:
   a. search for information
   b. analyze the situation
   c. develop alternatives
   d. none of the above

_____ 12. One of the following is out of place with the others:
   a. excessive reliance on experience

   b. resistance to change
   c. top management support
   d. objectives not clear

_____ 13. Which is not included in the situational analysis?
   a. organizational policy
   b. environmental factors
   c. potential user profile
   d. site location

_____ 14. These are concerned with establishing specific and detailed programs of action for attaining specific organizational goals:
   a. strategies
   b. policies
   c. tactics
   d. missions

_____ 15. Which statement is true?
   a. Long-range plans precede short-range plans.
   b. Short-range plans precede long-range plans.
   c. Planning and organizing are developed at same time.
   d. Planning is similar to fortune telling.

CASE 7.1 PLANNING A NEW FITNESS CONSULTING ENTERPRISE

Bill Phillips, Teresa Abrams, and Jody Janeke were looking forward to their June graduation. Jody would be receiving her master's degree in wellness and fitness management; Bill and Teresa would receive the bachelor's degree in commercial and corporation fitness. They had been very close friends for four years and had talked frequently during the past year about staying in the university city of Paradise Hills and starting a new fitness testing and consulting service in the town of forty-three thousand residents. Their parents were willing to consider assisting them in obtaining $45,000 in capital to begin the venture. The parents were not sure the business was a wise move, but each recalled how they had started out in small businesses under similar circumstances.

In early February, Bill, Teresa, and Jody made arrangements with their parents for all of them to meet in Paradise Hills to further discuss the entrepreneurial idea. After three hours of discussion, each parent agreed to help their excited children with a loan only after seeing and approving a well-documented prospectus of the enterprise.

The following Monday, the three fitness students met to make plans for preparing the prospectus.

Your Response

1. What are the issues and problems in this case?
2. What barriers may stand in the way of the best decisions?
3. What actions are recommended?
4. What action guides lead to the decisions relating to the proposed business venture?

CASE 7.2 NEEDED: A NEW PHYSICAL EDUCATION BUILDING

Sally White, hired to teach physical education at Oaklawn High School seven years ago, was appointed to chair the department one year after her arrival. The indoor physical education facilities were twenty-five years old and inadequate for the activity program needed at Oaklawn.

Sally had been expressing the need for a new facility for the past three years to Gil Troy, the principal, and two of the school board members with whom she had become acquainted. All listened attentively and promised to give their attention to the need. The principal discussed the problem with the superintendent of schools, and the two board members succeeded in getting the matter on the agenda for discussion.

After discussing the issue in a formal board meeting, the chairman told Gil to have Sally present preliminary plans for the facility to the board at the March meeting, which was two months away.

Your Response

1. What is the central issue?
2. What problems does Sally White face?
3. What specifically should she prepare and how should she proceed?
4. List some generalizations that can provide direction.

BIBLIOGRAPHY

Bialkowski, Carol. "Launching a New Club." *Club Industry* 7 (April 1991): 22–34.

———. "Small Club Survival Guide." *Club Industry* 7 (July 1991): 17–31.

Bullaro, John J., and Christopher Edginton. *Commercial Leisure Services: Managing for Profit, Service, Personal Satisfaction.* New York: Macmillan, 1986.

Cohen, William A., and Nutrit Cohen. *Top Executive Performance: 11 Keys to Success and Power.* New York: Wiley, 1984.

Johnson, M. L. *Functional Administration in Physical and Health Education.* Boston: Houghton Mifflin, 1977.

Koontz, Harold, and Heinz Weihrich. *Essentials of Management.* 5th ed. New York: McGraw-Hill, 1989.

Schwartz, Alan. "The Art and Science of Feasibility Studies." *Athletic Business* 10 (April 1986): 36–39.

"Sports Club Design: Fitting Facilities to Program Plans." *Athletic Business* 9 (April 1985): 22–30.

8

Organizing for the Activity-Based Program

All good organization tends to simplicity.
Sir Arthur Helps

Chapter Objectives

After reading this chapter and completing the exercises, you should be able to:

1 Explain what organizing and organizational structure really mean

2 Define formal and informal organization and tell why each is important

3 Describe two methods of departmentalization

4 List the advantages and disadvantages of narrow and wide spans of control

5 List the steps in organizing

6 Describe what function authority is

7 Explain the difference between line and staff authority

8 Discuss the purpose of delegating and decentralizing authority

9 Identify tasks that a sports director should not delegate

10 List two types of barriers to effective delegation and discuss how to avoid them

At what point does planning end and organizing begin? The answer to the first half of the question is that organizational planning does not end. It is an ongoing process, and in the administrative cycle, planning flows smoothly into organizing. Because planning is continuous, to draw a well-defined line between the two functions is difficult and unnecessary. The key to identifying the beginning of the organizing function is *action*. When organizing takes over from planning, action begins. The purpose of organizing is to make human cooperation productive.

WHAT DOES ORGANIZATION MEAN?

Organization is a term that means different things to different people. Some would refer to a professional baseball team as an organization; but sociologists often use the term in referring to the total system of social and cultural relationships. Others insist that it includes the total behavior of all members of a participating team. In this text, organization most often refers to the planned and intentional structure of roles or positions in an identified unit that seeks to achieve established purposes and objectives. On occasion the term is used in referring to an institution or enterprise, such as a university or a private fitness club.

Organizational roles, as described by Koontz and Weihrich, must have three characteristics if they are to exist and be meaningful. They must (1) identify verifiable objectives, which are a major part of planning; (2) include a clear idea of the major duties or activities involved; and (3) incorporate an understood area of discretion or authority, so that the people filling the roles know what they can do to accomplish results. When people work together they must fill certain roles, and it is absolutely essential that these roles be intentionally planned and designed. Intentionally structured roles can be fitted together so that the

people filling the roles may, as a group, pursue the goals of the enterprise smoothly and effectively, with a minimum of wasted effort.

FORMAL AND INFORMAL ORGANIZATION

The type of organization we have just described is formal organization. The word *formal* connotes to some people a very confining circumstance with little room for flexibility and creativity. That connotation must be set aside, because it is critical for organization to allow for flexibility and encourage creative endeavors by individuals as they work together as a group. Formal in this sense refers to a planned structure that is identified and made known to all who relate to the productive unit. Formal organization enables the individual to understand the roles of group members as they strive for common objectives and thus makes the individual's effort and contribution more meaningful to him or her. Cooperation and unity are indispensable keys if formal organization is to fulfill the intended purpose.

Sports or fitness directors must not only thoroughly relate to the formal organization, but they must also recognize the informal organization that exists in their realm of authority. Informal roles, lines of authority, and chains of command do not appear in operating codes and organizational charts, but it is most important that the director recognize the informal organization and not antagonize it.

An informal organization is any group (large or small) that contributes to joint outcomes without a conscious joint goal. For example, a small group of coaches or fitness instructors who get together each morning for coffee may represent an informal organization. A group of four members of the staff who get together socially every two or three weeks along with their spouses may constitute an informal organization. The participating em-

Regular coffee groups may be a part of the informal organization.

ployees may even be unaware of the influence their group may have on enterprise results. Wise administrators, as they manage subordinates, use informal structures to the advantage of the department or institution.

DEPARTMENTALIZATION

A very important aspect of organizing is establishing organizational divisions. The division with which people in the field of physical education, fitness, and sports are most familiar is the department. The department is a distinct area or division of an enterprise with a director who has authority and responsibility for the performance of specified activities. If it were not for departmentalization, the size of an enterprise would be restricted to the limited number of employees who could be directly supervised and controlled. Grouping activities and people into departments makes it possible for an enterprise to expand almost indefinitely.

No single best method of departmentalizing can be recommended for all organizations or situations. The nature of the institution or enterprise and the requirements for best achieving the established objectives usually determine the way an organization is departmentalized. If top management decides that one pattern of departmentalization will yield better results than other patterns, then that pattern is adopted.

Departmentalization by Numbers

In departmentalization by numbers, a division is formed once a specified number of people are gathered. At that point a manager is appointed to direct the department's activities. The Israelites were divided in this manner as Moses led them from Egypt toward the promised land. The military still uses this technique for its basic training units. This method has certain applications in modern administration but is not used often.

This method is declining in use for three reasons: (1) Technology has advanced, requiring different and more specialized skills; (2) grouping by

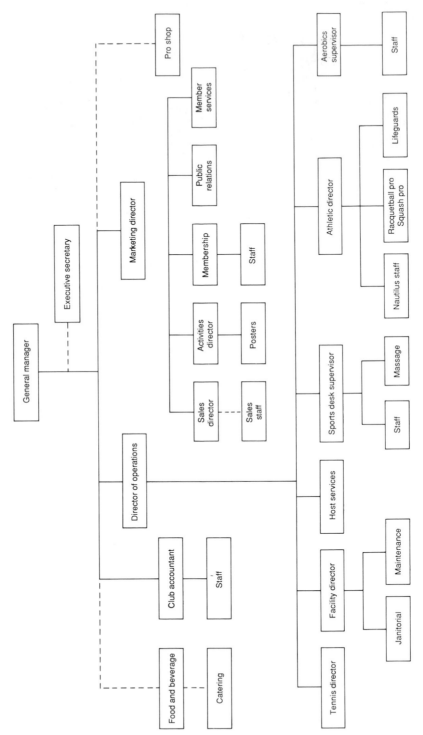

Figure 8.1 *Organizational Chart for a Large Athletic Club*

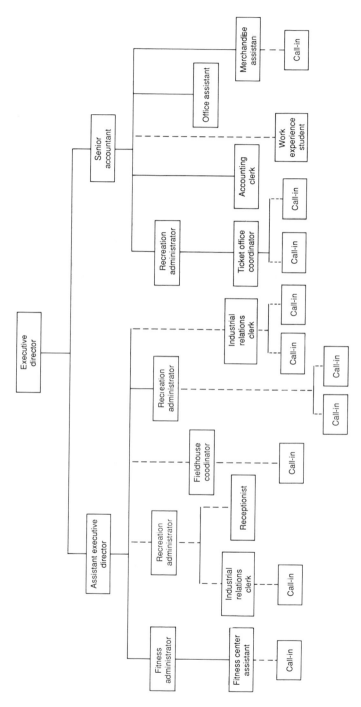

Figure 8.2 *Organizational Chart for a Corporation's Recreation and Fitness Department*

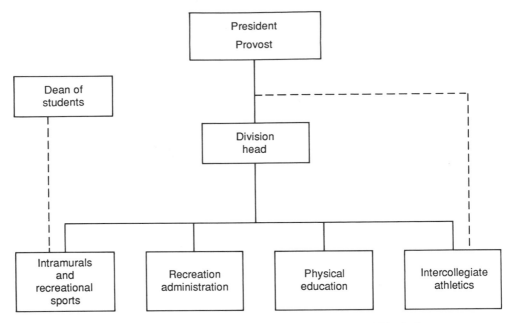

Figure 8.3 *Organizational Chart for a University's Division of Physical Education, Recreation, and Sports*

specialized interest and task is more efficient than designating groups by mere numbers; and (3) this method is useful only at the lower organizational levels.

Departmentalization by Function

In physical education, fitness, and sports endeavors, functional departmentalization is the most widely employed basis for organizing activities. It is a logical method of division, and time has proven it to be very effective. It follows the principle of task specialization, thus using efficiently people with similar interests and goals.

This method of departmentalizing is illustrated in the organizational charts in Figures 8.1, 8.2, and 8.3. Figure 8.1 illustrates the functional grouping for a large private health and fitness club; Figure 8.2 displays the functional grouping of a corporation's recreation and fitness department; and Figure 8.3 shows the functional group-

ing of a university's health, physical education, recreation, and athletics division. Workers concentrating on a particular task or aspect of the operation are grouped under a single director, and these directors in turn report to the head administrator.

SPAN OF CONTROL AND ORGANIZATIONAL LEVELS

The purpose of organizing, as we stated earlier, is to make human effort productive and effective. An important consideration in the process is how to make the control function most efficient. That consideration relates to span of control and organizational levels.

Span of control refers to the number of subordinates that a manager supervises. There is a limit to the number that one person can effec-

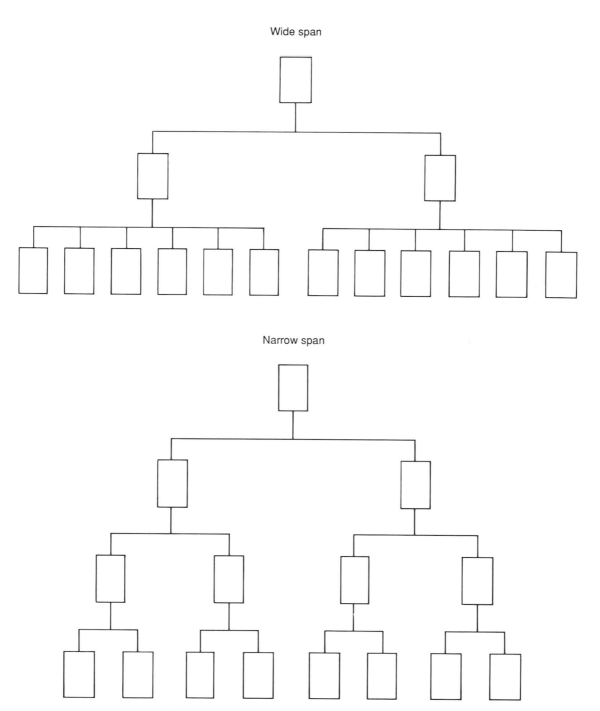

Figure 8.4 *Narrow and Wide Spans of Control*

OK! SIGNAL HOWARD. IT'S TIME TO START THE FUN RUN.

A wide span of control can make communication more difficult.

tively direct, varying from four to fifteen, or possibly more, depending upon the nature of the situation. At the upper levels of organization, the ideal number may be as low as four, and at the lower levels, it may be as many as fifteen or more. Such factors as task complexity, experience and maturity of the personnel involved, and task relationships determine whether the span is narrow or wide. Complex tasks usually require a narrow or short span, whereas a wider span may be indicated if the personnel are more experienced and mature or if the tasks are closely related.

Decisions about span of control determine the number of levels an organization has. If the span is narrow, more levels result, and, conversely, fewer levels exist if the span is wider. Figure 8.4 illustrates this concept.

The advantages of the narrow span of control are greater control, close supervision, and fast communication between subordinates and superiors. The disadvantages are the high cost due to a multitude of levels, involvement of superiors in subordinates' work, and the great distance between the top level and the lowest level of the organization.

The advantages of the wide span of control are that delegation of authority is forced, a positive feeling of responsibility and worth results for subordinates, policies must be developed clearly and in detail, careful selection of subordinates becomes critical, the distance between the lowest level and the top level is small, and operational costs are minimized. The disadvantages of the wide span are that it is more difficult for managers to maintain control, and inefficient managers may cause decision delays.

The key to deciding on the appropriate span of control and the appropriate number of organizational levels is that work units must be small enough to be manageable and large enough to be cost efficient.

STEPS IN ORGANIZING

We've stated that organizing begins when planning ends, but that precise line of demarcation is not always easy to identify. However, since organizing is an action process, the logical place for organizing to begin is after the objectives have been formulated and the course of action determined. The organizing process is sandwiched between planning and controlling, and consists of these four steps: (1) identifying specific tasks or activities; (2) grouping the tasks or activities; (3) assigning resources and responsibilities; and (4) coordinating activities and relationships.

Identifying Specific Tasks or Activities

The effort necessary for achieving organizational objectives must be broken down into specific activities so that the personnel in the organization with the specialized skills to perform the activities may be assigned the responsibilities. If the people presently employed do not possess the specialized skills needed, then those who do must be hired.

Consider, for example, the planned athletics program of a new high school. Specific tasks or activities necessary to operate effectively include not only organizing and directing the sports that will be offered, but also organizing and issuing equipment, training athletes, operating off-season conditioning programs, promoting the program, and selling tickets. Each one of these areas of responsibility must be assigned to someone with relevant skills.

Grouping the Tasks or Activities

Efficiency as well as effectiveness must be of prime concern when grouping related activities into workable units. Care must be taken to ensure that the units are not too large to be effective or too small to be efficient. In an athletics situation, the grouping of activities does not appear at first glance to be very difficult. Each sport may constitute a logical division or group, and organizational charts always reflect this type of grouping. However, deciding on the divisions for servicing the various sports may not be as simple. Where will the head coach's responsibility begin and end in providing ancillary services such as athletic training, off-season conditioning, and promotional programs? The athletics director must identify the specific needs of all sports and group them so that each sport will receive the greatest benefit.

Assigning Resources and Responsibilities

After the tasks or activities have been grouped, resources must be provided and responsibility assigned so that the goals of the particular unit may be achieved. Resources include funding, personnel, time, and facilities. Unless reasonable conditions and appropriate resources are provided, success cannot be anticipated. Authority must be delegated along with responsibility if good working relationships, high morale, and optimum productivity are to result.

Coordinating Activities and Relationships

Coordinating is the fourth and final phase of organizing, and it is a critical one. Coordinating is very similar to communicating in an organization in that it must permeate every phase of the operation. It must go up, down, and sideways, so that all parts may smoothly move together toward the common goals of the institution or enterprise. The verb *coordinate* means to harmonize in a common action and effort.

The director must be sure that assigned activities and relationships are specified and described in detail. Job descriptions and operating codes must be written, distributed, and fully understood by every instructor, coach, coordinator, and supervisor so that overlap of responsibility and authority is avoided. Authority relationships must stay within bounds. A volatile situation can quickly explode if a supervisor begins to exert authority outside her or his designated area of responsibility.

LINE AND STAFF RELATIONSHIPS

Confusion seems to abound in administrative circles about what *line and staff* really means. From the outset, it should be understood that the line and staff concept relates directly to authority in an organization.

Line and Staff in Theory

The *line* function is supervisory in nature. Line authority is what a supervisor, director, or administrator exercises over a subordinate. In an organization, lines of authority run uninterrupted from the top executive down to the least responsible employee—from the top level of an organizational chart to the lowest level. Persons serving in the line function are often thought to be those

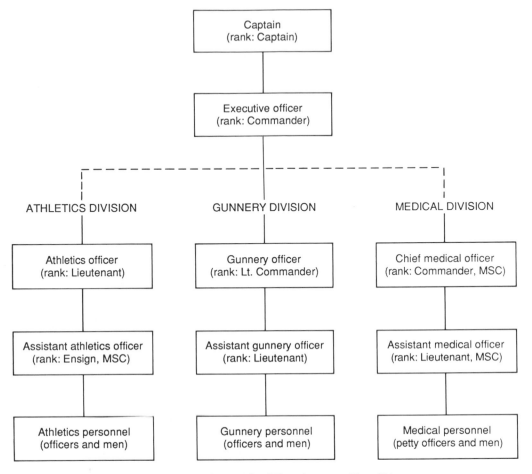

Figure 8.5 *Line and Staff Functions on a Navy Ship*

who are most responsible for meeting the objectives of the enterprise. This concept is partially true; however, line relationships may also be present in a service or staff department within an organization.

The *staff* function is advisory in nature. Those who serve in a staff role provide line administrators with information, special advice, and counsel. The authority of persons in staff roles stems from their expertise rather than from their position in the hierarchy.

Because the idea of line and staff functions originated in the military, a military example can best illustrate it. Figure 8.5 depicts line and staff functions on a Navy ship. The lowest-ranking officer in the gunnery division would take over the command of the ship before a higher-ranking officer from the medical division would, in the event that all officers above the ensign in the line function were killed in battle. The gunnery division is a line division and the medical and athletics divisions are staff divisions (denoted by broken lines) in that they provide services to help make the line division more effective. Note that line relationships exist within the athletics and medical divisions even though they are staff divisions. In each

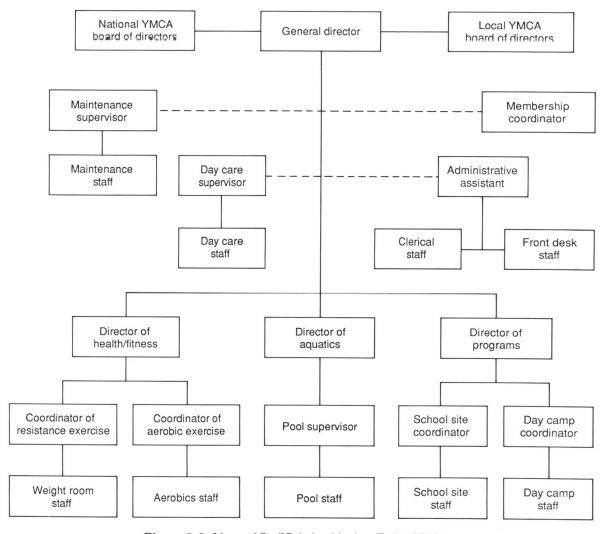

Figure 8.6 *Line and Staff Relationships in a Typical YMCA*

division, the officer serving in the superior position can give orders to those serving below him.

Figure 8.6 illustrates line and staff relationships in a typical YMCA. The lines of authority and staff roles are readily observable (again, broken lines denote staff relationships).

The line may devise, but the staff must advise. This statement summarizes the line and staff re-

lationship. It means that the staff has the right to counsel and advise, but the line has the authority to make the decisions and act on them. If everyone understands this premise and is willing to operate by it, optimal results may be expected from the coordinated effort.

Especially in the decision-making process, it is important for all line and staff personnel to have a

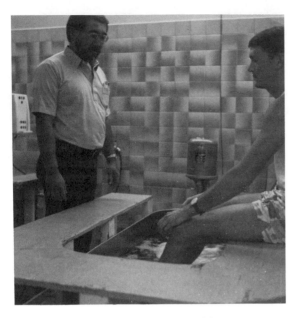

The trainer fills a staff position.

clear understanding of the relationships between line and staff authority and of the role that each plays. For example, the head trainer with twenty years of seniority does not make a coaching decision for the first-year assistant football coach, because the decision is a line decision in football, and even though the trainer is a senior staff member, his responsibility and authority are confined to the specialized area of athletic training. In a reversed situation, a seasoned head football coach should not have authority over a first-year trainer if the decision is an athletic training one, even if the decision relates to an injury to a football player.

Functional Authority

Functional authority is a right delegated to a person by a top-level administrator to perform a line function in a department or administrative unit of which he or she is not a member. This person is usually a staff person from a specialized area who is given a portion of some line manager's authority to perform a specialized task. For example, a financial specialist might be given the responsibility to move into a university athletics department that is having financial problems. The specialist would not be working under the athletics director but would make decisions and report directly to the provost. No new authority would be created, but a portion of the athletics director's authority would be assigned to the specialist.

Using functional authority means taking a risk even under the best conditions. An administrator may be unwilling to relinquish a portion of his or her authority. An outsider may be resented by the personnel of the entire department and receive very little cooperation in carrying out the assignment. Management has a tremendously important responsibility to smooth the way and lay the foundation for assigning functional authority. The administrator, the department personnel, and the specialist must be fully educated as to the purpose of the move and the role of the specialist in the decision-making process. The specialist must maintain a low profile and make a concerted effort to relate positively to all department personnel.

Benefits and Limitations in Using Staff

Technological advances have permeated the field of physical education, fitness, and sports, as well as other fields. Such areas as exercise physiology, sports medicine, fitness testing and prescription, and coaching have become so sophisticated and the skills so specialized that an administrator needs advice and counsel from staff specialists to move ahead knowledgeably. Advice is the contribution that staff can make in assisting the director, a line manager, in being effective. Where highly specialized knowledge is required, specialists may need the functional authority to make certain decisions without consultation with the line manager.

Although the benefits derived from effective staff use more than justify it, because of its nature and the difficulty of understanding it, staff authority leads to certain problems in practice.

Too much staff authority can create confusion for workers and complicate the role of the line manager if not adequately controlled. As the saying "No man can serve two masters" indicates, workers can only truly be responsible to one manager. Even if it means the sacrifice of a valuable specialized service, staff authority may need to be restricted in order to prevent the problem of too many bosses.

Besides the potential danger of having employees and supervisors reporting to more than one superior, administrators must be mindful of the following concerns when assigning responsibilities and authority to staff personnel:

• Staff specialists may undermine line authority if they are clothed with enough authority that they begin to dictate instead of counsel.

• In some situations, when a plan recommended by staff fails, staff may blame line for poor implementation and line may blame staff for a poor plan.

• Staff may have a tendency to think in a vacuum, and since they are so engrossed in their own specialization they may fail to see how their recommendations will fit into the total operation.

Making Line and Staff Relationships Productive

Administrators must make a major effort to establish the conditions for productive line and staff relationships. Getting line personnel to listen to the specialized advice of staff personnel is not always easy. Some people in authoritative positions are not willing to take the advice of experts, whether out of fear of losing their power, for some other psychological reason, or because of wanting to save money. Regardless of the reason, an unwillingness to listen can create problems and cause the loss of valuable enterprise resources. A smoother effort will result if superiors can establish mutual respect and appreciation between line and staff personnel. If this condition cannot be achieved, the line person may have to be told to listen to the staff expert. The staff must realize also that they have an obligation to be thorough in preparing their advice. Advice based on inadequate research and lack of thoroughness can destroy a healthy line-staff relationship.

Administrators must establish ever-flowing lines of communication with the staff, especially in conveying information related to decisions that may affect the specialist's role in the organization. Failing to keep the staff informed is a common complaint in organizations. Good communication can prevent accusations that the staff think in a vacuum.

DECENTRALIZING AUTHORITY AND DELEGATION

Decentralizing authority means providing key decision-making opportunities for lower-level administrators. It is a concept and practice that has received a lot of attention in this country in recent years, and in cases where top executives have really given authority to those closer to the place where production actually occurs, very positive results have been observed. Besides improved product quality, other benefits have included improved morale, reduction of red tape and operating costs, and more time for top-level executives to be more involved in those activities that can best be done by them, such as public relations and development.

Delegation is the means by which decentralization is achieved. As a concept, delegation has probably been practiced on this planet since prehistoric times. Anthropologists speculate that tribe or group leaders were present in early

JUST DO YOUR JOB — I CAN HANDLE THIS.

*Anthropologists speculate that delegation of authority
has been around for a long time.*

times, and the responsibilities for survival were apportioned or divided among the group members. The leaders were probably those tribe members who were either larger or stronger than the other members, and those who were capable of seeing that the group objectives could be met, i.e., those who could delegate.

Today, the concept is basically the same. *Delegation* can be defined as authorizing a person or persons to act in one's behalf. That authorization carries with it accountability and responsibility for results. For the administrator, delegation becomes an important tool to involve the staff in executing basic functions geared to meet defined objectives of the organization. It is through delegation that directors are able to free themselves from the tasks and activities that others can perform as well as, or better than, they can. Directors can use reacquired time in performing activities that can best be carried out by them. This turning loose of tasks and activities is often one of the most difficult decisions for directors, because most directors move up from positions that require attention to details, and old habits are sometimes hard to change.

The Delegation Process

Engal (1983: 11) lists eight distinct parts to the delegation process:

1. The superior determines that some objective he seeks may not be accomplished or is better accomplished by another.

2. The superior determines the need to shift to another person the obligation for an objective's accomplishment.

3. The superior selects a delegate who will do what the superior cannot or should not do.

4. The superior explains to the delegate the scope of the objective and the nature of the delegate obligation. Time constraints, if any, are clarified.

5. The superior shifts or loans enough of his authority to the delegate to achieve the objective. The obligation is accepted by the delegate.

6. The scope of the objective may be narrowed or broadened with the delegate given wide latitude. Levels of support are understood.

7. The delegate then achieves, fails to achieve, or partially achieves the objective.

8. Finally, the superior evaluates the results. He may or may not withdraw his loaned authority from the delegate and terminate his obligation.

Besides this process, other elements of delegation must be understood by both administrator and subordinates. McConkey (1974: 13) states that "delegation takes place when the subordinate is given the widest possible latitude to determine his own destiny" in the following areas:

Responsibility: jurisdiction or scope of his job

Accountability: specific results he must achieve

Planning: doing the planning for his own organizational unit

Authority: having the authority necessary to make the decisions and take action appropriate to his job

Decision Making: making decisions that need to be made for his unit

Directing: within a minimal monitoring or control system, being left alone to direct and manage his own organization and its resources

Monitoring: receiving the tailor-made feedback and data necessary for [him to monitor his operation's] progress and take corrective action as required

When the administrator decides to give a subordinate a responsibility, that responsibility must be accompanied with the authority to carry out the assigned task or activities. It should be made very clear to the subordinate that he or she is accountable for accomplishing the objectives of the assignment. And whenever possible, the director should delegate a total job to one person and let the subordinate delegate some of the responsibil-

ity while remaining in charge of the assignment. This creates better control and coordination, and minimizes confusion during the course of the job.

McConkey (1974: 15) defines what he calls "no-nonsense delegation" as "delegation by objectives and for results." He echoes Engal's eight-part delegation process by describing two conditions that must be met before effective delegation can occur. The first is that the organization must determine its priorities and objectives and adhere to them. The second is that the subordinate must be allowed to "play his proper role in achieving the necessary objectives."

It must be pointed out that even though Engal and McConkey believe that subordinates should be allowed the freedom to achieve objectives by their own methods, an atmosphere of total permissiveness should not exist. Freedom for the delegate exists only within the confines of the organization's priorities and objectives; if all subordinates are allowed to do their own thing without restraining guidelines, organizational chaos will result. Further, it should be understood that even though the director can delegate to a subordinate a task or responsibility, permit her or him to assume the authority necessary to achieve the objectives that accompany the responsibility, and then hold the subordinate accountable for the results, the ultimate responsibility for the accomplishment of the objective still remains with the director.

The Danger of Overdelegating

Drucker (1966: 37–38) points out that delegation can be overemphasized and that this is the danger in heeding such phrases as "The laziest manager is the best manager." He believes that people should get paid to do their own work without pushing it onto someone else to do it for them. Drucker does go on to clarify that the executive may not have enough time to do all the things he or she considers important, and in these cases should delegate any work that can be done by others so he or she can pay attention to really important matters.

The administrator must determine which functions to handle and which to delegate. Gardner and Davis (1965: 36) suggest a set of guidelines to help determine what should and should not be delegated. The administrator should

- handle his or her own "hot potatoes":
  —emergency situations that require his or her skill and knowledge
  —extremely important matters that have serious consequences
  —matters of exception to general policy and routine procedure
- conduct appraisals of his or her subordinates
- reward or punish subordinates
- do jobs requiring his or her status and position.

The administrator can usually delegate

- routine and inconsequential details to his or her secretary and staff assistants
- tasks and duties that others can handle as well as or better than he or she can—jobs that use the specialized skills of subordinates
- activities that will lead to the development of subordinates and their skills.

For example, the physical education department head should handle the annual staff evaluations and review, but facility scheduling can be handled by a staff assistant or one of the members of the physical education department.

The administrator should avoid overdelegating unpleasant and undesirable tasks because doing so defeats the key objectives of developing subordinates' abilities and motivating commitment. And when beginning in an administrative position, the administrator should avoid delegating too much at first. He or she should take time to gradually develop to an appropriate level of delega-

tion. This allows subordinates to get used to the administrator's delegative process. By the same token, a new subordinate must be brought along slowly and delegated tasks gradually so he or she will not feel buried by too much responsibility.

Barriers to Effective Delegation

Barriers to effective delegation are caused in most situations by the director's reluctance to let go, but sometimes they result from subordinates' reluctance to accept responsibility.

The director may be unwilling to delegate and then move out of the subordinate's way because he or she

- is insecure in her or his position
- believes he or she is more competent than subordinates
- is afraid of not knowing how to lead in delegation
- is fearful of developing someone to replace him or her
- feels incompetent to adequately define objectives.

Subordinates may be hesitant to accept responsibility because they

- do not understand the requirements of the task
- are too dependent on others
- feel uncomfortable with the organization
- do not believe in themselves
- fear criticism
- already feel overworked.

The director can create an atmosphere that either hinders or promotes effective delegation. The following action guides can help the director do the latter.

Action Guides for Effective Delegation

In the delegative process, the administrator must first decide what is to be delegated and then what steps to follow to delegate effectively. He or she must be aware of problems and must not avoid them.

To give delegation an opportunity to succeed, the director should follow these widely accepted guidelines:

- Set job standards that are fair and attainable.
- Understand the concept of delegation.
- Know subordinates' capabilities.
- Develop meaningful goals and objectives.
- Correct subordinates' mistakes with tact.
- Reward subordinates with greater responsibility.

- Show genuine concern for what subordinates are doing.
- Provide training for handling responsibility.
- Delegate authority along with responsibility and accountability.
- Be aware of areas that should not be delegated.
- Acknowledge the importance of the results.

The delegative process may be only one of the functions of a director, but it is a very important and complex process that requires people to work together in achieving objectives. Its use can affect the morale of an organizational unit in a positive or negative way. Hence, it is imperative for the activity director to develop and practice effective delegating skills.

KEY WORDS AND PHRASES

Organization	Departmentalization by numbers	Staff authority
Formal organization	Wide span of control	Delegation
Informal organization	Narrow span of control	Accountability
Departmentalization by function	Line authority	Overdelegating

QUESTIONS FOR REVIEW

1. Give an example of a formal and an informal organization.
2. Construct an organizational chart of either a physical education or athletics department, a commercial fitness enterprise, or a corporation fitness department. How can this chart help or hinder organizational efforts?
3. What are the steps in organizing? How would you follow them to organize a fun run or weekend tournament?
4. What are the advantages of departmentalization?
5. What are the disadvantages of a narrow span of control?
6. Explain the difference between line and staff authority.

7. List several guidelines for successful delegation.

8. Why do efforts to decentralize authority fail?

SELF-TEST

Corrected True-False

If the statement is true, mark it T. If the statement is false, mark it F and change it to a true statement by adding or deleting words.

_____ 1. The purpose of organizing is to make human cooperation productive.

_____ 2. The methods of organization and management of schools and industry are very similar in nature.

_____ 3. Administrators agree that the number of people one person can effectively supervise is five to seven.

_____ 4. Formal organization is the intentional structure of roles.

_____ 5. The first step in organizing is to formulate objectives.

_____ 6. Departmentation according to function is a widely accepted practice in physical education, fitness, and sports programs.

_____ 7. Line personnel devise; staff personnel supervise.

_____ 8. People in an organization with staff functions will fall in the direct line of command on the organizational chart.

_____ 9. Functional authority delegation means that line managers or administrators are deprived of some authority.

_____ 10. It is okay for the fitness director to ask his or her associate director to punish his or her subordinates.

Multiple Choice

_____ 11. A greater number of important decisions are made at the top when the span of control is:
   a. narrow
   b. eliminated
   c. wide
   d. minimized

_____ 12. Directors may be unwilling to delegate when they:
   a. are secure in their jobs
   b. feel they are experts in doing many things
   c. are very well organized and controlled
   d. none of the above

_____ 13. Athletic trainers in high school and college are usually:
   a. line personnel
   b. staff personnel
   c. functional authorities
   d. independent

_____ 14. Organizational charts are:
   a. not recommended in a participatory organization
   b. ineffective in smaller- and middle-sized units
   c. primarily a communication tool
   d. both a and b

_____ 15. Which is part of the organizing function?
   a. formulating objectives
   b. coordinating activities
   c. developing premises
   d. all of the above

CASE 8.1 WHO NEEDS A CHART?

Fred Clegg, general director of the Stone City YMCA, declared, "I will have no organizational charts or job descriptions of any kind in this organization. We are a successful and fast-growing nonprofit service organization, and I want all of our directors and staff members to feel that they are part of the team. Those charts and operational codes have a way of making people feel that they own a position—a box on the chart—and become very possessive about it. We do not need that sort of thing. We grew from a small YMCA with three hundred members and four employees to one that now has thirty-five hundred members, seven departments, and twenty-three employees. We experienced that growth because we all pulled together and came up with outstanding programs, reasonable membership fees, and a good marketing program. We have experienced this growth without complicated charts and codes, and I don't think we need them now."

In discussing Mr. Clegg's opinion of organizational charts and position descriptions at lunch one day, Mitch Rudy, chairman of the YMCA Board of Directors, strongly defended the director, making the point that true teamwork is essential to success. Nicki Swisher, director of the health and physical fitness department, did not hesitate in saying that Mr. Clegg's attitude was from the dark ages and totally unrealistic. "I could not run my department without an organizational chart and operational code," she continued, "and I have them hidden in my desk where Fred Clegg never sees them."

Your Response

1. Do you agree with Clegg or Swisher?
2. If no charts or job descriptions exist at the YMCA, what do you expect might happen with the relationships of employees there?
3. What are the issues and problems here?
4. What actions are needed?
5. What are the action guides that one must consider?
6. Are there any barriers or hurdles that could stand in the way of the best solution?

CASE 8.2 ACCOUNTABILITY

Earle Page, principal at Eastwood High School, received a call from the mother of a member of the freshman class, Jack Braden. She was somewhat upset because Jack had stepped in a hole on the softball field the previous afternoon and sustained a chip fracture of the left ankle. She was concerned about the safety conditions of all the physical education facilities at the school.

After expressing his regrets to Mrs. Braden for Jack's fractured ankle, Earle hung up the phone and began to slowly get angry. Previous injuries had occurred as a result of poorly maintained physical education facilities, and he had specifically assigned Harold Boster, chairman of the physical education department, the responsibility of seeing that the activity facilities were safe and properly maintained. He felt that Harold had let him down, and he asked the secretary to have him come to his office as soon as possible.

Your Response

1. What is the main issue?
2. What are the problems?

3. What barriers or hurdles may stand in the way of the best solution?

4. What actions are needed?

5. List the action guides that led you to take such action.

BIBLIOGRAPHY

Drucker, Peter F. *The Effective Executive*. New York: Harper & Row, 1966.

————. *The Frontiers of Management*. New York: Harper & Row, 1987.

Engal, Herbert M. *How to Delegate: A Guide to Getting Things Done*. Houston: Gulf Publishing, 1983.

Gardner, Neely D., and John N. Davis. *The Art of Delegating*. Garden City, NY: Doubleday, 1965.

Koontz, Harold, and Heinz Weihrich. *Essentials of Management*. 5th ed. New York: McGraw-Hill, 1989.

McConkey, Dale D. *No-Nonsense Delegation*. New York: AMACOM, 1974.

9

Controlling the Activity-Based Program

*People cannot change truth—but truth
can change people.*

author unknown

Chapter Objectives

*After reading this chapter and completing the exercises
you should be able to:*

1 Explain how controlling, supervising, and evaluating relate to each other and to planning

2 List the basic steps of controlling

3 Explain the importance of feedback in the controlling process

4 State several principles of effective control

5 List several indirect techniques of control and state the principle of direct control

6 Delineate several supervisory methods for improving the performance of instructors, coaches, and fitness professionals

7 Explain how the director can alleviate the fear or apprehension that usually accompanies personnel evaluations

8 List the six steps for evaluating—the SCORER procedure

To *control* is to *coach;* to control is to conduct; to control is to empower; to control is to regulate. Control often connotes the unpopular idea of suppressing freedom or individual rights, which may be why some administration texts ignore or only sparingly discuss the topic. Whether we use the word *control* or the seemingly less suppressive *regulate* to describe this aspect of administration, the meaning is the same: to verify or regulate performance and results with established standards and objectives. *The ultimate purpose of controlling is to produce a quality product or service.*

Controlling is a function of every administrator from the bottom to the top of the managerial ladder—from the least powerful project coordinator to the top executive of the enterprise. Although the authority to control varies among supervisors and administrators, managers at every level have the power to ensure that plans are being followed and objectives are being achieved.

It is important to understand how controlling dovetails with planning and organizing as administrative objectives are being pursued. Control is the essential managerial process that ensures that planning and organizing function effectively. When a mistake occurs in either of these processes, effective control will identify the error and correct it.

In this chapter we will look in detail at the controlling process and at the processes of supervising and evaluating, which it encompasses. We hope our discussion will make the controlling process less formidable and mysterious.

Getting in control is a balancing act.

function: (1) establishing measurable standards; (2) measuring performance and accomplishments against the standards; and (3) revising or correcting variations from the standards when they occur. The following discussion of these three basic steps should enhance your understanding of how the controlling process works.

HOW THE CONTROLLING PROCESS WORKS

The controlling process is basically the same for an exercise and fitness center, a high school physical education department, and a local car-wash business. Regardless of the nature of the enterprise, three basic steps make up the controlling

Step 1 Establishing measurable standards. The basis for the initial step of controlling is established in the planning process when objectives are first considered. As a project moves from planning to implementation, the controlling process begins. At this point, goals are formalized and shaped into standards so that everyone involved fully understands the expected outcomes.

For example, assume that you are the director of fitness for a large corporation, and you develop a weight-reducing program of exercise and diet for overweight executives. In the planning stage, you set a goal of having all participants reduce to within 10 percent of their ideal weight within a specified period of time. From that goal, you establish a standard that specifies the degree or level of the requirement or attainment—in this case, say one to two pounds of weight loss per week. That standard is recorded and serves as the expected outcome for each week an executive is in the program. As director, you assign a fitness specialist to coordinate the program, and that coordinator is responsible to you for seeing that the standard is properly pursued.

During this phase of establishing standards, involving everyone engaged in the project and integrating their knowledge and skills becomes very important. The director and coordinators should communicate so that there can be no misunderstanding among them as to what the standards are. By letting people know what is expected and encouraging open communication, the administrator can elicit greater commitment and performance from the project personnel who can make the effort successful.

As plans are being followed and standards are being pursued, someone must trigger the action, give instructions, oversee, and conduct the performance of the program personnel just as a conductor leads an orchestra. A director's effectiveness is determined by how well those who are being led meet the stated standards. Productivity is the objective that is most often used as the standard for effectiveness; therefore, the director must break the leadership responsibility down into more definitive functions in order to reach the production goals. An important func-

tion of leadership is supervising, which is discussed in detail later in the chapter.

Step 2 Measure performance and accomplishments. After project objectives have been refined into measurable standards and after personnel begin working toward the objectives, measurement begins. Performance and accomplishments are compared to the standards through various measuring means, such as observation and inspection. The results of these comparisons are recorded and judgments are made as to how well, or to what degree, performance and accomplishments match the standards. When the real and the ideal are not the same, the discrepancies are noted and the final phase of the three-step cycle is implemented.

Step 3 Revise and correct. Where discrepancies occur between standards and performance, changes must be made so that the project goals can be achieved in the most effective and efficient manner. Discrepancies may result from inadequate human performance, unsafe facilities, faulty or inappropriate equipment, and mistakes or miscalculations in programming. Once the source of discrepancies has been identified, revising and correcting can proceed and the standards can be upheld.

FEEDBACK AND THE CONTROLLING PROCESS

Feedback is essential to achieving effective administrative control. Whether the goal is to improve a batter's swing, increase a cardiac patient's aerobic capacity, or improve the curricular offerings in a physical education program, a system for feedback is critical. Let's look at a few examples of how feedback works.

An effective feedback system can prevent injuries.

a behavioral change and, ideally, an attitudinal change in the players. He called for a meeting with the coach and insisted that the coach teach sportsmanship and begin by improving his conduct on the field. After receiving this feedback, the coach began to change his behavior.

In another situation, a staff physician at a college infirmary called the head of the physical education department to inform her that more than ten intramural sports participants had come in with sprained knees and ankles and various lacerations during the past six weeks. An investigation revealed that the most commonly used activity field was unsafe. Some areas had become mini-swamps as a result of normal watering procedures, sprinkler heads protruded above the ground as they did not recede after the automatic switch shut them off, and ruts existed where the tractor and mower had passed through the muddy areas. As a result of that feedback, the department head contacted the supervisor of buildings and grounds, who corrected the safety hazards.

Insight through Illustration

The athletics director at State University wished to promote sportsmanship for all the school's athletes. As it stood, he was not satisfied with the attitudes expressed by members of the baseball team. He attended games and took note of the coach's and players' actions. He observed that the players in the dugout were unmerciful in their "bench-jockeying" tactics with the opponent's third baseman. When the insults stopped, the coach moved through the dugout encouraging the players to "pick up the jockeying." Coach and players alike always seemed to be looking for an argument with the umpire. Since neither coach nor players were good sports on the field, the athletics director reasoned that the coach was actually teaching the players to be rude and offensive. As a result of his game observation, the athletics director realized that to meet the established standard for player conduct, he had to bring about

Feedback can come from direct observation or from other sources, and it must be put to use quickly. The key to the proper use of feedback is to eliminate the lag between the time the information is available and the time it is put back into the system. Even the briefest delay can waste resources, or as we saw in the previous example, cause injury. In that example, an effective feedback system could have prevented the multiple injuries that the physician noted.

Instructors and coaches should be encouraged to watch for safety hazards and immediately report any to a designated individual who can expedite changes. A backup tactic, in case an instructor fails to carry out this daily responsibility, is to develop a safety checklist and appoint one or more staff members to walk through every facility, observe, and report any unsafe conditions. If the checklist is not turned in by an appointed time, the director then has an obligation to find out why. Once alerted to unsafe conditions, the director must inform the physical plant director or the grounds supervisor of them and secure his or her assurance that the problems will be corrected without delay.

PRINCIPLES OF EFFECTIVE CONTROL

To assure themselves that events, conditions, and performances conform to established plans, administrators must devise effective systems of control. Although it is important to tailor controls to specific situations, certain fundamental principles are universally applicable.

Tailor Controls to Specific Circumstances

Every planned effort has certain unique aspects, and it is important for control methods to relate specifically to the plans they are designed to monitor. The system for following the progress of a health promotion plan in a community will differ significantly from that needed to check the progress of a plan to improve crowd control at athletic events.

Controls should also be fashioned for specific personnel. Control techniques used by the director of athletics in a large university will be somewhat different from those used by the assistant basketball coach. The specific control methods that have been successful for the YMCA director may not be appropriate for the director of a corporation's fitness program.

The manner in which controls are applied must also vary according to the personalities involved. A few years ago a young man began his career as a college coach shortly after graduating with a master's degree. His college coach had been one

of the most successful college coaches in the history of the game. The young man tailored every technique of team and player control to match those used by his former coach. They did not work for him because his personality was very different from the personality of his coach. Each administrator must use a system of control that feels natural.

Use Both Subjective and Objective Means of Evaluation

Subjectivity can never be eliminated from the control system, and whenever possible, management should complement subjective methods of evaluation with objective techniques that maintain sensitivity to human needs. Objectivity, although more easily justified than subjectivity, has a tendency to be insensitive to human needs and is inappropriate for some exceptional and unusual circumstances. For example, a coach may not lead a team to many wins during a season, but this objective measure of his performance cannot take into account the fact that his performance was temporarily affected by the death of his son in an auto accident.

On the other hand, sometimes the difference between effective and ineffective administrators is the former's refusal to allow personality differences and bias to stand in the way of fair practice and justice. Regardless of whether subjective or objective judgments are expressed, it is critical for the information upon which the judgments are based to be accurate.

Be Flexible

Flexibility must be built into the controlling process as it is in the planning process. Failure to allow for flexibility can create frustration and mediocrity. For example, when 850 participants show up for a workshop designed for 550, the director must be flexible enough to revise and correct by scheduling additional classes, hiring the needed instructors, and increasing the budget as necessary. The additional income from the increased enrollment will more than pay for the additional expense.

Be Economical

Determining benefits in relationship to costs is sometimes difficult, but the costs of controlling a program should be in line with what is affordable. For example, it may not be economically feasible for an activity program to establish an elaborate control system involving printed evaluation forms to be filled out by participants and tallied and interpreted by someone whose time might be better spent on another task.

Aim to Improve Performance

The only way that a control system can be justified is by identifying deviations from the ideal and then making the necessary changes to improve performance. Only through adjustments and revisions to planning, organizing, and staffing can improvements become real.

DIRECT AND INDIRECT CONTROLS

Controlling consists of various decisions and activities that extend from the planning stage to the final product or service, and the process is totally dependent upon the performances and achievement of individuals. People produce results, and control involves changing the behavior of these people when the real results vary from the ideal.

Control must affect whoever has been making ineffective decisions. For example, a preparation program for physical education majors cannot be controlled by criticizing the poorly prepared graduates; a corporate fitness program cannot be controlled by lowering the fee for inferior programming; and a volleyball team cannot be controlled by ridiculing the players in the news releases. If results are unsatisfactory, the decision maker responsible for the inferior outcomes must be addressed in the hopes that future decisions will produce better results. More effective decisions may require retraining or replacing the responsible personnel or modifying the existing policies and strategies.

Two means of encouraging behavioral change exist: direct and indirect control procedures. *Direct control* attempts to eliminate errors of judgment made by incompetent leaders through developing or hiring new leaders who will skillfully apply proven concepts, principles, and techniques from the outset. *Indirect control* relies on tracing the cause of unacceptable results back to the managers or supervisors who caused them and getting them to correct their practices through retraining and various other methods.

Direct control is based on the premise that administrators who are well-prepared in administrative philosophy will make better decisions for ensuring positive results. Formal education through university courses, extensive on-the-job experience, and disciplined self-study are the most common means for learning to make effective decisions. The principle of direct control is as follows: *The higher the quality of managers and their subordinates, the less will be the need for applying indirect controls.*

Indirect control depends upon feedback gained through monitoring the performances and accomplishments that occur from the time plans are put into action until outcomes are achieved. The methods most commonly used for indirect control are budget empowerment, internal audits, statistical data analysis, and the various supervisory techniques.

Supervision is part of the controlling process.

SUPERVISING ACTIVITY-BASED PROGRAMS

Supervision is an administrative skill concerned with overseeing, guiding, and directing others as they pursue the unit or enterprise goals. It often does not get the attention that other administrative skills get, but its importance should not be underrated. It is through this function that the administrator or supervisor deals with subordinates on an everyday basis. Supervising comes fully into play when individuals and groups are cooperating and participating in decision making.

The Nature of Supervision

Supervision has many facets. It represents a measure of control and responsibility on the part of the supervisor for ongoing actions. Supervising activity-based programs should be viewed as a function primarily concerned with assisting teachers, coaches, and fitness-related professionals.

One goal of supervision is to provide for continuous improvement of the educational or productive process. The director constantly looks for ways to eliminate hindrances to effective performance and tries to bring out the creative ability of the professional in finding needed solutions to problems. Supervision is also concerned with organizing opportunities for the professional to gain proficiency in the skills basic to his or her position of responsibility.

Appropriate supervision is a delicate balancing act. The amount of supervision needed depends upon the situation, and successful supervisors know when to intervene and when to leave an employee alone. Teachers, coaches, and fitness professionals who are highly responsible, dependable, and skilled need only a minimal amount of supervision, and the supervisor needs only to provide general direction and support. In this situation oversupervision can lead to employee resentment and disenchantment because of the lack of freedom.

Some faculty or staff, however, may require close and constant supervision. People falling into this category are those who were recently hired and are perhaps young, those who are looking to take advantage of the employer, or those who may be incompetent. Close supervision is expected to bring about a positive change in the employee's performance, and if that does not occur, the alternative may be to fire the incompetent employee and hire someone who will be responsible and independent.

Supervision should be a pleasant and relatively easy relationship for all individuals involved. An overbearing boss or an incompetent staff person can upset an otherwise harmonious workplace. Replacement of the problem person—the employee or the boss—may be the only alternative.

The Link to Administration

Supervision is a link between action and administration, ideally providing communication for a functional and efficient program. Fundamentally, it differs from administration, but sometimes distinguishing between the two is difficult.

The administrator makes decisions, procures needed facilities, equipment, and supplies, and makes certain that materials and resources are available in suitable quantities. The supervisor functions best when he or she makes recommendations that may influence administrative decisions; recommends the best kinds of facilities, equipment, and supplies for the program; and assists in selecting and developing the types of materials and resources that will benefit the operation. The administrator assigns duties and responsibilities to teachers and/or staff members and is concerned with the general matter of efficient enterprise operations. The supervisor acts to improve the ability of teachers and staff members to complete their assigned duties and responsibilities and is concerned with developing curriculum and improving instruction, or in a

nonschool setting, improving the performance of coaches or fitness specialists.

The administrator and supervisor should work in complete cooperation with one another. When this does not happen it adversely affects the progress and accomplishments of the department members.

Supervision as a separate process is a delegated responsibility that requires administrative authority. Most of the time, however, in the physical education, fitness, or sports environment, the supervisor and the administrator are the same person. When this occurs, supervisory duties tend to dominate the administrator's time.

Duties of a Supervisor

Supervisors are generally responsible for the following duties:

- *Supervision.* They seek to improve the performance of employees through conferences and consultations.
- *Administration.* They organize and coordinate the work of others, make decisions, and direct.
- *Planning.* Supervisors participate in developing policies in their field and organizational unit.
- *Program development.* They participate directly in formulating objectives, selecting experiences, preparing instructional materials, and selecting equipment and supplies.
- *Demonstrations and lectures.* They give and arrange for demonstrations in techniques and methodology, they lecture, and they lead group meetings.
- *Research.* Through systematic surveys, experiments, and studies, supervisors explore current conditions and recommend changes in practices.
- *Evaluation.* They are significantly involved, along with the manager, in assessing perfor-

mance of personnel and conditions of facilities and equipment.

Techniques Used by Supervisors

Supervisors use a number of different methods and techniques in their efforts to improve the performance of faculty and/or staff. The following techniques appear to be the most commonly used:

- *Visitation.* The supervisor should periodically visit the places where services are being rendered or products are being produced. The visits may be scheduled prior to their occurrence, or they may be the drop-in type, without notice. The drop-in visit is viewed with disdain by some, but it can be a worthy method of gathering useful data.
- *Personal observations.* Observations are less formal than on-site visits. The supervisor just needs to be aware of what is going on around him or her as he or she moves about the department.
- *One-on-one conferences.* The supervisor can really get to know employees in these individual and personal encounters. Employees appreciate and respond more positively to personal instructions, evaluations, and reprimands in one-on-one meetings.
- *Group conferences.* These conferences are valuable for doing general business and passing information.
- *Workshops, retreats, and working conferences.* There is no better way to solve critical problems or develop programs than to leave the distractions of the workplace and go to some isolated setting for concentrated work efforts.
- *Assessments and reports.* The supervisor gathers assessments and reports from other people who are affected by the performance of em-

HOLD IT! I GOTTA RUN OUT AND HAVE A CHAT WITH MY CENTERFIELDER!

Employees respond more positively to reprimands in one-on-one meetings.

ployees in order to make fair and objective judgments.
- *Reviews of performance plans.* The supervisor reviews performance plans such as course syllabi in the educational setting or personal performance objectives in athletics and fitness settings.

EVALUATING ACTIVITY-BASED PROGRAMS

In its most general sense, evaluation involves determining the worth or value of something compared to some known quality, standard, or criterion. An inescapable part of life, evaluation occurs constantly. When a baby is born, a program is initiated, or a facility is built, the process begins. Where you live, what you do, and everything you own are constantly being evaluated for worthiness.

No other process or function of management is more critical to progress than evaluation. In fact, without it, there would be no progress. When comparisons are made between what actually is (the real) and what is hoped for (the ideal), deviations can be noted and judgments can be made. Progress will result as corrections are instituted.

What does the director of an activity-based program evaluate? Personnel, program, and facilities (including equipment) constitute the scope of administration, and each area must be carefully appraised.

There is no one best evaluation instrument recommended for evaluating either personnel, program, or facilities. Each organization is unique as to what is desired and expected, and most have developed their own instruments to be used in the evaluation process. If it becomes necessary for one to develop an instrument, the guides identified in the discussion that follows should be of significant value.

Evaluating Personnel

Understandably, personnel evaluation activates fear in most people. A quick look at some of the instruments used in gathering information and the forms used in reporting evaluation results can easily show why. Most seem to draw attention to the negative rather than the positive aspects of performance. Then, too, a person's reappointment, tenure, or promotion depends on the results of evaluation. That is usually enough to strike fear into an evaluee's heart. Then too, pride is at stake, and negative criticism can threaten it.

Personnel evaluation should, and can, be a positive and rewarding element of the work experience. Because people's careers and futures depend so heavily on the judgments of the evaluator, feelings of apprehension will never be totally eliminated from the process; however, an emphasis by management on the positive instead of the negative consequences can significantly affect employees' attitudes. This emphasis will not occur without an extended effort on the part of the administrator to emphasize the contributions of employees instead of their faults. Improved effec-

tiveness in performance should be the aim of personnel evaluations, and that theme of effectiveness is just as important for administrators or evaluators as it is for employees. The responsibility for promoting positive and effective evaluation experiences rests with the director.

Evaluation is most often based on observation and the reports of the staff person's peers and clientele (students in the educational setting) as gathered by the director. An employee's own involvement in establishing the criteria for the evaluation, along with self-analysis, can be an important part of the overall evaluation and can help establish a healthy relationship between the evaluator and the one being evaluated.

To alleviate much of the fear that always seems to accompany evaluation periods, a director might follow these steps:

1. At the beginning of each year, send a memo to each department member—instructor, coach, and support staff person—requesting that they submit a list of goals they hope to achieve during the upcoming year.

2. Schedule an individual half-hour conference with each person to review and discuss the goals submitted. In most cases, the director will need to encourage staff members to rewrite the list so that it is more challenging and more measurable. Typical of an unacceptable goal is "Be a better teacher than I was last year." Such a statement is not quantifiable and, therefore, is unacceptable. A more appropriate statement would be "Participate in a teacher effectiveness program of instruction on campus during the year." At the end of the evaluation cycle, this will be measurable.

3. By the end of the individual conference, agree upon a reasonable number of personal and professional goals to be attained during the year. The director may have to convince the staff member that the list submitted is too ambitious for a single year.

4. File a copy of the goals in the staff member's personnel file, and instruct him or her to place a copy in an observable place as a constant reminder of the challenge.

5. Schedule another half-hour conference toward the end of the year, and review the goals list to determine how well the employee is doing. The director should be sure to find some accomplishment for which to praise the employee. If the employee is only partially successful, the reasons why should be discussed, and suggestions offered for improvement.

The real advantage of this approach is the opportunity it offers for a two-way exchange of ideas and discussion of existing problems. It also gives the employee a chance at self-analysis.

Evaluation by those being served should also be part of the appraisal process. An appraisal is incomplete without offering the student or consumer an opportunity for input. The validity of these assessments is often questionable, however, and there are some legitimate reasons why they should be carefully applied. The most important factor that can affect the reliability of consumer or student evaluations is the emotional environment at the time the assessments are conducted. For example, a class that has just seen a movie is likely to appraise the instructor differently from a class that has just taken its final exam. Disgruntled students may take the opportunity to retaliate for a difficult test.

We recently asked a group of graduate and undergraduate students how valid they believed student evaluations were, and their responses indicated a low to moderate validity rating. The basic reason for this low rating was that they did not believe that the appraisals were taken seriously, because nothing ever changed as a result of them. The effective instructors continued to be effective, but the less effective instructors seldom did anything to improve. Unfortunately, their criticism is partially true.

Appraisals by the clientele of public and private fitness centers are probably no more valid than student evaluations. Personality and employee popularity affect the opinions of the clientele to such a degree that their judgments are colored, even if they do understand the difference between effective and ineffective performance. Nonprofessionals cannot be expected to really know how well job responsibilities are being met.

Peer evaluation is a procedure that is becoming more common, especially in educational institutions. Peer assessments can be more valid than student appraisals simply because associates have a better understanding of what constitutes an effective performance. However, many peer groups put very little effort into the process, and the validity of their reports is then questionable. If associates must take on the extra responsibility of conducting assessments without having an already heavy work load reduced, some may rebel.

Evaluating the Program

Program evaluation is essential to determine the degree to which the objectives of the organizational unit are being achieved. A cooperative effort by administrators, faculty, staff, and those being served can accurately determine the effectiveness of a physical education, fitness, or sports program.

The best means of determining just how good a program is may be to test it against some known value or standard or against similar programs of other institutions or enterprises. In athletics, making this judgment is not difficult. Wins and losses are not the only criteria for success, but provide the one measure that is most readily observable and most often pursued.

The product of a physical education program (the student) is most often compared to the pre-program student or to other students at local or national levels. Students may be tested before and after program participation to determine the amount of change that occurs as a result of the

Equipment as well as personnel and program must be evaluated periodically.

physical education experience. These measurements assist in assessing the achievement of the student in relation to the established goals or standards of the program. The only place where these results really make a difference is outside the educational institution; therefore, it is important for the students and the program staff to compare their scores to those of students from other schools. Similar procedures and comparisons may be conducted to evaluate professional preparation programs and fitness programs at various public and private enterprises.

Evaluating Facilities and Equipment

Because of the obligation to provide a wholesome and safe environment for conducting challenging and enjoyable activities, ongoing assessment of facilities and equipment needs to be a high priority for the director of an activity-based program. Few things can be more demoralizing to partici-

pants and instructors than going to an assigned space and finding it unclean and, in many cases, unsafe. Even when facilities and equipment are less than ideal, the situation can be made acceptable if the instructor has a positive attitude and proper attention is paid to cleanliness, tidiness, and state of repair.

Steps in Evaluating

Being familiar with and following a step-by-step procedure can make the difference between an effective evaluation process and an ineffective one. It seems that physical education, fitness, and sports directors have more demands on their time than most administrators. This is especially true on the educational scene and is most likely due to the amount of attention required for providing, maintaining, and scheduling heavily used facilities. Most academic department administrators are free of those time-consuming demands.

It can be tempting to cut corners in a process such as evaluation, which is legitimately a time-consuming effort.

The following step-by-step procedure is meaningful and complete for any type of appraisal. It can be easily remembered by the first letter of each step as SCORER.

1. Specify the intent of the appraisal to be made.
2. Communicate the purpose to those concerned.
3. Obtain the evaluative information.
4. Record and organize the information.
5. Examine the information and make judgments.
6. Report the evaluation results.

We will discuss each step in detail.

Specify the Intent   It is the director's responsibility to establish the intent and purpose of any type of evaluation under consideration. When the object of appraisal is the program or facilities, the expected objectives and standards must be clearly understood and stated. If the object of the evaluation is a person, then the administrator, the person being evaluated, and anyone else involved must be aware of the job description and understand the responsibilities attached to the position.

Different evaluations of the same facility or employee may vary in focus. For example, the cleanliness and safety features of a wrestling and mat room may be appraised rather than the space available there. By knowing this, the evaluator can adjust procedures accordingly. A director may wish to evaluate an exercise physiologist's ability to relate to people rather than overall performance. Whatever the case may be, the intent and purpose must be specified and understood by both evaluator and evaluee.

Communicate to Those Concerned   Directors often assume that everyone understands the par-

ticulars in a given situation. Experience has shown that it is best to assume nothing. Every detail, expectation, and direction needs to be clarified on paper and sometimes through discussion as well. When the evaluator(s) and the person being evaluated for promotion, for example, have a mutual understanding of the intent of the appraisal and how judgments will be made, the interpretation and the results of the appraisal may be less stressful and more positive and meaningful. Effective communication is the responsibility of the manager or director.

Obtain the Information   In this third step, it is important for the evaluator to describe the information needed, locate the information already available, decide when and how to obtain additional information, and then select and/or prepare the instruments for collecting the needed information. Following standard procedures at this data-gathering step is important to ensure that the information gathered is not biased. For example, when an instructor is being evaluated by students, it is important for her or him to leave the room or area where the questionnaires are being completed so that the students will feel free to express their feelings and beliefs.

Record and Organize the Information   After being gathered, observations and other types of information relating to the performance of a person or status of a program or facility must be compiled, recorded, organized, and categorized.

Examine the Information and Make Judgments   After the information has been analyzed, it must be examined in light of the established objectives, standards, or responsibilities. This is the time when the wisdom of the administrator is needed most. A wise judge will be able to weigh the significance of the information and evidence and ensure that a fair and unbiased determination of worth is achieved.

Report the Results   The last step in the procedure is to report the results of the appraisal. The key person to whom the results are reported is the one who can effect change if change is indicated. In most cases, a number of people need to be made aware of the evaluation results. If an evaluation of a facility indicates that some change in cleanliness or safety needs to be made, the key person may be the director of plant operations.

Evaluation results that indicate curriculum deficiencies should be reported to the principal, dean, or whoever holds the power to implement change. The most essential person to notify when a personnel evaluation is completed is the person who has been evaluated, if the primary objective of the evaluation is to promote growth and development.

KEY WORDS AND PHRASES

Controlling	Supervision	Indirect control
Measurable standards	Student evaluation	One-on-one conference
Feedback	Peer evaluation	Group conference
Subjective evaluation	Direct control	Evaluation
Objective evaluation	Effective control	SCORER procedure

QUESTIONS FOR REVIEW

1. Explain the relationships among controlling, supervising, and evaluating.
2. List and discuss the three basic steps in the controlling process.
3. Explain why feedback is so vital to achieving enterprise objectives.
4. Compare the direct control principle to the indirect control devices and explain their values.
5. Why are the authors supportive of subjective evaluation methods?
6. Which one or two of the supervisory techniques presented do you believe to be most beneficial for improving performance, and why?
7. How is the SCORER procedure related to evaluation?
8. Why are staff personnel so apprehensive about formal evaluations?

SELF-TEST

Corrected True-False

If the statement is true, mark it T. If the statement is false, mark it F and change it to a true statement by adding or deleting words.

_____ 1. The process relating to the measurement and correction of performance to ensure that the objectives of the enterprise are being achieved is called evaluation.

_____ 2. Before the control function can be put into operation planning must occur.

_____ 3. One principle of effective control is to design the controls for specific circumstances. Another is to be fully objective.

_____ 4. Budget empowerment is a significant indirect control.

_____ 5. The quality of managers has a bearing on the extent that indirect controls are applied.

_____ 6. Supervision refers to the act of overseeing.

_____ 7. In a quality management situation, to control is to both regulate and empower.

_____ 8. Generally, supervisors of activity-based programs have no responsibility for research.

_____ 9. Individual (one-on-one) conferences are more productive than group conferences.

_____ 10. A slight fear and apprehension associated with a personnel evaluation is a desired reaction.

Multiple Choice

_____ 11. The process of assessing status or determining worth is known as:
   a. measuring
   b. supervising
   c. evaluating
   d. controlling

_____ 12. The act of overseeing or inspecting the performance of a person or operation is termed:
   a. supervising
   b. evaluating
   c. directing
   d. dictating

_____ 13. A method of supervising that is *not* recommended is:
   a. unannounced observations
   b. public criticism
   c. demonstrations
   d. inspections

_____ 14. According to the authors, the first step in evaluation is to:
   a. specify the intent
   b. describe the info needed
   c. communicate
   d. set the goals

_____ 15. The last step in evaluating is to:
   a. make judgments
   b. meet with evaluee
   c. report results
   d. none of the above

CASE 9.1 ATHLETICS DIRECTOR OUT OF CONTROL

When Jeff Pace, assistant athletics director, and Mike Bailey, athletics business manager, walked into the office of Clara Henderson, athletics director of Metro University of the West, they were greeted with an unwelcome verbal explosion.

"Why can't you people keep me informed? I never know whether things in this department are going well or not. Problems seem to grow into insurmountable obstacles before I hear about them. You two go to work immediately on a plan whereby I am kept up to date on what goes on in this department. You are to report back to me with the plan one week from today. It is ridiculous for the most responsible person in the athletics department to be kept in the dark about things that are going on."

After Jeff and Mike left Clara's office, Jeff turned to the business manager and retorted, "If she would only read the reports stacked on top of her file cabinet and get out from behind that desk, she would know what is going on!"

Your Response

1. What is the primary issue?
2. What are the problems?
3. What barriers or hurdles may prevent the best solution?
4. What actions need to be taken?
5. What action guides support your suggested actions?

CASE 9.2 "I DIDN'T KNOW WHAT WAS EXPECTED!"

George Musselman, director of recreation and fitness of the Aero-Plus Corporation, was reflecting on the unpleasant tasks related to his position, when Judy Redd appeared at the door of his office for her appointment. Ten months ago, soon after receiving her degree in fitness management, Judy had been hired as the assistant coordinator of the fitness testing and exercise prescription laboratory. She was keeping her appointment for her job review.

George was not very comfortable as the meeting began, and he decided to get right to the point. He opened with a statement that visibly surprised and shook Judy. "Judy, I am sorry to have to inform you that we have decided not to renew your appointment for next year."

Before George could continue, Judy responded, "But why? I thought I was doing fine. I've worked hard and have been prompt in fulfilling my responsibilities. Mr. Hyde seldom talked to me, but he wasn't really critical of what I was doing. I felt somewhat intimidated by his possessive attitude toward the lab and the equipment, but I thought I was doing what I was supposed to do." (Clive Hyde was the coordinator of the lab.)

When Judy regained her composure, Mr. Musselman explained that Clive had reported that she did only as much as seemed necessary. She did not do anything extra or innovative in the lab and never secured and cleaned the equipment properly. Mr. Musselman told her that Clive had assumed that she really was not very interested in, and dedicated to, her position.

Before asking to be excused because of her emotional state, Judy stated, "Mr. Musselman, I really have never known just what was expected of me."

Your Response

1. What are the major issues and problems in this case?

2. Who made the biggest mistake from the beginning?

3. What should have been done to prevent such a circumstance?

4. What would you do at this point if you were George Musselman?

5. What action guides motivated your responses to questions 3 and 4?

6. What barriers or hurdles may stand in the way of the best solution?

BIBLIOGRAPHY

Drucker, Peter F. *The Effective Executive.* New York: Harper & Row, 1966.

Frost, Reuben B., and Stanley J. Marshall. *Administration of Physical Education and Athletics: Concepts and Practices.* 3rd ed. Dubuque, IA: William C. Brown, 1988.

Johnson, M. L. *Functional Administration in Physical and Health Education.* Boston: Houghton-Mifflin, 1977.

Koontz, Harold, and Heinz Weihrich. *Essentials of Management.* 5th ed. New York: McGraw-Hill, 1989.

Resick, Matthew, Beverly Seidel, and James G. Mason. *Modern Administrative Practices in Physical Education Athletics.* 3rd ed. New York: Random House, 1979.

Tenbrink, Terry D. *Evaluation: A Practical Guide for Teachers.* New York: McGraw-Hill, 1974.

10

Staffing and Leading Personnel in Activity-Based Programs

*The best way to change an enemy is
to change him into a friend.*

author unknown

Chapter Objectives

*After reading this chapter and completing the exercises,
you should be able to understand:*

1 The importance of hiring the right person for a job

2 How to write a good job description

3 The proper procedures in recruiting and selecting a
new employee

4 The importance of good orientation for new department
members

5 The importance of employee retention

6 The various means by which department members
can be encouraged to grow professionally

7 The key theories of motivation

8 How the director can motivate subordinates

9 The mistakes directors should avoid making in managing personnel

The success or failure of physical education, sports, and fitness directors may well be determined by the quality of their decisions in hiring and retaining staff. The performance of every employee, whether the equipment manager, custodian, coach, instructor, or coordinator, reflects positively or negatively upon the effectiveness of the director. That is a major reason why the chief, though not sole, responsibility for appointing department personnel should be with the department administrator. Details of the selection and hiring process vary with the structure and practices of an enterprise or institution, but a common need exists everywhere for sound administrative judgment in making personnel decisions.

Based upon an acquaintance with the profession and with the goals of the organization, staff, and clientele being served, the director has the major responsibility for judging the kinds of instructional or specialized staff needed. In this profession, the task goes well beyond just filling vacant slots with good people, though this practice still characterizes too many professional appointments. As Drucker (1966) has emphasized, an administrator should not set out to hire a "good" person. He or she should attempt to hire a person who can specifically meet the demands of the position. Without considering what a "good" person is good for, the hiring decision could very well be disastrous. Wiser decisions are made when a continuing and meticulous assessment of department needs, not only for the next year but for future years as well, serves as the basis for personnel decisions.

The scope of the administrator's responsibilities has been identified as encompassing three areas of concern: personnel, program, and facilities. Of the three, personnel management is the most challenging and intriguing, affords the most satisfying rewards, and presents the most time-consuming and serious problems. If directors of activity-based programs perform well in managing personnel, the time they need to spend with the other two concerns is minimized.

Clearly identify tasks before hiring.

RECRUITING AND SELECTING A QUALITY STAFF

Hiring people is very much like betting on horses at the Kentucky Derby. Before going to the window and placing the bet, the gambler reads the racing form, talks to the jockies, trainers, and anyone else who may know something about horses, and then carefully looks the horses over as they are led away from the paddock just before the race. Then he or she puts his or her money down and takes a chance. Selecting personnel may not be as much of a gamble, but there is often no way to be sure of the best candidate when hiring.

Locating and hiring an effective staff begins with good planning and organizing. Some very sincere attempts to find the best people to fill job vacancies often end in frustration because of a breakdown in properly relating the job descriptions to the purpose of the organization or unit.

Placement centers are an excellent source for filling entry-level positions.

Effective personnel management must be based on aims and objectives. Goals must be identified and tasks and activities grouped into positions before the right people can be placed in the right jobs.

In Chapter 7 we said that goals and objectives are the driving force behind every activity of a successful organization, and in Chapter 7 we explained that tasks and activities must be defined and then grouped into positions. In the next phase, funds are provided for filling the positions, and then the administrator is ready to initiate the process of selecting quality personnel.

Conducting an inventory of the interests, skills, and abilities of current staff may show that specific job needs and expectations can be met without an outside recruiting effort. In that case, reassignment and adjustment of present human resources may be the best alternative for meeting the position goals. If, however, adequately staffing the

needs from within is not feasible, a recruiting effort needs to be initiated.

The Job Description

Formulating an accurate job description is essential to finding the right person for a job. A surprising number of positions are advertised without the responsible administrator fully understanding and/or communicating the role expectations of the position.

Insight through Illustration

A recent recruiting effort by a university physical education department is a classic example of how an inadequate job description can result in wasted resources and frustration for department personnel as well as prospective employees.

Two years before funds were available for hiring someone, the department determined that another faculty member was needed in the area of exercise physiology and professional preparation of students in the corporate fitness option. When the position was formulated, before writing the job description, the exercise physiologist and coordinator of the human performance lab, with whom the new faculty member would be most closely relating, was on sabbatical leave. The department administrator mistakenly thought that the program coordinator, the search committee, and he were communicating well while the job description was being drafted. Everyone realized that the role would encompass not only teaching assignments in the fitness option but also in the activity and health service programs. But it was not discovered until the final stages of the recruiting process that prospects had been misinformed about the amount of time required for teaching in the service programs.

Once the misunderstanding was discovered, the director had to choose between two alternatives: hire from the three finalists interviewed or cancel the recruiting process and readvertise the position the following year after a valid job description had been formulated. He chose the latter alternative for two reasons: He did not believe the three finalists were the best qualified for the diversified assignment, nor did he believe the preferred candidate, who was highly specialized in exercise physiology, would be satisfied with a heavy assignment in the service areas.

The mistake was embarrassing and expensive, but the process when properly planned and implemented the following year resulted in the hiring of a highly qualified instructor with whom all department members seemed to be pleased.

This example illustrates the importance of defining, describing, and communicating the precise details of job expectations for recently created positions or those that become vacant as a result of staff turnover. The manner in which the job description is formulated varies from enterprise to enterprise. For a school, the department may have the most influence in the hiring process, or the personnel division may conduct the entire proceeding. In a YMCA, corporate fitness setting, or a small fitness business, the responsibility for defining a position may rest entirely with the manager, director, or owner. Whether the job description is formulated by an individual or a committee, the final responsibility rests with the administrator who has been delegated the primary role in hiring.

Job Formulation and Job Analysis   Job descriptions are normally prepared after new positions have been formulated or after job analyses have been conducted. Job formulation consists of identifying and grouping activities, tasks, and responsibilities into a titled position. A new position is normally created as the result of program expansion or user demands and after funding resources have been identified.

The job analysis is conducted after a position has existed for a period of time. It is a systematic investigation designed to consider every detail of an existing position to determine its validity and relevance to the objectives of the organizational unit. After the investigation is conducted, the individual or committee performing the analysis should know what tasks and activities are being done, how well they are being done, and whether or not the efforts are making a worthy contribution to organizational goals. The analysis may confirm the relevancy of the position as it is, or it may point to a need for redesigning the job. If the activities of the position are still appropriate, the job description is not revised, but if the analysis indicates that the current job content is inappropriate, the needed changes should be identified and a new description prepared. The job description resulting from a job analysis is likely to be more accurate than one being written for the first time because of the feedback available about a position that has existed for some time.

Positions in physical education, fitness, and sports should be analyzed informally and continuously by the director. A formal analysis is appropriate every year for new and less stable positions, and every three to five years for stable positions.

Who Prepares the Job Description?   Job descriptions for personnel in activity-based programs are normally prepared within the department or designated organizational unit. How the actual preparation occurs varies from place to place and usually depends upon the size of the operation. When the unit is small (fewer than ten employees), the unit director or responsible manager normally performs the total function; if the unit is midsize (ten to twenty employees), the director may have one or more members of the unit do the preliminary preparation; and if the unit is larger than twenty employees, a departmental committee of three to five members is usually elected or appointed to perform the task.

Regardless of who does the initial preparation, two specific action guides must prevail: (1) the preparer must have a thorough understanding of the organizational goals that the position is designed to fully or partially achieve, and (2) the director or responsible administrator is fully responsible for the job description and should be directly involved before it is finally approved. Figure 10.1 depicts the relationship among goals, job content, job formulation, job analysis, and job description.

Essential Contents of the Job Description   Preparing a job description is not a difficult task when the preparer knows the kinds of information it should contain and also knows how to logically relate activities to goals for both the short-range and long-range needs of the organization. Job descriptions are often of inferior quality or even nonexistent because many administrators are not aware of the essential contents of an effective description. Typically, job descriptions are written statements composed of two parts: job specifications and required job qualifications.

Job specifications are statements of expectations and information as to how the job is to be performed. They include job title, a list of overall responsibilities, specific duties and assignments, and a description of general and specific working conditions including relationships with key individuals such as the employee's supervisor and those whom the employee supervises. The job title should be accurate. For example, the title of a position that consists primarily of cleaning a facility is custodian, not maintenance engineer. A person who performs routine or perfunctory administrative tasks without line authority is an administrative assistant, not an associate director.

Overall responsibilities are listed to provide a general concept of the position's makeup. Specific job duties and assignments are described in detail to avoid misunderstanding between the employee and those to whom he or she relates—especially the supervisor. Any unusual working conditions

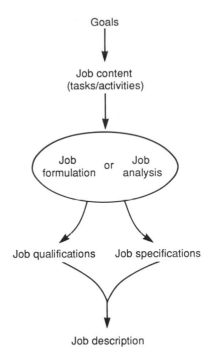

Figure 10.1 *Relationships Among the Ingredients in Formulating a Job Description*

associated with the position absolutely must be described. For cxample, if a coach is likely to be fired for failing to win the conference championship within the first three years after hiring, that expectation and probability should be specified.

The Job Announcement   After the decision is made to hire a new employee, a job announcement is prepared. The job announcement may be considered a condensed job description since very similar kinds of information are communicated. The purpose of the job announcement is to make the availability of a position known to a large number of potential candidates and provide information so that those who may be interested can decide whether or not they wish to apply. The following information should be listed:

- *Position title.* It is important for the title to be as accurate as possible.

- *Job specifications.* Major responsibilities and assignments should be listed. The job title alone is not enough to convey this information. Regardless of how much attention has been given to its accuracy, a job title does not always mean the same thing in different situations and to different people.

- *Minimum qualifications.* Minimum number of years of job-related experience, skills, abilities, and knowledge required to qualify should always be listed.

- *Education and special certification required.* Specific degrees and/or certificates are usually required for activity-based positions. Unless these requirements are met, potential candidates should be discouraged from applying.

- *Closing date for applying.* This date should be listed so that deadlines for appointments can be met. Whether the date represents the deadline for making the initial contact or whether it is the date when all materials must be to the employer should be specified. Legal problems may arise if the deadline date is not held to firmly. Sometimes it is practical for the closing date to be listed as "until position is filled."

- *Starting date of employment.* It is important to identify this date. Contractual obligations may be a barrier for some people, and they need to know if they cannot meet the conditions of employment before they go to the trouble of applying.

- *Salary and benefits.* The salary range should be listed and a general statement about benefits made. Candidates always are interested in this information. Many employers state the salary as "commensurate with qualifications and experience." That statement only takes up space and tells the candidate nothing. If the salary range is known, and it usually is, it should be listed so that potential candidates will know whether or not salary is a barrier to their interest.

- *How to apply.* Employers in the physical education, fitness, and sports profession prefer to receive letters of application only from interested candidates. The announcement should identify the information desired in the letter of application and to whom correspondence should be directed.

- *Description of the community and organization.* A brief description of the employing agency and the community in which it is located is of significant interest to most prospects.

Job announcements are usually a page long and contain as much information about the position as practical. The document should be easy to understand and attractive, so attention should be given to proper organization, spacing, and print size. A large number of job announcements are usually printed and distributed to various schools, agencies, and individuals who will make the position vacancy known to qualified and interested candidates.

Job ads are condensed versions of job announcements and only contain the most essential and basic information, due to the cost of advertising space in newspapers and professional journals. Figure 10.2 depicts a typical job announcement. The job ad in Figure 10.3 advertises the same position.

Locating Qualified Candidates

One of the important factors in hiring quality personnel is to convince a number of well-qualified people to apply. If an organization is truly sincere about hiring the best possible person available, it is logical to believe that the greater the number of qualified applicants, the better is the opportunity for hiring a top-quality employee.

There are six common sources of candidates for vacant positions in the field of physical education, fitness, and sports. These are the hiring organization itself, university placement centers,

POSITION	Lecturer for 1992–93 academic year, Physical Education Department, School of Professional studies. Responsibility includes teaching professional preparation and general activity courses in dance (ballet, folk, jazz, and social).
QUALIFICATIONS	Candidate must have a minimum of master's degree. At least two years of successful teaching in dance required.
SALARY	Range $26,500–$32,500, depending on experience and preparation.
HOW TO APPLY	Direct applications, accompanied by a resume, to: Dr. Will Hire, Head, Physical Education Department, Smith University, Smith, Kentucky 43499. Telephone: (616) 999-8888. Deadline for receipt of applications is May 1, 1988.
DEPARTMENT	The Physical Education Department offers bachelor's degrees in physical education and dance and a master's degree in fitness management. More than 400 majors are currently enrolled.

Figure 10.2 *A Typical Job Announcement*

LECTURER position for 1992–93 academic year, Physical Ed. Dept., School of Professional Studies. Salary range: $26,500–$32,500. Duties include teaching professional preparation and general activity courses in dance (ballet, jazz, folk, and social). Candidate must have master's degree and at least two years of successful dance teaching experience. Apply to Dr. Will Hire, Head, Physical Education Department, Smith University, Smith, KY 43499. Closing date: May 1, 1992. Affirmative Action/Equal Opportunity/Title IX Employer.

Figure 10.3 *A Typical Job Ad*

commercial placement agencies, professional organizations, professional associates and friends, and newspaper advertisements.

The Hiring Organization   Organizations usually can choose whether to hire from within or go outside to fill vacancies. Larger organizations tend to hire from within their current pool of full-time or part-time employees more than do smaller organizations. Hiring from within the organization has both advantages and disadvantages.

The three major reasons for hiring from within the organization are the following:

1. It fosters good employee morale by providing career ladders for advancement. Job opportunities become available as people move up in the organization. Employees know that when

someone retires or leaves the enterprise, they will have an opportunity for a higher-level position.

2. An organization knows the strengths and weaknesses of its own employees. It is easier to evaluate knowledge, skills, abilities, and work behavior of current employees. Working with known information reduces the risk of making poor hiring decisions.

3. The period of time for employee orientation is reduced when persons from inside the organization are advanced to fill vacant positions. Current employees are already familiar with the operation of the organization; therefore, they can devote their full attention to learning the new job. They immediately become more productive since their adjustment period is shorter.

The most common disadvantages of hiring from within are the following:

1. The organization may suffer from stagnation if there is too much inbreeding. Hiring new personnel from other professional settings and experiences keeps a flow of fresh new ideas coming into the organization.

2. Maintaining an in-house personnel training program is costly; it is often too costly for smaller organizations.

3. The limited number of qualified candidates from which to choose may result in the promotion of candidates who are less than ideal for the position.

4. Employees advanced from the ranks may have difficulty leading former peers who have become subordinates.

The most effective hiring practice seems to be to encourage applications from both within and outside the organization. When positions are open to all qualified candidates, a stronger pool of applicants from which to make the final selection will likely emerge.

University Placement Centers   Many believe that the most reliable source of qualified job applicants for entry-level positions is the university placement center. Many students receiving degrees and seeking employment register with their school's placement service, so the number of interested applicants is almost unlimited when the job is listed with several centers. School placement centers operate a service that is practically cost free to both the candidate and the employer. They have a reputation to uphold as they represent the university; therefore, they want both employers and their graduates to be satisfied with their service. An essential objective of any university is to place their graduates in satisfying positions, since their future enrollments depend upon that ability.

Commercial Placement Agencies   Commercial placement agencies are similar in many ways to university placement centers, but commercial agencies are profit-making enterprises. The person who obtains a job as a result of an agency's efforts must pay a sizable fee, usually based on a percentage of the first year's salary. The life of any business enterprise depends upon its ability to produce a quality product or service; hence, these agencies depend upon the reputation they establish as well. An advantage that the commercial agency has over the university service is that its pool of candidates is not limited to the graduates of a single school. Prospects moving into an area from another part of the country may establish a placement file with a local placement service. Through its preliminary screening and preparation of well-organized placement credentials, the commercial agency provides a very valuable service for employers.

Professional Organizations   The larger and more affluent professional organizations—such as the

Professional associates are a good source for locating qualified candidates.

American Alliance for Health, Physical Education, Recreation, and Dance, the Association for Fitness in Business, and the National Collegiate Athletic Association—have proven to be a very valuable source for locating position prospects. These organizations distribute to their members a list of position ads sent to them and paid for by the employer. The fee the employer pays is quite nominal for the breadth and quality of the distribution the ads receive.

At their national conventions and conferences, some professional groups also provide a placement service that can bring employers and interviewers face to face with a large number of applicants. These placement services provide employers with volumes of one-page resumes for their perusal, and they provide registered candidates with catalogs of job announcements for

their review. Assigned contact boxes, similar to post office boxes, are provided for employers and candidates so that they can conveniently communicate with each other to set up interview sessions. Interview booths may also be part of the service provided.

Professional organizations are an excellent source for locating candidates for everything from entry-level positions to top-level administrative posts.

Professional Associates and Friends Another source for identifying position prospects is through personal contact with professional associates and friends. Employing directors commonly contact reliable friends and counterparts at other institutions and enterprises to ask them to recommend known candidates who have proven themselves as quality performers. This method is most often used for locating candidates for positions requiring a high level of expertise and experience; however, many high school administrators and fitness organization executives use this method for hiring most of their entry-level personnel.

Employers using this approach do need to be sure that they can trust the person making the recommendation. An administrator may jump at an opportunity to unload an undesirable employee; this is one of the few ways an administrator can eliminate ineffective permanent employees without a major confrontation.

Classified Advertisements Advertising in local and selected major newspapers is the method most generally used by employers to locate candidates. The classified ad section is used widely by people looking for employment, and newspapers have a wider circulation than any of the other media sources listed.

Equal Opportunity for Employment and Affirmative Action

Employers are showing more concern than ever before for being fair to minorities and women in their hiring practices. These practices did not evolve voluntarily but as a result of several class-action suits and direct pressure from the federal government. However, discriminatory hiring still occurs, for three basic reasons: (1) Many employers are still prejudiced against certain minorities and/or women; (2) employers may not be fully aware of what constitutes nondiscriminatory hiring practices; and (3) the initial costs involved in implementing a sincere affirmative action plan, such as for additional advertising in periodicals and placement services that cater to minority groups and women, is significant.

In some instances, reverse discrimination has occurred when employers have been overzealous in hiring minorities, but these cases are few compared to those involving discrimination against minorities. The issue is an emotional one, and opposing views are quite common when employers attempt to justify certain hiring actions.

There is still a great deal of misunderstanding and confusion related to civil rights legislation for hiring and promotion; therefore, a list of questions and answers are presented in an effort to dispel that misunderstanding and confusion.

1. What legislative act is the basis for eliminating discrimination in the workplace?
   Answer: Title VII, Civil Rights Act of 1964, as amended in 1972.

2. What do equal employment opportunity and affirmative action mean?
   Answer: Equal employment opportunity refers to the right of all persons to apply and be evaluated for opportunities without regard for their race, color, religion, national origin, age, sex, sexual orientation, pregnancy, disability, or veteran status. *Affirmative action* refers to positive actions initiated by an employer to ensure that equal employment opportunities exist for minorities, women, and Americans with disabilities. Positive action generally is directed toward two major areas: (1) Affirmative action to identify and remove artificial barriers which may be built into personnel policies and procedures, and (2) recruiting activities designed to ensure that minorities, women, and Americans with disabilities are aware of employment opportunities and become part of the applicant pool.
   The purpose of affirmative action is to achieve equal employment opportunity.

3. Will affirmative action mean that people will be hired on the basis of their race or sex rather than on the basis of who is best qualified for the job, thereby undermining the merit system?
   Answer: Quotas can undermine but goals and timetables should not. Prior to EEO and AA

programs the hiring decisions of many employers were based in large measure on subjective and unproven criteria. As a result, racial and sexist stereotypes operated to exclude women and minorities without regard to their actual qualification. Such criteria were institutionalized within the "merit system." With equal employment opportunity and affirmative action guidelines, employers must take steps to assure that job qualifications are accurately appraised.

4. Do affirmative action plans establish preferential treatment for minority groups and women?

Answer: No. The purpose of affirmative action is to undo a preferential system many years in the making and to redress the historic imbalances now favoring white males in the job market. Redressing this imbalance requires that discriminatory patterns be eradicated and some measure of equity be established for persons who have been discriminatorily excluded in the past. Implementation of affirmative action plans must, therefore, necessarily involve a selection process aimed at achieving these goals.

5. Are goals and timetables aimed at achieving a proportional representation of minorities and women?

Answer: The concept of goals and timetables is not synonymous with proportional representation. Rather, the concept comes into play when it has been determined that women or minorities are underutilized or underrepresented in one or more job classifications. When underutilization has been established, affirmative action programs are employed to bring minorities and women into the labor force in the numbers that "would reasonably be expected by their availability."

6. What groups are protected from discriminatory practices under Title VII of the Civil Rights Act?

Answer: All prospective employees are covered under Title VII.

7. Why then are there so many well-educated and knowledgeable people who believe that reverse discrimination is occurring as a result of affirmative action?

Answer: In some instances, reverse discrimination has occurred, not because of the legislation but because of the implementation procedures of the employer. Many employers are so intent upon achieving a proportional balance, they forget about the rights of the white male population. The real problem lies in how the qualifications for a position are advertised. Traditional qualifications, such as years of experience, advanced degrees, and publication records, are still being listed as requirements for jobs without any evidence that such requirements are necessary for quality performance. Employers must be up front with prospective candidates when identifying job requirements.

8. How can diversity in job classifications be achieved?

Answer: Employers need to realize that proportional diversity in the work force usually cannot be achieved immediately. It may take five, six, or ten years in some cases. Federal legislation allows for extended periods if the employer can provide evidence that a strong effort is being made that will result in equality. Employers are obligated to initiate and finance programs of education and training for minorities and women that prepare them for fields that have traditionally been the domain of white men.

Personnel Involved in the Selection Process

The nature of an organization dictates who is involved in hiring personnel. A small fitness promotion business with three full-time and six part-time employees will not follow the same selection guidelines as a school district that has two hundred employees and a large personnel department. In the small fitness operation, only the owner and/or the manager may be directly involved in hiring, and the results may be very effective; in a large school district, the personnel in the district office as well as the principal, athletics director, physical education director, and coaches at a particular school are likely to be directly involved in the process. Whatever practices is fair and effective should be followed.

In a democratic society, a decision-making action guide for the hiring process that seems to work well is this: *Those affected by the decision should be involved to an equitable degree in making the decision.* The administrator whose job will be most affected by the hiring decision should have the controlling authority in making the selection. In health and fitness clubs, corporate fitness programs, and physical education and athletics programs that have fewer than eight full-time professional employees, one would not expect the staff to be very involved in the selection process. In larger organizations and programs, the director often uses search and screening committees to assist in the selection of new personnel.

For larger programs and departments, search and screening committees can be an invaluable aid to the administrator if delegated the appropriate responsibility and authority and provided with the proper guidance to proceed. The committee may consist of as few as two members, but not more than five. A three-member committee is recommended for most position searches, for three reasons: (1) A three-member committee is large enough to divide the responsibilities and review the applications without undue stress; (2) each member will feel significantly responsible for carrying his or her share of the load; and (3) it is not difficult for three people to find a common time available for regular meetings.

The role of a search and screening committee is to represent the views of the entire faculty or staff as they work with the director throughout the process. They prepare the job announcement, the list of criteria for assessing candidates, and the itineraries for those invited for interviews. They also carry out, with the assistance of a secretary, the details of advertising the position, receiving applications, corresponding with the applicants and references, and following through with phone calls to present or former supervisors of the finalists. Their most critical responsibility is paring down the list of candidates to three to six finalists for on-site interviews. Their final responsibility is to rank and present recommendations about the finalists to the other staff members and/or the responsible administrator.

Sources of Information about Applicants

Once a position has been advertised, applications and other kinds of information will be either volunteered or sought by the committee. Some sources are reliable and some are not. The following sources of information usually have a bearing upon the decision to hire.

Completed Official Application Form Every candidate should complete an official application form. Comparing candidates' qualifications is much easier if the information is presented in the same form. Comparisons are difficult when information is presented in the candidates' personally designed resumes without the benefit of a standardized format. The official application should have places for

- personal information
- educational background information—including degrees, dates attained, and certifications
- data about related experience—including dates, employers, and names of supervisors

Part of the interview process may be to observe the prospective instructor in action.

- brief statement of philosophy
- names and addresses of references.

Transcripts Copies of all college transcripts should be part of the applicant's file. The overall grade point average is usually not as important as the nature of course work and the pattern of progress and success.

Letters of Recommendation Letters of reference are normally required for application files. Actually, they are of very limited value, for two reasons. First, they only represent the views of the people the applicant chooses, from whom positive recommendations are expected. Second, very few references are willing to be totally frank and honest when writing a letter. They have a tendency to dwell on, or create, strengths, and fail to make comments regarding weaknesses.

From these sources, the committee or administrator decides who will be on the list of finalists or semifinalists. If a list of semifinalists is developed, the next step is to either gather more information, more closely review the information

available, or do both. If further information is needed before the final list is developed or before candidates are invited for the preemployment interview, phone calls to present and former supervisors are strongly recommended.

Supervisors' Assessments In our experience, supervisors and former supervisors will be more candid and truthful in a phone or face-to-face conversation than they will be in a letter of reference. The person is likely to feel more comfortable if open-ended questions, rather than digging inquiries, are presented. If the open-ended responses are not satisfying, then questions regarding specific concerns should be asked. The supervisor may be hesitant to criticize, but in many cases may convey messages by how he or she states things or by what he or she obviously omits. Talking with supervisors is considered to be a very worthwhile technique.

Observed Performance Although this is not a widely used source of information in our field, some program directors prefer to see the candidates in action. Candidates may be informed prior to their interview visit that they will be expected to present a prepared lecture to either a class or a group of department members, or to actually lead a physical education or exercise group through a prepared lesson of their choice. Observation in a real situation can be very beneficial and is recommended when appropriate.

Interviews   The final source of information is the preemployment interview. Contrary to reports and research evidence that interviews are not reliable predictors of future success for employees, we have been very pleased in our use of this final step. Some assert that very few interviewers are prepared to conduct an effective interview, but when an extended effort is devoted to making the interview a meaningful basis for making a decision, it can be of tremendous value.

Before or during the interview, we recommend the following:

- A standardized set of questions should be developed for use by all who will be involved in the interview. This will contribute to equitable treatment of all candidates and will add effective structure to the process.
- Both group and individual interview sessions should be scheduled.
- Attempts should be made to put the candidate at ease.
- Mental notes should be registered during the interview and immediately written down as soon as the candidate leaves the room. If an interviewer's memory does not serve well, then it is better for her or him to inform the candidate that "memory joggers" will be jotted down during the interview and to do so rather than forgetting important responses. Candidates realize that they are being closely scrutinized, and this procedure should not disrupt the responses of a confident person.

- Those who will be asking questions should be reminded that certain questions are illegal and grounds for a grievance. Some of these are:
  "What does your husband do?"
  "Are you a member of NOW?"
  "With what church are you affiliated?"
  "How old are you?"

Lists of discriminatory questions to avoid are available at most placement centers and personnel offices.

Screening and Selection Criteria

Making screening and selection decisions to fill positions in the health and fitness fields is not an easy task. Developing a list of criteria upon which screening decisions will be based is not difficult, but determining how well candidates meet certain criteria and how heavily each factor should be weighted in the decision *is* difficult. How much weight each factor will have must be determined for each position under consideration. The value of a pleasing personality, for example, is greater for an instructor than it is for a laboratory researcher.

In the selection process, two sets of criteria should be developed. The initial screening criteria are used to pare the original list of candidates down to a list of finalists. The interview criteria are used as a basis for judging those who are invited for the on-site interview, and supplement the screening criteria.

Screening Criteria   The search and screening committee or the director develops the screening criteria and uses them without having the advantage of seeing or talking to the candidates. The criteria should reflect the factors listed in the job description. The committee should identify each factor and decide the weight each factor will have in the decision. For example, a candidate may be given zero to ten points for experience directly

APPLICANT QUALIFICATION FORM

Applicant _Wally Tanner_   Date _May 15, 1992_
Position _Fitness Instructor_   Department _Fitness_

(List the total points awarded for each factor.)

Factor	Points Possible	Points Awarded	Remarks
Personality (from references)	0–20	18	Positive in all references
Appropriate role model	0–10	9	Hero type
Academic achievements (degree, GPA, etc.)	0–10	8	BS – Fit Mgmt GPA – 3.3
Scholarship activities (research, publ., etc)	0–6	1	Limited
Professional activity (memberships, offices)	0–4	2	Member, two organizations
Success: recent past	0–16	15	High praise by supervisor
Job-related experience	0–10	9	Four years
Other experiences	0–4	1	Insignificant
Philosophy	0–4	4	Good
Personal fitness level	0–10	10	Runs marathon
Past participation	0–6	5	Track athlete
TOTAL POINTS AWARDED		82	

Figure 10.4 *Screening Criteria Form*

```
INTERVIEW ASSESSMENT FORM

Applicant  Wally Summer              Date  June 10, 1992
Position  Fitness Instructor        Department  Fitness

(List the total points awarded for each factor.)

                    Points      Points

Factor              Possible    Awarded      Remarks

Personal            0–10          10         Neat and clean
appearance

Presence/           0–14          12         Reserved
personality

Communication       0–10          9          Verbal good
skills

Interest in         0–12          12         Highest
position

Knowledge           0–14          12         Good on several accounts
level for
position

Attitude            0–10          10         People oriented
toward
clientele

Professional        0–10          9          Life-style supportive
philosophy

Overall             0–20          18         A really good interview
appropriate-
ness for job

TOTAL POINTS AWARDED              92
```

Figure 10.5 *Interview Assessment Form*

related to the position but only zero to five points for academic achievement.

Criteria normally used in screening candidates for activity-based positions appear in Figure 10.4. Such a form can provide structure in the screening process. If a determination of worth for each factor is established and related in terms of points (one to five, for example), the points each candidate is awarded by each committee member can be totaled, thus establishing a ranking order.

Interview Criteria   The second list of factors that should be developed as a supplement to the screening criteria is the interview criteria. A sec-

ond assessment of an applicant's qualifications is made for the candidates who are interviewed. After the interview, the committee members and/or director may wish to adjust their point totals on the screening criteria form. Figure 10.5 is a completed sample interview assessment form.

In the sample forms we present, note that for the instructor's position, which involves daily contract with those being served, personality was rated highest, with successful experience also weighted heavily. As we stated previously, the nature of the position will determine how heavily or lightly each factor is weighted in the hiring decision.

Building on Strengths   Peter Drucker, in his classic *The Effective Executive* (1966), presents an outstanding discussion of building on strengths when selecting personnel. The essential points he makes are as follows:

- Staffing decisions should be made to maximize strengths, not minimize weaknesses.

- Whoever tries to avoid weakness rather than making strength effective is a weak person. He or she probably sees strength in others as a threat to herself or himself.

- Whoever tries to place a person or staff an organization to avoid weakness will end up at best with mediocrity.

- There is no such thing as a "good person." The person must be good *for something*.

- To focus on strength is to make demands for performance. Each job is made big and demanding.

- Effective executives know that their staff is paid to perform and not to please them.

- The immediate task of the administrator is not to place a person; it is to fill a job.

- Except in rare cases, structuring jobs to fit a particular person is almost certain to lead to favoritism and conformity.

- To get strength one must learn to tolerate certain weaknesses.

Insight through Illustration

When author Jim Railey was serving as assistant baseball coach at Arizona State University, there was so much talent that it was not necessary to tolerate bizarre behaviors and problem players to have one of the top teams in the nation. After moving on to Utah State University as head coach, he soon discovered that baseball talent was not that abundant there, and he had to keep what he had. One scholarship center fielder could run, throw, hit with power, and cover his position like a blanket, but his personality was terrible. He could not relate to the coach, and his teammates did not like him. Rather than giving up on him, Coach Railey counseled, tolerated, and stretched his ways to the limit in keeping the player on the club. It paid off. The center fielder not only led the team in several offensive categories, but he also developed into a good citizen. Especially for that achievement, Railey has always been pleased that his decision was not to boot the player off the team. The player had some unusual strengths, and the club needed them.

The Selection

After the preemployment interviews have been completed, it is decision time. In education or in any other work setting where people other than the administrator have been involved in the screening and selection process, all those involved should have their opportunity for input. Although the director should be the authority in making the decision to hire, to involve faculty or staff members in the detail work of screening and then not give them the opportunity to vote or advise in the final selection would violate the very foundation of the democratic process.

After those involved have voted, written their recommendation, and sent that recommendation to the responsible administrator, that administrator must either agree or disagree with the recommendation. If he or she agrees, the staff should be so notified and the hiring recommendation forwarded to the final approving authority of the organization. If the administrator does not agree with the recommendation of the staff, he or she should call the group back in session and explain why. They should be given the opportunity to further justify their selection. Consensus should be sought, and if a sincere effort is extended, it usually can be achieved. If the director is still unable to persuade the staff to support his or her decision, and cannot be convinced by them that their recommendation is best, the right of authority dictates, and the director makes the final decision with justification. The director, not the staff, must be responsible for the actions of the person hired, and in light of that fact, he or she must be the responsible decision maker.

IMPROVING STAFF PERFORMANCE

A director can help improve staff performance both by making sure that new employees get off on the right foot and by supporting seasoned staff members' participation in developmental activities.

New Employee Orientation

A productive performance begins with a good orientation. That orientation actually begins with the interview and continues with the contractual letter of appointment. The letter should be accompanied by the organization's staff or faculty handbook, which provides details about the working conditions of employment, such as sick leave, accrual of vacation time, health insurance, and general policies regarding expectations of the employee.

By the time the new staff member arrives for work, a plan should be ready for acquainting the person with the other members of the department or unit, key persons and offices in other divisions of the organization, the detailed policies and procedures of the unit, and the employee services available. A person within the department may be relieved of normal responsibilities in order to conduct the formal orientation. The foundation for a positive feeling toward an organization and the administrator can be established at this time. In contrast, nothing can be more frustrating and demoralizing than for a new employee to be put to work not knowing his or her associates nor understanding the organization's mode of operation. A well-planned and conducted orientation pays high dividends.

Employee Retention

For years corporate America has known that employee retention is vitally important for maintaining a high level of productivity. Just recently the fitness club industry has realized that a direct correlation exists between employee retention and member retention. For many years club owners operated with the belief that for most economical results they should hire mostly part-time employees as cheaply as they could. They were also hesitant to invest in their professional development and training because of the high rate of employee turnover. Because research has established that membership stability and employee stability are so closely related, employers are now investing in the professional development of their employees even though many are still employed on a part-time basis.

Graham (1991:24–31) suggests six factors that will help fitness club management retain productive staff members:

- *Recruit wisely* by improving the interview procedures.
- *Offer training* so that the employees will feel confident in their jobs.
- *Communicate and evaluate* so that the employees will feel like valuable members of the team.
- *Promote from within* and the employees will display a greater degree of loyalty to their organization.
- *Offer financial incentives* and the employees will strive to be more productive and experience a higher degree of morale.
- *Provide meaningful benefits and perks* such as consistent schedules and stipends for attending workshops.

In-Service Training

The wise director will provide and/or arrange in-service training opportunities for staff improvement. By *in-service training,* we mean any professional development activity that occurs during employment that is supported wholly or in part by the employer. The degree of support may range from releasing the employee from job responsibilities for an hour a week to giving the employee a sabbatical leave at full salary. Certain in-service development activities may occur within the organization, but many require travel to other places.

In-service training activities within the department or organization can give a tremendous boost to staff development and improvement, and they can be conducted for very little or no cost. Encouraging staff members to share creative and innovative ideas and techniques is one example, and all directors should consider doing this regardless of the type of program being conducted.

One method of in-service training is for experts to teach fellow instructors.

Insight through Illustration

When Jim Railey was a teaching assistant at Indiana University, a lunch-hour sharing of expertise was scheduled every Friday for the benefit of both faculty and graduate teaching assistants. The learning sessions included reviews of recent research, lectures on special topics, and learning through participation in various activities. For example, during one lunch hour participants were taught how to fly cast, even though some had never had a fly rod in their hands before. These sessions were invaluable for learning new knowledge and skills.

Other in-service professional growth activities that often are provided from within are teacher improvement classes at no cost to the staff member, reviews of new books, and one-day or weekend retreats for such activities as cardiopulmonary resuscitation certification renewal or curriculum development.

Directors can improve the productivity of their staff by not only providing in-house growth opportunities, but also by supporting other kinds of professional development activities that take staff members away from the work site, such as the following:

- *Professional organization membership and participation.* Administrators can have a significant effect upon the involvement of their staff members in professional activities. For example, some directors have initiated campaigns promoting participation by all employees in state and national organizations. Others have contacted professional colleagues and friends in key positions and asked that their staff members be placed in presenting roles at state, regional, and national conventions. It takes some effort, but everyone experiences the positive results of involvement.

- *Conference/convention attendance.* Directors can make a difference also in their staff's attendance at conferences and conventions. Administrators have budget power, and providing financial support for traveling to conferences can be a big morale booster. Administrative support is also needed for getting substitutes to take over the staff member's responsibilities while away.

- *Sabbatical leaves.* In the past, sabbatical leaves have been identified more with college and university faculties than with public and private schools or health promotion and fitness enterprises. However, more and more, these other agencies are recognizing the benefits of supporting leaves with pay for their permanent employees who have proven themselves worthy. Leaves for professional research, writing, travel, and promotion can put new life into the productive efforts of the mature or older staff member.

- *Workshops and clinics.* Professional workshops and clinics provide very valuable opportunities for teachers and fitness employees to renew and learn new techniques from master teachers. The administrator needs to support inducements for participation in these experiences.

MOTIVATION AND THE DIRECTOR

Directors of physical education, sports, and fitness programs need to be as concerned about motivating their staff members as does a production manager for a large automobile manufacturer. In fact, since health and well-being are more important than a product or profit in activity-based programs, maybe they should be more concerned. Motivated employees are more successful, more productive, more ambitious, and enjoy life more than those who are not motivated. Unmotivated staff members are substandard performers, experience friction on the job, and have a high rate of absenteeism and tardiness.

Research and Theories on Motivation

We do not have space here to discuss in depth the various research studies and theories on motivation, but we will briefly consider the findings and proposals of recognized leaders and studies on the topic.

Scientific Management Theory   In the early 1900s, Frederick Taylor proposed the theory of scientific management. He initiated time-and-motion studies directed toward establishing efficiency in the organization, and when the tasks were efficiently organized he used various incentive plans to satisfy the economic concerns of the workers. He concluded that the main focus of the manager was not on the needs of the individual but on the needs of the organization.

The Hawthorne Studies   At the Hawthorne, Illinois, plant of the Western Electric Company, a group of efficiency experts conducted a study in 1924 of the effects of improved illumination in the workplace. Illumination was improved for a test group, while the illumination level for a control group was kept within the normal range. As the illumination level for the experimental group was increased, that group's productivity also increased, as expected. An unexpected finding was that when as the result of an error, the lighting for the control group was decreased, their output also increased.

Baffled by these findings, the researchers conducted a follow-up study involving a group of women who assembled telephone relays. For more than a year and a half, the working conditions for the group were improved, including shorter work weeks, scheduled rest periods, and company lunches. As expected, the productivity of the women improved. The researchers then took all the added privileges away from the group, expecting a significant decline in their output. They were amazed to find that even after the added privileges were taken away, the women's productivity continued upward to an all-time high.

The researchers concluded that the increased output was not due to the physical working conditions but was a result of the attention given to the group. Because the women were made to feel as though they were an important part of the company and participating members of a cohesive work group, they were motivated toward achieving unusually high goals. Being identified as working partners with management is a recognized motivator. As a result of these findings, the human aspect was recognized as an important part in motivating and managing people within the organization.

Theory X and Theory Y   Douglas MacGregor, a Harvard University psychologist, developed Theory X and Theory Y, which are concerned with human behavior and managing people. Theory X proposes that people are motivated by fear, money, and fringe benefits. It further assumes that most people prefer to be directed and closely controlled in their performance effort and that employees are irresponsible, unreliable, and immature.

Theory Y is directly opposed to Theory X. Theory Y assumes that employees are basically reliable and can direct themselves, that people actually want to work and are creative if motivated and given that freedom, and that people can best accomplish organizational goals as they directly achieve their own goals through self-direction.

Most administrators in a democratic society, in developing their own modes of operation, incorporate both theories into their styles. A director may hold Theory Y assumptions about human nature but find it necessary to be more coercive and directive with younger and less-experienced staff members.

Maslow's Hierarchy of Needs   Abraham Maslow, a noted psychologist, developed a theory of motivation in which people's desires and needs are arranged in a hierarchy of importance. The needs are arranged into five categories:

1. *Physiological needs,* which are the basic needs for food, clothing, and shelter, and which must be satisfied before a person is motivated to satisfy other needs
2. *Security needs,* those related to self-preservation and physical safety
3. *Social needs,* such as the need to belong
4. *Esteem needs,* related to feelings of power and control, prestige, respect from others, and self-confidence.
5. *Self-actualization needs,* the desire and need to reach one's highest potential or capacity

A person's desires and needs must be satisfied in the order presented, from the basic needs to self-actualization. According to Maslow, people, desiring better consequences, always want what they do not have. Since satisfied needs can no longer motivate, new needs arise after lower-level needs have been satisfied.

In reflecting upon the theories presented, it is important to realize that precepts from each can help in understanding motivation and why it is important in the workplace. Each situation and each employee's personality is different, and that understanding should inform the director's concern with staff motivation, performance, and productivity. In one situation money may be the primary motivator; fear may motivate in one case and not in others; and praise and challenging assignments may be motivators in another situation. These are important factors of which the director needs to be aware.

Morale and Motivation

Morale is a spiritual or emotional state indicated by the degree of cheerfulness with which a person is willing to perform assigned tasks and responsibilities. Every administrator talks about the importance of morale, but most have difficulty in controlling it. Regarding morale and motivation, Cohen and Cohen (1984: 54–55) make these observations:

High morale in the organization does not always contribute to high productivity. It may not sound logical, but it's true. Happy workers are not necessarily the most productive workers. But this doesn't mean high morale is to be avoided. High morale may not ensure high productivity, but it is usually a necessary condition for it. The advantages of high morale include low turnover, less absenteeism, and a better climate for supervision (criticism and instruction are likely to be more effective). Cohesive decision sharing by the group usually implies high morale. The morale of your subordinates will most likely be more influenced by your treatment of them as their manager than by the behavior of higher management. The reason is that you are closer to them, and people are more affected by personal contacts. You can therefore have a greater impact on them than anyone else in the firm.

Ways the Director Can Motivate

The primary responsibility for motivating the staff toward achieving organizational goals lies with the director. The director who is sensitive in helping individuals achieve realistic personal goals will find that organizational goals, if properly related, will be accomplished in the process. We will list twelve important ways the director can motivate. The first letters of each of these twelve keys to motivation spell the words CRITICAL CORE. We believe these to be the critical core of motivation.

Communication   The director must communicate to make sure the staff understands what is needed and expected from their performance. The director cannot assume that staff members are on the same wavelength as her or him. It is better to overcommunicate than to fail in properly relaying information.

Responsibility   When directors accept administrative posts, they accept full responsibility for that position. That includes a commitment to excellence, a willingness to take risks, and a readiness to accept the blame for failures.

Independence   The staff must be encouraged to be independent and self-reliant. To this end, the director should make sure employees know what to do but allow them to exercise their own creativity and ingenuity in how to do it. The director must be there if needed for suggestions and corrections but must allow the person with the assignment to be responsible for its successful completion.

Truthfulness and Honesty   The results of truthfulness must be trusted. There may be times when confidential matters cannot be discussed, and if that is the case, the director should simply make that statement. Attempts to deceive will lead to a lack of trust. Wise people know as long as they tell the truth, they never need to be concerned about what they told someone yesterday.

Initiation   It is important for the leader to take the initiative and set the example for others. Good administrators train themselves to see the things that need attention and do them without being told.

Courage   It takes courage to make tough decisions, accept the blame when a subordinate makes a mistake, and take risks in order to excel. A staff can be motivated in their pursuit of excellence by observing a courageous leader in action.

Assignments of Interest   When staff members are doing what they want to be doing, they are more motivated to succeed. There are occasions when staff members must take less desirable assignments to fulfill the goals of their agency, but the director should make every reasonable effort to make their assignments enjoyable and rewarding.

Listening   A motivating director must be willing to listen to what subordinates have to say. It is essential that both suggestions and complaints be heard. A director who listens to the staff is appreciated. A classic example of a demotivating act is when an administrator asks someone for advice and then does not truly listen when it is given.

Constructive Criticism   A staff member will appreciate and respond positively to constructive criticism. Some questions the director needs to ask in order to keep criticism constructive are the following:

- Do I get the facts before criticizing?
- Does the person understand what is wrong?
- Do I criticize in private?
- Do I praise before criticizing?
- Do I control my temper?
- Do I protect the dignity of the criticized person?
- Do I make specific suggestions for preventing a recurrence?
- Do I forgive and forget?

Openness   Motivating directors make sure that no barriers exist between the staff and themselves. Maintaining an open-door policy, getting out from behind the desk and circulating among the staff with a sincere effort to be open to their needs, and not allowing rules and regulations to become obstacles are ways to keep barriers down.

Awards are a way to say, "Thanks!"

Rewards and Awards of Praise   Rewards should be as concrete as possible. For an exemplary effort, a monetary bonus or time off should be given. This is not always possible, but an award that every administrator can give is one of praise. When an employee does something deserving, the effort should be recognized. A verbal word of praise in private is important, but something in written form is even better. Many people believe that "a 'thank-you' is worth only as much as the paper it is written on."

Enthusiasm   Staff members can be motivated by an enthusiastic leader. The director needs to get excited about the profession. The things that happen in activity-based programs, such as learning new skills, improving levels of fitness, losing weight, and winning athletic contests, are exciting. Remember, enthusiasm is catching.

Some other things that the director can do to motivate staff are leading by example, keeping abreast of new advances in the field and informing the staff, judging fairly, keeping assignments basic to the goals, being flexible, fighting for top salaries and good fringe benefits, and delegating responsibilities that are challenging. Fear is used quite often to motivate subordinates and in certain situations can be effective. However, it should be used only as a last resort to get a job done.

Guarding against Demotivating Practices

The director must guard against actions that are demoralizing. Because of the frequency with which they occur, we have selected seven administrative failures for emphasis.

Belittling Subordinates The dignity of the staff is important, and the director should not criticize employees in front of others or talk down to them.

Playing Favorites Sometimes administrators do not realize this fault, but other staff members notice when preferential treatment is given to one in particular.

Failing to Help Entry-level employees, especially, need help from the director in their professional growth and development.

Being Insensitive Being sensitive to needs and to those things that are important to employees must be a high priority for the director. Insensitivity usually is not planned, but it is not uncommon

when directors allow themselves to become overloaded with detail and fail to show proper concern.

Lowering Standards Holding fast to high standards of performance and achievement is necessary for maintaining the staff's respect. To ease up and accept what has previously been decided is unacceptable can negatively affect motivation.

Vacillating on Decisions Employees look up to a leader who can make a firm decision and stand with it. Frustration is common when the decision maker is unsure of his or her ability to make the right move.

Forcing Views on Others Recently we heard a fellow who was reminiscing about his good old days in the Navy refer to a common slogan of petty officers: "The right way, the wrong way, the Navy way, and my way." Unless staff members are given freedom to think and act within certain parameters, enthusiasm and motivation to excel will be stifled.

Managing personnel can be the most challenging and fulfilling function the administrator performs. The director's ability to select quality performers and to motivate them toward achieving the objectives of the organization can make the difference between success and failure in any activity-based program. The personnel function requires more of the director's time than functions relating to facilities and program, but the results justify the time and effort invested.

KEY WORDS AND PHRASES

Job description

Job analysis

Equal employment opportunity

Affirmative action

Screening and interview criteria

In-service training

Hawthorne studies

Maslow's hierarchy of needs

Theory X and Theory Y

Motivators

Morale

Demotivators

QUESTIONS FOR REVIEW

1. List the parts of a well-prepared job description.

2. To attract the best candidates available for a position, where and how would you advertise?

3. In your opinion, which factor(s) should be weighted most heavily in screening job candidates for activity-based programs? Least heavily? Why?

4. Discuss the concept of building on strengths when hiring for a position.

5. What should a new-employee orientation cover?

6. List ten ways to motivate employees.

7. Of the various employee motivators, which four do you believe would be most effective? Why?

8. Of the various demotivators, which four do you believe should be most avoided?

SELF-TEST

Corrected True-False

If the statement is true, mark it T. If the statement is false, mark it F and change it to a true statement by adding or deleting words.

_____ 1. The time directors need to spend managing programs and facilities is minimized when personnel are well-managed.

_____ 2. As soon as a position is filled, it is essential to formulate an accurate job description for that position.

_____ 3. Aggressive affirmative action is often in conflict with equal opportunity employment.

_____ 4. Staff members should not be given an assignment unless they have a keen interest in the task.

_____ 5. According to the text, letters of reference are one of the most reliable screening devices or sources of info on a candidate.

_____ 6. A director should be more concerned about filling a position to meet the job requirements than placing a good professional.

_____ 7. A good orientation for a new fitness specialist should begin with the interview and include the assignment of a mentor.

_____ 8. An in-house teacher improvement session is considered in-service training but a sabbatical leave is not.

_____ 9. Fear can be an effective motivator for improving employee performance.

_____ 10. *Critical core* is a mnemonic device associated with twelve things a director can do when writing a job description.

Multiple Choice

_____ 11. This theory of motivation concludes that increased output was a result of the feeling for being "partners with management" rather than physical working conditions:
   a. Scientific Management Theory
   b. Maslow's Theory
   c. The Hawthorne Studies
   d. Theory X and Theory Y

_____ 12. Which action guide would be inappropriate for Case 10.2 *Employee Problems in the Fitness Center?*
   a. Subordinates should be reprimanded privately, not publicly.
   b. A corporate fitness director

should impress upon his employees that they should not expect pay raises similar to other corporate employees.
   c. It is essential that communication channels stay open between director and employees.
   d. Instructor's tardiness to class should not be tolerated.

_____ 13. Which of the following is not an important part of a job description?
   a. job title
   b. exact salary
   c. list of responsibilities
   d. specific duties

_____ 14. "Is your family willing to move?" is a question that should:
   a. be asked in the interview
   b. be asked behind the scenes
   c. not be asked
   d. only be asked by the CEO

_____ 15. Which is most unlikely to motivate a fitness employee?
   a. vacillating superior
   b. praise
   c. relating assignment to goals
   d. delegating responsibility

CASE 10.1 TROUBLE WITH STALE TEACHING METHODS

Kioko Suzuki had just settled into her new position at Seaview High School as director of physical education, and everything seemed to be on the rise for her. She had been appointed to a director's position a couple of years ahead of the schedule she had planned three years ago for her climb upward in her profession. Seaview was a school of twenty-eight hundred students located on a large campus with outstanding physical education facilities. There were eight other health and physical education teachers in the department, and the school district was supporting a four-year requirement for physical education. The salary schedule was good and class enrollment was limited to no more than thirty-two per class. "This is a physical education teacher's paradise," Kioko thought.

But her elation was cut short when Bud Bailor, senior teacher on her staff, and Cindy Waymire, volleyball coach and racquet sports instructor, made an appointment to discuss a "serious problem." As they proceeded to voice their complaints about working conditions, they seemed to focus on the fact that the faculty members were all specialists in one or two activities, and innovative teaching methods were practically nonexistent except in team sports. The lessons teachers of most of the individual and dual activities taught gave every evidence of coming right out of the textbook. The school board and superintendent seemed to be opposed to supporting sabbatical leaves, conference attendance, and other renewal programs. In most cases, they would not permit teachers to be absent from school to attend a conference even when the teachers were willing to pay their own expenses.

It did not take Kioko long to get the picture, but her response to the problem was going to require some careful planning.

Your Response

1. What are the issue and problems in this case?

2. What barriers or hurdles may stand in the way of the best solution?

3. What should the director of physical education do about it?

4. List the action guides that can offer Kioko some direction and support as she works toward a solution.

CASE 10.2 EMPLOYEE PROBLEMS IN THE FITNESS CENTER

Tim Dowling had been serving as the director of fitness and recreation for the Aeroflyte Corporation since the program was initiated four years ago. He was instrumental in selecting every staff member in the department, and during the hiring process, he was particularly careful to hire only those applicants who displayed excitement and showed past evidence of being motivated toward outstanding achievement.

For the first three years, the instructors and staff seemed to be enthusiastic about working for Aeroflyte, and Tim had felt very good about his hiring decisions. During the past year, however, he received complaints from the program participants that the instructors and support personnel alike had become less helpful and more irritable than in the past. Tim also noticed that three or four of the instructors were often late for their classes, and instructors were calling in sick more often.

As he reflected back over the past year to see if he could identify any reason for the change in performance and attitude, Tim did recall that the recent pay increases and fringe benefits for his employees were below those of most of the other employees at Aeroflyte. He also recalled having to reprimand Eric Vann and Jill Hollen in the hallway for childlike behavior and excessive loudness. He had talked to all of his instructors and office personnel, and they all seemed hesitant to openly discuss problems on the job.

Tim Dowling wanted more than anything to see his nine staff members performing well and enjoying their jobs. He pondered his next step.

Your Response

1. What are the issue and problems in the case?

2. What barriers may stand in the way of the best solution?

3. What administrative actions need to be taken?

4. What guides motivated you to decide on your actions?

BIBLIOGRAPHY

Boucher, R. Bruce. "The Utility of the Pre-Employment Interview: Insight for Sports Administrators." *The Physical Educator* 41 (December 1984): 195–99.

Bucher, Charles. *Administration of Health and Physical Education Programs Including Athletics.* 8th ed. St. Louis: Mosby, 1983.

———. *Management of Physical Education and Athletic Programs.* 9th ed. St. Louis: Mosby, 1987.

Cohen, William A., and Nutrit Cohen. *Top Executive Performance: 11 Keys to Success and Power.* New York: Wiley, 1984.

Dougherty, Neil J., and Diane Bonanno. *Management Principles in Sport and Leisure Services.* Minneapolis: Burgess, 1985.

Drucker, Peter F. *The Effective Executive.* New York: Harper & Row, 1966.

Frost, Reuben B., and Stanley J. Marshall. *Administration of Physical Education and Athletics: Concepts and Practices.* 3rd ed. Dubuque, IA: William C. Brown, 1988.

Graham, Lamar B. "Employee Retention." *Club Industry* (June 1991): 24–31.

Harris, Ben M., Kenneth E. McIntyre, Vance C. Littleton, Jr., and Daniel F. Long. *Personnel Administration in Education.* Boston: Allyn & Bacon, 1979.

Jensen, Clayne R. *Administrative Management of Physical Education and Athletic Programs.* Philadelphia: Lea & Febiger, 1988.

Tucker, Allan. *Chairing the Academic Department: Leadership among Peers.* Washington, DC: American Council on Education, 1981.

11

Managing the Budget and Program Finances

. . . wealth from hard work grows.

Proverbs 13:11

Chapter Objectives

After reading this chapter and completing the exercises, you should be able to:

1 Explain why many sports directors are inefficient in managing program finances

2 Tell what a budget is

3 Name three types of budgets and explain the differences among them

4 List and describe the various budgeting systems

5 List the characteristics of an effective budget

6 Tell how to properly prepare and present a budget for approval

7 Name three types of accounting systems and explain how they differ

8 Explain the purpose and importance of audits

9 Suggest six ways to add to budget income

10 Describe the general procedure for purchasing supplies

Financial management is one of the most important responsibilities of administrators. In managing their departments or enterprises, they are concerned with preparing budgets, making all types of financial transactions, and accounting for large sums of money. In handling these financial matters, effective and simple procedures are available and should be used. The director who is responsible for fiscal matters is expected to follow sound business practices. To do otherwise may lead to severe criticism or even dismissal. No person who handles public funds can afford to be careless or fiscally ignorant.

Despite the recent recession, there still seems to be plenty of discretionary money available for sports, fitness, and leisure activity, possibly because the public continues to maintain a very strong interest. Yet, directors in schools continue to complain about their lack of financial resources and struggle to keep their programs intact. With the amount of money available and the accelerated interest in leisure, sports, and fitness activities, one must wonder why physical education, fitness, and athletic programs in schools are struggling for survival. In contrast to the financial dilemma being experienced in the schools, commercial and corporate fitness programs are growing at a rapid rate, and most appear to be financially successful. The reason for this seeming paradox becomes apparent when a comparison of the two types of operation is made.

Although program financing is a major concern for directors of every kind of activity-based program, directors in school settings differ greatly from directors in commercial and corporate settings in their attitudes and actions related to marketing and acquiring funds. We can note three major differences in these areas. First, commercial and corporate fitness directors recognize the necessity of aggressive marketing and/or fund-raising efforts and are willing to undertake them, whereas physical education and athletics directors rely heavily on the general funding from their institutions, and many seem to abhor outside fund-raising efforts. Second, physical education and athletics directors in the schools spend too many hours on fund-raising efforts that produce very little income; commercial fitness managers spend their energies only on those campaigns capable of significantly increasing their income. And third, commercial enterprises hire personnel educated and trained in marketing a product or service, whereas most school administrators expect their teachers, coaches, and sports administrators to raise the needed supplementary funds.

In addition to these differences relating to marketing and fund raising, other reasons account for the financial crises that school sports administrators are experiencing: (1) Many school administrators do not realize the benefits derived from physical activities and sports and fail to adequately support them (support not only includes funding but also keeping classes to a reasonable size and other scheduling considerations); (2) a number of teachers and coaches of physical education and athletics are not dedicated to the needs and interests of the students, whereas commercial fitness managers must be, or their jobs cease to exist; (3) many athletics programs are competing at levels that they cannot afford; (4) school officials have had difficulty in funding equitable programs for girls and women after Title IX was implemented without cutting back on existing programs for boys and men; and (5) many sports administrators are very poorly prepared to manage program finances and are ineffective in their efforts. They usually learn by the trial-and-error method, which is quite inefficient. Experience is a good teacher, but in the case of fiscal concerns, it is a very expensive teacher.

The aim of this chapter is to look at the function of managing program finances and to suggest ways in which it can be made more effective.

A new facility is a major capital outlay item.

WHAT IS A BUDGET?

A budget is simply a written estimate of anticipated income and expenditures. Some experts refer to the budget as a numberized plan—a plan that serves as an essential instrument of control. Directors of activity-based programs in schools and commercial settings alike find that the budget is basic to the financial management of their programs.

TYPES OF BUDGETS

Fitness and athletics directors need to understand and manage three types of budgets: the operational, equipment, and capital outlay budgets. The degree of control the director has over each type of budget varies from program to program. In most situations, the director is fully in charge of the operational budget, largely responsible for the equipment budget, and only has input in developing the capital outlay budget.

The *operational budget* normally has a life span of one fiscal year, but some entities operate on a two-year budget. Therefore, it is considered to be a short-term budget. Costs of salaries, office supplies, travel, phone, and advertising are paid from this budget.

The *equipment budget* is sometimes included in either the operational or the capital outlay budget, depending on the cost and anticipated life span of the equipment. Equipment can be considered to be any object that has a predetermined minimum life span as well as a predefined minimum value. For example, any item that costs more than $500 and has a life span of more than five years may be classified as equipment rather than supplies. In contrast, a line marker, even though it may last more than five years, is only valued at $140 and thus is likely to be classified as a supply item. The equipment budget is considered an intermediate or long-term budget. Examples of items purchased from the equipment budget are bicycle ergometers, video and audio equipment, pitching machines, and typewriters.

The *capital outlay budget* is usually intended to

enhance existing facilities, either through new construction or renovation. Sometimes, high-cost equipment such as an automobile may be purchased from the capital outlay budget. This depends upon how each enterprise or institution defines capital outlay. Capital outlay budgets may be broken down on the basis of cost into two categories: major capital outlay and minor capital outlay.

Normally, money funded for one budget category cannot be expended for items in one of the other categories. Towels and balls, for example, being operational expense items, cannot be purchased from the equipment or capital outlay budgets unless they are identified with the initial cost of equipping a new or renovated facility.

SYSTEMS OF BUDGETING

Several different budgeting systems have been used effectively in industry, public administration, education, and private business. Considerations such as organizational size and purpose, number of employees, sources of funding, product or services rendered, and requirements of reporting or control agencies heavily influence which budgeting system is most appropriate.

Directors other than those employed by small private or public enterprises are unlikely to have much input in determining which method is used; still, they should know the advantages and disadvantages of each of the more commonly used systems. We should note that these systems are not necessarily mutually exclusive and can, in fact, be combined in some cases to produce a more functional approach to budgeting in a given organization.

Line-Item Budgeting

The most commonly used form of budgeting is the line-item method. In this format the budget is separated into budget categories and objects (line items), both identified by numerical codes. For example, a category identified as Operating Expense 8400 may encompass common line items such as Salaries 8410, Travel 8420, and Supplies 8430. Figure 11.1 shows a condensed line-item budget. Specified dollar amounts are planned for and allocated to each object for the total operation of the administrative unit rather than for each program or project within the unit.

The greatest criticism leveled at line-item budgeting is that the relationship between expenditures and a specific program cannot be identified. One cannot tell by examining the budget which projects within the administrative unit are cost-effective. The focal point of a line-item budget is the budget category itself rather than the cost of individual programs or projects.

The reason line-item budgeting is the method most often used relates to its advantages. It is simple; it requires less time to administer than the other methods; and it encourages cooperative use of resources. The major disadvantage, as previously mentioned, is that one program may be a financial drain on the resources of other programs without being identified as such. The athletics director, for example, can financially favor one sport over another without the budget's reflecting that favoritism. Consequently, that disadvantage for those who examine the budget is sometimes considered an advantage for the budget administrator.

Incremental Budgeting

Incremental budgeting procedures are most often combined with line-item budgeting in determining item amounts for a new budget. If more funds are expected for the upcoming fiscal year, then each budget item is increased by specified increments. Conversely, if funding allocations decrease, then each item may be decreased by specified decrements. To balance funding needs in the object cat-

```
UNIVERSITY FOUNDATIONS

PHYSICAL EDUCATION WORKSHOP BUDGET

FISCAL YEAR: 1992

DIRECTOR: Bill Deficit

ACCOUNT: 8432       OBJECT#  ACCOUNT DESCRIPTION        BUDGET
_____         _____   _____      _____

                    8032     Conference coordinator    $1,600.00

                    8033     Instructors                  150.00

                    8075     Student assistants           200.00

                    8091     Benefits: taxes & W/C        220.00

                    8140     Honorariums                6,100.00

                    8210     Postage                      600.00

                    8261     Travel                       200.00

                    8405     Printing                   2,000.00

                    8563     Facilities rental          1,816.00

                    8602     Audiovisual rental            50.00

                    8606     Insurance costs              387.00

                    9000     Financial services           554.00

                    9020     Contingency reserve        1,162.00

                    9030     NET FOR DISTRIBUTION       6,031.00

                             TOTAL BUDGET             $21,070.00
```

Figure 11.1 *Condensed Line-Item Budget*

egories, a combination of increments and decrements are used.

Incremental budgeting is safe and easy. Its biggest disadvantage is that program mediocrity may result when adequate attention is not given to the relative value or merit of each project that is funded.

Formula Funding

Formula-funding budgets are quite common on the educational scene. In this method of budgeting, a formula is applied that relates funding to production. For example, in public schools, average daily attendance is the key to receiving state funds. Some colleges and universities have developed very complex formulas to determine the distribution of funds from the general fund to each program, but the basic element is the production of student credit units (SCUs). On the surface, formula funding appears to be a very equitable means of distributing funds, but it may not be unless those who control budget distribution introduce certain indices into the formula to make it equitable. For example, science courses may produce only half the SCUs of history courses, and yet laboratory courses cost more to operate because they need expensive equipment and a

```
POLYTECHNIC STATE UNIVERSITY          PROGRAM  Coaching Workshop

DIVISION OF BUSINESS AFFAIRS          DATE  July 18 - 31

CONFERENCE SERVICES                   SPONSOR  P. E. Department

                                      COORDINATOR  Joe Ray

BUDGET SUMMARY

Project # 8433                        Proposed        Actual


INCOME

    Registration   400 × $95         $38,000
                    160 × $60           9,600



TOTAL INCOME                         $47,600


EXPENSES

    Program                          $21,435
    Facilities                         3,007
    Food service
    Housing
    Services                          14,940


TOTAL EXPENSES                       $39,382


NET                                   $8,218
```

Figure 11.2 *Condensed Program Budget*

smaller student-teacher ratio. The formula must take this into account. To achieve parity in funding, each course or program must be coded with varying value indices. The same process can apply to organizations offering recreation or leisure activities.

Planning-Programming Budgeting System (PPBS)

The planning-programming budgeting system is a system of budgeting that gained a great deal of popularity and support a few years ago when the public became very conscious of the need for governmental and military agencies to be more financially accountable. It is a system that was designed for very large operations or organizations. Although certain practices common to the PPBS may be used by physical education, fitness, and athletics entities, the system in its pure state does not seem practical in those settings. The system is goal oriented and directs one's attention to planning and programming rather than to individual expenditures, which is an advantage. Each program within a department is separated from other programs, and items such as instruction and supplies are funded separately for every program. Figure 11.2 is a condensed version of a PPBS budget format. The biggest advantage of the method is that it requires managers to justify what they wish to do.

The disadvantages are that it is time consuming, very complex, quite expensive to implement and operate, and discourages sharing of resources between programs or projects.

Zero-Base Budgeting (ZBB)

Another goal-oriented budgeting system is the zero-base budget. Its most distinguishing feature is that each year's budget is viewed as an isolated unit that is planned and justified from a zero base, independent of what has previously existed. It was first introduced into industry during the 1970s, and its purpose was to eliminate some of the problems of line-item and incremental budgeting.

Basically, there are two major steps in putting the zero-base budget together: First, the decision package must be developed. The package includes a description and a cost analysis of each program or activity in terms of how it will contribute to the achievement of the overall objectives. Alternative levels of funding are presented in relationship to how well the goals can be achieved at each level. This presentation of alternatives gives the approving authorities options other than just flat approval or disapproval.

The second major step in developing a zero-base budget is the ranking or prioritizing of the individual decision packages according to how well they meet the needs and objectives of the department. At each subsequent level of budgetary authority, a reordering of the decision packages may occur if the authorities believe such reordering is appropriate for meeting the objectives of the total organization.

The major advantage of zero-base budgeting is

that funding requests must relate program costs to goal achievement. Through the constant appraisal of activities and programs that this makes possible, administrators are fully aware of the benefits of each.

The major criticism of the system is that it is unrealistic to go back to square one for ongoing programs each budget cycle. Other faults of the system are that it is very complex, it is time consuming, and many resources are required for its implementation.

PRINCIPLES OF EFFECTIVE BUDGETING

Certain specific principles of budgeting make the difference between an effective budget and an ineffective one. We will consider the five most important principles here.

The Budget Must Be Based on Program Objectives

A budget must be based on program philosophy, objectives, and priorities; it must address the important issues of the unit's mission. This principle is of utmost importance, and constant monitoring is required to assure the budget's continuing compliance with it. To illustrate how a department may violate this guide, we will consider an example of what is happening in athletics programs at both the high school and college levels.

Insight through Illustration

At a large midwestern university, the objective of the athletics program was to provide a broad-based program of sports that equitably fulfilled the needs and interests of both sexes in individual and team sports. Another was that no sport would be designated as major or minor. These guides were usually followed. However, as a result of the persuasive power of a particular coach, booster pressure, and the difference in gate receipts for football as compared to other sports, the budget authority was convinced that football deserved a larger slice of the budget pie. Soon the athletics were not being treated equitably. The members of the football team were eating steak when they traveled, and the members of the other teams were eating fast-food hamburgers.

I JUST CAN'T BELIEVE THAT DUMB BUSINESS MANAGER COULD FORGET TO BUDGET FOR PLANE FARE!

Budget for anticipated needs.

If this kind of thing happens, then the director of athletics is not adhering to the stated philosophy, and the budget becomes an ineffective plan for achieving the adopted objectives.

The Budget Needs to Be Realistic

When developing the budget, administrators must be realistic in their estimates of anticipated expenditures and income. When establishing budget figures or changing those already established, sound reasoning is basic to action. For example, if a new marketing or fund-raising plan is implemented and the experiences of other agencies indicate that a 40 percent increase in income can be expected as a result, then it is realistic to budget for a 40 percent increase in income. On the other hand, to budget the same figure for salaries as that budgeted the previous year and expect to retain the same employees when the cost of living has been on the rise for the past twenty years is not being realistic at all.

The Budget Should Be Flexible

It is important to remember that the budget is a guide and plan, and plans are subject to change. If unforeseen circumstances occur, the budget must be flexible enough to allow for change. It is not unusual for program priorities to change even

within the life span of a fiscal-year budget, and if that occurs, the director should be able to transfer funds from one budget item to another. Though caution should be exercised in allowing this option, it is often to the overall benefit of an operation to make it available. Sometimes, however, legislation or policy established by the funding source restricts such flexibility. For example, funds provided for services, equipment, or facilities for the handicapped are restricted to that specific use.

The Budget Should Be Prepared Early

A more effective budget will materialize if those who are responsible for budget preparation allow adequate time. Budget preparation ordinarily requires thorough analysis, concentrated thought, and involvement of several people, and unless adequate time is allowed for such thoroughness, some item of importance is likely to be overlooked. Too often budgets are presented to reviewing and approving authorities with incremental increases for every budget item, and the director is unable to plausibly explain how the inflated request will meet program goals. Responsible reviewers have an obligation to require justification for funding requests, and budget administrators are often unprepared for the review because they were too rushed to meet the budget deadlines.

The Budget Needs to Be Easily Understood

Another quality of a good budget is that when presented it is easily understood. Some administrators seem to find security in complexity and develop budgets that only accountants can understand. Such a practice is absurd! The budget is a tool of communication, and if the message cannot be understood by the receiver, no communication transpires.

Insight through Illustration

A new department head asked his dean and several other department heads to explain how the formula-driven budget of the institution worked. Most had some knowledge about the value of certain formula ingredients, but none had an adequate understanding to make the budget work for his or her department. The new department head went to the director of operations with the same question. He asked if the department head had three or four hours for the indoctrination. It took almost that much time for the explanation, but it was worth the effort. For three years, the department head was able to play their budget game by making a few changes in class scheduling that created the necessary ingredients for increased department funding according to the formula. Until the other department heads became inquisitive as to how his department was getting an unusually large portion of the school budget, funds were plentiful.

Simplicity is a key word to remember when developing a budget. A properly prepared budget is not difficult to understand.

BUDGET DANGERS

Budgets can be a hindrance instead of a valuable tool of planning and control if enterprise and institutional authorities lose sight of budgeting purposes. *One common danger is that program goals may become less important than budgetary goals.* Directors and their administrative superiors must not lose sight, in their zeal for staying within the budget, of the primary importance of program and enterprise objectives.

Insight through Illustration

A few years ago when the officials at one college were forced to resurface the running track because of its eroded and unsafe condition, a decision was made at the upper administrative level to resurface with a rubberized asphalt product instead of a quality synthetic surface. The reason for resurfacing with a less than adequate product was that the department budget fell 40 percent short of the cost of the quality surface. At the time, the manufacturer of the synthetic surface was offering a 50 percent reduction in cost of installation to have its product at a strategic location and showplace in the area. Institutional funds were available for the better surface, but officials held rigidly to the budget limits of the department. The asphalt surface was barely adequate for two years. At that time the rubber ingredient began to break down, as predicted, because of the heat and other weather conditions. Five years later a new synthetic surface was installed at a cost of 300 percent more than the original introductory offer.

Overbudgeting is another hindrance to effective budgeting practices. Program administrators are deprived of the needed freedom to manage their departments when budget lines are established in such specific detail that flexibility is lost. Over-budgeting results from an overzealous effort to control spending by the person directly responsible for the financial operation.

Budgeting by precedent can also create some real problems for efficiency and goal achievement. Some budget makers look at past budgets and carry certain past expenditures over into the new budget as a minimum line without examining the need to readjust for updated programming. Some budgeting authorities also have been known to pare down every budget request by a certain percentage without reexamining the standards and factors by which planned action is translated into numerical terms. When the people making the budget requests learn that this malpractice is being followed, they simply inflate their requests to allow for the standard cutback to get the realistic funds needed. Under such circumstances, the budget becomes a shelter under which a lazy and inefficient administrator can hide.

Inflexibility may be the greatest hurdle for conscientious directors to overcome. Sometimes income will exceed or fall short of expectations, as will the cost of certain budgeted items. When that occurs, the manager must be permitted to adjust up, down, or crosswise in directing expenditures toward the accomplishment of objectives. Numbers in a budget should not be viewed as concrete and unchangeable.

PREPARING AND PRESENTING THE BUDGET

The principles we have just discussed should be followed in each phase of preparing and presenting the budget. The budget preparation and presentation process itself consists of certain identi-fiable steps, regardless of the budget system or format being followed. We will briefly describe these steps.

Budget Preparation

Budget preparation consists of five steps: (1) reviewing organizational goals; (2) analyzing present and alternative programs; (3) deciding upon program status for the new budget request; (4) estimating costs; and (5) writing the budget request.

Reviewing Organizational Goals It is surprising how many budgets are prepared from previous ones without closely reexamining the organization's purposes for existing. Complacency and mediocrity are inevitable unless new goals and challenges are established and pursued. To pursue new projects requires adequate funding, and adequate funding should be granted only when justification reasonably assures goal achievement. To do otherwise would be as foolish as blindfolding a basketball player, putting him on a court, and telling him to practice his shooting techniques.

Analyzing Present and Alternative Programs Every existing program must be reviewed by talking with those directly involved to determine the cost-effectiveness of each program relative to the overall objectives. If the program is to continue, the adequacy of the existing equipment and supplies must be appraised. Program expenses can be expected to vary from year to year. From the onset of budget preparation, the director needs to give consideration to programming and funding alternatives. To do otherwise represents incomplete planning and could prove embarrassing later when the director is asked to justify the budget request. Conscientious authorities who make decisions on budget requests can be relied upon to inquire as to whether alternative approaches could meet the same objectives at a lower cost.

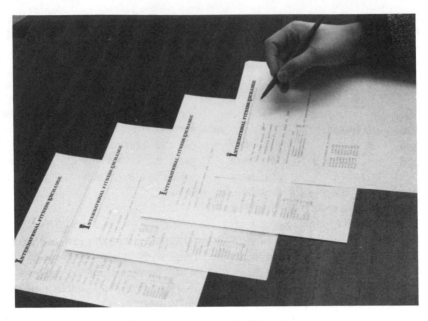

The budget is prepared in light of goals.

Deciding upon Program Status for the New Budget Request   Each year decisions must be made about which programs to continue or terminate and whether or not new programs will be added. These decisions will be based on the results of the assessment conducted in the previous step, the anticipated funding level of the new budget, and the relative value of each program in fulfilling organizational goals. Even if the funding level is not increased, worthy new programs or projects may sometimes be undertaken by significantly modifying and adjusting the budget without dropping existing programs.

Estimating Costs   After programming decisions are made, the budget administrator must attach costs to each line item of each program. Even if the planning-programming method of budgeting is not used, the cost for each program must be considered separately and each line for each program developed. Items such as salaries, supplies, equipment, travel, insurance, printing and dupli-

cation, utilities, and facility maintenance are typical expenditures associated with most projects. Cost figures for each item are estimated by analyzing past expenses in light of present conditions.

Writing the Budget Request   By the time the director gets to this final step, the most difficult tasks of budget preparation are past. Putting the budget into the formal request format is usually a matter of completing a standard form that has been adopted by the organization for all departments to use. Specific instructions and guidelines normally accompany the budget form.

Budget Presentation

No single procedure for budget presentation is common to all organizations and agencies. Sometimes formal budget presentations are scheduled and are open to anyone who wishes to attend; at other times directors may be asked to present

Justification is needed for high-cost equipment.

and justify the budget in a closed session with only a review board present; and under other circumstances, directors are asked only to present their budget requests to their immediate supervisor, who takes the request to the next level for approval, modification, or denial. The nature of funding sources and the amount of interest and concern the people supplying the funds have in the programs usually determine the procedures for the presentation.

Whether the presentation is before a large audience in a public hearing, before a review board, or only before the administrator at the next level, certain guidelines should be observed. Many times the quality of the presentation and the thoroughness of the presenter are more instrumental in getting a budget approved than the worthiness of the budget itself. The director should follow these guidelines in presenting the budget:

- Prepare the budget without error exactly as the instructions specify.

- Provide copies of the budget request to those in authority well in advance of the formal review.

- Be thoroughly prepared and knowledgeable about every aspect of the budget before the review hearing.

- Be confident and decisive during the delivery.

- Use a well-organized, simple, and logical format in the verbal presentation.

- In an open hearing or board review it may be appropriate to have present one or more supporters of the budget (students, athletes, parents, staff members, or clientele) who are prepared to speak on certain aspects of the budget and whose opinions would be respected by the review team.

- Maintain a mature and composed presence throughout the review session regardless of the nature of the inquiries. Some present may attempt to draw the director into an argument and even be insulting.

THE BUDGET IN ACTION

After the budget has been approved, the implementation phase of financial management continues for the entire budget cycle and requires a significant portion of the director's attention. The budget does not drive itself, and unless properly attended to, can cause administrators as much grief as any of the other administrative tasks. Failing to administer financial matters as higher-level authorities deem appropriate has been the basis for replacement of many directors. Consequently, anytime a person is authorized to be the steward of funds belonging to someone else, it behooves that person to be open and meticulously accurate in carrying out that responsibility.

Accounting Systems

Maintaining control over the budget is an essential requirement in financial accountability, and a systematic approach must be adopted that will provide an up-to-date awareness of budget status. In keeping with one of the stated objectives of an effective budgeting system—that is, to serve as an instrument of control—a good budgeting system must be complemented by a good accounting system. The accounting system tracks the acquisition (income) and consumption (expenses) of the resources identified in the budget.

Several methods of accounting are commonly found in organizations. The nature and complexity of the agency and/or the preference of the person ultimately in control normally determines which system is adopted.

Cash Accounting System   The cash accounting system tracks income as cash is received and expenses as payment is made. The tracking of transactions is related to the disbursement or receipt of cash regardless of the time period in which the commitments are made. As with any accounting system, a cash accounting method

documents transactions that occur during a set period of time, typically a fiscal year. It is considered to be the simplest of the various accounting systems.

Accrual Accounting System   Unlike the cash accounting method, an accrual accounting system tracks transactions on the basis of the period to which the transaction applies and not when the transaction takes place. For example, if equipment is ordered against the resources budgeted in one fiscal year, the transaction is reflected in the books as a commitment of resources in that year regardless of when the equipment is received and payment made. The accrual accounting system thus does not consider the exchange of cash as the mechanism that triggers an accounting transaction.

Cost Accounting System   While not constituting an accounting system in the same context as a cash accounting or an accrual accounting system, the cost accounting system is a concept that merits explanation. A cost accounting system attempts to identify the components that make up the cost of delivering a product or service. Typically, labor, materials, and overhead are the components that are evaluated in a cost accounting system. A cost accounting system is particularly useful in cost analysis studies when one wishes to assess the relative worth of continuing to offer a service or deliver goods in a given manner. It has less application in a service-oriented concern than in a manufacturing concern.

Audits

Audits are a form of evaluation that ensures the financial operation of an organization is being conducted according to regulations, policies, and good business practices. Contrary to the belief of some, audits are not conducted for the purpose of keeping the director or employees honest; still, if there is reason to believe that financial irregularities exist or that some employee is misusing funds, a special audit may be conducted to investigate that suspicion.

Audits may be compared to personnel evaluations in that the intent is to improve performance. They should not be viewed as an investigative process for the purpose of finding something wrong. They are a routine procedure conducted periodically, and the results usually tend to reinforce the position that the financial procedures are appropriate for achieving the organizational goals. Audits may be internally or externally conducted. External audits are more common for governmental or tax-supported agencies such as schools. Officials have a responsibility to assure the public that tax monies are being used as intended.

PROGRAM FUNDING

Physical education programs receive a funding base from the school's general fund. This base may range from barely adequate to very satisfactory for conducting a required and/or elective activity program. But seldom do tax dollars provide the income necessary for the program quality desired by highly motivated physical education teachers. Therefore, identifying and raising more funds for such items as resistance-exercise and testing equipment and facilities can make a difference in program quality and level of student morale.

Athletics programs must depend more heavily upon funding sources other than the general fund. Most states and school districts place rigid restrictions on the use of tax monies for interschool athletics; thus, outside funding sources are an absolute necessity for their conduct. Equipment, supplies, travel, facilities, officials' salaries, scholarships, and conference fees are some of the items that must be paid for by nontax funds.

Health and wellness programs for profit and nonprofit organizations are expected to be largely or totally self-supporting. Commercial and private agencies are motivated toward a profit and are characterized by aggressive marketing efforts. Unless these enterprises make a profit, they will not be operating for long. The same goes for the fitness and wellness programs of nonprofit organizations such as the YWCA and YMCA. Although gifts and endowments constitute a significant portion of their incomes, those donations are restricted to operating programs for the underprivileged and needy, such as summer camps for the mentally and physically handicapped.

Corporate fitness programs may be more like school athletics departments than like the other organizations listed. Most corporations that operate fitness and wellness programs provide the site, sometimes the basic facility, and they may pay certain salaries, but costs of operating and facility expansion are expected to come from some kind of fee structure.

Memberships and Fees

The basic income for public and private fitness enterprises is generated by membership and usage fees. In exchange for paying a fee, the customer or member is granted certain privileges and services by the organization. Members of an athletics booster club, in a like manner, may join the club and donate a specified amount, and in exchange be allowed to attend athletic contests and participate in some social functions without additional charge. A similar option is usually available for members of commercial or corporate enterprises. The advance fee structure is preferred to the per-use fee structure, because the organization can plan with more confidence when it has a guaranteed income paid or committed in advance. The practices of per-use clientele are unpredictable and do not offer a sound base for planning. For example, only a small percentage of the people who join a fitness center continue with their good intentions for more than a few weeks.

Fun-run income may be a needed supplement to general funding.

On the athletics scene, attendance at contests drops off drastically if the team is not a consistent winner.

For years, sports clubs and athletics departments have depended on memberships and fee structures for income. More recently, physical education and recreational sports departments have realized that they are able to offer a more effective program when fees are charged for services and privileges that extend beyond the curriculum. For example, towel and locker fees and charges for using facilities before and after school may be appropriate and can be a significant funding source.

Regardless of whether the organization is a school or profit-making enterprise, it is essential that strict policies regarding fees be established and followed. The philosophy of the organization

must be reflected in these operational guidelines. Collection, use, and accounting techniques must be in accordance with the regulations of state and local governments.

Fund-raising Events and Activities

Fund-raising events and activities such as weekend competitions, raffles, bake sales, door-to-door sales, and camps and clinics can be a good source of funds for activity-based programs. Weekend competitions, for instance, are a relatively new and often used activity for generating additional funds for clubs, departments, and nonprofit enterprises. Walk-a-thons, jog-a-thons, lift-a-thons, fun runs, and tennis and racquetball tournaments have become means of support for many groups that sometimes struggle for existence. It

Table 11.1 *Fund-raising Activities*

Activity	Considerations
A-thons (swim-a-thon, bike-a-thon, cartwheel-a-thon, dance-a-thon, dunk-a-thon)	• Require little initial cash outlay. • Use professionally printed pledge cards for credibility. • Set minimum dollar or cents amount per lap or repetition. • Collect pledges and send thank you's within a few days of the event.
Door-to-door sales (candy sales, magazine sales, cookie sales)	• Usually earn 30–50 percent profit on retail cost through fund-raising organizations. • Divide sales areas into sections to avoid numerous sellers calling on one residence or business. • Ages twelve to fourteen most effective in door-to-door sales. • Promote peer competition. Give a prize for most money raised.
Raffles/lotteries	• Check with authorities for legal ramifications. • Solicit donated prizes from local merchants. • Set minimum number of tickets to be sold by each member. • Offer cost of ticket refund by printing coupons good for cost of ticket off pizza, dinner, etc., through local merchants.
Bake sales Car washes Rummage sales Auctions Camps and clinics	• Use busy location to generate walk-up/drive-by sales. • Advertise with flyers, posters. • Minimal cost to organization. • Need committed members for labor and donations. • Teams can sponsor clinics at own gyms and fields for local youths to learn sport skills. • Greater profits (requiring greater expenditure) earned by week-long or weekend camps at distant location. • Big-name athlete will generate greater interest and profit.

```
ACTUAL COSTS FOR FUND-RAISING PROGRAM

Printing of brochures . . . . . . . . . . . . . . .   $_____

Preparing mailing (___ hours @ $___/hr) . . . . . . .   $_____

Postage . . . . . . . . . . . . . . . . . . . . . .   $_____

Printing thank-you letters . . . . . . . . . . . .   $_____

                              TOTAL COSTS      $_____
                              TOTAL INTAKE     $_____
```

Figure 11.3 *Sample Cost Accounting Form*

is not unusual for two hundred or more participants to pay a fee of from $10 to $40 each to compete in one of these weekend competitions. We don't need an advanced course in math to realize why these events have become so popular: significant income results from most. As long as the masses are physically and competitively oriented, this will continue to be a worthwhile type of fund-raising effort. Table 11.1 lists various types of fund raisers and some considerations for each.

The fund raiser should be prepared for in a step-by-step manner. Present income from all sources should be reviewed and realistic goals should be set for the amount of money to be raised. Bearing in mind that it takes money to make money, the budget for the fund-raising program should be examined to determine whether it is realistic. Costs for printing, mailing, and labor should be included. Decisions should be made as to whether employees will be paid overtime for extra work or whether all work will be voluntary. Writing down all expenditures will help to determine actual total costs (Figure 11.3). Only when all costs are weighed against the income derived can the worthiness of the fund-raising program be truly evaluated. Once a course of action is decided upon, the responsible person should make sure that sufficient funds and willing organizers, leaders, and staff are available to execute the plan. Staff should be divided into committees to handle the variety of tasks at hand and so that people can work in the area in which they are most comfortable, behind the scenes or up front. Ones with many business contacts would be of most advantage in generating sponsorships, whereas detail-oriented staff members might prefer to handle accounting or writing assignments.

The methods presented here for generating increased funding for sports and activity organizations are only a sampling of the myriad means available. Often, the most successful fund raisers are those that are original and create enthusiasm for all involved. Campus organizations are constantly coming up with innovative fund-raising ideas. One campus group at a small college chose an obscure holiday, Sweetest Day, to sell roses. The flower idea was chosen because the family of one member owned a flower shop and agreed to obtain the flowers at wholesale cost. This fresh idea generated so much interest (and money!) that seven years later, Sweetest Day is celebrated as fervently as Valentine's Day on that campus.

When planning any fund raiser, but especially an event such as a banquet or "a-thon," every VIP possible should be invited. A noted personality as guest speaker will help draw a larger crowd for banquets or other events. Accoutrements such as programs, tickets, decorations, sound systems, and prizes should not be skimped on. Printers, merchants, and rental agencies should be approached about donating equipment, printing, sound systems, prizes, refreshments, raffle/auction items, and any other needs for the event. All sponsors should be acknowledged with a letter of appreciation and, if appropriate, in the program or verbally at the event itself.

Concessions

Concessions can be a significant funding source when properly managed. Concession stands have been a fixture at athletic contests for years, but their full potential as a means of supplemental income has come into focus only within the past few years. Concessions are still poorly managed in too many situations.

Successful concessionaires have learned to cater to the spending habits, appetites, and desires of the American public, who are eager to buy caps, shirts, and other items with a logo stenciled on them. Some sports enthusiasts bring as much to spend to the scene of the activity as they pay for the main attraction. Concessionaires can take advantage of those habits and make customers happy while making a profit. At special events, fair trade pricing yields to demand pricing. People have money and want to spend it, and those who help them can make a profit.

Concessions may be directly administered by the organization, or they may be let out to professional concessionaires. There are advantages and disadvantages to both methods. Most profit-making enterprises do their own selling, as do many athletics departments. More profit can be realized by this method if the manager gives proper attention to the function. A well-trained and reliable staff is a prerequisite for a fully successful concession operation. If the director of operations or athletics does not have adequate time or staff to oversee the concession function, it will be more profitable to let a specialist take charge of it in return for a fixed percentage of the gross sales.

The advantages of an entity's administering its own concessions are twofold: (1) with a reliable system, a greater profit can be realized, and (2) full control over that aspect of the program will probably give patrons a more positive image of the organization. A business person motivated only by profit may be less sensitive to patrons' feelings. The major advantage of letting a professional concessionaire handle the selling is that the director is relieved of a major headache that he or she may not have the time or staff to deal with.

Contributions and Endowments

Directors should be aware of the potential funding that can come from interested persons or organizations. An unlimited number of people usually are willing to donate from $25 to $200 annually to a physical education or athletics department or a nonprofit community agency such as the YMCA or a cardiac research center. A few will contribute up to a million dollars or more if properly motivated.

The key to this source of funding is motiva-tion through involvement and/or recognition. Whether an individual or organization donates $25 or $250,000, the director must make sure that the donors are involved in such a way that they feel they play a very significant role in the program. Strength in a program can be attained by satisfying a large number of people; therefore, the ego involvement of several $25 contributors can be just as important as providing satisfaction to a few who provide much larger gifts. Program administrators need either to spend a portion of their time keeping contributors informed and happy or to hire a good public relations person for that purpose.

Most institutions can locate at least one or two individuals or agencies willing and able to make a sizable contribution to a program if the proper persuasive techniques are used. Gifts in the range of a million dollars or more usually are given in the form of an endowment or for a special project such as a new facility bearing the name of the donor. Large gifts often carry with them certain restrictions. For example, the gift may be given on the condition that matching funds be obtained or provided, or the gift may be a building or property given for a specific purpose without consideration for daily maintenance and operating costs. The recipient must be careful when accepting restricted gifts, and must make sure that important program goals are not compromised when accepting them.

Grants

Grants have become such a significant source of income for schools and nonprofit organizations that it is a common hiring practice to investigate the prospective director's grant-writing ability and experience. Contrary to the managerial concerns of a few years ago, today's administrators must keep aware of available grants by constantly reviewing professional, government, and foundation publications. Government agencies that

Taking regular inventory shows what you have and what you need.

provide grants in physical education, fitness, and sports include the President's Council on Physical Fitness and Sports, the U.S. Department of Health and Human Services, and Action (a funding source for seniors). Aquatic programs for arthritics, par-courses for the handicapped, and sports camps for youth are examples of programs funded by government or private foundation grants.

Bond Issues

Bonds are a primary source of funds for capital outlay expenditures. Municipalities and institutions of learning commonly take advantage of this funding source. Authorization for a bond issue is subject to a legislative act or public vote. The total debt that any one municipality or system of education can accrue at one time is limited by state law. The limits for each state are different. Student governments at colleges and universities have exercised this option for building sports centers and activity complexes.

PURCHASING SUPPLIES AND EQUIPMENT

The specific procedures for purchasing supplies and equipment vary from organization to organization, and most large operations have detailed directions for making purchases. Nevertheless, some general guidelines apply and should be recognized for all purchases whether the organization is large or small.

Taking Inventory

The purpose of taking inventory is twofold. First, it is an act of accountability that ensures that equipment and supplies are being properly maintained and are located where they best can be used as organizational goals are being pursued. Second, it is the basis for purchasing new items for the ensuing year. We will focus on the latter purpose here.

Before new equipment and supplies are purchased, an inventory of present equipment must

INVENTORY CHECKLIST

Activity _____ Location _____ Date _____

Completed by: _____

ITEM	CONDITION					Total usable	Number needed	Date ordered	Date received
	New	Good	Fair	Discard	Reconstruct				

Figure 11.4 *Equipment Inventory Form*

be taken. The formula for purchasing is quite simple: Needs for next year are determined, and equipment on hand is subtracted from that figure (needs − number on hand = number to purchase). That logic is so simple it may seem silly to even mention it; however, one of the major errors directors make in purchasing is to let last year's requisitions determine the number of equipment items they order for the upcoming year. Their practice is to pull out last year's requisitions from the files, change the dates, and submit them again. There is no rationale for such a practice, and directors who follow it are irresponsible.

Although purchasing should be a continuous function to meet needs as they arise, most equipment and supplies are ordered as soon as the budget for the new fiscal year becomes effective. Before then, those directly responsible for maintaining the equipment and supplies should update the inventory and submit it to the director. A sample inventory checklist is illustrated in Figure 11.4.

Purchasing Considerations

When purchasing equipment and supplies, directors must make every effort to get the most and the best for the organizational dollar. In fulfilling

REQUEST FOR QUOTATION
THIS IS AN INQUIRY,
NOT AN ORDER.

VENDOR: PLEASE QUOTE PRICES ON ITEMS LISTED. NOTE DELIVERY REQUIREMENTS, AND STATE FIRM DELIVERY DATE

DATE	P.O. NO./REQN. NO.	REPLY DUE	DELIVERY REQUIRED BY	QUOTATION NO.
5/29/91		6/21/91	30 days ARO	RFQ P90/67

VENDOR: SEE REVERSE SIDE FOR
QUOTATION INSTRUCTIONS.

			Unit Price	TOTAL
5	EA	ARMLESS STACKING CHAIRS Weight: 12 pounds each Seat dimensions: 32H x 19W x 24D Finish: polished chrome Fabric: 40%-nylon, 30% acrylic, 30% olefin 3M Scotchguard REF: CHAIRWORLD #7737 FABRIC: CHATHAM #C605, "HONEY" MANUFACTURER _____ MODEL _____ FABRIC _____		

VENDOR—MUST COMPLETE THIS INFORMATION FOR FINAL CONSIDERATION.

DATE DELIVERY PROMISED	TERMS OF PAYMENT	DATE OF QUOTATION	
			[ ] F.O.B. Destination [ ] Prepay Freight and add to invoice Estimated Freight Costs: _____

If freight is to be paid by Cal Poly, please estimate costs and note on quotation.

REPLY TO:
PURCHASING DEPARTMENT
CALIFORNIA POLYTECHNIC STATE UNIVERSITY
SAN LUIS OBISPO,
CALIFORNIA 93407
  X Pat Harris   FAX: (805)756-1279
  ___Mike Johnson   PHONE NO.: 805-756-2231

SIGNATURE AND TITLE OF COMPANY REPRESENTATIVE _____

TELEPHONE NO. _____

FAX No: _____

Figure 11.5 *Sample Bid Request*

this responsibility, they need to realize a balance between the quantity purchased and the quality of the product. Circumstances often dictate a sacrifice in quality to get the quantity required. For example, if an organization needs a hundred dozen towels for next year, and top-quality towels are $25 per dozen, but the same size and brand of towel with minor flaws in the material ("seconds") can be purchased for $12.50 per dozen, the director must decide whether fifty dozen top-quality towels or a hundred dozen of the seconds will best serve the goals of the organization if only $1,250 is budgeted for towels.

Product safety is an overriding consideration that cannot be compromised in purchasing supplies and equipment. For example, racquetball eye protectors that only partially protect should not be chosen over a type that fully protects just because they cost less and meet rulebook requirements.

Competitive Bidding

Most governmental agencies and schools require that purchases exceeding an established dollar figure, such as $200, be subjected to the compet-

BUT COACH, THE SALESMAN ASSURED ME
THEY HAD ONLY **VERY SLIGHT** IMPERFECTIONS!

Product specifications must be in detail.

itive bidding process. Typically, a minimum of three bids from reputable companies is required. The company submitting the lowest bid usually becomes the supplier of the requisitioned product. We say *usually* because most agencies or institutions permit enough flexibility in their purchasing procedures to allow for unusual circumstances. If the low bid is not accepted, a statement explaining why should be required. For example, a fitness center may be purchasing a product that requires frequent servicing, and the company submitting the low bid may be located so far away that it cannot guarantee the service required. In that case, buying from a dealer who can guarantee the service required may be a justifiable reason for buying from someone other than the low bidder. Again, the key consideration is to follow the procedure that is best for the particular program. A sample bid request is illustrated in Figure 11.5.

Writing Specifications Product specifications, written in explicit detail, are an absolute must when the bidding method of purchasing is used. A description specifying the exact color, model, composition, and capabilities needed is suggested. If one loophole is left open, dealers may substitute a product that is to their advantage to sell, even though they know it is not best for the purchaser or what the purchaser intended to buy. The purchaser may be forced to accept an inferior product unless exact specifications are submitted with the requisition.

Buying from Local Merchants Administrators often prefer to buy from local merchants whenever possible. Although buying from local dealers has some advantages, caution should be exercised in the practice. The purchaser must make sure the advantages are for the organization, not for the dealer nor the purchaser personally. The most common advantage is that more efficient and better service is probable, because the local merchant is likely to have more interest in the success of a local program than dealers at a distance.

Some merchants may strongly believe that because they are a patron, an alumnus of the purchasing organization, or a member of its board that the organization has an obligation to buy from them. That is not true. A "you scratch my back and I'll scratch yours" practice can create more problems than a director can control. A sample purchase requisition form is illustrated in Figure 11.6.

Accepting Gifts It may be difficult for a coach or a director to decline the gift of a new set of golf clubs or a portable television set from a company representative, but professional ethics and sound administrative practice require a firm refusal. Sales representatives may insist that there are no strings attached, but the director should not believe for one minute that the gift is not intended to sway business in their direction; and in most cases, it will. Advertising products or activities, such as a pen with the company's name and telephone number, or an invitation to dinner, are offers that are acceptable, because these are ethical selling techniques that all companies use to sell their products.

Figure 11.6 *Sample Purchase Requisition*

Summary of Purchasing Guidelines

The guidelines discussed or alluded to in this section can be summarized as follows:

- Purchasing should be based on program needs after an inventory has been conducted.
- For large purchases, competitive bidding results in getting more for the money.
- Product safety is an overriding consideration when purchasing.
- Purchasing responsibility may be delegated to a competent and interested staff member.
- When purchasing equipment and supplies, service and replacement of purchased items must be considered.
- Items should be purchased well in advance of need.
- Product specifications must be explicitly written.
- Products should be purchased at the lowest cost possible without sacrificing either safety or quality.
- A purchaser should not accept gifts and favors from sellers.
- The needs of the physically challenged should be considered.
- Purchase only from reputable vendors.

KEY WORDS AND PHRASES

Manager's fiscal duties

Budget

Operational budget

Capital outlay budget

Line-item budgeting

Incremental budgeting

Formula funding

Planning-programming budgeting system (PPBS)

Zero-base budgeting (ZBB)

Cash accounting system

Budget preparation

Accrual accounting system

Cost accounting system

Audit

Inventory

Competitive bidding

Inventory checklist

QUESTIONS FOR REVIEW

1. What is a budget?

2. What are the three types of budgets? Explain the differences among them.

3. If an organization's funds are inadequate to meet its goals, what six sources might it look to for additional income?

4. Name five systems of budgeting.

5. List the five stages or steps in budget preparation.

6. Name three accounting systems and describe each briefly.

7. What is the purpose and value of an internal audit?

8. What is the first step in purchasing supplies and equipment?

9. Why is the writing of specifications for purchases so important?

10. What are the advantages and disadvantages of purchasing through local dealers?

11. Name five principles of effective budgeting.

SELF-TEST

Corrected True-False

If the statement is true, mark it T. If the statement is false, mark it F and change it to a true statement by adding or deleting words.

_____ 1. The budget in a very large operation out of necessity becomes a very complicated plan to understand.

_____ 2. A budget is merely a financial plan for meeting the objectives of an organization.

_____ 3. All staff affected by the budget should have an opportunity for input in its formulation.

_____ 4. Exceeding the budget is sometimes an acceptable practice and can be justified.

_____ 5. The primary purpose of an internal audit is to keep the director honest.

_____ 6. The operating budget is oftentimes referred to as the equipment budget.

_____ 7. The crossing over from one budget line to another prohibits growth and is not permitted.

_____ 8. Padding the budget is just one "trick of the trade" and is an accepted practice.

_____ 9. The inventory should be the last step in purchasing procedures.

_____ 10. Building support for your program and budget should begin about two months before budget presentation.

Multiple Choice

_____ 11. Most important criterion for purchasing equipment:
   a. safety and quality
   b. specifications
   c. best bargain
   d. competitive bidding

_____ 12. The best means for getting the most for your money:
   a. buy from big companies
   b. competitive bidding
   c. buy from local dealer
   d. personal negotiating

_____ 13. The most often used accounting method by sports and exercise entities:
   a. cost
   b. actual
   c. cash
   d. accrual

_____ 14. The most commonly used form of budgeting is:
   a. formula
   b. line-item
   c. incremental
   d. PPBS

_____ 15. Regarding the budget, one of the following does not belong with the others:
   a. must be based on facts
   b. should be flexible
   c. needs to be realistic
   d. should be prepared early

CASE 11.1 PLAYING THE BUDGET GAME

Paula Pearce had been serving in her new position as director of health, physical education, intramurals, and athletics at Brent Community College for five months. It was now February, and she had initiated the budget cycle for the following year. Paula noticed during the year that men's sports seemed to be well supplied and equipped, but the physical education, intramural, and women's sports inventory was substandard.

After receiving and reviewing the supply and equipment requests from all head coaches and division coordinators, she saw that the requests from the men's sports coaches were unreasonably high whereas the other budget requests appeared at first glance to be well within reason. Paula talked with Pat Akers, head football coach, and Jerry Keller, head baseball coach, to see if they could offer a reason for the unusually high requests. Jerry's first remark was the only explanation needed. He said, "It was common knowledge among the men's coaches that John Roberts, former director, would take all budget requests and reduce them by 30 percent and approve them at that figure. Therefore, we overestimate our needs intentionally to get what we want."

After the meeting, Paula told her secretary to

call a staff meeting. She began outlining those things that she knew had to be discussed.

Your Response

1. What is the primary issue in this case?
2. What are the problems?
3. What barriers or hurdles may stand in the way of the best solution?
4. What actions are needed?
5. What action guides support the actions you have suggested?

CASE 11.2 PROVIDING THE EXTRAS

The Continental Fitness Corporation decided to open its first fitness center on the West Coast. The corporation had six other centers in various locations in the Midwest, and all were profit-making operations. The president and marketing vice-president spent a good portion of five months in Corydon, a city of fifty-seven thousand residents, getting the new facility ready for operation.

Christie Eliot, who recently had completed her master's degree in fitness management, was hired as the director of the new enterprise. The top-management officials returned to Chicago three weeks after the grand opening and after they were satisfied that Christie had the operation under control. Initial membership enrollments were satisfactory.

Two months after Continental Fitness West opened its doors, Christie surveyed the staff and the members for suggestions on how to improve the services and working conditions. Three suggestions seemed to be worthy of further consideration:

1. The male members suggested that after-shave lotion, shaving cream, razors, and hair spray be provided in the locker and dressing room area.
2. The clients who came from work at midday for their workout requested that sandwiches, fruit, and drinks be made available for sale.
3. The staff suggested that in addition to the after-hours cleaning service, a part-time custodian be hired to keep the facility neat and tidy during the day. The staff were not happy that they had to mop water and spills, pick up trash, and maintain the jacuzzi.

Christie notified company officials of these suggestions, but she was disappointed with the response. They simply stated that these things were not provided at their other establishments, and they did not feel that they could increase membership fees at this time for these provisions. They did tell Christie that if she could come up with an acceptable plan for providing these extras, she could add them. Christie felt strongly that the suggestions were good ones, and she retired to her office to consider what she should do.

Your Response

1. What is the primary issue in this case?
2. What are the problems?
3. What barriers or hurdles may stand in the way of the best solution?
4. What actions are needed?
5. What action guides support the actions you have suggested?

BIBLIOGRAPHY

Austin, L. Allan, and Logan M. Cheek. *Zero-Base Budgeting*. New York: AMACOM, 1979.

Berg, Rick. "Shaking the Money Tree." *Athletic Business* 15 (March 1991): 23–28.

Bronzan, Robert. "Student Fees: The New College Facility Funding Source." *Athletic Business* 8 (March 1984): 18–22.

Bucher, Charles. *Management of Physical Education and Athletic Programs*. 9th ed. St. Louis: Mosby, 1987.

Bullaro, John J., and Christopher Edginton. *Commercial Leisure Services: Managing for Profit, Service and Personal Satisfaction*. New York: Macmillan, 1986.

Cohen, Andrew. "Concessions Come of Age." *Athletic Business* 15 (May 1991): 61–64.

Dougherty, Neil J., and Diane Bonanno. *Management Principles in Sport and Leisure Services*. Minneapolis: Burgess, 1985.

"Has the 'Fitness Boom' Gone Bust?" *Athletic Purchasing and Facilities* 7 (July 1983): 13–16.

Horine, Larry. *Administration of Physical Education and Sports Programs*. 2d ed. Dubuque, IA: William C. Brown, 1991.

How to Do It Series #6: Fund Raising for Local Sports Organizations. Centre for International Sports Management.

"How to Make Your Concession Operation Pay Dividends." *Athletic Business* 8 (September 1984): 40ff.

Lopiano, Donna A. "New Ideas for Promotion and Fund-Raising in Non-Revenue Sports." *Athletic Purchasing and Facilities* 7 (October 1983): 14–19.

McKenzie, William. "Money Woes? Here Are 10 Golden Rules for Fund Raisers." *Athletic Business* 9 (August 1985): 20.

Olson, John R. "Improving Your Fund-Raising Sales." *Athletic Purchasing and Facilities* 6 (July 1982): 28–33.

———. "Is Poor Equipment Management Costing You?" *Athletic Purchasing and Facilities* 7 (September 1983): 42–46.

Palmisano, Mike. "Fundraising Ideas That Really Work." *Athletic Business* 8 (November 1984): 34–35.

VanderZwaag, Harold J. *Sport Management in Schools and Colleges*. New York: Wiley, 1984.

12

Marketing the Activity-Based Program

*The process of promoting is the power to persuade plenty
of prospects to purchase your product at a profit.*

Mikki Williams

Chapter Objectives

*After reading this chapter and completing the exercises,
you should be able to:*

1 Describe the scope of marketing

2 List the five basic components of the marketing mix

3 Delineate the questions that market research seeks to answer and suggest possible data sources

4 Discuss the difference between core and peripheral products or services

5 Discuss considerations of place from a marketing angle

6 Name and describe at least six pricing methods

7 List and explain the basic types of promotion as well as the steps involved in developing a promotion plan

8 Discuss the importance of public acceptance of a product or program

9 List and explain the steps in the consumer adoption sequence

10 Discuss the role of the administrator in marketing

In the past, if someone provided a needed product or service, as the only doctor or grocery store in town did, there was little need for marketing. When consumers needed the service or wanted the product, they knew where to find it. Today, however, with stiff competition in all areas, a working knowledge of marketing is not only good for business but necessary for the survival of profit and nonprofit organizations.

The term *marketing* is often misunderstood and misused. It does not mean just advertising, recruiting, selling a product, or being nice to everyone. It is these factors and more. In reality, marketing includes all the activities involved in producing and moving goods and services from the producer to the consumer. Stoddart (1982) defines sports marketing as "the total management of sports activity that directs the flow of events, services, and goods from the sport to satisfy the needs of an existing or potential public that has been identified." The cost of aggressive marketing may be considered too high by some, but the cost of poor marketing is even higher.

As consumer income increases, a smaller percentage of total personal income is required for the basic necessities of food, clothing, and shelter. This leaves more money for leisure spending, and vast numbers of businesses have sprung up to offer a variety of opportunities for such spending. In this climate, a business must operate on a marketing concept, meaning it must cater to the wants and needs of the consumer. In this chapter we explore the various dimensions of marketing as it relates to the activity-based program.

THE MARKETING MIX

Marketing a service or activity-based program differs slightly from marketing a product like a candy bar or an automobile. But overall, the same basic components of marketing apply. These basic marketing components are (1) product, (2) place,

(3) price, (4) promotion, and (5) public. The "product" offered by an activity-based enterprise is actually a program, service, or event, but the same marketing considerations apply. Mullins (1983) terms the distribution component "place," and refers to the first four elements of sports marketing as "the four P's." Stoddart (1982) adds a fifth element, timing, to the marketing mix. We have expanded the idea of timing to encompass other considerations.

The marketing mix can be considered as a set of tools used by a producer or a provider of a service to secure and increase sales volume. Although we will discuss each element individually, it is important to remember that these components are all part of an integrated whole, and each element must be used to balance the other parts of the marketing mix.

The basis of any marketing effort is market research. Such research should inform every part of the marketing mix, so we will discuss market research before turning to a detailed look at each of the five basic marketing components.

MARKET RESEARCH

The first step in any marketing effort is market research. If a business wants to meet the needs of the consumer, that business must first determine what those needs are and what its resources are for meeting them. Some areas to research are suggested by the following questions:

- What is the firm capable of offering (labor, funding, other resources)?
- What competition will it face?
- What means are available for program testing and research?
- How will the program or service function?
- Who will the consumers be, and what is their motivation to buy?

- How will the program or service be priced and promoted?
- How will the program or service be packaged (this includes consideration of facility design and location)?
- If the program is seasonal, what will carry the organization through the off season?
- What long-range trends can be predicted?
- What is the market potential of the program or service?

The Scientific Method

Market research should be based on the scientific method of inquiry, which is characterized by objectivity (the absence of bias), organized and systematic inquiry, maximum care and accuracy, and control. Consulting an unbiased outside opinion will provide clearer thinking and promote objectivity.

American philosopher John Dewey formulated a list of the five steps of the scientific method of inquiry (Clarke and Clarke, 1984): (1) perceive that a problem exists; (2) identify the cause of the problem; (3) formulate a hypothesis or plan of action to solve the problem; (4) expand and develop the plan of action; and (5) test the plan by experimentation and observation. This approach is frequently used by large companies to develop new products. Before launching a new product on the market, companies usually test market it in limited regions to observe the market response and gauge market potential. All organizations should use this approach. For example, an organization that wanted to develop a corporate fitness program might proceed as follows: (1) Realize that many people's health care costs are excessive; (2) identify poor fitness and nutrition as a probable cause of high medical costs; (3) plan a corporate fitness program with nutrition and exercise components; (4) open a corporate fitness center; and (5) track health care costs of participants versus nonparticipants in the program.

Data Sources

Various sources of data are available to the researcher. In many cases, organizations or individuals may have already collected and compiled data for the researcher to draw on. These secondary sources should be used whenever possible. A good place to start looking for these secondary sources is in the library. Often university libraries have a greater selection of professional journals and reports to offer than do public libraries. Other secondary sources include census data, business papers, university research reports, business directories, professional association reports, and government reports. The researcher can look up material by subject or title in the card catalog. Bibliographies often list sources that may be helpful. Indexes and guides such as the *Reader's Guide to Periodical Literature,* the *Education Index,* and the *Public Affairs Information Service* list sources of data. Of course, the librarian is a very good starting point if the researcher has no idea of where to begin.

If the information needed is not available from some secondary source, then the researcher must gather data himself or herself by such means as surveys, questionnaires, and "man on the street" interviews. In the case of doing market research for a corporate fitness program, the logical starting place would be company records, to determine how many and what type of employees would likely be interested in participating in the program.

Promotional competitions and giveaways can assist in compiling a consumer list. Each entry form should include blanks for name, address, and phone number so that follow-up contact can be made. In a school setting, lists of alumni, members of fraternities, sororities, and clubs, season ticket holders, and recreational sports participants can be useful in determining who to target for special programs or events.

A variety of sources can be consulted in monitoring marketing trends. Employees, customers,

AS BAD AS SALES ARE HERE, I MIGHT AS WELL BE TRYING TO SELL THESE THINGS IN SOME ISOLATED SPOT LIKE FLAGSTAFF!

Know your market.

suppliers, trade and technical journals, professional associations and societies, colleges and universities, government agencies, conventions, and civic organizations all provide good contacts and opportunities for idea pooling.

Market Position

Positioning is not something you do to the product, it is something you do to the mind of the consumer—creating an image of the product in his or her mind. There are various market positions including:

- the low-cost leader
- the technology leader
- the quality leader
- the service leader

To be the low-cost leader, an organization positions that the goods and/or services they offer are the lowest price around. The explosive growth of warehouse grocery stores and buyer's clubs, such as The Price Club and Sam's Club, indicate that in times or areas of economic hardship, low-price leadership is a good market position. An example of the low-price leader position in sports is a recent promotion by a Southern California

university athletic department. The promotion positions a Saturday football outing as a low-cost, family-oriented activity. The tag line in radio advertisements states that a family of four can attend all home games for as little as $120 for the season. What an entertainment bargain!

The technology leader is exemplified by a company which positions itself on the leading edge of technology. In highly technical fields, such as computers, being the technology leader is often a tenuous position. All it takes is a new invention by a competitor, and the competitor can leapfrog into the lead. A sports rehab center can adopt this position by promoting its highly technical exercise and diagnostic equipment, and the credentials of the staff.

The quality leader positions its product as the finest available to the consumer. Cadillac and Mercedes-Benz position their automobile products as quality leaders. In the field of recreation, many private golf and country clubs utilize this position. Usually the quality leader can command a higher price for its products.

The service leader position entails positioning not the product that is being purchased but the service that goes along with the sale. In retail clothing chains, Nordstrom is the undisputed king of the hill. Nordstrom employees are known for remembering customers' names, writing thank-you notes to buyers, and even going so far as to shop in other stores if a customer cannot find what he or she needs in Nordstrom. Shoppers are very loyal to service leaders. Some shoppers are so taken with the service provided, they call themselves "Nordies." This loyalty creates a return base of customers who are willing to forego the discount clothing outlets in order to receive the personal attention lavished on them at Nordstrom. A recent visit to a hotel and spa in Palm Desert, California, exemplifies the service attitude in sports and recreation. There are numerous hotels and spas in Palm Springs and Palm Desert, so differentiation is key. A day at the spa included being picked up at the door of one's villa and driven by golf cart to the door of the spa. Once inside, each customer was addressed by name by the attendants, who provided all necessities and luxuries such as robes, towels, slippers, toiletries, bottled water, and even various levels of sunscreen for the pool area! Each customer was toured around the spa to become familiar with all amenities, and while the client exercised or utilized other treatments, the staff remained courteous and helpful. This type of pampering was evident in all areas of the resort, from golf courses and restaurants to housekeeping and front desk. Does this resort cost more than a Motel 6? You bet! But the hundreds of guests obviously felt it was worth it.

To develop a market position for a new product, or to recreate a position for an existing product, the administrator needs an idea of the group of consumers that the program will target. The first step is to identify the different marketing segments of the population. These segments are often determined by demographic information such as age, sex, income, residence location, profession, and hobbies. This kind of information is readily available in census form at libraries and from chambers of commerce, local business organizations, magazines such as *Business Week,* professional journals, and national and regional associations like the American Alliance for Health, Physical Education, Recreation, and Dance (AAHPERD); the American College of Sports Medicine; the Association for Fitness in Business; and the National Collegiate Athletic Association. Marketing segments are also determined by psychographic information, which reflects the life-styles, activities, and opinions of the population. This type of information can be obtained from opinion polls and from fitness industry magazines and trade journals. When implementing a new program in an already existing organization, information about how often a facility is used or the amount of money donated to a certain program is useful in determining the new program's market position.

Determining the benefits a consumer can expect to derive from a program or service is also part of developing to a market position. The market researcher needs to find out what aspect of the program, event, or service is most important to the consumer. For example, an ex-football player may attend an athletic contest because of the enjoyment of watching the game, whereas his spouse may enjoy the social contacts made with other spectators. At a YMCA, the reasons for participation in programs can range from a desire for increased personal fitness to enjoyment of competition to a desire for increased social status to enjoyment of the social aspects.

Once this information has been collected, it should be stored in an organized and systematic way. Small organizations may find an index card system adequate. Computers are invaluable in organizing and storing this type of information. A variety of software packages are available for virtually every type of computer. All types of marketing information, from simple address lists to complete demographic files, can be easily sorted, stored, and called up for use.

COMPONENT 1: PRODUCT OR PROGRAM

With the market research completed, development of the product or program—the first component of the marketing mix—may begin. The core product or service should be developed first. In the case of a health club, the core product or service would be the exercise equipment and the life-style counseling offered. The peripheral products or services, such as food or juice bar service, saunas, and locker room facilities, are also a very important part of the product or program as a whole and cannot be neglected. When considering a football bowl game, the game itself is the core product or program, whereas cheerleaders, concessions, and halftime entertainment are the pe-

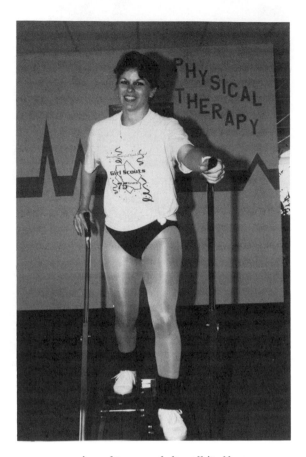

A good program helps sell itself.

ripherals. A core product or service can be promoted on the basis of the peripherals, and often this approach is used when there is heavy competition in the field.

Attention must be paid at this point to program or product image. The image that is created for the program should reflect the image consumers have of themselves. The core and peripheral products or services should be considered and designed to appeal to the consumers' real or perceived needs. All components of the marketing mix come into play in creating an image, as will become clear.

COMPONENT 2: PLACE

The second component of the marketing mix for an activity-based program is place. Where the manufacturer of a retail product must concern itself with distribution—moving the product from the factory to the consumer—the administrator of an activity-based program must focus on the *place* where the contest, program, or service is to be offered. This includes determining the location of a fitness facility, a sports medicine clinic, or the campus location of a school athletics program, and designing the look of the facility.

First impressions die hard, so it is imperative to make the consumer's first impression of a facility a good one. This could mean a cheerful reception area and helpful staff, a clean and well-equipped facility, ample supplies, and foresight to anticipate and eliminate potential problems. Most people do not take special notice of amenities but do note broken equipment, empty towel and soap dispensers, and showers with inadequate hot water.

The look of a facility is like the packaging of a product. A high-tech look for a sports medicine facility or an attractive, comfortable office for the athletics department will help to create good impressions, but the costs must be weighed against the benefits derived. Limited capital and credit may force managers to be more conservative than they would like to be with a facility's look.

COMPONENT 3: PRICE

The third component of the marketing mix is price. Often, price equals quality to consumers. The price established depends upon whom the provider of a program or service wishes to appeal to and the image the organization wishes to project. For example, does the provider want to project the image of a bargain or an expensive and

First impressions are important.

exclusive service? Is the program economical or elegant? Whatever the position taken, the overriding factor in price setting is that consumers must receive greater perceived benefit from the program or service than it costs them. A few factors that can be manipulated in producing consumer satisfaction are the benefits derived from the core product or service, the peripheral product or service, price promotions, and special promotions. Giveaway contests, two-for-one deals, and holiday promotions are common tools used in producing increased consumer satisfaction.

The determination of the consumers' cost must consider all factors of expense to the consumer. For an athletic event, not only the price of admission but also travel time and cost, parking fees, and program costs should be tallied up to ascertain the actual cost to the spectator. For a chic spa, often women feel they must dress in colorful and stylish leotards and workout gear. The cost of aerobic shoes, tights, duffle bags, and other items all add to the real cost of membership. Because consumers rarely add up the cost of these extraneous items, pricing promotions are

effective ways to attract business. If a person sees that she can save fifty dollars on the cost of membership in a new spa, she will not automatically consider the forty or fifty dollars she will end up spending on new exercise shoes. Nor will the alumnus who comes back for a homecoming game consider first the cost of travel and time away from work when he is offered a special package price for his game tickets, dinner, and dance.

Various methods can be used in determining the initial price of new or special services or items. Full-cost pricing is used when the actual cost of production can be determined; then a predetermined percentage or markup is added to the actual cost. This method is useful in pricing a tangible product, such as an exercise bicycle.

Demand pricing is used in a situation where the actual costs of production cannot be determined accurately, or when the difference between production cost and price to consumer is so great that fluctuations in costs do not matter. Demand pricing, as the name implies, depends on the consumer demand for the product. For example, the cost of ski equipment rental depends directly on the season. The cost of the skis, poles, and boots is far exceeded by the income generated by renting each item a number of times.

In margin pricing, a fixed markup is added to the cost of the product. This markup covers operating expenses and profit. The drawback to this type of pricing structure is that operating expenses may fluctuate and cut heavily into the profit. Margin pricing should be used only when the profit is large enough to cover fluctuations in operating expenses. Many products and services are priced in this manner. A set fee is established with the actual costs of materials far below the cost to the consumer. A rehabilitation session at a sports medicine clinic may involve a variety of modalities or medical supplies, but these fluctuations in cost are covered by the fee paid by the patient.

Externally guided pricing is rarely encountered

in sports and physical education settings. A common example is the government control of gasoline prices. In some professional sports, the cost of tickets must be approved by a governing board, but there is no established cost for all organizations.

Customary pricing is, as the name implies, charging the usual and customary price for an item. An everyday example would be the cost of twenty-five cents for a candy bar or fifty cents for a can of soda pop. In the field of sports and fitness, conferences and conventions are often priced in a customary manner.

Prestige pricing is the setting of a high price for the sake of being chic. A good example is the cost of exclusive health spas such as those in Palm Springs, California. This pricing structure is directly related to the establishment of a product image as discussed earlier in this chapter.

Odd pricing is fixing a price at a few cents less than an even dollar amount to give the appearance of a lower cost. Think of how many times you have heard a sales pitch like "your cost is under $50"—usually meaning that it is $49.95.

Skim-the-cream pricing is a method of pricing an item or service high when it is first introduced on the market. This only works when there is little or no competition, and lasts only until competition comes in and eventually forces the price down.

In contrast to skim-the-cream pricing is penetration pricing. This is the establishment of a low introductory price to help a product get its foot in the door against competitors. After a share of the market has been obtained, prices are raised to be more in line with competitors. One drawback to this method is that it can start price wars if competitors lower their prices to prevent loss of consumers to the new company.

In light of the variety of pricing methods possible, it is important to choose carefully which method will work best in a given situation. All influences (cost of production, cost of delivery, demand for product or program, market response to price changes, and competitors' prices) should be considered in deriving the final cost to consumers. Consumers, employees, and professional literature are good sources of information about pricing trends and reactions to changes.

COMPONENT 4: PROMOTION

The fourth component of the marketing mix is promotion. Promotion is often confused with marketing. In fact, promotion is just one part—albeit a very important one—of the total marketing mix. The objective of promotion is to stimulate a primary demand for a *type* of product, and then to generate a secondary demand for a *particular* product.

The key to successful promotion is innovation. Trend setters succeed. Creativity is as important in promotion as it is in product creation and improvement. A creative sales campaign has often made an ordinary object or service into an extraordinary success. Remember the Pet Rock? That is a classic example of taking a nothing and turning it into a million-dollar success story. Another example of good promotion was the market storm of Teenage Mutant Ninja Turtles. This is an example of taking a group of movie characters and turning them into an international sensation. Turtles appeared on lunch boxes, t-shirts, water bottles, and at least a dozen turned up at the authors' residence on Halloween! The core product was the movie, but the peripheral products generated massive revenues.

Consumer Adoption Sequence

When developing a plan for promotion, it is wise to understand how a consumer makes a decision to purchase or utilize a product. This is known as the consumer adoption sequence. By understanding the four steps of consumer adoption, the marketing manager can plan promotional activities to move the consumer more rapidly through the earlier stages and into the last, and in most cases, profitable stage.

The first step in consumer adoption is *awareness*. A customer in this stage will say, "Yes, I know the name," but will not have taken any action regarding the product. This is passive participation on the part of the consumer.

In the second step, *interest,* the consumer begins to see a product as answering a personal need. Here a customer will not only recognize the name but will desire to know more about the product or service.

The customer is moved to action in the third phase, *trial.* Here the customer actually tries the product. This trial can assume many forms. In grocery stores, a trial may involve buying a small package of the desired good, hence the name "trial size." A weekend athlete may try a new type of golf or tennis ball. A trial can also be a telephone call to, or tour of, a fitness or weight management center. In order for a person to reach this third phase, he or she must not only know where to locate the desired product but also be moved to action. This call to action is achieved by coupons, free trial memberships, discounts, free samples, open houses, campus tours, incentives, anything that moves the consumer to take action *now.*

The successful culmination of these steps is *adoption.* This is the time when a customer actually decides to use the product again. That may mean enrolling in a fitness center after a free workout or paying the initial fee for a smoking cessation program. In education, adoption is the enrollment and attendance at a school or university. In the case of tangible goods, adoption would be a repeat purchase of the balls, cereal, shoes, or laundry detergent. Most people are creatures of habit. Think about what toothpaste and deodorant you use—are they often the same brands? What is your favorite fast-food restaurant? By repeatedly patronizing a business or product, a person "adopts" this product as part of his or her life.

In marketing a product, program, or service to influence consumer adoption, an administrator can use four basic types of promotion: advertising, publicity, personal selling, and special promotions. The mark of a successful marketer is the ability to find the right mix of methods to achieve the best promotional results.

Advertising

Advertising is any form of paid media announcement. This is an appropriate form of promotion when contact with a large number of people is desired. The advantage of low cost per person contacted should be weighed against the disadvantage that adjusting the sales approach to individual needs is impossible.

What about the size, type, and number of advertisements to run? The same ad that will catch the eye of a student may do nothing to attract a busy executive's attention. One large, well-timed advertisement is more dramatic and effective than a series of small ads. The cost of a full-page or half-page newspaper ad may initially seem too high, but when weighed against the impact and cost of a series of smaller ads, the larger advertisement may be a better value for the investment.

It is important to consider all forms of media when contemplating advertising. Newspaper or magazine advertising may be the best way to reach one population, whereas a television or radio commercial may reach more and different people and be a better choice for the advertising dollar. In addition to radio, television, and newspapers, other areas should not be overlooked. Magazine advertising can reach specific populations like no other medium can. Many cities and states have their own magazines, such as *Los Angeles Magazine, My Old Kentucky Home,* or *Sunset,* which targets the western United States. A new health club or sports medicine clinic in a city might find that advertising in a regional magazine would yield good results.

Business papers can reach executives and secretaries in specific areas of business. This would be a wise choice for advertising conferences, resorts, or postgraduate educational programs. A few examples of business papers are the *NCAA News* and publications by the Association for Fitness in Business, the American College of Sports Medicine, and the American Alliance for Health, Physical Education, Recreation, and Dance (AAHPERD). Outdoor advertising in the form of billboards can reach many people, but the ad must be eye-catching and convey the desired message in a limited space and number of words. Many arenas and stadiums now sell advertising space that is not only seen by spectators in the facility but also may appear in televised coverage of the contest.

A variety of other publications solicit advertisements. In a school or college community, yearbooks, athletic event programs, and club publications defray the cost of publication by printing advertisements. Businesses can offer special deals to anyone bringing in a ticket stub or program from a particular athletic event.

Direct mail is a growing form of advertising. Individual circulars and announcements can be sent to homes and offices, and also can be included in packets of advertisements that companies now prepare and mail out. The cost of being included in this type of direct mail packet is substantially less than doing individual mailings for a business.

Publicity

Publicity is a second form of promotion. Public relations can be described as planned persuasion, a conscious effort to motivate people, via nonpaid media exposure. Again, there are various avenues to be explored. One of the most overlooked forms of publicity is word of mouth referrals by current customers. Some businesses work very hard to promote this type of publicity, via special offers and events, but a word of mouth referral is,

in most cases, generated by providing quality products and service to existing customers. A wise director will bear in mind that publicity can be negative as well as positive and strive to promote positive publicity through good customer and public relations. In the school setting, physical education, athletics, and recreation will perhaps play a more visible role in publicity than any other departments due to community interest in activities sponsored by these departments. It is imperative to maintain an image of providing a sound and respectable program. This will create interest in the programs and lead people to try, and possibly adopt, the services provided. Athletic events bring people on campus and heighten visibility of a school. Public recreation programs and facilities can provide the same type of publicity for an institution.

Public service announcements on radio and television can be used to promote seminars and speakers. Many newspapers have community sections telling about upcoming events. A good professional working relationship with a reporter or newspaper staff person may entitle the business owner or academic administrator to obtain news coverage of special events and speakers. When a media contact has been cultivated, announcing new equipment, services, or speakers can be as simple as making a phone call.

News releases or articles sent to periodicals should use the proper form for each. If a special news release form is available, it should be used. Often if news releases or articles are submitted in improper format, they get no farther than a waste can. If illustrations or logos are used, they should be simple, easy to print, and eye-catching rather than complex. Using consistent logos on all correspondence will encourage consumer recognition.

If frequent requests are made for information about programs or services, a press/promotional kit should be prepared and stockpiled. This kit should include any pertinent information about the program or service, prices, business address, phone numbers, names of persons to contact, and if applicable, photos, magazine reprints, and endorsements. This system will save time and money spent on individual duplication, packaging, addressing, and mailing, since reduced postal rates are available for mass mailings.

Personal Selling

Personal selling is any person-to-person contact which occurs between a potential or current customer and a member of the organization. Personal selling can take the form of traditional sales such as face-to-face and telemarketing or in the wide range of activities defined as customer service. Traditional face-to-face sales are often the best way to tailor the marketing approach to the exact needs of the consumer. A variety of considerations enter into developing successful selling tactics. The most important aspect is to remember who the sales people are in a business: The sales force is not limited to the person or group of people in charge of marketing. Anyone connected with the organization is a potential salesperson, and every individual should be trained or cultivated to become a good representative of the business. The key to successful selling is in successful communication. Unless an employee knows the needs of the customer, it is impossible to meet those needs.

The Front Line The public's first contact with a business, especially a clinic or club, is often with a secretary or receptionist. This "front line" handles walk-in customers and telephone contacts. These individuals should be trained to make a good first impression so that potential customers are given the image of a professional, competent staff. A great mistake made by many companies is thinking that the front office staff is there only to handle housekeeping tasks such as making appointments, typing, bookkeeping, and screening telephone calls. In reality, the secretaries and receptionists are often the make-or-break factor

in turning a person with a question into a satisfied customer. The people who staff the front office or telephones should be knowledgeable enough about the operation of the business to field most questions from potential customers. Teaching these people about the business is crucial. This can be enhanced by taking them through a rehabilitation or aerobics session, in the case of a clinic or club. In a school setting, the front office staff should be kept abreast of all new information, and in an athletics setting should be knowledgeable about the sport or sports represented by the organization. The potential for increased sales due to the "front liners" should not be overlooked.

Sales Reps Sales representatives are key personnel in recruiting new customers. Many training seminars, books, and courses exist to develop the potential of a sales staff. Administrators should make funds available for continuing education in the field through conventions, seminars, and training workshops. This principle should also apply to other staff and faculty members such as administrators, instructors, and technical crew.

Sales Training Training of salespeople is key to successful marketing. Remembering that everyone in the business is a potential salesperson, it is important to train everyone in two areas: understanding the needs of consumers and understanding the business and its operation. Training in these areas will not only reduce turnover by promoting a positive feeling among the staff, but will serve to reduce errors and misunderstandings, which will mean less supervision for the administrator, allowing more time for important decision making.

Staff training can be accomplished in many ways. Conferences are a good way to inform large numbers of people. A working orientation, such as an apprenticeship or trainee-staff meeting, is useful when the trainee must learn a variety of things to become qualified. Modular or programmed learning is an excellent method of training a small number of individuals in a variety of areas. An informative employee-training manual can serve as a guide for self-paced learning. Choosing the most appropriate form of training is the first step in creating a good sales force.

The Skill of Selling We have discussed who the salespeople are in a business (everyone) and how to cultivate their potential. What remains is to briefly touch on the principles of good selling. Good communication is essential to selling. Listening to the consumer will not only help the salesperson to mold the promotional approach to that consumer but will also alert the salesperson to problems with the program or service and help the organization to plan for improvements or changes in the future.

Persuasion is secondary to good communication. Very few products or services will sell themselves. Someone with knowledge of the product must point out to potential customers why they need the product. This can only be done if the salesperson has listened and asked probing questions of the customer to determine his or her motivations, desires, needs, and wants. Many people cringe when they hear the words "sales" and "persuasion" together. They envision a tenacious used-car seller with a bad suit and fake smile trying to sell a car. Most people love to buy, but few people like to "be sold." A successful sales person will simply enhance the customer's desire to buy and facilitate the transaction from shopper to owner. Often in sales, more emphasis is placed on buying rather than ownership. The advantages of ownership should be stressed. If motivated highly to own, people will find a way to buy.

Sales skills are difficult for some people, but there are numerous books, videos, consulting and training firms which will provide training in the art of persuasion. Often, employees are uncomfortable with the term "sales." They may feel, "I'm a secretary, not a sales person," or "I didn't attend four years of college to become a sales person." Think for a moment about a job interview. That is

nothing more than one person selling his or her talents, and another person selling the organization. Even personal relationships involve selling. People "put their best foot forward" on dates, negotiate where they will eat dinner, and even debate with and persuade a spouse on how to praise or reprimand their children. Once staffers realize that every person sells, every day of his or her life, they should be able to understand the need to represent the organization properly.

The first step in any sale is to qualify the customer. This means that the salesperson must determine if the person with whom he or she is dealing has the ability to pay for services or benefit the program in any other way such as donations and sponsorships. The second step of the sales process is showing the customer the need for the program or service. If the need is not immediately apparent to the potential consumer, persuasion must be used to emphasize the need. Turning the perceived need into a sale is the goal of persuasion.

Closing the sale is a crucial step in the sales process. This is the point when a customer takes the adoption step. The role of the sales person is to facilitate this step by answering questions of financing, need, benefits, and other issues the customer may have. Closing the sale involves reiterating the features of the product and how those features will meet the needs of the customer. These are commonly referred to as *features* and *benefits* in sales language. Persuading the customer may involve overcoming objections, which are really just questions in the mind of the consumer. Once all questions have been addressed, the sales person makes the call to action and consumer adoption occurs.

Unfortunately, in some businesses, managers feel that the sale ends with consumer adoption. That is not true. In fact, it has just begun. The selling must continue after the initial adoption, or the customer may try, and adopt, another product or business. This ongoing selling is the basis of customer service. Customer service is the ongoing selling to a customer that reinforces his or her decision to purchase. Customer service involves any activity or action that enhances customer satisfaction. The section titled Component 5: Public covers various aspects of customer service.

Other Selling Opportunities   Besides using front office staff and sales reps, two other areas for increased personnel selling are often overlooked. The support staff, including custodial, delivery, and repair personnel, can be a great asset or hindrance to a business. Though a repair person is rarely asked a professional question, if by chance a potential customer is given a bad impression of a business by a disgruntled employee, the result could be a questioning of the quality of service provided. One other area that can be successfully cultivated for increased business contacts is public speaking and membership in special civic and professional organizations such as the Lions Club, the Elks Club, athletics booster clubs, the American Red Cross, and AAHPERD. The list of these types of organizations is endless. Not only will the director and staff of an activity-based program that lends speakers benefit from an improved social and professional image, but the contacts made through these organizations can go far to bring in new clients. Members of civic organizations often prefer to patronize businesses represented by people they know from this kind of contact. Mention on radio, television, or in the newspaper of a business name in connection with public speaking engagements is valuable free publicity.

Special Promotions

The fourth category of promotion includes any method not mentioned previously. Some typical examples include giveaways, special campaigns, and fund-raising events or activities. T-shirts, visors, caps, workout bags, and imprinted towels are often given to participants of races, tournaments, and camps. These giveaways not only provide a tangible reward for participation, but

also serve to further promote the event whenever the item is worn or used.

Special campaigns and offers also are an excellent way to encourage consumers to try a new product or service. It is important to limit the length of time on introductory offers. Six months after launching a new product, that product is no longer new, and so the introductory offers should be discontinued and other promotional strategies should be implemented.

Offering a cost break for advance sales will help in projecting the number of participants for a program. Special prices for memberships sold before a health club opens are related to introductory offers. Most athletic events offer price breaks for preseason ticket sales or pre-event sales. Most people have heard pitches like "$10 in advance or $12.50 at the door" in reference to dances, concerts, and sporting events.

Group sales are another area of promotion. Offering a price break for season tickets over per-event pricing and allowing tickets to be sold in blocks of seating to corporations, clubs, or groups will encourage greater attendance. Other ideas are to offer special corporate memberships at a fitness facility or sell a team a contract for preseason evaluation and in-season injury prevention and rehabilitation at a sports medicine clinic. These are just a few of the many group sales tactics currently used.

Community lectures or seminars can be used to generate member and nonmember interest in a service or program. A popular method used by one fitness center is to offer monthly free lectures to explain its program of diet and exercise. A sports medicine clinic might present monthly or quarterly lectures or slide presentations on the prevention and rehabilitation of particular sports injuries. A health club can offer lectures or panel talks on the benefits of circuit weight training or cardiovascular health. A golf or tennis club could present a well-known professional as a guest lecturer/instructor. All who attend these events should be asked to fill out a list with their names and addresses, and this list can be used for follow-up mailings. Attendees can be introduced to the services a business has to offer through short talks, slide shows, tours of the facilities, or whatever method best works into the presentation.

Fund raisers such as raffles and amateur tournaments are frequently used in promoting athletics and generating support. One example of a well-known and successful campaign is the annual Jerry Lewis Telethon to generate funds, interest, and support for muscular dystrophy research.

COMPONENT 5: PUBLIC

The fifth and final component of the marketing mix is the public. Ultimately, the public decides whether a product, program, or service succeeds or fails. Remembering this, the overriding concern of every business must be to keep the customer satisfied. Customer satisfaction is the objective of customer service.

Customer Relations

Once a sale is made, the organization needs to continue to "sell" the customer that his or her decision was a good one. Customer relations, also called public relations, is a long-term process, not a one-time-only contact. Albrecht (1985) identifies four elements found in most successful customer service-centered organizations: (1) a well-conceived strategy for service; (2) delivery systems oriented to customers and employees; (3) customer-oriented front-line people; and (4) an understanding of the customer's moments of truth, those points at which a customer comes into contact with any aspect of the organization and has an opportunity to form an opinion of the quality of service provided. Figure 12.1 shows how these elements combine to form the Service Triangle.

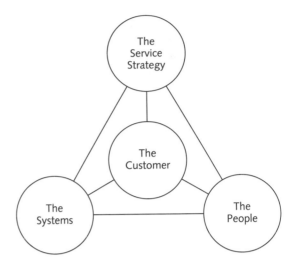

Figure 12.1 *The Service Triangle*

High quality customer service involves problem solving, planning, and teaching and training if necessary. Also, a knowledgeable salesperson will have the ability to speak to all levels of intelligence. The salesperson will be able to explain the product to a person with little or no knowledge of the subject area and also converse with someone who possibly knows more about the general subject than the salesperson. Good public relations depends entirely on two-way communication. Opening and maintaining those communication channels is crucial to continual upgrading of consumer/producer relationships.

Many fitness facilities are plagued with a high rate of attrition. Members need to be continually informed and encouraged through newsletters, seminars, bulletin boards, and the best method, person-to-person contact. Without this continuing contact, a high attrition rate will continue to be a problem.

Public relations should go beyond just members, team members, or participants. Many groups need to be informed. In school or recreational athletics, parents, opposing team members, ad-

Long-term public relations cover all aspects of life.

ministration, and support staff need information as much as the athletes themselves. Many problems in program administration stem from a lack of communication with those having an indirect but noticeable influence on the program.

There are several ways that customer service can fail to perform. Zeithaml, Berry, and Parasuraman (1990) refer to these as service quality gaps. They cite five gaps which can cause a breakdown in customer service. The first occurs when management fails to identify or understand consumer needs. Poor market research, lack of interaction and communication, and multiple layers of management all contribute to this problem. Upper management may feel that their desires reflect the desires of customers, but this is often

not the case. Only by conducting ongoing market research and facilitating upward and downward communication will the gap be closed.

A second service quality gap exists when there is inconsistency between what management perceives to be consumer expectations and the translation of those perceptions into service quality. For high quality customer relations to occur, management must possess a commitment to service quality, and the entire organization must believe that high quality service can be achieved. This will involve goal setting and communication with all levels of the organization. Standardization of tasks will help to build in-service quality at all levels of an organization.

When service quality specifications are not translated into service delivery, gap three occurs. For plans to become reality in customer relations, teamwork, training, and empowerment of frontline employees must occur. If too much red tape hinders an employee from satisfying a customer, this service gap will widen. One way to encourage high quality customer service is to support employees who exhibit positive attitudes and actions. Rewards for customer service can be in the form of money, recognition, special parking places, or special badges and plaques.

The last two service quality gaps again relate to communication. However, these involve external communications with customers. If external communications do not accurately reflect the capabilities of an organization, gap four will exist. This can be a case of promotions promising more than an organization can deliver.

Insight through Illustration

Two regional airlines competed for the same segment of business and vacation travelers. One was positioned as offering "cheap rates and no frills"; the other touted free drinks and high quality customer service. The "quality leader" airline held a special promotion offering free companion passes and deeply discounted fares for a traditionally slow travel season. Unfortunately, the response to their offer was overwhelming. There was much more demand than this airline system could handle. What resulted was severely overbooked flights, bumped passengers, lost luggage, irritable ticket and gate agents, and irritable passengers. Many people who flew this airline for the first time (they were in the trial stage) made a decision never to fly this carrier again. When they were bumped from scheduled flights, many customers were happily accommodated on the empty seats of the competing airline. A promotion intended to show high quality customer service to potential customers resulted in negative public relations and the loss of future revenues.

Gap four can also occur when different divisions of one organization fail to communicate. An example of this would be failure to inform reception and switchboard staff that a large ad was to run in the Sunday paper. If many telephone calls and walk-in shoppers were anticipated, the manager of this department might bring in additional staffing. If uninformed of the potential for a busier than usual Monday, the receptionists may be swamped and stressed with an overload of customers.

The final gap, and possibly the most frequent, is the problem which occurs when there is a difference in a customer's expectation of what he or she will receive and that customer's perception of what he or she actually receives. Satisfaction level is determined by comparing one's expectations to what actually occurs. Sometimes, customers are pleasantly surprised to receive more than they bargained for. Unfortunately, the reverse is often true. Paying premium price for a product which is of poor quality, being treated rudely by an employee in a business, and finding hidden costs in a purchase are all examples of the fifth service quality gap.

Unfortunately, most businesses never hear from 95 percent of unhappy customers (Davidow & Uttal, 1989). Complainers are much more likely to tell others about their experiences than are satisfied customers. The positive aspect of complainers is that those who feel their complaint was handled and resolved are very likely to become repeat customers. What does a manager or administrator need to enhance high quality customer and public relations? Here are a few suggestions:

- top management commitment to quality service
- internal evaluation of service costs
- willingness to de-emphasize short term profits and emphasize long term performance
- determination of customer requirements
- goals and performance measures
- recognize and reward high performance
- customer driven management
- customer champions within the organization
- employee motivation—management should treat employees as they would like to see customers treated
- empower and train employees
- communicate feedback in a timely manner
- treat other departments within an organization as customers
- communication, communication, communication

Timing and Public Acceptance

The saying "an idea whose time has come" refers to a product or service that is well-accepted by the public, whereas a product or service that is ahead of its time may flounder and fail on the sports market. Timing as it relates to reception by the public is important to keep in mind when choosing promotional strategies or introducing a new product or program.

Appropriate time scheduling is critical for filling classes.

When a new class is introduced at a health club, it should be scheduled during peak hours to generate interest. At one particular fitness center, Monday is by far the busiest day, especially in the early morning and from 5:00 to 7:00 P.M. One theory held by the staff is that most participants are guilty about their overindulgent weekends, so they come in on Monday to atone for their transgressions. The same principle of timing can be applied to all sports or recreation programs. How many entrants would register for a 10K race on a Tuesday? Most 10K runners are students or business people who have other commitments during the week. A weekend race would gather more participants. The public should be kept in mind and the program adapted to suit them rather than vice versa.

Some sports or recreational programs are seasonal, and this should be considered. If an event is to be held outdoors in a stadium or field, it is wise not to schedule that event during a rainy or snowy time of year. Indoor events (such as basketball) are more popular during inclement weather, whereas many spectators greatly enjoy viewing a baseball game from the sunny side of the stadium during the early days of spring. Indoor temperatures should also be considered when planning an event. The unpleasant memory of a festival held in a gymnasium without air conditioning during a 101-degree July day can stay with a participant forever.

To a certain extent, the knack for proper timing is inherent. The courage to follow instincts is required to become a trend setter. Being the first one with a new idea is more desirable than being the last one with an old idea. But as we have illustrated, there are ways to anticipate the attitude of the public by doing some research and careful consideration.

THE ROLE OF THE ADMINISTRATOR IN MARKETING

The role of the effective administrator in marketing can be briefly summed up in three steps: goal setting, planning, and maintaining.

REHABILITATION AND SPORTS CONDITIONING CENTER

Where we are now (Jan.)	Where we want to be (Dec.)
MD referrals 65%	MD referrals 70%
Word of Mouth 20%	Word of Mouth 25%
Advertising 15%	Advertising 5%

STRATEGIES AND TACTICS TO INCREASE PHYSICIAN REFERRALS

1. Strategy: Increase physician referral by increasing awareness of new services.
   Tactics:

   A. Develop new brochure highlighting all services—March
   B. Open House—May
   C. Presentation at Orthopedic Dept. meeting—June

2. Strategy: Increase visibility via direct mail to physicians and allied health professionals
   Tactics:

   A. Send letter of reintroduction—February
   B. Quarterly newsletter mailed to office—ongoing

3. Strategy: Increase confidence in services via personal contact with potential referrers
   Tactics:

   A. Schedule three meetings per week for Director to meet with potential referrers
   B. Attend medical staff meetings—monthly
   C. Informal talks with physicians during rounds—ongoing

Figure 12.2 *Promotional Planning Worksheet*

The director's role in developing a marketing or promotion plan begins with a clear understanding of the business. A director is not required to be an expert marketer but needs to identify the resources available to him or her and assemble a marketing team. Development of the plan should be a product of this team and should involve everyone. The final responsibility is to manage the implementation and monitor progress, changing and adapting as necessary.

Development of the Plan

Resources available to a manager can be people or objects, including the marketing budget. In physical education or athletics these resources may include the public information officer of a university, other faculty members, consultants, writers from the school newspaper, a professor of business management, yearbooks, athletic booster organizations, desktop publishing software and computers, marketing planners; even the school library can offer a wealth of information on market segments. In a hospital or health care organization, marketing directors, physician liaisons, other managers, patients, and consultants may compose the marketing team.

Development of the plan is different for every type of product and location. However, there are four basic steps to follow, which will guide even an individual entrepreneur developing his or her own promotional strategy. First determine where current marketing efforts are. What is the market penetration in various segments of the target

	Jan.	Feb.	Mar.	Apr.	May
ADVERTISING:					
newspaper					
radio					
television					
PUBLICITY:					
PSA's					
newspaper story					
health fair					
OTHER:					

Figure 12.3 *Promotional Planning Calendar*

population? Where do referrals come from? Are they 90 percent advertisement generated or 60 percent word of mouth? Tracking and market research are crucial to knowing this information.

After a determination has been made as to the current status of marketing efforts, a determination of goals is needed. If an organization primarily serves adults but wants to enter the adolescent market, what percentage of adolescent customers is desired: 50/50 or 30/70? If an athletic director desires to increase attendance at basketball competitions, how many spectators or season tickets will mean success?

As in all planning, turning a goal into action requires identification of strategies to achieve goals, and the selection of appropriate tactics needed to carry out the strategy. Figure 12.2 shows a sample planning tool for a sports training and rehabilitation facility. The assignment of time lines to each tactic is necessary for the implementation of the plan. Figure 12.3 shows a simple method for planning promotional timelines.

Implementation of the Plan

The role of the manager in implementation is to delegate tasks to all members of the marketing team as well as to other appropriate staff. Meetings with consultants, approval of advertising copy, and monitoring of adherence to timelines are steps in this stage of marketing. Staff training may be necessary in the areas of selling and persuasion, customer service, new product specifications, or new delivery systems. It is important for the manager not to shoulder all the responsibilities for implementation but to maintain accountability that the tactics are completed as planned.

Monitoring Progress

Monitoring is an ongoing process in all areas of management. In marketing it is especially crucial. If an organization has a limited marketing budget, it is imperative that promotional tactics be tracked for effectiveness. For example, if a coupon offer is made, it is necessary for staff at all levels to track the usage of coupons. If a $600 investment attracts $60,000 of new business, that is a tactic that may be employed again. On the other hand if a $600 investment attracts only $450 of new business, this is a tactic that needs to be modified or eliminated. Monitoring opportunities for unplanned promotion is also important. If an opportunity arises for participation in a health fair or sponsorship of a fun-run, and this item was not

in the marketing budget, a shift of marketing dollars may need to be made. Staff training may need to be held if new problems arise as a result of a change in strategy. Also important is the monitoring and rewarding of employees who perform at or above expected levels in areas of sales, customer service, or other promotion. With continual monitoring and adjusting, the promotional plan is transformed from a few pieces of paper into a handbook for success.

KEY WORDS AND PHRASES

Marketing

Market research

Dewey's scientific method

Secondary data sources

Primary data sources

Customer service

Service quality gaps

Service triangle

Market position

Core product

Peripheral product

Product image

Pricing methods

Promotional plan

Persuasion

Satisfaction

Promotion

Advertising

Publicity

Personal selling

QUESTIONS FOR REVIEW

1. Define the term *marketing*.
2. Name and define the four P's.
3. What is demographic information?
4. What is psychographic information?
5. How does distribution of sports programs differ from that of other products?
6. Name and define seven pricing methods.
7. List and discuss four different types of promotion.
8. What is the role of a sales person?
9. How is timing related to public acceptance of a product or service?
10. Why is customer service important for educational institutions?
11. Who is "the customer"?

SELF-TEST

Corrected True-False

If the statement is true, mark it T. If the statement is false, mark it F and change it to a true statement by adding or deleting words.

_____ 1. As consumer income increases, a smaller percentage of total personal income is required for essentials of food, shelter, and clothing.

_____ 2. The first step in product positioning is market research.

_____ 3. Gathering data from company records (such as data relating to involvement in a corporate fitness program) is an example of primary research.

_____ 4. Using census or government report data is an example of primary research.

_____ 5. Professional journals are good primary sources of data.

_____ 6. Persuasion is the most important skill for selling.

_____ 7. Public relations and publicity are the same thing.

_____ 8. Demand pricing is often used where actual costs are hard to determine.

_____ 9. Skim-the-cream pricing cannot be used until a product is established among competitors in the market.

_____ 10. Advertising in a newspaper is a good form of publicity.

Multiple Choice

_____ 11. Special introductory offers should be offered no longer than:
a. two months
b. four months
c. six months
d. four weeks

_____ 12. Television news coverage is a good form of:
a. publicity
b. advertising
c. both a and b
d. neither a nor b

_____ 13. Which of the following is not a basic component of the marketing mix?
a. potential
b. product
c. promotion
d. public

_____ 14. Creating an image of a product in the mind of the consumer is a form of:
a. market mixing
b. market positioning
c. market research
d. market publicity

_____ 15. Which of the following is not one of the four steps of consumer adoption?
a. awareness
b. interest
c. trial
d. adaptation

CASE 12.1 "MAKE THIS CLUB GO!"

Hal Baer walked out of Hugo Walk's office in the Westside Shopping Center and stopped at the Westside Health and Fitness Club, which was three doors down from Mr. Walk's office. He had just been hired by Mr. Walk to manage the health and fitness club. Mr. Walk started the club when the shopping center opened four years before, hiring Ned Baker, a former Olympian, as the first director. But he recently fired Ned because the club had lost an average of $15,000 per year during those four years. There was no indication that Ned was going to get the financial situation turned around.

There were only 450 members, and they were mostly weight training and lifting enthusiasts. In fact, the club had very few women, senior citizens, or young people as members, because those groups felt intimidated by the "muscle beach" type guys between the ages of eighteen and thirty-five who seemed to cluster in the lobby to vocally admire the women coming from and going to the aerobics sessions.

Mr. Walk told Hal that he would pay him $29,000 per year, but he expected to see the club's membership double in the first six months and triple by the end of his first year. As Hal walked through the facilities, he was excited about his new position and believed Mr. Walk's expectations were well within reason. The club held six racquetball courts and a huge weight-training area that included the latest equipment and free weights. There also were eight top-line computerized stationary bikes in the resistance-exercise area. The facilities included an aerobics room, a fitness testing area, hot tubs, sauna, steam rooms, and adequate dressing rooms and office space. There was also a 160-meter sport-tread track on top of the building.

Hal knew he had a big marketing job in front of him, and he now had to determine what specific strategies were needed to "make this club go!"

Your Response

1. What are the issues and problems?
2. What would you do if you were Hal?
3. List the action guides that offer direction for what must be done.

CASE 12.2   CAN THE SENIOR CITIZENS HELP?

Bernice Hopkins had been a secretary at Providence High School for twenty-three years. She was planning to retire at the end of the current year, and some of the staff felt that it was about time. Bernice was a very helpful woman but had become somewhat headstrong during the past couple of years.

Lyle Shields, recently appointed as director of physical education, was eager to improve the extended curricular program with some attractive, exciting, and wholesome activities. Bernice had always been supportive of the various activity programs, and she had known Lyle since he was a student. She knew that Lyle wanted to make some improvements, and she wanted to help. She told Lyle that she and her husband were mem-bers of a senior citizens group, and the seniors often talked of getting involved and helping with school and community efforts. She told the young director that if they could help him in any way, he should let her know, and she was sure she and her husband could get ten to twelve committed helpers.

Lyle mentioned Bernice's offer to Mr. Coles, assistant principal. His advice to Lyle was to steer clear of "that bunch of old cronies," because they didn't have financial means or influence to help anyone. Coles thought they would be more of a hindrance than a help.

Coles's advice bothered Lyle, but he didn't have time to waste on the group if they couldn't help the program.

Your Response

1. Identify the issue and/or problems in this case.

2. What would you do if you were in Lyle's position?

3. What action guides are central to the issue and problems?

BIBLIOGRAPHY

Cannie, Joan K., and Donald Caplin. *Keeping Customers for Life.* New York: AMACOM, 1991.

Clarke, David H., and H. Harrison Clarke. *Research Processes in Physical Education.* 2nd ed. Englewood Cliffs, NJ: Prentice-Hall, 1984.

Cohen, William A., and Marshall E. Reddick. *Successful Marketing for Small Business.* New York: AMACOM, 1981.

Converse, Paul D., Harvey W. Huegy, and Robert V. Mitchell. *Elements of Marketing,* 7th ed. Englewood Cliffs, NJ: Prentice-Hall, 1965.

Davidow, William H., and Bro Uttal. *Total Customer Service: The Ultimate Weapon.* New York: Harper and Row, 1989.

Fram, Eugene H. *Small Business Marketing.* Dobbs Ferry, NY: Oceana Publications, 1968.

Frye, Robert W. *Introduction to the Marketing System.* San Francisco: Canfield Press, 1973.

How to Do It Series #1: Promotion. Centre for International Sports Management.

Mullins, Bernard J. *Sports Marketing, Promotion, and Public Relations.* Amherst, MA: National Sport Management, 1983.

Nesbitt, Keith. *Fundraising Made Easy.* Ottawa, Ontario: Coaching Association of Canada, 1982.

Stoddart, Ian. *Marketing Your Sport to Others.* Ottawa, Ontario: Coaching Association of Canada, 1982.

Zeithaml, Valarie A. *Delivering Quality Service: Balancing Customer Perceptions and Expectations.* New York: The Free Press, 1990.

Ziegler, Earle F. and Gary W. Bowie. *Management Competency Development in Sport and Physical Education.* Philadelphia: Lea & Febiger, 1983.

13

Managing Physical Education, Fitness, and Sports Facilities

Work hard and become a leader;
be lazy and never succeed.

Proverbs 12:24

Chapter Objectives

After reading this chapter and completing the exercises, you should be able to:

1 Identify seven of the ten general criteria for planning facilities

2 List three factors to consider when planning the location of a new facility

3 Name three limiting factors in facility design

4 Explain why fences are needed in outdoor activity areas

5 Compare the advantages and disadvantages of using natural and artificial turf surfaces

6 Discuss the importance of air-quality control in indoor activity areas

7 Name three good disinfection systems for swimming pools

8 Delineate two important considerations in setting up juice bars or concession stands

9 Name and discuss three aspects of facility management

Today the facilities for sports and fitness programs resemble less and less the old gymnasiums and stadiums of the past. As competition increases among fitness centers and athletics and recreation programs, the quality of facilities must improve. Multiuse facilities, designed to accommodate a variety of activities, are almost a necessity for profit and nonprofit organizations. The criteria for planning, constructing, and managing these facilities will be discussed in this chapter.

PLANNING THE FACILITY

A quality facility, like a quality program, begins with thorough planning. There are certain general criteria that guide facility planning, construction, and maintenance. Ten of the most important are listed below.

General Criteria for Planning Sport/ Activity Facilities

Serves the Identified Needs Meeting the needs of the clientele who will be using the facility is at the top of the list of criteria. If this criterion is not met, the expended resources will have been wasted. The planned facility must contribute to the objectives of the program for which it is to serve whether these be developmental or profit making in nature.

Quality Construction and Safety Considerations There is an adage, "You get what you pay for." This old saying certainly applies to facility construction. Most organization planners who have tried to cut corners and construct a facility which is less than what is needed or desired usually have had regrets. Nothing can be more expensive than failing to adhere to safety considerations. If someone is seriously or fatally injured because of an unsafe feature of a facility, the costs of paying for a negligence settlement are astronomical.

Multipurpose It has not been too many years ago when schools built a gymnasium strictly for basketball. In "basketball country" there were no other lines on the floor except those needed for basketball. Those times are gone forever! Because of the high cost of construction, consideration must be given in the planning stage for any facility to be used optimally. The gymnasium, for example, must be planned for all indoor sports that have a need for a large open space as well as for all types of convocations, exhibits, and concerts.

Secluded Location Facility location is discussed more fully in the following paragraphs, but planners must maintain an awareness that activity facilities need to be isolated from classrooms, libraries, or any area where the noise factor associated with sports would be a disturbance.

Easily Accessible This criterion is also discussed more fully in the page that follows.

Cost Effective Quality construction, safety considerations, and multipurpose criteria must be considered along with this criterion—a balanced and reasonable approach. For example, it would be convenient in a school locker room to have individual shower stalls and full-length lockers for everyone, but one would be hard-pressed to find such extravagance.

Easily Supervised Supervision is an important consideration for the safety of the users. This is one reason why in many fitness and activity facilities, you are seeing more open space and fewer obstructive walls.

Custodial/Maintenance Efficient If planners will give proper attention to this criterion, maintenance costs can be significantly reduced and a healthier and more orderly facility will result. Selecting the proper materials for floors and walls is an example of how this criterion can be met.

Expansible   Most physical education and sports facilities planned during the 1950s and 1960s were too small by the time they opened for use. Some planners had the foresight to allow for expansion by building in non–weight-bearing (false) walls on one side of the structure and allowing open space for the expansion to take place. This is why activity facilities should be constructed on the perimeter of a school campus rather than in the central core.

Aesthetic Presentation and Ambiance   Just how high this criterion should rank on the list depends upon the clientele being served. In most schools, utility would be more important than aesthetics and ambiance; however, in a country club setting, aesthetics and ambiance would more than likely be very important to the users. This criterion refers to mood-setting qualities such as a nice thick carpet on the locker room floor and wood-grain lockers instead of gray metal ones.

Location

Where to locate a new facility is a crucial decision. Factors that should be considered in the choice of location include accessibility, environmental quality, and the possibility of sharing existing facilities.

Accessibility   For school athletics and recreational facilities, accessibility to students is a key concern of facility planners. On many college campuses, students living in campus housing must rely on bicycles or public transportation to travel to an off-campus facility. Therefore, it is crucial that if facilities cannot be located near campus, they should be easily accessible by public transportation.

Accessibility is also a factor for fitness and sports businesses. A fitness/racquetball club can draw a large crowd of lunch-hour participants if it is located near a professional office park or business district. Heavy walk-in and drive-by traffic can help to generate increased exposure and

sales. Recreational programs for children and young teens must be easily accessible by public transportation, bicycle, or parental car pools.

Environmental Quality   For facilities accommodating outdoor activities, several environmental factors should be considered, including noise levels of surrounding areas and proximity to airports and traffic patterns. In El Segundo, California, there is a beautiful recreational and camping area at a beach near the end of the Los Angeles International Airport runways. Every few minutes jets roar overhead, making conversation impossible. This is not the best example of site location.

A good example of dealing with noise pollution is found at an urban fitness and racquet club located at a very busy intersection. An outdoor jogging track and lap pool are surrounded by a tall brick wall and lush landscaping. This helps to dampen noise levels of traffic and create a more serene environment for exercise.

Air pollution levels should be monitored for outdoor facility sites. Activities requiring cycling or running can be hampered if located near factories or other sources of air pollution. If spectators will be involved, the odors of a landfill or dairy farm can decrease their enjoyment. These areas should be avoided whenever possible.

Sharing Existing Facilities   If an organization has outgrown its current quarters, there are alternatives to new construction. Joint occupancy of existing facilities is one option. For example, when a city YMCA was in need of an indoor swimming pool, rather than constructing this pool, the Y exchanged racquetball court time for pool time with a local university. This arrangement benefited YMCA members, and the university was able to offer its students racquetball activity classes. Another innovative example of joint occupancy is in a large eastern city, where a school is built on the ground floor of a high-rise office complex. The recreational facilities are used for school physical

Overcrowding can become a safety hazard.

education classes during the day, then opened to business people on evenings and weekends.

Unconventional Sites   Imaginative and unconventional uses of space should be considered when a school or business requires a recreational area. Portland State University built tennis courts on the roofs of buildings. This would be a good idea for a crowded urban area. In New York City, some creative entrepreneurs turned two abandoned piers into a plush tennis club just blocks from Wall Street. An elegant racquet club was erected in the "dead space" underneath the Brooklyn Bridge. An abandoned supermarket in the inner city became a neighborhood gymnasium. In a small rural town in Kentucky, an abandoned auto service station and garage was converted to a health club and named "The Body Shop."

Virtually any level, vacant lot can be transformed into recreational space with a few baseball bases, playground equipment, or portable swimming pools. The only limits to space availability are in the imagination.

Facility Design

The best facility for most organizations is a multipurpose facility. Fields should be planned to accommodate a variety of activities such as football, field hockey, lacrosse, and soccer. Gymnasiums can easily be designed to handle basketball, volleyball, gymnastics, and special events such as concerts. The main point to remember is that all facilities should be designed to promote health and safety and to enhance the activities of all participants.

Sources of Ideas   Field trips to existing facilities and photos of other facilities are good sources of ideas and information about facility design.

Blueprints of facilities that are too distant to visit can be borrowed, but caution should be exercised in evaluating a design from the blueprint alone. In one new corporate fitness center facility, what appeared to be a good design on paper was impractical in reality. The design shown in Figure 13.1 appears to be a good use of space. In reality, however, if the doors to both locker rooms happen to be open at the same time, men and women in the sauna/jacuzzi area have no privacy. The design shown in Figure 13.2 corrects that problem as well as illustrating a more convenient relationship of the dressing/locker area to the ancillary areas.

Other sources for ideas and information about facility design are textbooks and journals such as *Athletic Business* (1842 Hoffman St., Suite 201, Madison, WI 53707). Researching these sources may prevent costly errors or point out money-saving plans for facility design.

Limiting Factors   In determining the best design for a new or remodeled facility, one must be realistic. The optimum plan as well as what is minimally acceptable should be defined. One must also be realistic about financing. If financing is unavailable for a deluxe facility, planners can research what can be done to meet current needs

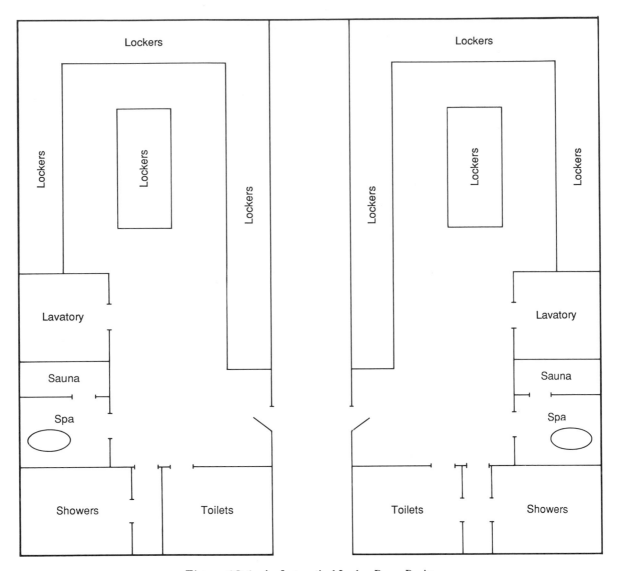

Figure 13.1 *An Impractical Locker Room Design*

and keep the design flexible for future expansion and improvement.

Other factors that must be considered in facility design include safety and adherence to federal and state codes. Features such as sprinkler systems and handicapped access may be required. Exterior signage, the building itself, and parking space must adhere to city, state, and federal regulations. Equality for male and female facilities should be designed into the plan.

Construction Materials   Perhaps the most traditional material for athletics and fitness facilities is brick. Wood, concrete, and steel can also be

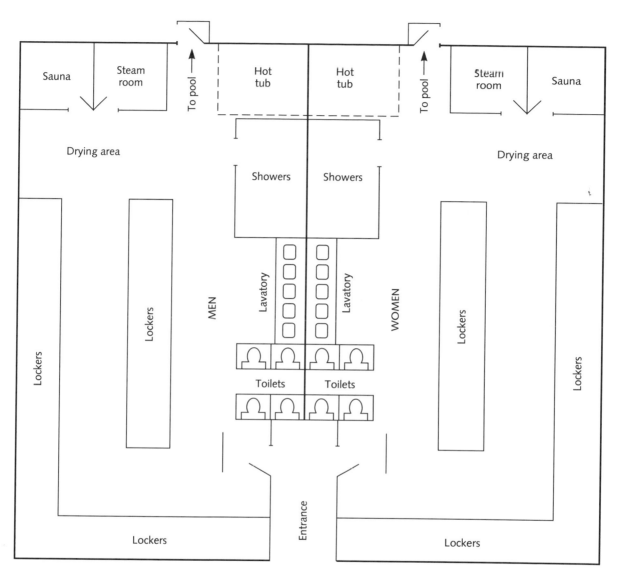

Figure 13.2 *A Practical Locker Room Design*

used. These traditional materials offer great flexibility in facility design. The material chosen for a new facility should suit the facility's location.

In addition to traditional materials, new air-support structures have become available. These structures have several advantages and disad-

vantages. They easily can provide a large unobstructed space fast and at low cost. Air-support structures can be erected seasonally to accommodate weather changes. Their transparency or semitransparency allows them to be easily lit, and maintenance costs of these structures are low

Facilities must be designed to meet the
needs of the handicapped.

Who Plans the Facility?

In a college or university setting, a large number of people should be involved in facility planning. The board of trustees, regents, and school administrators, as well as campus planning committees and maintenance personnel, all have valuable input for consideration. Of course, an architect and contractor should be involved in the planning. Others include space planners, facility planners, and marketing research consultants. The planning should be coordinated by department personnel. In the case of a physical education/athletics facility, all teachers, coaches, and administrators should have input through committees or other channels. Public schools should involve people in similar positions.

For fitness and sports medicine facilities, investors, operators, and other advisors such as physicians, physical therapists, and exercise physiologists should consult with architects and contractors to design the best possible plan. It is important in all settings, whether academic or business, for the architect to work closely with the professional sports advisors. It is up to the administrators and the planning committee to convey the requirements of the facility to the architect and follow up with contractors to ensure that the design is carried through to completion.

when compared to traditional cleaning, painting, and repair costs of other structures. Two other advantages are that they are fire- and earthquake-resistant.

Disadvantages are few when compared to advantages. The life span of air-support structures (about twenty years) is shorter than that of traditional building materials. Some climates are not suited to air-support structures, as the indoor temperature is hard to control. The potential for vandalism is also a serious consideration with these structures.

OUTDOOR AREAS

An examination of any college catalog today shows that about half of all physical education classes are held outdoors. Add to this use the requirements of athletic practices and contests and recreational use, and the importance of outdoor activity areas in an academic setting becomes very clear. Other public and private recreational facilities also rely upon outdoor facilities for many of their activities.

Fences

Because participants in outdoor activities display high levels of excitement and energy, fences can be considered as a safety measure for participants. In addition to the obvious role of keeping nonparticipants out of activity areas, fences serve other purposes. If activity areas are located near roads, railroads, drainage ditches, and parking lots, a fence will help protect participants in a variety of ways. When access to these hazards is reduced by a fence, less supervision is required. Playing implements such as balls, bats, and helmets are less likely to get lost or stolen. Fences can provide privacy for participants and help isolate them from spectators. Keeping spectators off playing fields will decrease the amount of maintenance necessary, especially on natural turf fields. Fencing can also aid in traffic control to channel crowds toward exits.

The choice of materials for fences ranges from simple chain link fencing to wood, block, and brick. The choice of materials should be based on security, privacy, safety, and cost requirements.

Fenced facilities are safer and more secure.

Surfaces

Proper drainage of fields and activity areas, especially those with natural turf, is crucial to the safety and enjoyment of participants. Surfaces should be graded so the center of the field is approximately 2 percent higher than the edges. This will encourage water to drain away from heavily traveled areas to prevent participants from slipping. Some areas may require subsurface drainage tiles to funnel water away from fields and other areas.

Nonturf Surfacing Many schools and recreational organizations require some form of concrete, blacktop, or other synthetic material for activity areas. These surfaces are desirable for year-round usage, and have reasonably low instal-

lation and maintenance costs. Their resilience, durability, and cleanliness are ideal for such activities as tennis, basketball, and three-wall racquetball.

Many running and cycling tracks are being converted from old-style cinder and blacktop to state-of-the-art rubberized surfaces. Not only are these surfaces visually appealing, but the surfaces are more comfortable for athletes and help decrease shin splints and shock to joints. Artificial surfaces such as blacktop can be combined with rubber, cork, or granite to increase or decrease firmness. A variety of colors are available for increased attractiveness.

Natural Turf Because many activities and sports require turf, either natural or artificial, it is important to be aware of the considerations for these surfaces. Maintenance of natural turf is difficult and expensive when one considers seeding, fertilizing, watering, cutting, and lining with paint or chalk. Water drainage can cause real problems in rainy areas. With so many disadvantages, why

WHERE'S THE GROUNDSKEEPER !

Proper grading of surfaces is very important.

do so many organizations choose natural turf? Their reasons probably include the following: (1) It has a pleasing appearance when well groomed; (2) it is versatile for multiple uses; (3) it is nonabrasive and safe for contact sports; and (4) it costs less to install than artificial turf.

Artificial Turf   In many situations, artificial turf is being chosen over natural due to its durability, year-round usability, and low cost of maintenance. There are many kinds of artificial turf available, and specific uses require specific piles. The face material should be at least 1/2 inch thick; backing and pads should be water-resistant and shock-absorbing, and should be a minimum of 9/16 inch thick. Turf can be permanently applied or removable. If permanent, the adhesive should be temperature/moistureproof and guaranteed for the turf's life. Cleaning methods include brushing, washing, and vacuuming. Answers to the following questions also have a bearing on which type of turf should be chosen:

- Will turf be applied over dirt or pavement?

- Will seams be sewn, taped, zippered, or welded?

- Will playing field lines be permanent or temporary?

- Does manufacturer guarantee color against fading?

Orientation

Outdoor playing areas and fields should be oriented so that during daytime competition, players are not looking into the sun. For basketball, football, soccer, and rugby, the goals should be oriented so players run perpendicular to the sun's light. Baseball and softball fields should be oriented so the batter looks north or south when facing the pitcher.

In a complex such as a school or recreational facility, fields may be located near commercial buildings, housing, gymnasiums, or classrooms. Fields should be located so as to minimize class disturbance and reduce travel congestion and distance between buildings, locker rooms, and fields. Flowcharts should be prepared to analyze traffic patterns and congestion among participants and spectators.

Buildings should not interfere with sight lines of players. This also applies to signs along walls and fences. No graphics or posters should be placed behind backboards or in such a manner as to distract players and/or spectators.

Lighting

Due to the public's demand for extended recreational hours, many outdoor facilities are being built with lights or converted to lighted fields and courts for night use. Night activity is especially popular in hot areas where midday activity is undesirable due to heat and humidity. Providing lighted outdoor facilities is a good way to increase revenue at many fitness and recreation centers. Because many factors are involved in lighting, it is best to consult lighting engineers and examine the lighting plans of similar facilities.

One precaution in lighting is to avoid placing lights in direct sight lines, or at field level. The visibility of players and spectators must be considered.

INDOOR FACILITIES

In school settings, teaching stations are required for physical education classes. The number of teaching stations depends upon many factors, including the number of students, numbers of days per week stations are in use, the number of school periods per day, and the types of programs to be provided. In some areas, climate is a factor requiring an increased number of indoor teaching stations for snowy and rainy seasons.

Because of the numerous factors influencing indoor facilities, our discussion will focus primarily on general considerations for various areas within facilities. For specific recommendations on playing court requirements, refer to periodicals and other publications.

Surfaces

Because the primary concern for any sports or fitness facility is the safety and enjoyment of participants and spectators, the surfaces that affect these groups are key concerns.

Flooring   The type of flooring used in facilities depends upon the activities to be conducted there. The kinds of flooring are as numerous as the activities held. Many buildings are constructed with concrete floors. Some activities can safely be conducted on concrete, but many require a more resilient surface such as hardwood or matted surfaces.

Strength-training areas in schools and fitness and sports medicine centers can safely be placed on concrete floors. The floors should be clean, smooth, and free of obstructions. Although concrete-floored areas are easily maintained and inexpensive, applying carpeting with a moderate amount of padding will create a more attractive and comfortable surface. Carpeting also absorbs sound better than hard flooring, thus keeping exercise areas quieter.

Other activity areas, such as those for basketball, wrestling, and volleyball, require special flooring. Due to the cost and space necessary to construct a gymnasium, most sports and fitness organizations are focusing on multiuse facilities which can be equipped with bleachers and goals for basketball and volleyball and then converted to a wrestling area by covering the floor with mats.

Many fitness centers conduct aerobics classes on their wooden-floored basketball courts. With the current concern for safety and injury prevention, the flooring for aerobic dance areas is being scrutinized more carefully than ever before. Several alternatives to carpeted concrete or wooden floors should be discussed. One type of wooden floor gaining popularity is a suspended gymnastic-type floor. This floor is actually a flexible wooden platform built on top of springs. When participants bounce, step, jump, and dance, the floor gives beneath their feet, reducing the jarring impact on joints and relieving shin splints. Another advance in flooring is the foam-padded covering. This has similar advantages to suspended flooring.

No matter what type of flooring is used in a facility—concrete, carpet, wood, tile, or linoleum—each area should be evaluated for safety features such as slipping and tripping hazards, attractiveness, durability, and maintenance to determine whether it is suitable for the intended activity.

Walls   Walls are often overlooked in facility planning, but they can have a positive or negative impact on participants. Walls should be smooth and easily cleaned, without sharp corners. Equipment such as fire extinguishers and drinking fountains should be recessed into walls to prevent injuries; however, they should be clearly marked and easily accessible.

COACH, ABOUT THOSE LIGHTS
YOU INSTALLED...

A variety of alternatives are available to make bare walls look appealing. Mirrors are a good choice for aerobics, dance, and strength-training areas. Mirrors can create an open feeling in a small room and assist participants in performing activities with proper body mechanics. Mirrors also help instructors in monitoring classes and activity areas. Paneling, paint, wallpaper, and poster art can all help to brighten activity areas. On the other hand, wall treatments should not be visually distracting to athletes or spectators. Painted graphics are an inexpensive way to dress up activity areas and can also be used to convey information.

Ceilings Ceilings should be light in color and treated so that acoustics are of the highest quality. In gymnasiums and volleyball and racquetball areas, where balls may hit ceilings, lighting should be recessed for safety.

Lighting

When facility lighting is assessed, both natural and artificial lighting should be taken into consideration. If areas depend on windows for some lighting, provision should be made so that night activities are adequately illuminated. A lighting engineer or architect should be consulted when planning and upgrading facility lighting. Burned out bulbs should be replaced and other problems corrected immediately to prevent safety hazards.

Air-Quality Control

Air quality is one aspect of facility design that should not be overlooked. When heating, cooling, and ventilation systems are in proper working order, they create a safe, comfortable environment for sports and fitness activities. Inefficient ventilation, however, can make activity and locker areas extremely unpleasant. Adequate ventilation is necessary to remove odors and decrease humidity in damp areas such as showers, pools, and hydrotherapy areas.

Air temperature should be maintained at approximately seventy degrees Fahrenheit. If an area is too cold it can cause chilling of sweaty participants; if too warm, it will promote dehydration and heat illness. Clearly, indoor air quality should be a major concern of facility administrators so that it will not become a concern for athletes and other participants.

Corridors

Hallways and doorways should conform to safety codes and be accessible to handicapped people. Emergency exits should be clearly marked, with all doors opening outward to speed exiting in case of emergency. Handicapped accessibility not only means providing ramps and elevators as well as stairs, but also making sure the width of doors and passages is adequate to accommodate wheelchairs, and outfitting doors with easy-to-manipulate handles. Passages should be kept free of obstructions at all times.

Passages should be roomy enough to accommodate dollies and equipment transports, if necessary. In a gymnasium or stadium, segregating opposing teams, officials, and spectators in different halls and lobby areas will help prevent overcrowding and decrease the possibility of confrontations. Removing restrooms and concession stands from exits will also decrease overcrowding.

Storage and Office Areas

Storage facilities and, in most cases, offices should be easily accessed from activity areas. Offices of activity supervisors may need to be built with large windows or even glass walls for easy supervision. Blinds or curtains should be provided for privacy when necessary.

The director's office should not be easily accessible by activity participants. Having a secretary or receptionist to screen visitors will help ensure uninterrupted time for the director to produce, as covered in our earlier discussion of time management. All offices and work spaces should be equipped with security features. When unattended they should be locked.

Locker Rooms

Dressing Areas   In facilities where athletic contests are to be held, separate dressing areas should be provided for each team, and another for officials. Should this be impossible, and should opposing teams be forced to dress at another location, a team meeting room should be provided.

To prevent congestion, dressing areas should be semi-isolated from showers, sinks, and toilets. If full-length mirrors, counters, and outlets for hair dryers are provided in dressing areas, the sink areas will be less congested for those needing a washbasin. In a large facility, it is practical to provide toilets and basins in separate restrooms. This will decrease the amount of traffic through locker rooms and provide more privacy for those who are showering and dressing.

Many fitness centers are increasing their member services by providing hair dryers, curling

irons, and ironing boards. Fire codes and insurance coverage should be checked to make sure they allow for these amenities. If so, these appliances can and should be attached to the wall to allow easy access while preventing loss or theft. One step further in personal service is making available hair spray, cologne, deodorant, aftershave, and lotion. This can be an inexpensive provision for members and is one way to elevate the image of an organization.

Lockers   The first objective of lockers is to safeguard clothing and personal items. In an area where business people will be coming from or returning to work, full-length lockers provide a way to store clothing without causing wrinkles.

All lockers should be adequately ventilated to allow moisture to evaporate and prevent mildew of clothing and equipment. Locking baskets provide adequate security for clothing while maintaining proper aeration. Lockers should be arranged to provide easy access, while using space in the most efficient manner.

Wet Areas   As mentioned earlier, toilets, sinks, and showers should be separated from dressing areas to decrease congestion and promote drying of locker contents. Flooring should be nonslip and treated to reduce the spread of athlete's foot and other germs. The choice of private, semiprivate, or communal showers will depend on the clientele and budget available. Facilities should provide toilets, sinks, and shower seats that are accessible by handicapped persons. Proper disinfection and cleaning are especially crucial for maintaining wet areas.

POOLS

Swimming pools can be either indoors or outdoors. The depth of pools should be governed by the type of activity to be conducted there. If a pool is to be used for teaching beginning swimming, it must be shallow enough for students to touch bottom while standing. For more advanced swimming lessons and competitions, a deeper lap pool is needed. Diving requires even deeper water, and many facility planners provide a deepwater diving area at one end of a lap pool rather than a separate diving pool.

Decks

The area surrounding a pool should be considered as carefully as the design of the swimming pool itself. Decks should be made of a nonslip, easy-care surface such as concrete. Proper drainage must be provided so that any water that splashes out of the pool will drain away and dry quickly instead of forming puddles, which are a slipping hazard. A secured storage area should be provided for floats, lane markers, and maintenance tools. Proper use of a storage area can prevent theft and help maintain uncluttered decks.

Lighting

An important consideration for indoor and outdoor pools is lighting. If windows provide light to indoor pools, the glare hazards should be assessed. Glare can cause problems for lifeguard supervision and competitive events. Wide roof overhangs or awnings can provide enough shade to minimize the problem. Windows also represent a source of heat loss, and this problem must be considered when planning. As far as artificial lighting goes, lighting fixtures placed directly over water are difficult to service.

Maintenance

Proper maintenance of pools for disinfection and pH levels is essential. Chlorine, bromine, and ozone generators are all good disinfection systems. Bromine and ozone generators provide adequate disinfection while eliminating chlorine gas problems in enclosed areas. Local departments of health should be consulted to determine which systems are approved in a particular area.

FOOD SERVICE

In all facilities, whether beverages are sold or not, plenty of drinking fountains should be available to prevent dehydration of participants. Fountains are usually preferred to a water cooler and cups for two reasons. First, water fountains are faster to use and do not create a litter problem. Second, when the opportunity is available to carry water into activity areas, there is an increased chance of spilling.

If food and beverages are to be provided in a facility, the concession stand, juice bar, or cafe should be easily accessible by participants to increase revenues from this source. However, care should be taken to make it inconvenient to carry food into the activity areas, where spilled drinks and food can create safety hazards. Many fitness clubs and sports medicine clinics have a wealth of expensive computerized equipment. If any drinks or wet food are spilled on these machines, they can be severely damaged.

Juice bars provide a good opportunity for relaxation and socializing, and many clubs are finding them to be a great way to earn added income. When setting up a cafe or a juice bar, a professional restaurant manager or planner should be consulted to assist in decisions about the type of food, service, utensils, and cooking appliances required.

In gymnasiums and stadiums, concession stands are a popular way to provide refreshments for spectators. Many schools turn over concession management to boosters or other campus clubs. It is important to locate these concession stands so they are convenient to bleachers and seating areas, but consideration must be given to congestion problems when crowds of fans are gathered around the concession area. Will they block traffic or visibility for athletes and other spectators? Careful planning can prevent this problem.

FACILITY MANAGEMENT

So far this chapter has covered information of concern to managers and administrators in planning, updating, or renovating facilities. What about the day-to-day operations? Facility management is crucial in keeping any organization running smoothly and efficiently. A facility that is well maintained and managed is one of the best public relation tools a director has.

Policy Guide

A policy document can be of great value in the operation of a facility. Statements addressing topics and items such as those below need to be included:

1. General Policies: Policies need to be established for any recurring problems, and they must be developed for each facility and area.
2. Facility Hours and Scheduling Procedures: These must be well-thought out and then adhered to.
3. Availability of Facilities and Equipment: Is there a use fee or is it free?
4. Leasing Arrangements and Contractual Agreements: Such items as advertising, signs and posters, ticket office service, program development and distribution, and concessions operations must be addressed.

It is essential that the policy document that is developed offers information and direction for all employees. It is an absolute necessity that the staff personnel who deal with the users of the facility thoroughly understand the rules, regula-

tions, and operating philosophy. In certain instances, compromising policy may be the best approach in resolving conflicts and providing the most beneficial service to the patrons; however, there are some policies that cannot be compromised. It is important that the supervisor and security team know when compromise is appropriate and when it cannot be considered. Consistent policy interpretation and application are vital to the effective operation of any facility.

Facility Supervision and Security

Activity-based facilities are used for many different events and by many individuals and groups, and the primary objective should be to meet the needs and desires of all patrons as easily and comfortably as possible while ensuring their satisfaction and safety. The clientele may include individuals who desire a personal workout, a group that has a reservation to play volleyball for one hour, or a large crowd of spectators who are in the facility for several hours to watch the progress of a tournament. Regardless of who the users are, supervisors or security teams are necessary for meeting the needs of the patrons.

To ensure that an effective service is provided for the individual user or a large spectator group, effective communication is absolutely essential. When the communication lines are open, the supervisor can work with the patron, but when those lines are closed, problems occur. The success of a good facility and crowd control program is only as good as the director responsible for the actions of the supervisor or security team. The director is responsible for good communication, and good communication results from following sound guides such as those that follow:

1. A written set of rules and regulations, including a statement to clarify them, should be available to all employees. Identify the common problems and clarify the eviction policies.
2. Facility rules and regulations should be posted

*Clean and neat facilities are a good
public relations tool.*

at all entrances and in strategic places such as spectator areas.

3. The supervisor or security team should be easily identifiable. The means of identification may be a name badge clipped to the shirt for the daily supervisors, a blazer or jacket for low-profile events, or uniformed police when high visibility is desired for crowd control purposes.

4. A friendly and helpful attitude should be displayed by the supervisor and security team members. They need not intimidate, snub, or abuse patrons either verbally or physically. They must always exercise caution and restraint and not over-react in stressful situations. There are times when they must be firm but never rude.

5. The facility manager needs to provide a training program to fit the needs of the facility. New ideas for improving the service should be encouraged, and reports should be maintained for future reference.

Facility Maintenance

In addition to promoting pride in an organization, proper maintenance is necessary to extend the life of and decrease the necessity for repairs in a facility. Some people may think that maintenance of a building, field, or pool is the responsibility of the janitorial and maintenance crews. In reality, every employee—from the director to instructors to secretaries and receptionists—should take pride in and help maintain the cleanliness of the facilities in which they work. Whenever employees see a burned out light bulb, spill, leak, or other concern, they should report it. Employees can also be responsible for frequent walk-throughs of locker areas, exercise areas, and restrooms to check for dirty towels, trash, or other small clean-up jobs that they can easily perform. Any large jobs requiring a janitor or maintenance person should be referred to a central maintenance coordinator who is ultimately responsible for all facility maintenance.

There are several key qualities to look for when selecting a maintenance coordinator. An ability to work well with others is essential. Responsibility, organization, and mechanical ability are also important qualifications.

Providing quality supplies and maintaining equipment well will prolong the life of equipment and make facility care easier and less expensive. Consider the savings from performing a small repair today at a cost of ten dollars, versus waiting until a piece of equipment breaks down and having to pay for a major repair. The savings in time and money are well worth the effort to perform routine maintenance.

JUST HAVE YOUR AEROBICS AROUND THE TABLES... HOME EC MEETS HERE NEXT...

The scheduling of facilities may appear simple but requires thoughtful planning.

Inventory Control

Careful inventory control is as essential to schools as it is to businesses or other organizations. Keeping precise records of all equipment, uniforms, and resale items will not only help in controlling loss and theft but will make ordering and reordering of stock and equipment easier.

All equipment and clothing should be clearly marked with laundry markers, pens, stencil, decals, stamps, branding, or engraving tools. This will help inventory personnel identify property.

Any equipment issued for use should be issued or lent on a check-out basis. For any inventory system to work, a routine protocol for issue of equipment should be established and rigidly enforced. Many organizations use special inventory forms to track equipment issued or purchased. Any person requesting the use of equipment, towels, or clothing should provide proper identification, such as a student or member ID card or a driver's license. Many inventory systems can easily be computerized to make tracking property easier. Refer to the chapter on computers for a discussion of these systems.

Facility Scheduling

The final topic to discuss relating to facility management is scheduling. On the surface, facility scheduling may seem like an easy task, but it is not as simple as group A goes here at 9:00, and group B goes there at 10:00. Consider the case of a university that has seven fields, one stadium, two gymnasiums, two strength-training facilities, three dance/gymnastic rooms, and many people and groups vying for the use of the facilities. One person should coordinate this scheduling.

Just as in inventory control, a standard procedure should be established for requesting use of facilities. Organizations should create and adhere to a standard request form and establish priority guidelines for authorizing use. The following is a priority list used by a major university. It could be adapted to suit any school or organization.

Priority List for Physical Education/ Athletics Facilities

1. scheduled physical education classes
2. athletic practices and contests
3. intramural/recreational sports
4. other campus groups—academic
5. other campus groups—nonacademic
6. off-campus groups

With this priority system in effect, a gymnasium request submitted for an intramural basketball tournament would be approved by the facility coordinator over a request received from the music department for a recital. Strict adherence to priority guidelines and request protocol should be stressed to all groups using facilities.

In smaller organizations such as racquet clubs, fitness and health spas, and clinics, scheduling may be less complicated, but there is still a need for protocol and proper authorization for facility use. Computer programs for facility management are available to assist in scheduling.

KEY WORDS AND PHRASES

Ambiance

Environmental quality

Accessibility

Air-support structures

Nonturf surfaces

Artificial turf

Orientation

Expansibility

Air-quality control

Scheduling priorities

QUESTIONS FOR REVIEW

1. When planning a sports facility, what environmental factors must be considered, and why?

2. List three unconventional sites for locating activity facilities and explain why the sites are logical.

3. What are the advantages and disadvantages of concrete as a floor or surface?

4. What are the advantages and disadvantages of air-support sports structures?

5. Who should be involved in planning for a new sports facility? What are one or two principal

roles of the physical education, fitness, or athletics director?

6. If you were an athletics director, would you prefer natural or artificial turf for your outdoor fields? Explain why.

7. What are some crucial considerations concerning outdoor facility orientation?

8. Why is it so important to establish priorities and scheduling protocol for activity facilities?

9. List several reasons why proper maintenance of sports facilities is critical.

SELF-TEST

Corrected True-False

If the statement is true, mark it T. If the statement is false, mark it F and change it to a true statement by adding or deleting words.

_____ 1. Accessibility should be the key concern of facility designers.

_____ 2. Because of the safety hazards involved, fencing should only be considered when absolutely necessary.

_____ 3. The trend in building activity facilities today is to construct a specific facility for a specific sport.

_____ 4. The center of a playing field should be approximately 2 percent higher than the edges for proper drainage.

_____ 5. Natural turf has many advantages over artificial turf for multiuse athletic fields.

_____ 6. A football/soccer field should have an east-west orientation.

_____ 7. Spring floors are creating too many problems for the health and safety of participants to be recommended.

_____ 8. Mirrors are recommended for aerobics facilities but not for weight-training facilities.

_____ 9. Air temperature in a fitness facility should be about seventy-five degrees Fahrenheit.

_____ 10. Water fountains are preferred to water coolers and cups for indoor activity areas.

Multiple-Choice

_____ 11. One of the following is not a criterion that would give direction to a facilities planner:
a. expansible structure
b. secluded location
c. accessibility
d. ambulatory

_____ 12. Who should have the responsibility for facility scheduling for campus gyms and athletic fields?
a. an appointed scheduler
b. physical education director
c. athletic director
d. none of the above

_____ 13. Which or who presents more problems for the manager?
a. program
b. facilities
c. staff
d. budget

_____ 14. Which statement is not true?
a. Facilities are a good public relations tool.
b. The architect should have the final word on plans.
c. The architect should talk with the custodians.
d. Facilities should be designed for the revenue sports.

_____ 15. Which statement is true?
a. Concrete is not recommended for pool decks.
b. Water coolers/cups are preferred to water fountains.
c. Concession stands should be easily accessible.
d. none of the above

CASE 13.1 CONFLICT IN GYM SCHEDULING

Jeff Roberts, director of physical education at Bradenville High School, received a letter signed by twelve intramural volleyball players who were obviously venting their anger: On Saturday morning they had had an intramural match scheduled at 10:00 A.M., but it had been canceled because of a conflict in gym scheduling.

Upon investigating the incident, Jeff discovered that the intramural director, Don Campbell, had scheduled the gym for the match. Further inquiry revealed that Earl Mitchell, boys' basketball coach, was practicing when the volleyball players arrived. Earl told Mr. Campbell that because his

team played so poorly on Friday night, he had decided to call a 9:30 to 11:30 A.M. practice that morning. He apologized for the "inconvenience" it caused, but (according to him) since the basketball team had a higher priority for gym use from December to February, he felt he had to exercise his priority. Mr. Campbell was furious because he knew his program was on the gym schedule and should rightfully be there; however, rather than create a scene and argument in front of the students, he conceded his right and sent the girls home.

Your Response

1. What are the issues and problems?

2. Was Campbell right in avoiding the argument or should he have taken another action?

3. What should Roberts do now that the incident is over?

4. List the action guides evolving from this case.

5. What barriers may stand in the way of the best decision?

CASE 13.2   INCREASED MEMBERSHIP CAUSES LOCKER PROBLEM

Membership at Sequoia Athletic Club had tripled in the past five years. When the club facilities were built in 1987, one hundred full-length lockers were installed along with six hundred half lockers. The intent was to provide a half locker for every member to store his or her personal workout clothing. The full-length lockers were provided for use while the members were working out. With the club membership grown to 800 members, newer members were unhappy that they were unable to leave their court and aerobic shoes at the club in a permanently assigned locker.

Larry Matson, club manager, presented the problem at his next regular staff meeting to see what suggestions seemed to be most applicable.

Your Response

1. What is the primary issue?

2. What is (are) the problem(s)?

3. What barriers may stand in the way of the best solution?

4. What actions are needed?

5. List your action guides.

BIBLIOGRAPHY

Bannon, Joseph J. and James Busser. *Sport Club Management.* Champaign, IL: Management Learning Laboratories, 1985.

Frost, Reuben B., Barbara Lockhart, and Stanley Marshall. *Administration of Physical Education and Athletics: Concepts and Practices.* 3rd ed. Dubuque, IA: William C. Brown, 1988.

Jensen, Clayne. *Administrative Management of Physical Education and Athletic Programs.* Philadelphia: Lea & Febiger, 1988.

Kinder, Thomas M. *Organizational Management Administration for Athletic Programs.* Dubuque, IA: Eddie Bowers Publishing, 1987.

Meagher, John W. "Eliminating the Negative in Sports Facility Design." *Athletic Business* 9, no. 1 (1985).

Olson, John, et al. *Administration of High School and Collegiate Athletic Programs.* New York: Saunders College Publishing, 1987.

Patton, Robert W., et al. *Developing and Managing Health/Fitness Activities.* Champaign, IL.: Human Kinetics Books, 1989.

Redican, Kerry, Larry Olsen, and Charles Baffi. *Organization of School Health Programs.* New York: Macmillan, 1986.

Resick, Matthew, Beverly Seidel, and James Mason. *Modern Administrative Practices in Physical Education Athletics,* 2nd ed. Reading, MA: Addison-Wesley, 1977.

Voltmer, Edward F., and Arthur A. Esslinger. *The Organization and Administration of Physical Education.* 4th ed. New York: Appleton-Century-Crofts, 1967.

14

Managing Risks and Legal Concerns

by
Dr. Betty L. Mann and Dr. William Considine
Springfield College, Springfield, Massachusetts

Carelessness leads to the courtroom.
author unknown

Chapter Objectives

After reading this chapter and completing the exercises, you should be able to:

1 Name the four sources of legal responsibility

2 Define *negligence* and list the four elements that must exist in a negligence case

3 Delineate four areas in which negligence cases arise in activity-based programs, and suggest ways of preventing negligent behavior in each area

4 List at least three defenses that can be used in negligence cases

5 Explain the purpose of accident reports, permission slips, and waivers

6 Define *contract* and give examples of the types of contracts directors normally enter into

7 Name and briefly describe three types of insurance important in the business of delivering services to others

8 Describe the rights to which an athlete is entitled under the Constitution

Physical education, fitness, and sports programs place participants at relatively high risk of injury. Activities that involve people moving, sometimes at high speed, possibly using implements, in a confined area are inherently risky. When an injury does occur and the question of liability is examined, the director, who is judged to be professionally trained to conduct all activities in a reasonable and safe manner while providing for and protecting the civil rights of all connected with the program, is sure to come under scrutiny.

In our increasingly litigious society, it has become common practice to sue all parties possibly related to an injury incident, including administrators of programs in which the injury occurred. If fault can be found, it may be prorated among the parties named. Depending upon the severity of the wrong, particularly when the wrong involved personal injury, the award amount can be astronomical. Personal injury suit awards have been known to exceed millions of dollars. When such high awards are granted, insurance policies may cover much, if not all, of the amount, but damages in excess of the coverage can be passed on to the individuals found at fault. Personal lives and careers as well as businesses have been ruined due to involvement in lawsuits.

For these reasons, it behooves the director of an activity-based program to become familiar with issues related to legal liability and risk management. Responsibilities and expectations in this area more than any other are likely to be left undocumented in the director's job description, but that does not absolve him or her of the responsibility to be knowledgeable about this important aspect of the director's position. Not only is it important to know what to do, but it is equally important to know what not to do. Laws, statutes, rules, regulations, policies, practices, expectations, duties, and common sense all impose direction on the administrator's actions as he or she strives to deliver quality programs and to ensure a safe environment for all participants. This chap-

SO MANY PEOPLE ARE BEING SUED, I BETTER HAVE A LAW DEGREE TO BE A SPORTS DIRECTOR.

ter is intended to provide a basis for development of fundamental knowledge in these areas.

SOURCES OF LEGAL RESPONSIBILITY

Four basic sources dictate the legal responsibilities of the director of an activity-based program: common law, the Constitution of the United States, state constitutions, and statutory laws. American law, as defined by the Constitution of the United States and the state constitutions, is founded on the common law of England. Common law is based on principles proclaimed in court decisions as rendered by judges and may be defined as law that emerges from case decisions. Whereas common law relies upon precedents established by earlier decisions in similar cases, statutory laws are written laws, drafted and adopted by federal, state, or local legislation.

Cases involving liability for injury most often fall within the domain of common law, whereas cases involving rights of individuals to freedom of speech and due process, for example, fall within the domain of constitutional law. We will discuss cases of both kinds in this chapter.

Directors of activity-based programs in a public educational setting have a somewhat different legal responsibility from those in private and commercial settings. State governments have primary jurisdiction over public education, and all states have an agency that is responsible for drafting and maintaining educational policy, usually the state department of education. These boards of education authorize local boards of education, school administrators, and teachers to adopt and enforce reasonable procedures, rules, and regulations for the effective and efficient operation of the local school system, subject to state and federal constitutional limitations. Directors in a public educational setting should be familiar with these procedures, rules, and regulations, just as directors in private and commercial settings should be familiar with the statutory and common laws that apply to them.

UNDERSTANDING NEGLIGENCE

The primary legal responsibility of the director of an activity-based program is to avoid negligence. Negligence is the failure to act as a reasonably prudent person would under the same circumstances. Negligence is part of tort law and tort law exists within the concept of common law. A tort is a civil (not criminal) wrong against an individual. Assault, battery, libel, trespassing, slander, and defamation are all torts and violations of personal rights. Courts distinguish between civil and criminal law in that crimes are wrongful acts against society such as murder, arson, theft, drunken driving, or driving to endanger. A tort is generally brought to a civil court. A tort, however, may also be a crime, in which case two separate legal actions are taken against the accused: the individual's action and the state's action.

Generally speaking, a tort is committed if someone without just cause injures an individual physically, or damages another's reputation, or misuses someone's property, or deprives another of freedom of action. The degree of intent to harm another person, according to Wong (1988), is differentiated on three levels: An intentional tort such as assault and battery describes a situation in which the actor intends to commit the act and intends to harm another person; reckless misconduct is characterized by one's intent to commit the act but no intent to harm; and an unintentional tort, or negligence, is one in which there is no intent to commit the act nor is there intent to harm. To recover damages for a tort, it must be proven that the act was deliberate and intentional or that it was the result of negligence and that actual damage or injury did occur.

In negligence cases, a lawsuit is initiated when a person files a complaint or a petition alleging facts that indicate a law has been violated. The person who is injured or the one who initiates the action is called the plaintiff, whereas the individual against whom the action is brought is the defendant. The plaintiff must set forth the information under which the court would declare that the facts warrant a trial. The facts of the case are explored by both parties during a "discovery period" that usually lasts at least six months.

After a verdict is rendered, the case may be appealed. The individual who files for the appeal is called the appellant. The other individual is the appellee. The appellate court reviews the written record of the lower court decision and can affirm, reverse, or modify the judgment of the lower court, or can order that the case be retried. Once the case is decided by the highest court having jurisdiction to do so, it may not subsequently be brought to court for further litigation. The case is then pronounced *res judicata* or "thing judged."

In a case concerned with negligence, four elements must exist: (1) a duty, (2) a breach of duty, (3) causation, and (4) damages. The concept of duty is based on the nature of the relationship between the parties involved. Teachers stand *in loco parentis* or in place of the parent. The duty the teacher owes to a student varies with the degree of responsibility inherent in the relationship; thus, a teacher is considered to have a higher duty when teaching very young or physically challenged children. In order for negligence to occur, this duty must not only exist, but it must be breached. In addition, the negligent act or behavior must have directly or indirectly contributed to the injury. This is causation or proximal causation. Finally, to recover for damages, an injury must have occurred.

Negligence is based upon foreseeability. Teachers, coaches, and administrators have a duty to protect students and players from reasonably foreseeable risks of harm. In other words, "the risk to be perceived defines the duty to be obeyed" (Weistart and Lowell, 1979: 687).

Establishing where negligence begins and ends is a matter of judgment. Suppose that during a gymnastics lesson, a physical education instructor fails to use an appropriate spotting technique. A student is hurt and the teacher faces a jury. Did his negligence cause the injury? Or a physical education instructor allows a student to participate in a relay race without appropriate footwear—just this one time. The student slips and is injured. Is the teacher negligent? Let's review an actual case in which it became clear that the courts were going to start taking a closer look at the negligent behavior of the teacher and give less credence to the defense of governmental immunity.

Insight through Illustration

In the case of *Miller* v. *Cloidt and the Board of Education of the Borough of Chatham* (1964), Stanley Miller, a fourteen-year-old student, was seriously injured while using a springboard to vault over parallel bars. The teacher had left the gymnasium for a few moments, and it was during his absence that the injury occurred. Is it foreseeable that when a teacher leaves the room, the students may tend to get rowdy or misuse equipment? If so, does this not increase the likelihood of injury? Although the act of the teacher did not, in this case, directly cause the injury, proximate causation could easily be established. The court costs alone for this settlement in 1965 amounted to approximately $10,000, which the insurance company paid in addition to the $200,000 in damages. The school board paid the remaining $135,140 from its own funds.

AVOIDING NEGLIGENT BEHAVIOR

How can directors, instructors, and coaches avoid negligent behavior? We will examine in detail the four important areas where sound teaching and administrative practices can help prevent negligent behavior.

Instruction and Supervision

The instructor or coach is responsible for what happens in his or her gymnasium, classroom, playing field, swimming pool, or locker room. This responsibility cannot be delegated to a student teacher, an aide, or to a student leader.

Insight through Illustration

The teacher and school district were found negligent in a case in which a junior high school boy named David was fatally injured. A student teacher had been allowed to substitute for one of the regular teachers who was absent from school. The coeducational class of approximately sixty students was supervised by one regular teacher and the student teacher. David had been absent from school during the two days of the unit on golf when safety instructions were discussed. The skill that was being taught, the golf swing, was unfamiliar to David. A fellow student volunteered to demonstrate the golf swing to David while the regular teacher was working with a small group of students and the student teacher was helping another student. David was struck in the head when he stepped too close to his classmate who was demonstrating the swing.

There are implications in this particular case not only for proper instruction principles but also for supervisory concerns and wise use of credentialed personnel. Can you identify the elements for which the court found the teacher and school district negligent?

Instruction   Instruction and selection of activities must be based upon sound, widely accepted educational practices. Injuries often occur when inappropriate practices are followed. A game called "murder ball" may be difficult to defend in court. Calling into action twelve of the fifteen participants in a line soccer game may be considered an illogical deviation from the established curriculum. Matching wrestlers from different weight classes is certainly inappropriate. When in court, the plaintiff's attorney will use the testimony of expert witnesses and school and state curriculum and syllabi. If the practice was not sound, the defendant may be found guilty of negligence.

Similarly, care must be taken not to make a safe facility unsafe by the manner in which lessons or drills are planned and designed. Using the bleachers or the wall as a finish line in a relay race is not a wise practice. Using students as markers for the javelin throw of their classmates would never be considered sound teaching.

Students must be taught appropriate safety precautions and the proper use of protective equipment. For example, football coaches must institute proper conditioning and training programs. Further, they must educate the players to the dangers of the game through explicit warning. The National Collegiate Athletic Association (NCAA) has developed the following statement regarding sports safety for college football players (Nygaard and Boone, 1985: 29–30):

Serious head and neck injuries, leading to death, permanent brain damage, or quadriplegia (extensive paralysis from injury to the spinal cord at the neck level), occur each year in football. The toll is relatively small (less than one fatality for every 10,000 players, and an estimated one nonfatal severe brain and spinal cord injury for every 100,000 players), but persistent. They cannot be completely prevented due to the tremendous forces occasionally encountered in football collisions, but they can be minimized by manufacturer, coach, and player compliance with accepted safety standards.

The rules against intentional butting, ramming, or spearing the opponent with the helmeted head are there to protect the helmeted person much more than the opponent being hit. The athlete who does not comply with these rules is the candidate for catastrophic injury.

For example, no helmet can offer protection to the neck, and quadriplegia now occurs more frequently than brain damage. The typical scenario of the catastrophic injury in football is the lowering of one's head while making a tackle. The momentum of the body tries to bend the neck after the helmeted head is stopped by the impact, and the cervical spine cannot be "splinted" as well by the neck's muscles with the head lowered as with the preferred "face up, eyes forward, neck bulled" position. When the force of impact is sufficient, the vertebrae in the neck can dislocate or break, causing damage to the spinal cord they had been protecting, and thereby produce permanent loss of motor and sensory function below the level of injury.

Because of the impact forces in football, even the "face up" position is no guarantee against head or neck injury. Further, the intent to make contact "face up" is no guarantee that the position can be maintained at the moment of impact. Consequently, the teaching of blocking/tackling techniques which keep the helmeted head from receiving the brunt of the impact are now required by rule, and coaching ethics and coaching techniques which help athletes maintain or regain the "face up" position during the milieu of a play must be respected by the athletes.

Insight through Illustration

The Seattle School District and its football coach were found negligent when a fifteen-year-old sophomore suffered an injury that left him a quadriplegic. At the time of the injury, the young boy was running with the football and had lowered his head to avert the tacklers. He was hit on the top of his helmet and consequently sustained injury to his spinal cord. The coach was sued for failure to warn and improper instruction.

Warnings of danger or possible harm similar to the NCAA football statement have been issued for other sports. Coaches should read these warnings with players and parents, and such statements should be signed by the parties involved. This procedure reinforces the function served by permission slips, consent forms, or liability waivers, which we will consider later in this chapter.

Teachers, coaches, and administrators need to provide instruction according to the age, maturity, and ability level of the students. Consideration must be given to the nature of the task and the anxiety level and health status of the player. It would be unwise to conduct a golf lesson for the 2-iron shot using a circular formation. One might consider excusing the young child with a bad head cold from performing on the balance beam. The doctor of the eager student just returning to class following a long-term illness should be consulted before the child is permitted to return to full participation.

Proper instruction can be verified by the consistent use of lesson plans that indicate teaching methodology, the progressions used, and anti-cipated problems. Keeping alternate plans for rainy days or absences is strongly recommended. The time it takes to write these plans will be well spent should an accident occur. You will be amazed at what you think you remember about an incident and what you do, in fact, forget.

Supervision Besides instruction, another area that the courts will investigate when deciding if negligence has occurred is supervision. Requesting one teacher to supervise five hundred fourth graders on a playground is considered unreasonable. The courts distinguish between general supervision and direct supervision. General supervision is appropriate in the locker room or in the corridors as students are changing classes. Direct supervision is what is normally required during the conduct of physical education programs or team practices.

The importance of the supervisor's appropriately positioning herself or himself during activities cannot be overemphasized. A supervisor should be positioned so that he or she can clearly see all students. Some activities require closer supervision than others. The design of lesson plans and format for drills should reflect attention to this detail.

For proper supervision and instruction to exist, the employment of qualified, well-trained personnel is essential. The liability issue alone supports the need for certification of coaches and the need for administrators to take advantage of the benefits of in-service training to update and revitalize the skills of school personnel. This is illustrated in the following case presented by Appenzeller and Appenzeller (1980).

Insight through Illustration

Lowry Stehn was injured in a wrestling program supervised by a faculty member who had had little wrestling and coaching experience. Allegedly, the coach introduced a wrestling hold that he had

Most negligence suits in activity-based programs arise from lack of supervision.

learned in the Army and did not teach a method of escape from the hold nor a defense against it at that time. In addition, the coach was attempting to supervise two matches simultaneously, with his concentration directed toward the one in which Stehn was not wrestling. The plaintiff based his case on inadequate supervision and raised the question of the qualification of the coach for coaching boys of Stehn's age in a wrestling program. Stehn was awarded $385,000 in damages for his injury.

Most states require individuals to be certified by the state in order to be employed as teachers. Each state sets standards for certification eligibil-ity, usually taking the form of courses completed or competencies demonstrated. Some are begin-ning to require a passing score on a minimum competency test. While these requirements do not assure good teachers, they are an attempt to impose some type of quality control on education and the personnel who assume responsibility for educational programs. They also serve as a basis for expectations of behavior in the conduct of pro-grams under the auspices of school systems.

The conduct of a certified teacher must meet the general expectations of all certified teachers. Deviations from this expected standard may be grounds to claim some form of negligence. In as-suming responsibility for the conduct of specific athletic programs, coaches are expected to have higher standards of care and special skills than the ordinary and reasonably prudent person. If the conduct of a coach does not conform to standard and accepted practices, a basis for questioning competence may be present. The Oregon Supreme Court ruled that a football coach at the junior high school level would be expected to demonstrate a higher standard of behavior than a senior high school football coach due to the fact that junior high school players are younger, less experienced, less physically mature, and less capable of good judgment than their older counterparts. This interpretation is counter to the general practices of most school systems in the country.

Requiring particular qualifications of personnel to be charged with teaching, coaching, or supervisory responsibilities is the duty of the administrator in charge of those programs. In a court case, the question of how these individuals were selected may play an important role. Does the fact that a person is certified as a teacher automatically qualify her or him as a coach? Are there certification regulations in the state for coaches? What competencies are required for a person to be employed in this capacity? These questions and more may be the subject of investigation.

Although certification does not guarantee competency, it does demonstrate some degree of specialized knowledge and training. Hundreds of different certifications are available, pertaining to areas ranging from coaching/teaching, fitness, and first aid to aquatics, aerobic dance, and scuba diving. Certainly, no one individual can be expected to possess them all. However, if a person is to be assigned a specific activity in which a certification exists, it is in the best interest of the employer and the employee for the employee to obtain that certification. In the event of litigation, the question of currency of knowledge and qualification may arise. Current certification may help demonstrate competency to undertake a given supervisory role. Failure to possess a common and expected certification may leave an individual vulnerable to a question of competency.

In tort law, there is a concept that should serve as a principle for administrators: "One is ignorant in any field at his or her own peril." In the event of a jury trial involving negligence, it is not uncommon for the plaintiff to bring in expert testimony that will cast doubt on the qualifications or the adequacy of the conduct of the supervisor in question. If the expert witness testifies that certification is an expected qualification, the jury may be convinced that the level of competency of the supervisor was less than what it should have been. In this instance, fault may be found with the person who hired the supervisor as well as the supervisor himself or herself.

The director should take the following steps to minimize the chance of litigation focusing upon the qualifications of personnel under his or her supervision:

- Be sure all instruction is as current and consistent with the norm as possible.

- Make sure all participants are clearly warned of any dangers that might be inherent in the activities.

- Be aware of special skills needed by personnel for the conduct of any activity under the director's supervision.

- Document and verify qualifications of employed personnel.

- Where specialized certifications are available, make sure staff members have them.

- Provide periodic in-service training sessions for the purpose of updating staff techniques, methods, and practices.

- Evaluate staff competencies on a regular basis.

Equipment and Facilities

As part of the usual duties of the administrator, purchasing and maintaining sports equipment and inspecting and maintaining facilities may occupy only a small portion of time, but that time is of

Poorly maintained facilities may lead to injuries and lawsuits.

utmost importance in protecting against claims of negligence.

Facilities Concerns Facilities must be inspected regularly and thoroughly. There is no hard-and-fast rule about what is "regular." What makes sense according to the activity and participants involved is the best rule of thumb. The concept of actual notice implies that the director is responsible for inspecting the facility, eliminating dangerous conditions to the extent possible, and informing supervisors, in writing, of known defects or hazardous conditions. As professionals, administrators are responsible, as well, if they should have known of the existence of a dangerous condition. This is called constructive notice and is illustrated in the case of *Adroin et al.* v. *Evangeline Parish School Board* (1979). A young boy was playing softball and as he was running from second to third base, he tripped on an embedded piece of concrete. The court ruled that the coach should have been aware of this condition.

Product Liability The time a director devotes to equipment matters had better include a thorough investigation of sports products used, including quality, specific use, limitations, guarantees, and standards. In the event of an injury to a participant using any type of sports equipment, there is the chance of legal action focusing upon the use or misuse of that equipment.

In the early days of our society, products were bought by consumers at their own risk. That is, once the product was purchased, the user was responsible for its quality and performance. If the product failed in some way, there was little that the purchaser could do about it. How times have changed! Today, manufacturers must use special care to ensure safe use of their products, and these products must perform their functions as

Manufacturers of products may be held liable if injury results from poorly designed or inferior equipment.

intended. Product failure, particularly relating to protective products, and product malfunctions can be the focus of legal action. Football helmets, hockey equipment, and gymnastics equipment have been the target of numerous lawsuits. Millions of dollars have been awarded by juries convinced of a product failure or malfunction.

When a catastrophic injury in sports occurs, it is not unusual to see litigation follow that names as codefendants coaches, administrators, school districts, and product manufacturers. If supervisory negligence cannot be found, the case may center upon the performance of the equipment in contributing to the injury. For example, if a gymnast were performing on the high bar and in the middle of the routine a cable broke and the athlete was severely injured, litigation would most likely follow. Would the person who purchased the equipment be at fault? Would the person who erected the high bar be at fault? Would the manufacturer of the high bar be at fault? In this instance, all three would quite likely be involved to some degree in legal action.

Arnold (1978: 25) states that "The term product liability refers to the liability of a manufacturer

to the user of its products for personal injury or property damage resulting from the use of those products." A manufacturer must adhere to standards expected of a reasonable and prudent person in the design of any product. The product must be tested and meet or exceed any industry standard that applies. It is the current opinion of the courts that the consumer has a right to expect the product to perform as it was intended, and failure for it to do so can be viewed as a contributing factor in causing injury.

If a defect in design or materials could be detected and foreseen, and this product is made available to the consumer, the manufacturer could be held liable. If, however, the defect could not be detected through a reasonable inspection, the product manufacturer may not be held liable. States Arnold (1978: 25), "The plaintiff must prove that the product contained a defect unreasonably dangerous to their person or property, that the defect in the product existed at the time of the sale of that product by the manufacturer, and that the defect did cause the injury."

Any product, whether it is a sports-related product or not, can be misused. Many sports products have warning labels attempting to define the products' intended use and limitations. A baseball bat can be misused as a weapon, and in this instance, the manufacturer of the baseball bat would not be held liable in an injury case; but if that bat breaks when it is being used properly and as intended, and an injury is sustained, the question of liability could be addressed by the court. Appenzeller (1985: 224) states, "The lack of warning specifically directed to any hazard that results in accident or injury has been sufficient ground for courts and juries to find the manufacturer liable. Thus the overwhelming majority of product liability actions against manufacturers and school districts are based on failure to warn."

Although most administrators are not directly associated with the manufacturer of sports equipment, they are responsible for purchasing and maintaining that equipment. They therefore assume the responsibility for its adequacy in performing its intended use. Those responsible for the use of equipment in sports must exercise good judgment in allowing its continued use by participants. In his article on product liability, Arnold (1978) offers ten recommendations for administrators as precautions to avoid product-related liability actions:

1. Participate in the collection of information associated with illness and injury.

2. Purchase the best equipment your budget will allow.

3. Buy only from reputable dealers.

4. Rely upon reputable reconditioners to see that protective equipment maintains a level of protection which could reasonably be expected from such equipment.

5. Exercise a high degree of care in adjusting, fitting, and repairing all equipment, especially protective equipment, and in moving equipment and performing assembly tasks.

6. Have an organized emergency care plan ready to activate in case of serious injury.

7. Do not flippantly cast blame for an injury on someone or something.

8. Do a good job of teaching and supervising.

9. Make sure that accident and general liability insurance coverages on, or available to, participants, staff members, and schools reflect an appreciation for the current sports product liability situation.

10. In the event of severe injury, preserve possible items of evidence associated with the injury.

In the event of an injury where the performance of a product may be questioned, the dilemma of performance standards is confronted. For many products, there are no standards, or at least no standards other than those selected by the manufacturer. This void has been noted in many liability cases. There are two organizations, however, that have established performance standards for some equipment, particularly football helmets. The National Operating Committee on Standards for Athletic Equipment (NOCSAE) and the American Standards Committee Testing Material (ASTM) have initiated standards for the performance of football helmets. The NOCSAE seal on a football helmet indicates that the material has been tested and meets the standards established by NOCSAE. There are businesses that recondition football helmets to meet the NOCSAE standards. Administrators responsible for football programs should make sure no player uses a football helmet that has not been NOCSAE-approved. Failure to recognize this industry standard may lead to vulnerability in litigation.

Product liability has become a problem shared by manufacturers, school districts, administrators, coaches, suppliers, and consumers. The price charged for most sporting goods contains a portion attributable to product liability insurance costs. As juries award more and larger sums in such cases, costs of these products rise. Unless state or federal regulations establish some limits, there appears to be no end in sight to the escalating spiral.

Proper Medical Procedures

Physical educators and coaches are expected to know basic first aid procedures. If one applies hot water to a burn, he or she will be found negligent, and rightly so. It is the administrator's responsibility to be sure that all teachers and coaches are aware of planned procedures for emergency medical care, whether put into practice in the physical education class or on the playing field during practices or games.

Job descriptions for all personnel associated with physical education and athletics, including athletic trainers, nurses, and physicians, should clearly delineate who is responsible for what in terms of care for the injured. Trainers, for example, must know the limits of their responsibility in relation to the responsibilities of the coach and the physician. All personnel must exercise due care to prevent unreasonable risk of injury. Should an injury occur, legal duty becomes one of preventing further injury and activating the emergency medical system.

Keeping accurate records that document the circumstances surrounding the incident is essential and will be discussed in detail shortly. Accident reports should reflect an objective assessment of the incident. The record keeping includes medical histories and preseason medical examinations, appropriately updated according to season or year. All records should be filed and kept for a long time.

Generally, negligence is found when coaches allow or require a player to participate when they know or should know the athlete has not sufficiently recovered from an injury; when inadequate or improper medical attention is provided; when players are allowed to compete who are disproportionate in size or ability; or when coaches fail to give proper instructions or warnings.

Transportation

In many instances, transportation of participants in activity-based programs is required. State laws and regulations, agency, organization, or school system policies, and program procedures all influence the mode of transportation chosen and legal liability in the event of an accident.

When administrators are faced with the responsibility of arranging transportation for the conduct of programs under their authority, they must be conscious of the inherent risks involved. If the school system owns and operates its own bus system, this responsibility is shared with other administrators within the system. The buses must be maintained in a safe condition. The drivers must be judged to be safe drivers, possess the appropriate license, and possibly have

successfully completed a prescribed driver education/safety course. Unless state law specifically states otherwise, school districts do not assume the liability for negligent acts by persons hired to drive their buses. Insurance carried by the school district normally covers damages in the event of an accident, but this insurance may not cover damages should negligence be found.

Some school districts use commercial carriers to transport students to and from school, to athletic contests, band contests, and so on. In this instance, the company owning and operating the bus assumes the liability for the safety of passengers. If possible, this alternative is the best and wisest choice for transporting students. The administrator should check with the transportation companies for current licensing, safety records, and insurance coverage.

In some cases, staff members may be called upon to drive a bus as part of their assigned duties. All laws and regulations governing the transporting of passengers still apply. The individual may be required to secure the appropriate license and complete a safety course. The school district should provide adequate insurance protection to both the passengers and the driver. Only those trained and licensed to operate a bus should ever be allowed to drive that type of vehicle.

Many interscholastic and intercollegiate programs depend heavily upon transporting athletes in vans driven by coaches. Although the coaches are acting as agents of the school or college and are usually covered by liability insurance carried by the school, they are susceptible to suit as individuals if negligence is suspected. Even if a person is conducting officially assigned responsibilities, personal conduct cannot be separated from actions performed on duty. Administrators have an obligation to inform their staff members of the risks involved, check the driving records of assigned drivers, and, of course, ensure the mechanical adequacy of the vehicle in use.

At times, students are transported in private vehicles to participate in school activities. School

Administrators or coaches must check the safety features of privately owned vehicles when used for transporting others.

districts and their representatives may be held more liable in some circumstances than in others. If a student is riding in a private vehicle for his or her own pleasure or to conduct his or her own business, that student may be considered by law a guest, and in this circumstance, the limits of liability may not be extended to the school district, but be limited to the owner/operator of the vehicle. If, however, the student is assigned to an automobile, is required to ride in the vehicle as part of a class assignment or to complete an assignment or responsibility, the guest status is no longer in force. In this circumstance, the school district might be held liable in the event of an injury to a passenger.

Administrators using privately owned automobiles in the conduct of programs under their authority must exercise extraordinary caution. Driver records must be checked, mechanical conditions must be judged to be safe, routes should be predetermined, policies governing speed and driver conduct should be written and provided to drivers, and weather conditions taken into account. Students should not be allowed to drive

vehicles used to transport other students unless they are licensed to do so. Evidence of adequate insurance coverage should be on file and riders obtained if this mode of transportation is used on a regular basis. Faculty or staff supervision is essential under all circumstances.

Recommended administrative procedures governing transportation of participants in activity-based programs include (1) familiarization with the state laws and regulations governing transportation, (2) assessment of alternatives, including costs and risks, (3) presentation of this assessment to appropriate authorities for selection, (4) preparation of written policies, procedures, and regulations governing implementation, (5) procurement and verification of adequate insurance coverage, (6) continued diligence in the supervision of the transportation process, and (7) continuous evaluation of the adequacy and appropriateness of methods used.

Although thorough planning, care, and adherence to laws and regulations go far in protecting administrators and staff against liability claims, there have been hundreds of court cases involving negligence in the transportation of students. Unfortunately, transportation cases often involve multiple injuries and may be susceptible to multiple defendant suits. It is therefore advisable to purchase adequate professional liability insurance for all associated administrators and staff.

DEFENSE AGAINST NEGLIGENCE CLAIMS

If confronted with a lawsuit, what should one do? Appenzeller (1985: 6) says the answer is simple: "Call your insurance carrier and your lawyer, in that order. This will permit a prompt investigation of the entire case when all events are still fresh in everyone's mind, so that the actual facts may be accurately preserved for presentation later, perhaps years later. It will also protect you against taking any action that could prejudice your position at a later date." Appenzeller (1985: 6) cautions us to keep accurate and detailed notes on everything related to the incident, including the names and addresses of those who may serve as witnesses. "Be reluctant to discuss any aspect of the case without the advice of your attorney, particularly to the news media. This should not imply that you are trying to "cover up" or "hide" anything, but merely that any public statement should be delayed until all the facts are known."

Everyone has the right to sue or to file a lawsuit against anyone for anything. But as Appenzeller and Appenzeller (1980) suggest, winning is another matter. Liability must be proven. Many times the matter is settled out of court before a trial is scheduled or a lawsuit is filed.

In the event an individual or organization is sued and the cause of action is negligence, what defenses can be used? In the most obvious defense, one of the elements of negligence would be found missing. It would be shown that a duty could not be established, or that there was no breach of duty, or that the injury was not caused by negligent action on the part of authorities, or that there was, in fact, no injury.

Insight through Illustration

In *Nestor* v. *City of New York* (1961) a teacher was supervising a group of children. One student, Anthony, was trying to hit a ball with a bat while all the other children were playing catch. Another student was hit with the bat as he tried to catch the same ball that Anthony tried to strike with the bat. The teacher, while supervising the children playing, was also distributing milk. The court ruled that the teacher was not negligent because the injury was an unforeseeable accident. In the opinion of the court (Weistart and Lowell, 1979: 976):

Even if the teacher had had the game under steady observation and the measure of his supervision had been constant, an assumption that he could have anticipated what ensued would be without justifiable warrant. The teacher would be required to be invested with a profound prescience to have foreseen that Michael would attempt, after batting the ball, to run to catch it and that Tony would suddenly run towards the ball with bat in hand and, without warning, swing with his bat at the descending ball while Michael was endeavoring to snare it.

To urge that the teacher should have anticipated each of the separate occurrences constituting the link in the chain of events herein above recited, or that a blast by the teacher on his whistle would have frozen the two boys into instant immobility and averted the accident which ensued, is indulgence in pure speculation. This reasoning is fortified by the fact that Anthony said that he saw Michael at the last moment but that he could not check his swing. This was an accident that could occur equally in the presence or absence of the teacher.

Another commonly used defense is that of comparative and contributory negligence. Con-

ACCIDENT REPORT

1. PERSONAL INFORMATION OF INJURED PARTY

  NAME _____ AGE _____ SOC. SEC. # _____

  STUDENT _____ GUEST _____

  HOME ADDRESS _____

  _____

  CAMPUS ADDRESS _____

  _____

  HOME TELEPHONE _____ CAMPUS TELEPHONE _____

  INSURANCE COMPANY _____

2. DATE OF ACCIDENT _____ TIME _____

3. CLASS OR ACTIVITY _____ WEEK/DAY OF UNIT _____

  INSTRUCTOR _____ LENGTH OF UNIT _____ WEEKS

  WITNESSES: NAME _____

           ADDRESS _____

           NAME _____

           ADDRESS _____

           NAME _____

           ADDRESS _____

  LOCATION OF ACCIDENT _____

  (Attach diagram of playing area to identify location of accident, instructor, witnesses, other participants.)

4. What specifically was the person doing at the time of the accident? _____

  _____

  _____

5. What was done or should have been done by the injured to have prevented the injury? _____

  _____

  _____

6. Detailed description of the accident _____

  _____

  Part of the body injured _____

  Type of injury or accident _____

  What first aid was administered? _____

  _____

  Who performed the first aid? _____

Figure 14.1 *A Sample Accident Report Form*

7. Person was referred to:

HEALTH CENTER   Yes _____ No _____ Accompanied by _____

HOSPITAL   Yes _____ No _____ Accompanied by _____

PARENTS WERE CONTACTED   Yes _____ No _____ Time _____

8. IF TAKEN TO THE HOSPITAL:

Attending Physician's Name _____

Diagnosis _____

Physician's signature _____

9. SIGNATURE OF WITNESSES   _____ Phone _____ Date _____

_____ Phone _____ Date _____

_____ Phone _____ Date _____

10. SIGNATURE OF PERSON INJURED   _____ Date _____

11. SIGNATURE OF PERSON COMPLETING REPORT   _____ Date _____

Time _____

Figure 14.1 *(continued)*

tributary negligence is defined by a situation in which both the teacher and the student are in some way responsible for what has happened. If the student, in fact, in any way caused his or her own injury, some states will recognize contributory negligence and bar recovery of damages. Most states, however, recognize comparative negligence in which the fault is apportioned between the injured student and the teacher, or the injured student, the teacher, the administration, the school district, the architect, and the equipment manufacturer, and each responsible party pays accordingly. If, for example, the jury decides the student contributed to his or her own injury, the percentage of fault is determined through analysis of the situation. It may be determined that the student's behavior contributed to the injury to the extent of 30 percent, while 70 percent of the damage is assigned to the responsible school authorities. Generally, but not in all cases, recovery of damages is barred if the student is more than 50 percent responsible for the incident.

Though infrequently used, another defense against negligence claims is an act of God (Vis Major). Should lightning strike without warning, giving the instructor no opportunity to vacate the field, the teacher is clearly not responsible for any injuries sustained by students if it can be shown that he or she acted prudently under the circumstances.

Two remaining defenses against negligence have experienced diminished usage in recent cases. Governmental immunity ("the king can do no wrong") protects the state or an agent of the state who is fulfilling a state function from being sued without its consent. The law is a changing, relational concept, not set in concrete but dependent on societal trends, the bargaining power of the people, and other influences affecting the interpretation of the law. Through the post-Vietnam era and the decade of the 1970s, people have become increasingly aware of their rights and expect compensation for the victim. Thus, governmental immunity is being used less and less as a defense, and so is the "assumption of by law. Unless extenuating circumstances can be proven, the law assumes that both parties entered the contract with legal purpose when the contract was signed.

Resick, Seidel, and Mason (1975: 78) explain that "a contract is deemed to have been accepted when signed, prior to a withdrawal date, by a person of legal age and of sound mind. Prior to fulfillment a contract may be terminated for a number of reasons. Among these are: (1) either of the parties failed to perform without a legal excuse, (2) one of the participants made the contract while concealing pertinent information, and (3) the participants agree mutually to terminate the contract." All individuals who enter into a contractual agreement are obligated to fulfill the terms specified unless one of these three conditions prevails.

Administrators usually sign a professional employment contract. This legally binding agreement specifies the terms of employment, usually including tenure, duties and responsibilities, and, of course, salary. All other personnel not employed on an hourly basis also sign contracts in most cases. In some instances, such as in coaching, separate contracts in addition to the teaching contract may be used. These supplemental contracts may specify additional duties with additional compensation and terms of employment.

Coaching or other additional assignments can also be included in the basic employment contract. In this case, all responsibilities specified in the contract are binding. Should an individual wish to be relieved of a portion of those duties, such as coaching, the employer is not obligated to accommodate such a request. If a contract offered with those duties included is accepted, the coaching assignment is also accepted. If rejected, the entire contract is rejected and the employer is free to extend an offer of that contract to another individual.

Both the basic contract approach and the supplemental contract approach have advantages and disadvantages. It is important to both parties to fully understand the ramifications of the terms of the employment contract.

Other types of contracts the administrator is likely to encounter include equipment purchase contracts, facility construction contracts, interscholastic or intercollegiate athletic contest agreements and agreements about officiating for such, advertising contracts, and transportation rental contracts. Most commercial vendors have standardized contracts that are used in the normal conduct of their business. These contracts should be reviewed carefully so all conditions are fully known prior to entry. When an administrator enters into a contract with another party as a representative of his or her organization, that organization becomes legally obligated to fulfill the terms of the agreement. Thus, this administrative duty should not be taken lightly.

INSURANCE

Administrators charged with a responsibility to deliver services to others should be familiar with at least three types of insurance: liability insurance, property insurance, and medical or accident insurance. No one expects the administrator to be thoroughly knowledgeable about the intricacies of particular policies, but familiarity with the need for and purposes of insurance is essential.

Liability Insurance

Liability insurance does not offer protection against negligence! Nor does it guarantee protection against being sued or being named as a defendant in a lawsuit. The purpose of liability insurance is to protect personal assets in the event that legal action is initiated against an individual or agency.

Most school systems purchase liability insur-

risk" defense. The limitations of the assumption of risk defense were brought to light vividly in the Seattle decision discussed earlier involving the fifteen-year-old football player. According to Weistart and Lowell (1979: 936), this defense rests on the principle "that a party who voluntarily assumes a risk of harm arising from the conduct of another cannot recover if harm in fact results." A participant in an athletic contest makes this assumption when he or she "is explicitly aware of a risk caused by the potential negligence of another, and yet proceeds to encounter it voluntarily." Further, "it may be stated as a general rule that voluntary . . . participants . . . in lawful sporting activity assume, as a matter of law, all of the ordinary and inherent risk in the sport, so long as the activity is played in good faith and the injury is not the result of an intentional or willful act." Appenzeller (1985) suggests that to assume the risk of participation, students must know the full extent of the risk. Risks inherent in a sport for experienced athletes may be very different than for novice players. Clearly, the importance of explicit warnings for players and parents of the potential dangers involved cannot be overstated.

RECORD KEEPING AND ACCIDENT REPORTS

Any enterprise that delivers a service to consumers needs to develop and use a system of record keeping. Records should be kept on each consumer of the service. For example, in the school setting, records of attendance, health status, grades, equipment issue, participation, and developed competencies may be required. Other forms of records may be used in the normal conduct of curricular and extracurricular programs. Careful attention to detail in any record-keeping process is essential to assure accuracy. But special care must be taken when the records document the event of an injury or accident.

An accident report form should be viewed as a legal document that might become just that should it be entered into the court record as evidence in a negligence suit. Completing an accident form should therefore not be taken lightly. Most school districts and other organizations have developed standardized reporting forms for accidents.

Betty van der Smissen (1990) suggests that an accident report should include the following information: name, address, social security number, age, phone number, and accident insurance agency or family policy of person injured; date and time of day accident occurred; name of instructor; names and addresses of witnesses; location of the accident within the playing area and a statement and/or diagram which describes where the instructor, witnesses, and other participants were located at the time of the injury; a factual statement, without reference to cause, about what the injured was doing and how the accident occurred; the sequence of the activity in relation to the unit plan (e.g., the accident occurred the seventh week in a ten-week unit or at the end of a lesson following a fifteen-minute presentation on safety regulations); what was done or should have been done by the injured to have prevented the injury (do not include statements about what you as the instructor could have done to have prevented the accident); procedures utilized in providing first aid and who performed the first aid, who phoned for emergency help, when help arrived, and who contacted the physician and the name of the physician; the signatures of the instructor, witnesses and, where possible, the signature of the injured party; and a record of any follow-up information pertinent to the incident (see Figure 14.1). Van der Smissen warns us to avoid including information that would, in effect, be an admission of negligence. For example, if you are approached by the media, avoid statements such as "If only I had done. . . ." The information on the accident report is a factual account of what happened with no reference to cause or inferences about what *should* have been done.

risk" defense. The limitations of the assumption of risk defense were brought to light vividly in the Seattle decision discussed earlier involving the fifteen-year-old football player. According to Weistart and Lowell (1979: 936), this defense rests on the principle "that a party who voluntarily assumes a risk of harm arising from the conduct of another cannot recover if harm in fact results." A participant in an athletic contest makes this assumption when he or she "is explicitly aware of a risk caused by the potential negligence of another, and yet proceeds to encounter it voluntarily." Further, "it may be stated as a general rule that voluntary . . . participants . . . in lawful sporting activity assume, as a matter of law, all of the ordinary and inherent risk in the sport, so long as the activity is played in good faith and the injury is not the result of an intentional or willful act." Appenzeller (1985) suggests that to assume the risk of participation, students must know the full extent of the risk. Risks inherent in a sport for experienced athletes may be very different than for novice players. Clearly, the importance of explicit warnings for players and parents of the potential dangers involved cannot be overstated.

RECORD KEEPING AND ACCIDENT REPORTS

Any enterprise that delivers a service to consumers needs to develop and use a system of record keeping. Records should be kept on each consumer of the service. For example, in the school setting, records of attendance, health status, grades, equipment issue, participation, and developed competencies may be required. Other forms of records may be used in the normal conduct of curricular and extracurricular programs. Careful attention to detail in any record-keeping process is essential to assure accuracy. But special care must be taken when the records document the event of an injury or accident.

An accident report form should be viewed as a legal document that might become just that should it be entered into the court record as evidence in a negligence suit. Completing an accident form should therefore not be taken lightly. Most school districts and other organizations have developed standardized reporting forms for accidents.

Betty van der Smissen (1990) suggests that an accident report should include the following information: name, address, social security number, age, phone number, and accident insurance agency or family policy of person injured; date and time of day accident occurred; name of instructor; names and addresses of witnesses; location of the accident within the playing area and a statement and/or diagram which describes where the instructor, witnesses, and other participants were located at the time of the injury; a factual statement, without reference to cause, about what the injured was doing and how the accident occurred; the sequence of the activity in relation to the unit plan (e.g., the accident occurred the seventh week in a ten-week unit or at the end of a lesson following a fifteen-minute presentation on safety regulations); what was done or should have been done by the injured to have prevented the injury (do not include statements about what you as the instructor could have done to have prevented the accident); procedures utilized in providing first aid and who performed the first aid, who phoned for emergency help, when help arrived, and who contacted the physician and the name of the physician; the signatures of the instructor, witnesses and, where possible, the signature of the injured party; and a record of any follow-up information pertinent to the incident (see Figure 14.1). Van der Smissen warns us to avoid including information that would, in effect, be an admission of negligence. For example, if you are approached by the media, avoid statements such as "If only I had done. . . ." The information on the accident report is a factual account of what happened with no reference to cause or inferences about what *should* have been done.

Several copies of this record should be made and kept on file for an indefinite period of time. Lawsuits have been initiated several years after injuries have occurred, when memories have faded, witnesses have moved, and even administrators have taken different positions. In these circumstances, the accident report form becomes invaluable.

Whenever an accident occurs, it is in the best interest of all parties to complete an accident report form. This should be done as soon as possible after the incident to avoid loss of accuracy. All policies and procedures specified by the school or organization should be followed explicitly. If the accident involved equipment failure, the equipment should be set aside and labeled, detailed records should be made describing the performance of the equipment, and the faulty equipment should be inspected by several appropriate individuals prior to repair or disposal. Photographs may also be considered as documentation to be included in accident records where feasible.

Accident records may serve as a basis for insurance claims, evidence in litigation, and a stimulus to improvement of programming or safety measures. All personnel in any organization should be familiarized with the procedures for filing and the importance of such reports. Few other reports may prove to be as valuable.

PERMISSION SLIPS, WAIVERS, AND CONSENT FORMS

Sports administrators often encounter institutional policies that require the use of permission slips, waivers, or consent forms. It is important to understand the use and value of these items in relation to legal interpretation.

Permission slips simply provide the school or organization with documentation that the individual has the right to participate in an activity. Forms granting permission to participate are commonly used by schools for their interscholastic athletics programs. Parents are asked to sign the form indicating that their child has the right to participate in the sports activity. Some forms include a warning about the inherent risks involved in participating in that sport. Permission slips are of little value other than in providing evidence of parental knowledge that the child is participating in the extracurricular program.

In contrast, a waiver form requests that the participant waive the right to bring suit against the school or organization for damages suffered while engaged in an activity. It should be noted that because parents cannot waive the rights of their minor children, waivers are of little value when the participants of a program are under legal age.

A waiver is an attempt to relieve one individual or organization of responsibility for another. For adults, signing a waiver is generally considered as entering into a contractual agreement, since it involves giving consent to engage in some activity. Hence, when the issue of waiver forms is taken up by the courts, contract law comes into play. At times, contract law and negligence theory come into conflict. While a contract is a legally binding document, it does not absolve either of the parties of responsibility for negligent acts. If a consenting adult signs a waiver form that details its full consequences, and there is no evidence of fraud, misleading information, or intent for deliberate misconduct on the part of the individual providing the services, the waiver may be viewed favorably in court.

Waiver forms may be included in membership contracts such as those used in fitness centers and health clubs. The fact that members contract for services and use of facilities for a fee may increase the value of waivers in relation to enforceability. When an accident occurs, unless obvious negligence is evident, the waiver clause may serve as some legal protection for the organization.

Waiver forms or clauses have been upheld by the courts for more highly skilled performers. But

WELL, SO MUCH FOR WAIVERS KEEPING
US OUT OF COURT...

Waivers do not always absolve one from
responsibility for negligence.

even in these cases, waiver forms may be voided if the following conditions are present:

- A strong public policy prohibits waivers.
- One party is in a clearly dominant position, as in a boss-employee relationship.
- Fraud or misrepresentation is present within the waiver.
- The waiver is signed under force or duress.
- Ambiguity is present in the waiver.
- The waiver is unreasonable.
- The organization's representatives are guilty of wanton, intentional, or reckless misconduct.
- The signature accepting the waiver is separated from the actual exculpatory clause.

Essentially, waivers serve to deter an injured party from filing a lawsuit and to educate the reader of the nature of the activity and the risks involved.

Consent forms are sometimes used by organizations as protection against claims of invasion of a person's right to privacy. Research activities involving the use of human subjects commonly employ consent forms. When assessment activities may require individuals to reveal personal information and that information cannot be held in confidence, documentation that the individual consented to the release and use of that information is necessary. The consent form must state clearly and accurately what information is required and how this information is to be used. It must be signed freely and with full disclosure of all consequences of voluntary participation.

Although permission slips, waivers, and consent forms are commonly used, in many instances the value of these methods may be questioned. It is important for the administrator to understand explicitly what use of these techniques accomplishes. Review of such forms by an attorney may be in order, especially to determine the effect of any local or state regulatory statutes. In practical terms, the use of these forms may discourage the initiation of a suit, but does not guarantee protection against such or absolve persons in authority of responsibility for negligent acts.

CONTRACTS

Contracts are legally binding agreements documenting terms of transactions such as employment, purchasing, payment, and delivery. Administrators may find themselves negotiating many forms of contracts in their professional careers, and due to their position of responsibility may be called upon to sign such legal documents representing either themselves personally or their employer. Fundamental knowledge of contract law is therefore essential.

Whenever a contract is used to document an agreement, it is assumed that both parties entered into that agreement by mutual consent and both parties read and understood the terms of the agreement. Contracts are binding on both parties for the specified terms and can be altered only by mutual consent. Should one party fail to live up to the terms of the contract, it can be enforced by law. Unless extenuating circumstances can be proven, the law assumes that both parties entered the contract with legal purpose when the contract was signed.

Resick, Seidel, and Mason (1975: 78) explain that "a contract is deemed to have been accepted when signed, prior to a withdrawal date, by a person of legal age and of sound mind. Prior to fulfillment a contract may be terminated for a number of reasons. Among these are: (1) either of the parties failed to perform without a legal excuse, (2) one of the participants made the contract while concealing pertinent information, and (3) the participants agree mutually to terminate the contract." All individuals who enter into a contractual agreement are obligated to fulfill the terms specified unless one of these three conditions prevails.

Administrators usually sign a professional employment contract. This legally binding agreement specifies the terms of employment, usually including tenure, duties and responsibilities, and, of course, salary. All other personnel not employed on an hourly basis also sign contracts in most cases. In some instances, such as in coaching, separate contracts in addition to the teaching contract may be used. These supplemental contracts may specify additional duties with additional compensation and terms of employment.

Coaching or other additional assignments can also be included in the basic employment contract. In this case, all responsibilities specified in the contract are binding. Should an individual wish to be relieved of a portion of those duties, such as coaching, the employer is not obligated to accommodate such a request. If a contract offered with those duties included is accepted, the coaching assignment is also accepted. If rejected, the entire contract is rejected and the employer is free to extend an offer of that contract to another individual.

Both the basic contract approach and the supplemental contract approach have advantages and disadvantages. It is important to both parties to fully understand the ramifications of the terms of the employment contract.

Other types of contracts the administrator is likely to encounter include equipment purchase contracts, facility construction contracts, interscholastic or intercollegiate athletic contest agreements and agreements about officiating for such, advertising contracts, and transportation rental contracts. Most commercial vendors have standardized contracts that are used in the normal conduct of their business. These contracts should be reviewed carefully so all conditions are fully known prior to entry. When an administrator enters into a contract with another party as a representative of his or her organization, that organization becomes legally obligated to fulfill the terms of the agreement. Thus, this administrative duty should not be taken lightly.

INSURANCE

Administrators charged with a responsibility to deliver services to others should be familiar with at least three types of insurance: liability insurance, property insurance, and medical or accident insurance. No one expects the administrator to be thoroughly knowledgeable about the intricacies of particular policies, but familiarity with the need for and purposes of insurance is essential.

Liability Insurance

Liability insurance does not offer protection against negligence! Nor does it guarantee protection against being sued or being named as a defendant in a lawsuit. The purpose of liability insurance is to protect personal assets in the event that legal action is initiated against an individual or agency.

Most school systems purchase liability insurance policies for their employees that provide coverage while they are engaged in the conduct of their assigned duties. Should a suit be brought and a judgment rendered against a school or an employee as a representative of the school, the monetary award is paid by the insurance carrier. However, if the amount of the award exceeds the limits of the insurance coverage, damages can be collected from other sources, including the employee or employees as individuals. There have been cases where the damage awards have been apportioned among defendants. Few individuals can personally afford to pay even a portion of the amounts awarded by juries today.

To protect employees as individuals, it is advisable to encourage the purchase of liability insurance on an individual basis. This practice extends the insurance protection beyond that provided by the school system and protects the personal assets of the professional employee. Many professional organizations offer as a membership benefit the option of purchasing professional liability insurance, usually at additional cost. The American Alliance for Health, Physical Education, Recreation, and Dance can serve as an example. Currently, members of this organization can purchase $1,000,000 worth of professional liability insurance based upon group rates for $70. Group rates are far less expensive than individual rates and can provide adequate coverage for a relatively small premium.

As one of their priorities administrators should investigate liability insurance coverage. The name of the carrier, the extent of the coverage, the adequacy of the coverage, and any exclusions should be known and communicated to all staff members. If necessary, a discussion with a representative of the insurance company from which the policy was purchased may prove beneficial. Adequacy of liability insurance is best known prior to its need. Discovery of noncoverage, or inadequate or limited coverage, after legal action is initiated can be a disaster!

Property Insurance

Property insurance provides coverage for school-owned or organization-owned equipment and facilities. Should a loss occur because of conditions covered by the insurance policy, such as fire or theft, the insurance company will pay for full or partial replacement. Again, policies vary in the extent of coverage for loss. Many have deductible clauses, which means that the school or organization must pay the first portion or part of the remaining monetary loss. Administrators responsible for facilities and equipment should be familiar with property insurance coverage and procedures to file claims with the carrier.

Periodic review of the adequacy of property insurance coverage is advised. In many instances, new equipment is purchased or facilities expanded and an assumption is made that the current policy will cover these new items. This is not always the case. Confirmation of coverage is always a wise action.

Medical or Accident Insurance

Many school districts provide students with some form of medical or accident insurance to cover the costs of medical care in case of injury. The extent of coverage and costs vary widely from school to school and community to community. Most school districts have regulations requiring medical insurance coverage prior to participation in extracurricular activities such as athletics. In some cases, the cost of policies is borne by the student and/or parents of the student, while in others, the school district pays the premiums.

Usually, school medical or accident insurance premiums are based upon group rates. Commercial insurance companies calculate the probability of accidents and costs, and set their premiums at a level that will ensure a profit for the company. Some school districts subscribe to medical insurance plans offered by state associations or organizations in an attempt to keep the costs to a minimum. Plans usually include two options: door-to-door coverage or full coverage. Door-to-door coverage generally limits coverage to activities undertaken while going to, during, and returning from school. Full coverage extends the coverage to all activities undertaken during the school year.

In most cases, the chief administrative officer of the school system or organization is responsible for procuring adequate medical or accident insurance options for the clientele served. Departmental administrators, however, should be familiar with the options available, the policies of the organization regarding the options involved, and the procedures required for filing a claim.

STUDENT RIGHTS

What constitutes a right? A right is a power or privilege belonging to individuals as a matter of law. Thus, by the First Amendment, we are guaranteed the right of freedom of speech. By the Fifth and Fourteenth amendments we are guaranteed the right to be treated fairly and not to be denied the privilege of life, liberty and property without due process, nor be denied the equal protection of the laws.

What are the implications of this for students, coaches, teachers, and administrators? Generally, courts agree that the right to participate in athletics is sufficiently substantial that it cannot be taken away without proceedings that comply with the procedural due process of law, thus protecting the athlete from arbitrary and capricious treatment; and it cannot be taken away for reasons that infringe on the participants' constitutional rights.

Insight through Illustration

In the case of *Tinker* v. *Des Moines Independent School District* (1969), several student athletes had been suspended from school for wearing black armbands in protest of the involvement of the United States in the Vietnam War. The court observed that a "student('s) rights do not embrace merely classroom hours. When he [she] is . . . on the playing field . . . he/she may express his [her] opinions." The court found no evidence that wearing armbands would cause disruption. The court held that

in order for the state in the person of school officials to justify prohibition of a particular expression of opinion, it must be able to show that its action was caused by something more than a mere desire to avoid the discomfort and unpleasantness that always accompany an unpopular viewpoint. Certainly where there is no finding and no showing that engaging in the forbidden conduct would "materially and substantially interfere with the requirements of appropriate discipline in the operation of the school," the prohibition cannot be sustained. . . . (Weistart and Lowell, 1979: 29)

On the other hand, a recent Supreme Court decision ruled that the guarantees of free speech under the First Amendment did not prevent disciplinary action against a high school student who delivered "an offensively lewd and indecent speech" at a compulsory school assembly. The court held that the First Amendment "does not prevent the school officials from determining that to permit a vulgar and lewd speech such as respondent's [student's] would undermine the schools' basic educational mission." (Fields, 1986: 11)

The relationship of coach and athlete is one in which the coach has broad authority to control, within reasonable and constitutional limits, those aspects of the athlete's life that directly relate to athletic performance. The coach has the right to establish and maintain health and training rules, to direct and conduct practice sessions, to issue during competition reasonable instructions that are to be followed without question, and to im-

Punishment for violating rules may violate a player's constitutional right to be treated fairly.

pose sanctions for violations of such instructions. Under this rationale, the hair length of athletes, a controversial issue in the 1970s, cannot be controlled by the coach unless it can be shown that a certain hairstyle (or lack of style) would interfere with performance. Coaches must be sure to explain rules, regulations, and expected procedures so that the players understand them. Should the rules be violated, players must be informed what they did wrong and be given ample opportunity to defend themselves. When a coach imposes punishment on a player for violating rules, these questions may legitimately be asked:

• Does the coach have the authority to impose the rule?

• Did the coach follow the appropriate process in implementing the sanction?

• Was the action taken by the coach justified and was the sanction related to the rule broken?

• Was the athlete given prior notice of the penalty for breaking rules, and was he or she notified of charges?

• Was the athlete deprived of his or her rights?

Certain other rights are guaranteed under the Fourteenth Amendment, Title IX of the Education Amendment of 1972, P.L. 94–142, and Section 504 of the Rehabilitation Act of 1973. Title IX provides that "no person . . . shall, on the basis of sex, be excluded from participation in, be denied the benefits, or be subject to discrimination under any education program or activity receiving federal financial assistance." But the 1984 ruling in the *Grove City College* v. *Bell* case, which stated that Title IX was to be applied *only* to programs that received direct federal funding, undermined the act's power to prevent sex discrimination. Since the ruling, we have witnessed a decline in women's sports programs and, increasingly, we are seeing fewer women in coaching and administrative roles. The Civil Rights Restoration Act of 1988 has strengthened civil rights legislation. With the passage of this act, we can expect to see an increase in complaints or lawsuits filed at schools and colleges. In addition, the Office of Civil Rights (OCR) of the Department of Education has developed the *Title IX Grievance Procedures: An Introductory Manual* that provides guidelines on how to proceed with an athletics complaint. Essentially, Title IX reflects a fundamental philosophical issue of fairness and simple, long overdue social justice designed to increase opportunities for boys and girls, and men and women, in accordance with sound educational practices and principles. Let us hope, regardless of the reluctance of federal authorities to take a stronger position for civil rights reform, that educators will profess equality and base their decisions on fairness.

Two additional pieces of legislation enacted in the mid-1970s, and again long overdue, are important to all educators and to those students and athletes with a disability. Public Law 94–142, the Education for All Handicapped People Act, essentially guarantees a free appropriate public education in the least restrictive environment for every child with a disability. Second 504 of the Rehabilitation Act of 1973 states that "no otherwise qualified individual in the United States shall solely by reason of his/her handicap be excluded from participation in, be denied the benefit of, or be subjected to discrimination under any program or activity receiving federal financial assistance." Section 504 applies to educational programs, extracurricular activity, and intramural, extramural, interscholastic, and intercollegiate athletics such that recreational departments, school boards, or other public agencies responsible for providing services cannot exclude any handicapped individual from programs or activities.

Insight through Illustration

A high school wrestler with one kidney was denied participation in a varsity wrestling program in the New Jersey courts (1980). Yet in another case, *Kampmeier* v. *Harris* (1978), the court noted that it was in a handicapped student's best interest to allow her to participate in the athletics program under the condition that she wear protective eyeglasses. And in a third case, the court ruled against a nineteen-year-old high school wrestler with a learning disability who brought suit against the State of New York when he was barred from the wrestling team for failing the ninth grade.

Courts are reluctant to allow individuals with a disability involving a vital organ to participate in contact sports. The risk of loss of life or permanent injury is too threatening. In situations where protective equipment can be used safely, the courts are willing to weigh the benefits of participation in athletics. The courts are usually consistent in ruling that students nineteen years of age or older desiring to compete in interscholastic programs are too mature physically, mentally, and emotionally to compete fairly with younger students.

Sports governing agencies are increasingly recognizing the rights, needs, and interests of individuals with physical and/or mental disabilities. The United States Olympic Committee established the Committee on Sports for the Disabled. The International Olympic Committee agreed to a full exhibition tournament for athletes with disabilities who participated in the 1988 Olympic Games in Seoul, South Korea. With appropriate rule adaptations, review of classification systems, better-trained coaches, and continued research, the sports world can provide significant opportunities for all athletes.

As teachers, coaches, fitness directors, and sport administrators, we must recognize the likelihood of being involved in a lawsuit. While we need to be aware of the possibility of such an occurrence, this awareness, at best, may translate into very positive reactions. Fortunately, we have responded to the explosion of lawsuits by using safer teaching methods and safer equipment. Betty van der Smissen (1990) speaks to the nature of these responses and suggests that our responses would be inappropriate if we deny students the right to take risks (not unsafe risks, but reasonable risks), if we deny students the right to be challenged, to solve problems, to make decisions, and if we curtail the ways in which we conduct programs. The legal experts look to tort reform, the reinstitution of governmental immunity, the move toward comparative negligence, and increased control over insurance carriers as positive responses to the litigation crisis. As teachers we need to examine our teaching style, methods, and objectives and communicate to our students the importance of assuming responsibility; that is, responsibility for learning about the activity and safety practices, responsibility for following rules and taking care of equipment, understanding of one's own capabilities, strengths, and weaknesses related to the skills, and awareness of what might happen if established rules are not followed.

Another appropriate response to the litigation crisis is the development of a risk management plan. As defined by van der Smissen (1990), a risk management plan is a "systematic analysis of the services offered for personal injury and financial loss potential." A plan to manage risk would include the following: policies which govern the hiring of personnel and required credentials, certifications, or licenses; insurance coverage of public liability, property, health and accident coverage; a plan for proper supervision and instruction of activities; identification of program scope and program evaluation; provisions for in-service training and proper credentialing of employees; a detailed plan for emergency procedures and an accident reporting system; transportation policies; provisions for regular inspection and maintenance of equipment and facilities; and purchasing policies for equipment and supplies. Safety is everyone's responsibility and may be facilitated by awareness of the laws and respect for the rights of others, effective communication, careful planning and implementation of sound policies, and enforcement of these practices.

KEY WORDS AND PHRASES

Duty	Liability	Comparative and contributory negligence
Negligence	Contract	
Lawsuit	Common law	Due process
Statutory law	Plaintiff	Waiver
Tort	Defendant	Right

QUESTIONS FOR REVIEW

1. As a director of physical education, athletics, or fitness, what five things could you do to reduce the possibility of a lawsuit claiming negligence?

2. Does the authority of a coach take precedence over a student's rights? Can the coach or director enforce participation restrictions and dress codes?

3. List the policies that should be included in a risk management program relative to transportation for athletes.

4. Should interscholastic coaches be certified? Explain.

5. Why are there more lawsuits today than ten to fifteen years ago?

6. Explain how product liability concerns the program director.

7. If you were in charge of an activities program for a group of school-age people, would you use waiver forms and permission slips? Explain.

8. Distinguish between common law and statutory law.

9. Why is it so critical for directors to concern themselves with legal knowledge and precautions?

10. What would your action plan be if you were confronted with a lawsuit?

SELF-TEST

Corrected True/False

If the statement is true, mark it T. If the statement is false, mark it F and change it to a true statement by adding or deleting words.

_____ 1. Legal cases involving liability for injury most often fall within the domain of statutory law.

_____ 2. Negligence is based upon foreseeability.

_____ 3. Regarding athletic-related injuries, as far as the law is concerned, coaches are expected to have higher standards of care and special skills as compared with other reasonably prudent people.

_____ 4. Most school districts and colleges carry liability insurance for their employees; therefore, coaches need not bother getting personal liability insurance.

_____ 5. As demonstrated by recent court cases, governmental immunity is not a reliable defense against negligence charges.

_____ 6. Liability insurance does not offer protection against negligence.

_____ 7. In general, courts have agreed that students have the right to participate in athletics.

_____ 8. A court would most likely rule that a student with only one kidney has the right to play football.

Multiple Choice

_____ 9. Most negligence charges relating to physical educators arise from:
   a. transportation
   b. supervision
   c. facilities
   d. equipment

_____ 10. The most important thing a physical educator can do to avoid a negligence charge is to:
   a. get waiver slips signed
   b. avoid risky assignments
   c. know the law and act prudently
   d. get a lot of insurance

_____ 11. The legal term most closely related to legal responsibility is:
   a. liability
   b. negligence
   c. due process
   d. common laws

_____ 12. Which of the following factors should not be listed with the other three?
   a. act of God
   b. assumption of risk
   c. contributory negligence
   d. prohibitive writ

_____ 13. You have helped a stranger whose life was endangered, and he has suffered a broken rib as a result of your action. If he sues, what is the best legislation for you to depend on for protection?
   a. common law
   b. save-harmless legislation
   c. good Samaritan doctrine
   d. act of God

_____ 14. The reason why physical educators, fitness professionals, and coaches are concerned about legal liability is:
   a. the risk in the business
   b. living in a litigious society
   c. most everyone has insurance
   d. all of the above

_____ 15. Which of the following is a true statement?
   a. Coaches can't be held to a teaching contract if they give two months notice.
   b. Coaches are usually released from contract responsibilities to accept better positions.
   c. Waiver slips have some value.
   d. both b and c

CASE 14.1 "HE DESERVED TO BE INJURED"

Jimmy Allen had the reputation of being a fourteen-year-old "gym rat." He always seemed to have a basketball in his hand and was shooting toward a basket if one was in the vicinity. Two men's volleyball teams were in the middle of a church volleyball league match when Jimmy came dribbling into the church gymnasium. He immediately started shooting his basketball at one of the main court baskets. After Jimmy's ball rolled onto the volleyball court, the men held up their volleyball game to remind Jimmy that the basketball goal was too close to the volleyball court for him to safely shoot while the game was in progress. Jimmy disagreed and continued to shoot baskets.

When his ball again bounced onto the volleyball court, one of the men went to the supervisor's desk in the adjacent area and asked if the young man could be told to leave the gym. Bob June, the supervisor, went to the gym and told Jimmy if he did not stop shooting until the volleyball match was over, he would have to leave the gym. Jimmy sat down, but as soon as Bob left the area, he defiantly resumed his shooting practice.

He had his back to the volleyball court about three feet from the end line getting ready for a jump shot when he suddenly was knocked to the floor. The 220-pound Craig Papp was backpedaling to return a high and deep lob when he crashed into the unwary Jimmy. As a result of the collision, Jimmy suffered three broken ribs and a punctured lung and spleen. Craig suffered a fractured wrist when he fell. Bob June responded like a programmed computer in administering first aid and arranging for the victims' transportation to the hospital.

When Marge Lofton, director of recreation for the local church, arrived the following morning, she started an immediate investigation to see if she could determine if negligence was a factor.

Your Response

1. What are the issues and problems in this case?
2. What actions should have been or should now be taken?
3. List the action guides related to this situation.
4. What barriers could stand in the way of the best decisions being made?

CASE 14.2 THE FITNESS CLUB INCIDENT

Tommy O'Connor was given a membership in a local fitness club for his fiftieth birthday by his wife. His wife thought this gift would be beneficial since he worked as an investment broker in a highly stressful environment, his work was largely sedentary, and he had steadily gained weight over the past several years. Tommy agreed with this rationale and was pleased with the opportunity to become more physically active.

On his first visit to the fitness club, Tommy was given the usual tour of the facilities, asked to fill out membership forms—including a membership agreement which released the club from all liability for injury which might occur through use of club facilities and equipment, and was given a basic fitness test battery. The club used four items as a basic fitness screening test battery: a flexibility test, a bench press, body composition, and an aerobic capacity test. Don January, the club manager, administered this series of tests and determined Tommy to be in sufficient enough condition to participate in the normal conditioning program for new members. Tommy was given a routine for the weight machines, allowed a fifteen minute session on the stair machine and placed in level two of the "aerobicize" conditioning class.

After his first night of full participation at the club, Tommy felt exhausted and complained of the intensity of the workout. Don, trying to motivate him to continue, informed him that it would get easier as time went on and that he would experience quicker results if he continued this program rather than modifying the workout to a lower level. Reluctantly, Tommy agreed to stick with the program.

During the second workout at the club two nights later, Tommy was three quarters of the way through the "aerobicize" session when he experienced severe chest pains and collapsed on the floor. The "aerobicize" instructor tried to administer CPR while another club employee called an ambulance. Tommy died on the way to the hospital.

Six months later, Mrs. O'Connor filed suit against the club, claiming negligence. The club attempted to invoke the waiver as its primary defense.

Your Response

1. What are the potential areas where negligence could have been claimed?

2. Are there actions which could have reduced the probability of this unfortunate event from occurring?

3. What are some of the usual practices which health clubs use to protect themselves from such potential litigation?

4. Prepare arguments for the plaintiff and the defense.

CASE 14.3 GYMNASTICS! WATCH OUT!

In a Massachusetts junior high school (grades 7–8–9), assignment to physical education classes was done in accordance with the principle of using free periods in the individual's schedule. This resulted in classes where students of all three grades participated together. Since coed physical education was mandated, separate classes for boys and girls were not possible.

One of the classes was involved with a unit on gymnastics. The thirty-two students had been working on various vaults from the springboard over parallel bars to a standing position on the floor. The teacher was a well-qualified woman with a BS and an MS from accredited institutions and with five years of physical education teaching experience. Her preparation and experience were characterized by personal competence as a gymnastics performer and effective teaching in this area, especially in girls' events.

There had been systematic progression in the gymnastics class in relation to this particular stunt and prior to the vaulting work, and the students had received instruction and practice in tumbling and body mechanics. They were first given a demonstration by the teacher of the workings of the springboard and then had a number of trials in which they practiced the approach, the spring from the board, and landing some distance in front on their feet. The entire activity was performed on mats. Following this, parallel bars were placed near the springboard, running perpendicular to the direction of the vault and covered both above and below with ample mats for protection of the students. The teacher discussed and demonstrated spotting techniques and assumed that spotters were present at all times during class, both at the point between the springboard and the near side of the parallels, and on the far side of the parallels where the vaults should terminate.

The students were taken through lead-up activities. Initially, they practiced going from springboard to a front kneel on top of the bars. Next, they practiced going from springboard to standing position on the bars. Only after these had been mastered did students proceed to vault completely over the bars to a standing position on the floor. Some boys expressed discontentment with the progressions, and occasionally completed the vault during the lead-ups.

Near the end of one class period, one of the seventh-grade boys who had had some gymnastic coaching at a private gym school and who had developed a liking for and reasonable competence in gymnastics indicated to the teacher that he wanted to incorporate something he had seen on TV with what they had learned. The instructor said emphatically, "No," and kept her eye on him during the remainder of the class. Another concern she had was with the equipment. Some of it had been purchased for girls prior to mandated coed physical education and perhaps was not strong enough for heavier boys, but the manufacturer had assured the department that the parallel bars were safe for both boys and girls when uneven as well as even.

Because she had responsibilities in the locker room at the end of class, the instructor left the gymnasium to go to the girls' locker room. Since there was another gymnastics class scheduled for the following period and the same equipment was needed, the male instructor for that class supervised the boys from her class and his class in their locker room, and everything was left in place on the gymnasium floor.

After the instructor's departure, the boy decided to try the stunt and a fellow student (seventh grade) agreed to spot for him. In the process of clearing the parallel bars, the vaulter hit an edge of the bars with his feet, lost his balance, and fell heavily on the spotter so that the latter suffered a serious back injury from the contact that required hospitalization and considerable subsequent medical attention with accompanying costs over the next two years.

The injured boy's parents had their lawyer file notice of claim six months after the incident, but as the expiration date for filing a negligence suit approached, they were undecided about whether to file against the school district, the teacher(s), the boy who performed the stunt, or the equipment company.

Your Response

1. Who is liable here? Why? Does negligence exist?

2. Prepare arguments for the plaintiff and the defense.

3. What administrative policies and procedures should be developed to prevent this from occurring in the future?

4. Identify good teaching practices employed by the physical education teacher.

BIBLIOGRAPHY

Acosta, R. V., and L. J. Carpenter. "Women in Athletics." *Journal of Health, Physical Education, Recreation, and Dance* (August 1985): 30, 37.

Adams, S. H. "Court Decisions Hit Hard with New Liability Twists." *Athletic Purchasing and Facilities* (May 1982): 12–16.

Alexander, R., and K. Alexander. *Teachers and Torts.* KY: Maxwell, 1970.

Appenzeller, H. (ed.). *Sport and Law.* Charlottesville, VA: Michie, 1985.

Appenzeller, H., and T. Appenzeller. *Sports and the Courts.* Charlottesville, VA: Michie, 1980.

Appenzeller, H., and C. T. Ross (eds.). "Sports and the Courts." *Physical Education and Sports Law Quarterly* 5 (Summer 1984): 13–14.

Arnold, D. E. "Sports Product Liability." *Journal of Physical Education and Recreation* (November-December 1978): 25–28.

Bolmeier, E. C. *Legality of Student Disciplining Practices.* Charlottesville, VA: Michie, 1976.

Bucher, C. A. *Administration of Health and Physical Education Programs.* St. Louis: Mosby, 1975.

Coughlin, E. K. "The Crits v. the Legal Academy: Arguing a Case against the Law." *The Chronicle of Higher Education,* 17 July 1985.

DAR Manual for Citizenship. Washington, DC: National Society of Daughters of the American Revolution, 1981.

Drowatzky, J. N. *Legal Issues in Sport and Physical Education Management.* Champaign, IL: Stysis, 1984.

Fields, C. M. "Rulings Handed Down in Cases on Race Bias and on Free Speech in High Schools." *The Chronicle of Higher Education,* 16 July 1986.

Frost, R., B. Lockhart, and S. Marshall. *Administration of Physical Education and Athletics: Concepts and Practices.* 3rd ed. Dubuque, IA: William C. Brown, 1988.

"Full Steam Ahead: The Women's Movement toward 2000." *The Graduate Woman* (January 1986).

"Here is What Liability Responsibility Means for Athletics." *Athletic Purchasing and Facilities* (August 1977).

Horine, L. *Administration of Physical Education and Sports Programs.* Philadelphia: Saunders College, 1985.

Jensen, C. R. *Administration Management of Physical Education and Athletic Programs.* Philadelphia: Lea & Febiger, 1983.

Kaiser, R. A. "Program Liability Waivers." *Journal of Health, Physical Education, Recreation, and Dance* 55 (August 1984): 54–56.

Klappholz, L. A. *Physical Education Newsletter.* Old Saybrook, CT: Physical Education Publications, 1977.

Lisbee, H. C. *Liability for Accidents in Physical Education, Athletics and Recreation.* Unpublished paper, 1952.

Marsh, R. L. "Be Aware of Standards as They Apply to Liability Cases." *Athletic Purchasing and Facilities* (May 1982): 20–24.

Nygaard, G., and T. N. Boone. *Coaches' Guide to Sport Law.* Champaign, IL: Human Kinetics Publishers, 1985.

Resick, Matthew C., B. L. Seidel, and J. G. Mason. *Modern Administrative Practices in Physical Education and Athletics.* 2nd ed. Reading, MA: Addison-Wesley, 1977.

Reutter, E. E., and R. R. Hamilton. *The Law of Public Education.* New York: Foundation Press, 1976.

Schwartz, B. *The Law in America.* New York: McGraw-Hill, 1974.

Seiter, M. M., and M. Goggin. *Shaping the Body Politic: Legislative Training for the Physical Educator.* Reston, VA: American Alliance for Health, Physical Education, Recreation, and Dance, 1985.

Short, J. S. "Litigation in Physical Education and Athletics: Basic Guidelines for Teachers and Administrators." *GAPHER Journal* 10.

VanBiervliet, A., and J. Sheldon-Wildgren. *Liability Issues in Community-Based Programs.* MO: Paul H. Brooks, 1981.

Van der Smissen, Betty. Legal Liability and Risk Management for Public and Private Entities. Cincinnati, OH: Anderson, 1990.

Weistart, J. C., and C. H. Lowell. *The Law of Sports.* Charlottesville, VA: Michie, 1979.

You and the Law. New York: Reader's Digest Association, 1971.

Wong, G. M. *Essentials of Amateur Sports Law.* Dover, MA: Auburn House, 1988.

15

Coping with Stress and Conflict

*No doubt there are other important things in life
besides conflict, but there are not many other things
so inevitably interesting.*

Robert Lynd

Chapter Objectives

*After reading this chapter and completing the exercises,
you should be able to:*

1 Define stress
2 Explain the difference between eustress and distress
3 Explain why stress is necessary in everyone's life
4 List at least ten warning signals of stress overload
5 List five steps to achieving deep relaxation
6 List at least three appropriate methods of coping with stress
7 Understand how visualization could benefit a manager
8 List three methods for adding lifestyle activity to a day
9 List key elements in choosing a lifelong sport
10 Explain why conflict management is important to the director
11 List eight to ten conflict resolution methods and explain how they are applied

Eustress . . . and distress.

Stress is a very popular term these days. Every administrator experiences stress and sometimes can create stress for co-workers. How well each manager deals with the different types of stress can differ radically. Although one manager can utilize stress as a tool for improving performance in himself or herself or within the organization, another can feel overly pressured by stress and let it decrease his or her ability to manage effectively. To understand how to cope with stress and conflict, it is necessary to recognize the causes of stress and learn the best ways to deal with them. This chapter will focus on providing that knowledge.

WHAT IS STRESS?

Stress can be defined as a physiological response to any demand placed on a person. Stress can be created by either pleasure or pain, and it can be either good or bad.

Good stress, also termed *eustress,* is a challenge that results in growth or positive development. This is the type of stress that is beneficial for employees and managers. Eustress can be likened to strength training. If a person takes a twenty-pound dumbbell and performs fifteen to twenty bicep curls, the bicep muscle is stressed. If the exercise is executed properly, the stress will help to strengthen that bicep and make it perform better. A moderate amount of stress is necessary to get us to perform at optimum levels. But if stress becomes too great to handle, it becomes distress.

Distress is the type of stress that can be damaging to mind and body. If a person takes a seventy-five-pound dumbbell and performs bicep curls until the muscle is strained, the skeletal muscle is damaged, which may result in a weakening of the muscle. So it is with stress. If the body is not allowed to return to a relaxed state after moderate stress, stress keeps building to a breaking point.

Everyone experiences a variety of stressors. Physical stressors are any changes in the body's internal or immediate external environment that cause a physical response. Some physical stressors include diet, noise, drugs, athletic activity, and physical trauma. Cognitive stressors are factors that require interpretation to trigger a stress response and stimulate emotional arousal. To some people, thunder and lightning are very frightening, but others find thunderstorms very beautiful. Overcrowded offices and relationships with co-workers are cognitive stressors that do not directly affect the body but must be interpreted to elicit a response. As previously mentioned, both pleasure and pain can elicit a stress response. The cardiac muscle doesn't know if the heart rate speeds up because of a surprise promotion or a layoff notice. Both, however, trigger stress responses within the body.

WHAT GOOD IS STRESS?

Stress in limited amounts is necessary for survival. In primitive times, the stress response was followed by some form of physical exertion to return the body to a normal relaxed state. This is the fight-or-flight reaction, which produces adrenaline, sends blood away from visceral and toward skeletal muscles, and increases heart rate and respiration, enabling the person or animal to flee from an attacker or fight off danger. But in today's workplace, seldom does a manager get to use the adrenalin and other bodily changes produced by the fight-or-flight reaction. It is therefore difficult for the body to quickly return to a relaxed state, or homeostasis.

Stress is necessary and beneficial to encourage growth and optimum performance. How often have you worked harder or given 110 percent because of pressing deadlines or an upcoming important presentation? This is an example of stress in its good form, eustress. But what happens when the stress response is triggered too often? When constant stressors occur over a prolonged period, the body is unable to relax and return to a more normal state. This is when stress goes awry, and it is this type of stress—distress—that concerns health care professionals. This type of stress can be damaging in many ways.

EFFECTS OF BAD STRESS

When stress overload occurs it leads to a variety of illnesses. Most managers have heard of brownout and burnout, particularly in the teaching and nursing professions. Burnout frequently refers to a psychological loss of direction and motivation. Brownout is a less severe form of burnout, a warning flag of impending overload. Brownout and burnout can lead to physiological problems.

Psychological Effects of Overstress

Overstress can manifest itself psychologically in any number of ways. Feelings of despair, disorientation, loss of direction, paranoia, irritability, and social withdrawal can occur in varying degrees of severity. Intellectual decay may appear in the form of stupid errors, frequent excuses, and feelings of inadequacy.

These psychological problems can lead to

physiological outlets such as substance abuse, eating disorders, violence, and the ultimate consequence of burnout, suicide.

Physical Effects of Overstress

Current research shows a relationship between many diseases and stress overload. Cancer and heart disease, two of the biggest killers in America, are being directly linked to stress. Other physical maladies such as respiratory disease, gastrointestinal problems, menstrual irregularities, and sexual dysfunction are even more easily traced to stress. The occurrence of high blood pressure, ulcers, and stomach upset is common among those under stress.

All of these problems, both physical and psychological, are warning signs to intervene with stress management. Table 15.1 summarizes psychological and physical symptoms of overstress.

Table 15.1   *Signs of Overstress*

Fatigue	Clumsiness
Inability to concentrate	Muscular tension
Boredom	Headaches
Restlessness	Dizziness
Decreased sex drive	Trembling/nervousness
Eating disorders	Heart pounding
Feelings of worthlessness	Sudden weight changes
Hopelessness	Forgetfulness

STRESS AND THE MANAGER

Managers are more prone to stress than other workers due to the problem-solving nature of their occupations. Whether in schools, fitness centers, or sports programs, managers are constantly faced with decisions, which cause stress. The more complex the choices, the more stress is created. Seldom are a manager's choices as simple as right or wrong, good or bad. If several viable solutions to a problem are apparent, it may be difficult to choose the best one.

Change is another cause of stress. Any life change, such as income increase or decrease, job change, illness or injury, or loss of friends and loved ones, creates stress within an individual's life. Even happy events such as marriage, pregnancy, and job promotions create stress.

Middle managers are even more prone to stress than top-level administrators. The feelings and realities of less control, coupled with pressures from above and below, force greater stress on middle managers. Intervention and stress management are clearly necessary for all administrators if they are to perform efficiently.

Managers can help or hinder the stress levels of their employees. Management can assist employees in managing their own stress levels in a variety of ways. Because feelings of lack of control generate increased stress, often in the form of distress, a manager can increase the sense of control among his or her employees by encouraging, and acting upon, input from subordinates. Another term for this is Team Building. Chapter Five discusses a variety of ways to facilitate this type of two-way communication.

Managers can also increase the feeling of distress in employees by acting as stress carriers. A stress carrier is anyone who causes another to feel stress. Many directors are stress carriers for their employees due to the director's responsibility to maintain and improve organization operations. If a director is not an efficient administrator, he or she creates greater stress for all members of the organization.

STRESS INTERVENTION

Stress is a cycle, and during that cycle, intervention is possible to keep stress overload from occurring. The director should be able to recognize

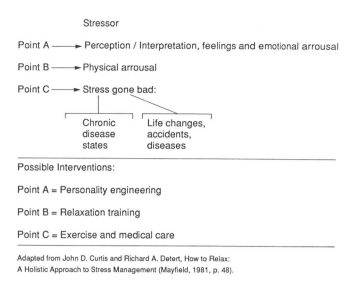

Figure 15.1 *The Stress Cycle*

these intervention points, and to distinguish inappropriate from appropriate ways to handle stress.

The Stress Cycle

Figure 15.1 depicts the cycle of stress and the possible points of intervention. Point A is the first point of intervention, where altering the individual's perceptions, or personality engineering, may be possible. A good example of this is the difference between Type A and Type B individuals. The Type A person can be characterized as a racehorse, constantly on the run, often spinning his or her wheels. Many managers are this type of person and, therefore, become stress carriers for their employees. The Type A person perceives everything as urgent and races about trying to accomplish everything at once.

The Type B person, on the other hand, carries out duties in a slower, more deliberate manner. This person is the more relaxed employee or manager who knows how to properly balance work and leisure. Often the Type B turtle accomplishes more than the Type A hare, and certainly ends up with less tension in the process.

Personality engineering involves retraining a person so that his or her perception of stressors allows a more relaxed approach. Although many people believe that it is impossible to change a Type A person into a Type B, there are ways to teach the Type A individual how to relax, deal with stress, and set positive, attainable goals.

The second point of intervention is point B, where the physical arousal that results from stress can be worked with. Relaxation training through meditation, hypnosis, biofeedback, and progressive muscle relaxation are all examples of this type of intervention.

Intervention at point C can be practiced when the other methods fail to reduce physical stress reactions. Exercise is the healthiest form of point C intervention. How many times have you gone out and run a few miles or played an aggressive match of tennis or racquetball to rid yourself of pent-up emotion? This is a classic example of handling stress at this point in the stress cycle, when stress has begun to cause physical symptoms.

Another, less desirable form of intervention is medical care to treat the symptoms of overstress such as ulcers and headaches. As you can imagine, it is better to intervene at the earlier points than to delay until medical care is required. More and more businesses and insurance companies are realizing that *prevention,* through stress management, is much less expensive than medical intervention. That is one reason why the fitness and wellness industry is currently booming.

Inappropriate Coping Methods

If stress or depression are experienced over prolonged periods, some people may turn to inappropriate methods of coping. One of these is using substances to alter their perception of stressors (point A intervention).

Many people envision substance abuse as involving cocaine or other illegal drugs, but many legal substances are more commonly abused in the workplace. One of these is tobacco. Fortunately, professionals in the fields of fitness, sports, and physical education have an awareness of the many problems associated with the use of tobacco. Nicotine acts initially as a stimulant, and then later as a depressant. The long-term effects include lung cancer and increased risk of heart disease.

Caffeine is another substance commonly used by people in the workplace. Caffeine is a stimulant found not only in coffee, but also in teas, chocolate, and many soft drinks.

Other substances such as cocaine, marijuana, heroine, and codeine create a euphoric feeling in the user. To continue experiencing this feeling, a person must increase the dosage, leading to addiction, which has physiological and psychological side effects too numerous to discuss here.

Alcohol, tranquilizers, and barbiturates are all drugs that are used in moderation by many people. They are central nervous system depressants. As the frequency or quantity of use increases, these drugs lose their effectiveness and must be used in greater quantity. This leads to physical and psychological dependence.

The frequency of substance abuse is often hidden in the workplace. What starts out as a medical prescription (point C intervention) may result in an addiction, which will only increase the problems faced by the abuser. When an administrator discovers a problem with substance abuse, either with himself or herself or with other employees, several basic steps can be followed for intervention. First, the abuser must make a commitment to stop; then, he or she must find a program designed to help stop the inappropriate behavior. Educating all employees about substance abuse will help to make them aware of problems and can help to increase support among co-workers.

Recognizing and admitting the need for help is a crucial step in recovering from addiction. Many employers offer employee assistance programs (EAP's) to increase awareness and recognition of substance abuse and to provide education on appropriate coping mechanisms. When needed, EAP's also assist employees in obtaining rehabilitation and support. If no formal employee assistance is provided, many medical insurance policies cover rehabilitation programs.

Avoidance of a problem, whether through alcohol, drugs, or denial, is not a way to solve it. There is no way to avoid everything that causes stress, and no real reason to try. Learning how to appropriately deal with stressors is a better answer.

Appropriate Coping Methods

There are many appropriate methods of stress intervention. We have already mentioned one, personality engineering, which consists of altering perceptions. We will suggest several other methods here.

In general, there are several steps to take when a business or personal incident becomes a stressor. First, one must identify what the stressor is. Is a lack of communication causing a problem? Possibly, poor time management is creating pressures at home and on the job. If the problem is simply a matter of how one perceives a situation, then personality engineering is indicated. After identifying what is causing the problem, one should define what aspect of the stressor causes the most problem. Sometimes this aspect can be avoided altogether. If one person in particular is the stress carrier, then altering one's perception can eliminate or, at the very least, lessen the problem.

If the stressor is not one that can be avoided, one must determine why the stressor is necessary and brainstorm to generate alternatives to the current method of dealing with it. All alternatives should be evaluated, even the absurd ones, then the best alternative tried. After the solution has been put into practice, the situation should be reevaluated. Has the stress been lessened? If so, the method has been successful.

Laughter and Stress Laughter has always been a way of reliving tension. The term "nervous laughter" refers to this release of tension and nervous energy. Laughter can also be a way of reducing boredom and guilt, and has been used to relieve muscle tension headaches. Many public speakers use jokes or humorous anecdotes throughout their speeches to relieve boredom and personal nervousness.

A sense of humor is based on feelings of self-worth. As self-worth increases, the sense of humor correspondingly increases. Other physical effects of laughter can also relieve stress. Laughter affects the pulmonary and respiratory systems by increasing aeration, expelling stale air, and helping to clear foreign matter from the respiratory tract.

The muscular effects of hearty laughter help relieve muscular tension in the face, neck, chest, abdomen, diaphragm, shoulders, and even pelvic areas. Circulation is beneficially affected by a brief increase in heart rate, circulation, and blood pressure. After the brief increase in the circulatory system, the heart relaxes, and these values drop below normal for a period. These effects are so beneficial that some people have called laughter

"sit-down jogging." The term "weak from laughter" indicates the muscular relaxation and corresponding positive effects in lessening tension that result from laughter.

The hormonal system also benefits from laughter through a rush of adrenalin and catecholamines, which trigger a release of endorphins, the body's natural pain killers. Endorphins can reduce pain and create a general feeling of euphoria, much like the runner's high. With all the benefits of laughter to physical fitness, mood, and stress reduction, it seems that he or she who laughs, lasts.

One very important aspect of job satisfaction is the feeling that one's workplace is a pleasant environment. Appropriate laughter helps to make the work environment more pleasant to employees and customers alike. Some managers encourage humor by periodically circulating cartoons or humorous anecdotes relating to the job situation and absurdities of life in general. Another tactic is to provide a bulletin board in an employee break room or other common area, where everyone can contribute to the collective funny-bone of the organization. While this can be an easy way to inject humor into the day, managers must take care to never encourage or allow racist or sexist humor to circulate in the work environment.

Other methods of providing "chuckle breaks" include:

- Keep cartoon collections or other funny books in desk or breakroom.
- Find simple wind-up toys or children's toys and keep on hand for your own enjoyment.
- When traveling, take a few minutes at the airport to watch a child. Try to capture some of the enthusiasm for the adventure the child exhibits.
- Tell a joke.
- Listen to a joke.
- Show a clip of a funny video or play a comedy

album at the beginning of a meeting to set a positive, relaxed tone.

Biofeedback   Biofeedback is any method of voluntary self-regulation. People who practice daily blood pressure monitoring practice a basic form of biofeedback. By reinforcing the relaxation response, biofeedback can teach people how to deal effectively with stress. Not only blood pressure, but also body temperature, heart rate, and muscular tension can be monitored to teach successful relaxation. Although biofeedback does not replace medical care, it is one way to get immediate, accurate, and continual reinforcement of positive behavior. Learning to use biofeedback is not difficult if taught by a professional. The daily practice of it can often be the hardest aspect of the program.

Relaxation and Visualization   Relaxation and visualization are ways to reduce distress and harness eustress for one's own benefit. Athletes, especially professional and olympic-calibre athletes, have used these methods to fine-tune skills and overcome negative techniques. But how can visualization assist the manager? The saying, "If you can't imagine achieving it, you probably won't," is applicable in all areas of life, personal and professional. Those people and those companies who lead the race are most often those who carry a goal and can visualize the achievement of that goal.

On a personal level, how does a person incorporate this tactic into daily life? Visualization can best be accomplished after deep relaxation has been achieved. There are numerous methods for achieving deep relaxation: deep breathing, hypnosis, progressive muscular relaxation, and meditation are a few. These relaxation techniques are discussed in depth in the sources listed in this chapter's bibliography.

Once relaxation is achieved, a person can visualize a variety of things, depending on that person's goal. If one wants simply to reduce stress, he or she can visualize a favorite spot such as the beach, the woods, or a favorite jogging path. Focus in your mind on how all your senses react to this location. Visualize the sights—swaying trees, green grass, waves lapping the shore. Visualize the scents—the salty air, the pungent odor of pine trees, the honeysuckle bushes that line the path. Visualize the sounds—the waves crashing and breaking, birds chirping overhead, bees buzzing, children laughing. Visualize the textures and feelings—warm sand against your back, cool grass against your skin, cold water from a stream dancing across your toes. By losing oneself in this little fantasy vacation, one's body reacts to the scene in the mind, not the external scene which may be causing increased stress. Comedian Steve Martin used a reference to this technique in his stand-up routine. He would pause on stage with a blank look on his face. After a few moments of this, he'd snap back into his stage persona and say "Sorry, just took a quick trip to the Bahamas!" A quick trip to the Bahamas is good for everyone.

Another use of visualization is to perfect or practice an upcoming event. Watch any professional athlete in competition. As the basketball player steps to the free throw line, he or she takes a few seconds to address the hoop. Is that person contemplating what's for dinner? Probably not. More likely he or she is visualizing the motions involved and completion of a perfect free throw. The golfer addresses the ball at the tee. The tennis player stares at the opponent's side of the court prior to the serve. These and other elite athletes all visualize the successful execution of the serve, tee shot, shot put, hammer throw, or baseball pitch.

So why does a manager use visualization? Like the athlete, the manager must successfully complete actions in order to be successful. A manager can take fifteen minutes to visualize an impending speech, the audience's reaction, the use of audio visuals. This will enable him or her to feel more at ease, as if this task has already been successfully completed. Another person might awaken in the morning, and before getting out of bed, or while taking the train to work, take a few minutes to visualize the activities planned for the day. He or she can rehearse opening lines for the meeting with the boss. He or she can envision the successful resolution to a conflict, or how to handle a surprise rush of customers. By taking time to "rehearse" the day, a person sets the tone of feeling in control, which will help throughout the day.

Insight through Illustration

Mark Hill hates flying. He hates the feeling of being out of control and likens air travel with being held prisoner at 30,000 feet. Today, however, he must fly to Chicago to lead a training seminar. As he walks onto the airplane he feels his palms growing sweaty, his heart racing, and his breathing becoming more rapid. His first impulse is to ask the flight attendant for a cocktail before takeoff. But since the seminar on substance abuse he attended last week, he knows that drinking is not a good method of stress management. Mark decides to try a stress management tactic that has been useful to his wife.

After Mark is settled in his seat and buckled in, he closes his eyes, leans back, and begins breathing deeply. As he concentrates on the sound his lungs make as they expand and relax and the rhythmic movements of his chest and abdomen, he feels his shoulders start to loosen up. Once he has focused all thoughts on his physical sensations and away from his environment, he begins by curling his toes and stretching them out again. Then, he flexes and stretches his calves, legs, abdomen and continues to progressively contract and relax all muscle groups until he is relaxed from toes to forehead. As he slowly opens his eyes, Mark realizes the plane has taken off and attained cruising altitude. "Well," Mark thinks to himself, "maybe this flying isn't so bad after all.

Now, I just need to stay relaxed until Chicago. I'll take awhile and mentally review my training presentation so I'll be prepared when I arrive."

Exercise Exercise is another method of stress reduction. Exercise reduces the aroused state by decreasing circulating hormones and returning the body to a more relaxed state. Regular exercise also aids in the reduction of body fat and other risk factors associated with coronary and other diseases. In addition to the physical benefits of exercise, there are specific benefits for the business person. By achieving satisfaction through improving sports performance, controlling weight, and/or increased stamina, that person often attains a more positive attitude and higher confidence level. This attitude crosses over the boundaries of exercise and sport into the realm of business, creating a more energetic, confident worker.

When developing a personal exercise regimen it is important to choose a sport that one enjoys. Exercise should not become an additional stressor in an already over-burdened life. How does a person add exercise when there is no spare time in the daily schedule? First, exercise must become a priority in the schedule. People always make room for priorities, such as work, church activities, grocery shopping, or physical activity. When adopting a new exercise regimen, it is wise to select an activity which can become a lifelong enjoyment. Criteria for choosing your sport include:

- Choose something you enjoy.
- Choose something which you do well or at which you can learn to excel.
- Is this sport accessible to you? For example, if you live in Florida, snow skiing may not be the best option.
- If you travel frequently, choose a sport such as

Exercise is a catharsis for frustration.

walking, running, or rope skipping, which are easily portable.

- Will you gain a sense of accomplishment from this, or will it be a frustrating experience?
- Can you grow gradually in this skill and remain challenged throughout your life?
- Does your chosen sport provide a complete workout for strength, coordination, and cardio-vascular system?
- Focus on the enjoyment experienced during the activity, not just on the health benefits.

One good example of a lifelong sport is golf. For most people, it meets the criteria listed above and provides both lifetime challenge and enjoyment. We know one avid golf coach who golfed several times a week, throughout his life. In fact, he took in 18 holes just days before his death . . . at age 92.

Additional exercise can be added to a busy life by simple, quick activities such as parking several blocks from work and walking to the door. Take stairs instead of elevators. Deliver your own memos instead of using inter-company mail. Not only do you get away from your desk and walk, but you gain visibility within the organization. While sitting at desk or in traffic, shrug and rotate shoulders. Point and flex feet while in meetings (but make sure your feet are concealed under a table). While sitting on the subway or bus, contract abdominals and press spine flat toward the back of the seat as you exhale. Release and inhale. Using creativity to incorporate activity is the key to achieving a more active lifestyle.

Companies that provide or support corporate fitness programs do so not only for the benefit of their employees but because they see the return to the company, also. Recent studies indicate that the more fit employees are, the less time they take from work for sick days and hospitalization. In 1990, Pacific Bell announced plans to spend $16.4 million over five years to build physical fitness centers for its employees at twelve sites throughout California. Pacific Bell officials estimated that adding this component to their existing wellness programs will save the company $10 million in health care costs over the first decade of use. Pac Bell also reported that its wellness program held increases in health care costs at 10 percent, when the national average was 20.4 percent.

Another successful corporate fitness program is exhibited by Canada Life Insurance Company in Toronto. They installed modest exercise facilities and established half-hour exercise classes for employees to utilize on their own time. In 1978, the company reported a drop in health care costs of $85 per employee (435 employees total). Additionally, absenteeism dropped 22 percent, and turnover rate fell by 15 percent. It is wise for administrators to encourage their employees to engage in cardiovascular exercise programs, thereby reducing lost work time.

Time Management   Much stress is created in the workplace by time pressures. Feelings of being rushed or not moving toward goals can create anxiety and worry, resulting in stress. The methods we suggested in Chapter 6 for improving time management can help reduce these stressors.

MANAGING CONFLICT

Often managers feel they cannot get any "real" work done because of all the time spent in problem solving and conflict resolution. For a manager, these people issues are "real" work issues. One of the major, and probably most time-consuming, jobs of the physical exercise, fitness, or athletics director is that of dealing with conflict situations. Conflict can concern equipment and facilities, programming, or personnel, but most often concerns the latter. Since the director is primarily responsible for the hiring, controlling, and terminating of employees, this is certain to be true for him or her.

After rising through the ranks of business on his or her own merits, a person taking on responsibility for others may find it a difficult adjustment. It is important to remember that a manager's output is, in reality, the output of his or her organization.

The importance of effectively dealing with employee conflicts cannot be overemphasized, since employees are the most valuable asset to any organization. It is the employee who makes the first impression and relates directly to the student or member of a fitness center. The coordinated effort of the total enterprise depends heavily upon keeping employees positive and satisfied. An angry and dissatisfied employee can do more damage to the reputation of a program than most can imagine.

Positive Uses of Conflict

Conflict is inevitable, and it cannot be avoided or ignored. It actually is necessary for the growth of employees and managers. It must be dealt with in ways that make it constructive rather than destructive.

Conflict within an organization provides a mechanism for survival and growth in a changing environment by affording the opportunity for dissent; reassessment of values, norms, goals, and power relationships within and between groups; innovation by existing personnel or through personnel changes; and reestablishment of cohesion and unity. The conflict itself can increase cohesion in a group or between individuals, and resolution of the conflict may increase unity between the conflicting groups.

If a business follows certain policies and procedures simply because "that's the way we've always done it," it is time to reassess and often adapt to changing environments.

The Need for Communication

Traditionally, the emphasis in managing organizational structures has been placed on maintaining a formal, hierarchical structure and authority. Today, though a structural framework remains important, the emphasis is placed much more on a human relations approach. When traditional forms of authority have been superseded by human relations, productivity has increased. The key to an effective human relations approach lies in the element of communication. Directing a fitness center or an athletics department by a positive human relations approach means opening up communications and involving staff in problem identification. As a result, the staff becomes more loyal and dedicated, and morale soars. In an open organization, where members are encouraged to take part in problem solving and decision making, everyone benefits as a clear decision is made and more confidence emerges concerning policies and procedures.

A first step in preventing conflicts is to have well-defined policies and procedures while empowering employees to be flexible as the situation arises. Establishing ground rules at the onset of employment is a wise method of preventing problems from occurring. These ground rules may cover topics such as expected business hours, performance expectations, filing and other office procedures, conducting personal business during business hours, and the correct way of greeting customers. Conflict then is much less likely to erupt, and when it does, is likely to be resolved quickly. In short, the manager or director who nurtures a system of open communication in the organization decreases the probability of conflict.

Conflict Resolution

Conflict resolution refers to a number of methods that can be used to deal with conflicts and problems. The following conflict resolution methods can be used by the director in a physical education, fitness, or sports setting. Using one method may be sufficient, but in some instances, more than one technique may be necessary for resolving conflicts.

Avoiding or Evading the Issue This method involves withdrawing or suppressing one's feelings or beliefs. It is sometimes referred to as the "ostrich approach," because it is much like sticking one's head in the sand and hoping the problem will go away; which it will occasionally but not very often. In reality, the basic cause of a conflict is not eliminated by ignoring it.

Pulling Rank or Using Pressure Tactics This technique involves the use of positional power, threats, or punishment. The one in the less powerful position is forced to give in or make concessions in the problem's resolution. The immediate results may seem to favor the oppressor, but because resentment usually accompanies the resolution, associated problems may be created.

Using Kid Gloves Differences are played down or ignored by not openly discussing them. Accusations and threats are avoided, the opponents express a desire for cooperation, and common interests and views are emphasized. This approach may temporarily avoid further escalation of hostility and disruption of work relationships, but latent differences may continue to exist.

Negotiation and Compromise Final agreement is reached by both parties' making concessions. The result is a decision that is acceptable to both opponents, yet optimal for neither; therefore, both may be considered winners without having to identify a loser. Confidence and trust must be part of the negotiations for reasonable compromises to be offered.

Persuasion This method involves an attempt to get an opponent to change a position. This may be

accomplished by providing factual evidence, discrediting the opponent's information, or by identifying pros and cons in relation to accepted standards. If both opponents are strongly committed to their goals and those goals are not compatible, this approach will not work. If the conflict is minor, the method may be very useful.

Problem Solving This approach also requires face-to-face discussion and analysis through open and honest exchange of facts, needs, and feelings. Trust and confidence are basic to the success of the problem-solving method. It is more scientific than the other methods.

Emphasizing Superordinate Goals This method emerges from the problem-solving technique and results in the formation of a shared goal that cannot be attained except through interdependence and mutual achievement. The conflict over incompatible goals is resolved through the substitution of a new shared goal. When conflicts are based on values, this method is unlikely to be effective.

Using an Arbitrator This technique involves the intervention of an unbiased third party. The arbiter is called in when the two sides are hopelessly deadlocked with no agreement in sight. The third party acts as a catalyst to get the opponents back to the bargaining table for the purpose of negotiation. Using an arbitrator may develop into a crutch and eventually result in a situation where conflicting parties are incapable of resolving their own problems.

Behavioral Change This technique relies upon resolving the conflict through education, analysis through group processes, and training to increase an individual's awareness of self. In some cases it may be a very effective method, but two drawbacks may render it ineffective: It is slow and costly, and some may resist attempts to change their attitudes.

Structural Changes in the Organization This method involves changing the organizational structure through position transfers or changes in job descriptions. By immediately relieving tensions and positions of control, structural change can make the conflict disappear. But the decision to make such a change is a critical one and may cause more conflict than it reduces.

These ten approaches to conflict resolution may be used in combination or succession to eventually bring about positive attitudes and behaviors on the part of employees. Ideally, a conflict's resolution should contribute to the achievement of the goals of the organization while also satisfying the people involved. If conflicts are viewed realistically and open and honest discussions are held, alternatives can be critically evaluated, and equitable solutions can be reached.

KEY WORDS AND PHRASES

Stress	Relaxation	Personality engineering
Distress	Corporate fitness programs	Biofeedback
Burnout	Eustress	Visualization
Cognitive stressors	Brownout	Conflict resolution
Stress carrier	Physical stressors	
Employee assistance program	Homeostasis	

QUESTIONS FOR REVIEW

1. What physiological effects does laughter produce and how does this affect a person under stress?
2. List three appropriate methods of intervention in the stress cycle.
3. List three inappropriate methods of intervention in the stress cycle.
4. How can positive life events such as marriage or job promotions create distress?
5. Why is stress necessary?
6. Give three examples of how you manage stress. Are they appropriate or inappropriate methods?
7. Describe the "fight-or-flight" syndrome.
8. How can a manager help reduce his or her employees' stress levels?
9. Explain why communication is so important when dealing with conflict situations.
10. When is conflict beneficial in management?
11. What is your preferred method of conflict resolution? Why?

SELF-TEST

Corrected True-False

If the statement is true, mark it T. If the statement is false, mark it F and change it to a true statement by adding or deleting words.

_____ 1. Time management is the key to stress reduction.

_____ 2. Stress is never beneficial for a person.

_____ 3. A person who causes others to feel stress is a stress carrier.

_____ 4. Personality engineering is an example of Point B intervention.

_____ 5. Hatha yoga and massage are examples of Point B intervention.

_____ 6. Hatha yoga and massage are examples of Point C intervention.

_____ 7. With proper training, a type A personality can successfully change and become a type B personality.

_____ 8. Tobacco acts as both a stimulant and a depressant.

_____ 9. Avoiding a problem is one appropriate way of dealing with stress and conflict.

_____ 10. A manager can use visualization to help relax and to solve problems.

Multiple Choice

_____ 11. Probably, the most time-consuming job of a director is:
   a. dealing with conflict situations
   b. dealing with his/her own stress
   c. getting the employees to exercise
   d. stopping eustress

_____ 12. Which of the following statements is most correct?
   a. Conflict can be avoided.
   b. Conflict is necessary for the growth of employees/managers.
   c. Conflict is not inevitable.
   d. all of the above

_____ 13. A structural framework in organizational management is still important, but today the emphasis is placed:
   a. on maintaining a formal hierarchy
   b. on insisting on loyalty and dedication
   c. more on the human relation approach
   d. exercise and social gatherings

_____ 14. The best method to use in conflict resolution:
   a. problem solving
   b. persuasion
   c. using an arbitrator
   d. depends on circumstances

_____ 15. Differences are played down or ignored in this method of conflict resolution:
   a. using kid gloves
   b. behavioral change
   c. negotiation and compromise
   d. emphasizing subordinate goals

CASE 15.1 Dilemmas Facing the New Manager

Dorothy Manning had been the Regional Director for Execu-Health for one month. Within this time she had identified five key areas in her region that needed to be improved. As she flew to Dallas for a meeting with the ten regional sales and account managers in her division, she knew this would be a difficult meeting, for a variety of reasons.

Dorothy had targeted one area in dire need of improvement: team building. The far-flung geography of the region, coupled with the ineffectiveness of the previous regional director, had led to the breakdown of any form of team spirit among the managers. There existed currently a strong competition among several of the account managers, especially Joan Whitsel and Mark Vohn. Rarely could they agree, and their animosity often erupted into arguments at group meetings. Some of the other account managers were taking sides in support of one or the other on issues. Dorothy knew she needed to manage and overcome this rivalry in order for the region to be productive.

Jeffrey Twines also posed a potential threat to the cohesiveness of the region. He had applied for the regional director position and was very resentful of Dorothy for having gotten the job. She would just have to wait and see what his behavior was like at this meeting.

Another topic on the agenda was the planned rollout of the new product line. This would require team effort, hard work, and close monitoring on Dorothy's part. She also needed the managers' input to decide the best method of training them on the specifics of the new products. Developing a rollout plan which everyone bought into would be crucial in the successful launch of these products.

As the pilot announced the approach to Dallas-Fort Worth Airport, Dorothy closed her briefcase and took a deep breath. She said to herself, "This should be an interesting week."

Your Response

1. What are the issues Dorothy faces in her task?
2. What methods of conflict management do you recommend she use?

CASE 15.2 A Matter of Stress

Jay Morrow, director of employee health at BRECKO, sat at his desk with his head in his hands. He felt lousy. He had been working so hard to get the new on-site fitness center open that his wife, Tara, had begun to complain about never seeing him. Sure, he'd been working twelve to fourteen hours a day, but didn't she understand that he was only trying to do well so they could have a better life? He'd been sleeping poorly and all that junk food he'd eaten had added ten pounds to his middle. Tara let him know about that, too.

Next week, however, the center would be completed. The grand opening was scheduled on Wednesday, and after that, he could move out of this dark, stuffy cubicle of an office and into his new office in the center. Maybe with the new situation, he'd be able to resume his exercise regimen, too. "Yes, maybe things will get better," he thought. "But today I've got the sniffles, a headache, and about nine more hours of work before I can go home and collapse in the recliner and watch a little television before bed."

Your Response

1. List the environmental, physical, and emotional stressors in Jay's day.

2. What symptoms of brownout/burnout does he exhibit?

3. What would you recommend Jay do to better manage his stress?

BIBLIOGRAPHY

Allen, Roger J. *Human Stress: Its Nature and Control.* Minneapolis: Burgess, 1983.

Bronzan, Robert T. "Communication Is the Key to Managing People." *Athletic Purchasing and Facilities* 5 (April 1981).

Curtis, John D., and Richard A. Detert. *How to Relax: A Holistic Approach to Stress Management.* Palo Alto, CA: Mayfield, 1981.

Hollman, Robert, and Barbara Hollman. "Managing Conflict." *Athletic Administration* 12 (Fall 1978): 17–20.

Wyle, Peter, and M. Groethe. *Problem Employees: How to Improve Their Performance.* Belmont, CA: Pitman Learning, 1981.

16

Using Computers in Activity-Based Programs

We give advice by the bucket, but take it by the grain.

William Alger

Chapter Objectives

After reading this chapter and completing the exercises, you should be able to:

1 Identify the three types of computer systems and describe their basic differences

2 List and explain how four types of computer accessories can expand the capabilities of personal computers

3 Explain how computers can be used to improve the fiscal operation of a department

4 Explain the advantages of word processing over conventional typewriting

5 Explain what data base management means and how it can improve management of activity-based programs

6 Discuss the role of computers in telecommunications and as educators

7 Knowledgeably compare software and hardware packages to select those best suited for your particular needs

In administration a large amount of information must be obtained, sorted, and stored so it is readily available for recall. Unless the manager has a photographic memory, keeping all pertinent information available for daily use is time consuming and often difficult. In recent years, management has begun to realize the value of using computers for many administrative functions. Because of the computer's great speed in processing information and its objective and exact memory, it has become an invaluable tool for performing routine or repetitive tasks and handling detail work.

Even though implementing a computer system has both its advantages and its disadvantages, a successful business operation today must have access to computers. Each manager must weigh the options to determine how a computer will benefit his or her own organization. The availability of word processing, data base management, spread sheets, telecommunications, graphics, and speciality programs can improve efficiency by increasing the quality and quantity of work produced. The availability of accurate data and the increased speed with which it can be sorted, calculated, and displayed can help motivate the staff, improve customer service, and decrease the amount of time required for routine tasks, leaving more time for creativity. A large investment of time and money is required to get a computer system operational and the necessary staff trained. Like any other machine, computers can break down, causing delays, lost information, and frustration for staff and clients. There is also the expensive problem of outgrowing this fast changing technology.

While administrators may not directly use all the software or hardware the organization purchases, it is imperative that they become knowledgeable about the various possible applications and about considerations in buying various systems. This chapter will give an overview of various types of computers and accessories, specific applications, and points to consider when buying or upgrading a computer system.

Access terminals to mainframe computers may be located in offices.

COMPUTER SYSTEMS

Computer systems are generally classified by size and capabilities as mainframes, minicomputers, or microcomputers. Short of owning one of these three types of computers, organizations can take advantage of service bureaus and timesharing to meet their computing needs.

Mainframes

In the 1950s, the birth of the mainframe computer started the computer age. Often in movies or television shows, data processing centers are depicted as housing a huge computer surrounded by a roomful of people at individual terminals. This is an accurate scenario in that mainframe systems do take up a lot of space and require a large staff of data processing and information systems professionals. They are also expensive, costing from one hundred thousand to a few million dollars. This type of system is designed to handle huge amounts of business information as fast as possible, but it is usually impractical for the type of applications found in fitness and sports.

Minicomputers

Like the mainframe, the minicomputer has a central processing center with multiple terminals. It does, however, take up less space, has a smaller memory for data storage, and has a considerably smaller price tag. The cost for a minicomputer begins around $10,000.

Microcomputers

The microcomputer is the type of computer with which most individuals are familiar. The microcomputer or personal computer (PC) can store, sort, recall, and display information with speed and ease. The PC differs from the previously mentioned computer systems in that it is not part of a large system, but can stand alone. As the name *personal computer* indicates, the microcomputer is self-contained. The best-known manufacturers include Apple and IBM. The basic microcomputer system usually consists of a central processing unit (CPU), a video display, a keyboard for data input, and a printer. Certain microcomputers use electronic pens or voice commands for data input. A microcomputer is affordable for most businesses or athletics departments at a cost as low as $1,000. The distinction in price between the low-end minicomputer and the high-end microcomputer has recently blended together. Also, a new concept called RISC (Reduced Instruction Set Computer) will eventually cause the differences between microcomputer companies like Apple and IBM to disappear. Many of the applications discussed later in this chapter will refer to the use of a microcomputer.

ON SECOND THOUGHT MAYBE I SHOULD HAVE PUT THOSE SURGE PROTECTORS IN THE BUDGET.

Protecting the investment pays in the long run.

Computer Service Bureaus

The computer service bureau has emerged to fill the need for data processing in small and medium-sized businesses. Computer service bureaus, often using a mainframe computer, receive and process data from many organizations. This service can be very useful for a business that has infrequent need for data processing. It can be used for payroll processing on a monthly or semimonthly basis, and for inventory information with monthly, bimonthly, or annual frequency. The cost for this service can be low when compared to the cost for an in-house computer system and accounting staff.

Timesharing

A timeshare computer system consists of a large data base, usually on a mainframe or a minicomputer, with multiple terminals connected. A timeshare user simply hooks up to the main data base through a terminal located in his or her own organization or home. This can be a good way to use a computer data base without the expense of purchasing a complete system. Timesharing is often used in schools and universities, and is one option for an athletics or physical education department to explore.

There are several points to consider when looking into timesharing. First, there are a limited number of lines into the data base, and occasionally a user is unable to access data due to high demand or downtime required for maintenance. Also, the equipment, programs, and printouts are preselected by the vendor, and the user must make sure that they mesh comfortably with her or his needs.

HARDWARE ACCESSORIES

Computer hardware is the physical machinery of the system. Software, on the other hand, is the instructions that run the machinery. A variety of hardware accessories are available to expand the capabilities of personal computers. We briefly discuss four types of accessories here.

Modems

A modem is a device that allows one computer user to link up, via telephone lines, with other data bases. This topic is covered in depth in our discussion of telecommunications later in this chapter.

Output Devices

The type of output generated by the computer should be governed by the applications of the system. Some systems are equipped with a computerized "voice" that allows the machine to answer inquiries through the audio medium. For printed output, the choice of printers can make a dramatic difference in the quality and quantity of output. Dot matrix printers create a series of tiny dots grouped together to form letters, numbers, and figures. These printers can be either thermal, using temperature differences to create the figures on special paper, or impact, as in a conventional typewriter. Another type of impact printer is commonly referred to as a letter quality printer. This creates documents that resemble those typed on a conventional typewriter. Ink jet printers use a series of pens similar to a cartridge pen to print words, figures, and graphs. These can print in one or more colors, and are useful in graphic displays where different data can be represented by different colors. A recent development in printers is the laser printer, which can turn out printed pages almost soundlessly and at lightning speed, much like duplication by a photocopier. This is the type preferred by many businesses for correspondence now that the price has dropped to a more affordable level.

Storage Devices

Instructions and information that have been entered into the computer can be saved either in main storage or in secondary storage. Main storage refers to storage within the computer itself, in an area called memory. Recently there has been a tremendous increase in the amount of internal memory of personal computers. It is not unusual to purchase personal computers with four to ten times the amount of internal memory compared to just a few years ago. In addition, special circuit boards called memory boards can be purchased and installed to enlarge a computer's memory even beyond the original amount.

Secondary storage refers to storage outside the computer. The best-known secondary storage device is the floppy disk, or diskette, a flat magnetic disk that the computer can write information onto. Floppy disks are portable and easily copied, making it easy for several users at different terminals to share information. Even though the amount of space on a floppy disk has doubled in recent years, applications are larger and the space still seems limited.

A hard disk can store a great deal more information. Most computers have a hard disk built in as part of memory; some hard disks are separate pieces of hardware, usually encased in a small rectangular plastic box, that can be added outside the computer.

Printers are equipped with a buffer, which is a storage area for a limited amount of data, so that the CPU can send data faster than the printer can print. If the printer's buffer capacity is insufficient for the system's purpose, separate buffers can be purchased. A buffer can be a separate piece of hardware or part of a software package that operates with some of the CPU's memory capacity.

Graphics Devices

Graphics display is another option that can be creatively used in many phases of business. A graph or picture can add impact to reports. Fiscal or physical areas can be shown in the form of bar graphs, line graphs, or pie charts. Some testing and training equipment uses an audible beep tone along with visual bar graphs to motivate and communicate progress during testing and workout sessions. This data can then be printed out or stored on personal diskettes for later comparisons.

COMPUTER APPLICATIONS

To determine current trends in computer applications in the sports and physical fitness field, we conducted a survey. We sent questionnaires to numerous sports medicine facilities, fitness/health centers, diet/weight loss centers, recreational sports organizations, and collegiate athletics and physical education departments. We found that most of these organizations do use computers. The overwhelming favorites among computer systems in use are microcomputers (70 percent of respondents), followed distantly by mainframes (17 percent) and minicomputers (13

percent). We will discuss the most common applications for computers in activity-based programs.

Fiscal

Computer systems have a variety of applications in the area of accounting, payroll, general ledger, and inventory control. Computers can help prepare budgets, storing the data and quickly generating budget proposals and reports. When accounts payable, accounts receivable, and inventory are linked to one system, one entry can update all areas of cash flow control, thus saving time and increasing accuracy. This precise cash flow control is especially useful in schools or small businesses where every penny counts. We will examine each area of fiscal applications in detail, with special emphasis on how a computer system can improve operations in activity-based programs.

Accounts Receivable   Computerizing the accounting operations of a business or athletics department takes a lot of time as equipment is installed and staff trained, but it can dramatically improve the speed and quality of cash flow control. Accounts receivable can be easily and accurately balanced by precisely programmed computer software. Account statements can be updated daily as payments are received, and credits and charges posted as they occur. These up-to-date invoices and account statements can be sent out promptly by routine, periodic generation of these documents. Accounts can be automatically aged as current, thirty, sixty, or ninety days past due, and applicable service charges can be calculated. Having this up-to-date information on hand can be very useful in managing athletic ticket records. And by including information on special events or promotions, an account statement can double as a marketing tool.

A relatively new concept in the fitness and sports industry is electronic fund transfer (EFT). This system allows a business to transfer a client's monthly dues, or any other type of payment, directly from a bank account into the business's own account. The capability to make this type of transaction must be established with a bank, much like a credit card account. The advantages to a business of electronic fund transfer are twofold. First, because the client or club member signs a contract allowing automatic monthly withdrawals for his or her dues, this eliminates the possibility of forgetting to pay dues on time. Second, unlike with many credit card accounts, there is no lag time between when money is received and when it is credited to the business's account. The necessary fund transfer requests can be automatically generated on a monthly basis by a small computer system.

Accounts Payable Computerization of accounts payable also has many advantages over manual calculation. Many vendors offer discounts of 2 to 5 percent for prompt payment. The computer program can flag or automatically pay those accounts, enabling the accountant to take advantage of these discounts. In cash planning, a computer system can help the accountant to choose the most advantageous payment schedule, whether for the total balance due or installments. Automatically printing purchase orders, checks, envelopes, and mailing labels can be a great time saver.

For security purposes, the data stored by the computer can provide audit trails to determine where, when, and to whom payments are made. One university athletics department has computerized its tracking of scholarship accounts. Vendor information, such as year-to-date and total purchases, is useful for tracking accounts and can be used in bargaining for volume discounts and in making other purchases.

General Ledger Special software packages are available for general ledger accounting. These can be used in any business or sports program for budget planning and tracking any deviations from the proposed plan. The general ledger can also identify sources of profit and loss in athletics departments, recreation departments, and fitness centers. The general ledger can provide an overview of any account, whether it is the amount donated to an athletics department by a booster, or the amount spent per season on women's softball. Having this precise information on hand is necessary for planning the budget and rationalizing any changes in cash disbursement.

Payroll Three areas of concern in payroll are (1) providing paychecks for employees, (2) figuring and reporting government tax information, and (3) tracking the costs of labor. A computerized payroll program, whether in-house or through a computer service bureau, can provide this information. The computer can be programmed to automatically deduct taxes and other withholdings from employee's paychecks, then automatically write those paychecks. In computing taxes, the system can generate reports, fill out tax forms, and generate mailing labels for each report. Other reports for tracking labor distribution and costs or payroll and attendance records can easily be prepared by simply calling up and printing any employee or departmental file. As mentioned before, a computer service bureau can handle payroll at a very reasonable cost. One organization with over twenty-five employees has its bimonthly payroll generated by a bureau at a cost of under fifty dollars per month. For the cost of six hundred dollars per year, the company saves the expense and time of an in-house accountant.

Inventory Inventory control is an important function in many areas of sports and fitness. The staff in a recreational setting must keep track of all sporting equipment to prevent loss or theft. In a physical education setting, a precise inventory must be kept to help in preparing budgets for purchasing new equipment and to ensure that the necessary equipment is available for classes. Sev-

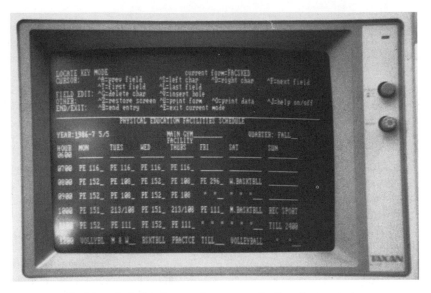

Facility scheduling is one of many uses for the microcomputer.

eral basic functions in inventory control can be aided by a computerized inventory system:

- maintaining a master count of each item (for example, 43 basketballs, 158 baseballs)
- maintaining current information on pricing, reorder levels, and delivery times by item or by manufacturer, to assist in preparing purchase orders
- locating any item in inventory by calling it up on the computer
- reviewing and assisting in planning and forecasting the use of equipment, prices, volume discounts, and other ordering and shipping information
- producing inventory lists and reports.

Many fitness centers have a snack/juice bar or sporting goods store. When the computerized inventory of these retail areas is linked to an accounting system, the inventory can automatically be updated with the daily receipts. This method not only saves time but also money.

One final note on computerized inventory is that it does not replace a manual inventory count. Although a computerized system can aid in tracking equipment, merchandise, and supplies, a routine manual count of all items in the storage room and all areas of the business or school department must still be performed.

Spreadsheets Another way of tracking budget accounts is through the use of a spreadsheet. A spreadsheet is a layout of cells identified by rows and columns and can be filled in with numbers, formulae, or labels. The data is entered and the spreadsheet does the calculating. Even if there is a fiscal management system for the entire organization (i.e., the University Budget Office), a spreadsheet is still an excellent way to track income and expenditures on the department level.

Insight through Illustration

Spreadsheets: Tracking a variety of budget accounts is a typical fiscal procedure common to administrators associated with physical education and sports programs. In this example, the physical education department has a budget of $7,080 for student wages. The situation is complicated by the fact that some students are on work study and the department pays only 20 percent of their actual wages. Each pay period is listed under date. The student's name, work status, social security number, supervisor's name, and hourly rate of pay are entered at the time of initial employment. Each week the number of hours the student works is entered and the spreadsheet calculates the weekly and year-to-date amount paid to the student, the weekly amount paid by the department, and a running balance is kept, based on previously entered formulae. In the case of work study students, the adjusted amount is calculated. This allows the administrator to track this budget on a weekly basis. Additional payroll information such as social security number and supervisor's name is an added convenience. The computer provides highly accurate calculations and if an entry mistake is made, it can be corrected and everything instantly re-calculated. (See Figures 16.1 and 16.2).

Word Processing

Word processing, vital to the smooth operation of a business or educational department, is the most popular personal computer application today. It is hard to imagine an office setting without word processing capabilities. There are many helpful features beyond the obvious ones of seeing your words on the screen, being able to store what you have typed, and changing it at a later time.

Word processing allows high-quality correspondence and documents free of errors, smudges, and liquid paper. Within the last few years, high resolution monitors can now provide a true "what you see is what you get" on the video display screen. This means that margins, line spacing, indentations, and justification in the text

will show up on the screen. Various fonts, sizes, and styles that will be printed on paper will also show up on the display screen. You can easily move drawings or graphs into word processor documents and see the product on the screen rather than a blank space where it will be added later.

There are many features to explore when purchasing a word processing package. The user should carefully consider the desired outcomes and make sure these features are available in the selected program. This might include such common features as: word wrap, justification, various styles, formatting, flexibility in specifying the margins, headings, footings, page numbers, line spacing, grammar checkers, and spelling checkers. Others might also include search and replace, page finders and graphics. These features can save many hours in proofreading, leaving time free for more productive uses.

Word processing has many other applications in the sports and fitness field. Athletics departments can use a mass mailing feature to draft a letter of recruitment, then insert names, addresses, and other pertinent information from the data base management file to send a personalized letter to prospective student athletes. This mass mailing feature can also be used to send fundraising letters. A booster is more likely to feel like an important part of the athletics program if her letter is addressed "Dear Dr. James" instead of "Dear Booster." All forms of athletics contracts can be typed and the information stored on a disk, eliminating piles and files of document photocopies.

The sports information director can use word processing to draft, proof, update, and print news releases. An electronic mail feature, which will be discussed in a later section, can be used to send the information to television, radio, and newspaper offices.

The marketing department of a fitness or sports medicine center can use word processing for preparing newsletters, reports, and personal-

A/1	B	C	D	E	F	G	H	I	J	K	L
2											
3						WEEKLY	YEAR TO DATE	WEEKLY	DEPT		
4	PAYROLL	STUDENT	WORK	HOURLY	# HOURS	AMT PAID	AMT PAID	AMT PAID	BALANCE		
5	DATE	NAME	STATUS	RATE	WORKED	TO STUDENT	TO STUDENT	BY DEPT	$7080.00	SS #	SUPERVISOR
6	=========	=========	=======	=======	=======	=========	=========	=========	=========	=========	=========
7											
8	31958	CHRIS WALL	Regular	$3.95	12.0	$47.40	$47.40	$47.40	$7032.60	887-60-7903	CAVANA
9	31972	CHRIS WALL	Regular	$3.95	11.0	$43.45	$90.85	$43.45	$6989.15		CAVANA
10	31988	CHRIS WALL	Regular	$3.95	10.0	$39.50	$130.35	$39.50	$6949.65		CAVANA
11									$6949.65		
12	31958	MICHELLE JONES	Work Study	$3.95	10.0	$39.50	$39.50	$7.90	$6941.75	645-90-8203	GAYLE
13	31972	MICHELLE JONES	Work Study	$3.95	12.0	$47.40	$86.90	$9.48	$6932.27		GAYLE
14	31988	MICHELLE JONES	Work Study	$3.95	11.0	$43.45	$130.35	$8.69	$6923.58		GAYLE
15									$6923.58		
16	31958	JEFFREY WALL	Regular	$3.95	19.0	$75.05	$75.05	$75.05	$6848.53	308-74-7082	JOHNSON
17	31972	JEFFREY WALL	Regular	$3.95	20.0	$79.00	$154.05	$79.00	$6769.53		JOHNSON
18	31988	JEFFREY WALL	Regular	$3.95	18.0	$71.10	$225.15	$71.10	$6698.43		JOHNSON
19									$6698.43		
20	31958	JAMES BROWN	Work Study	$4.15	15.0	$62.25	$62.25	$12.45	$6685.98	768-08-7103	FREDERICK
21	31972	JAMES BROWN	Work Study	$4.15	20.0	$83.00	$145.25	$16.60	$6669.38		FREDERICK
22	31988	JAMES BROWN	Work Study	$4.15	20.0	$83.00	$228.25	$16.60	$6652.78		FREDERICK

Figure 16.1 *Spreadsheet of Student Wages Showing Actual Values*

A/1	B	C	D	E	F	G	H	I	J	K	L
2											
3											
4	PAYROLL	STUDENT	WORK	HOURLY	# HOURS	WEEKLY AMT PAID	YEAR TO DATE AMT PAID	WEEKLY AMT PAID	DEPT		
5	DATE	NAME	STATUS	RATE	WORKED	TO STUDENT	TO STUDENT	BY DEPT	BALANCE 7080	SS #	SUPERVISOR
6	========	========	=======	=======	=======	==========	==========	==========	=========	=========	=========
7											
8	7/1/91	CHRIS WALL	Regular	3.95	12	=E8*+F8	=+G8	=E8*F8	=J5-I8	887-60-7903	CAVANA
9	7/15/91	CHRIS WALL	Regular	3.95	11	=E9*+F9	=H8+G9	=E9*F9	=J8-I9		CAVANA
10	7/31/91	CHRIS WALL	Regular	3.95	10	=E10*+F10	=H9+G10	=E10*F10	=J9-I10		CAVANA
11									=J10-I11		
12	7/1/91	MICHELLE JONES	Work Study	3.95	10	=E12*+F12	=+G12	=E12*F12*.20	=J11-I12	645-90-8203	GAYLE
13	7/15/91	MICHELLE JONES	Work Study	3.95	12	=E13*+F13	=H12+G13	=E13*F13*.20	=J12-I13		GAYLE
14	7/31/91	MICHELLE JONES	Work Study	3.95	11	=E14*+F14	=H13+G14	=E14*F14*.20	=J13-I14		GAYLE
15									=J14-I15		
16	7/1/91	JEFFREY WALL	Regular	3.95	19	=E16*+F16	=+G16	=E16*F16	=J15-I16	308-74-7082	JOHNSON
17	7/15/91	JEFFREY WALL	Regular	3.95	20	=E17*+F17	=H16+G17	=E17*F17	=J16-I17		JOHNSON
18	7/31/91	JEFFREY WALL	Regular	3.95	18	=E18*+F18	=H17+G18	=E18*F18	=J17-I18		JOHNSON
19									=J18-I19		
20	7/1/91	JAMES BROWN	Work Study	4.15	15	=E20*+F20	=+G20	=E20*F20*.20	=J19-I20	768-08-7103	FREDERICK
21	7/15/91	JAMES BROWN	Work Study	4.15	20	=E21*+F21	=H20+G21	=E21*F21*.20	=J20-I21		FREDERICK
22	7/31/91	JAMES BROWN	Work Study	4.15	20	=E22*+F22	=H21+G22	=E22*F22*.20	=J21-I22		FREDERICK

Figure 16.2 *Spreadsheet of Student Wages Showing Formulae*

ized correspondence. The manager will find that time saved in correcting and revising correspondence will lead to better customer service.

Data Base Management

Although the term *data base management* may sound very technical, it simply means storing information (data) in an organized and systematic manner. In computerized data storage systems, information is stored often on disks or tapes. Data base management finds a wide variety of applications in athletics, fitness, and educational settings.

Records can be stored and easily retrieved by zip codes, towns, alphabetically, or by using any label to differentiate the information. Mailing lists can thus be stored and retrieved. Client files can be quickly called up onto the video display screen or printed on demand. Letters, reports, or even book manuscripts can be stored very compactly. Imagine the convenience of condensing the information contained on hundreds of printed pages into one easily stored five-inch-square flat disk. A data base management system also allows the user to conduct a search for information by asking the system to display all files containing a certain label, such as a name or school affiliation.

The applications for computerized data storage are endless. We will look at a few that relate to activity-based programs.

Uses in the Athletics Department   An athletics director can use a data base to store team schedules, recruiting files, physical education class schedules, athletes' schedules, practice schedules, statistics, banquet lists, personnel files, or information on season ticket holders. This information can easily be changed and updated by inserting the new information and commanding the computer to file it in its proper order, whether alphabetically or using another method.

The sports information director can use the computer to store statistics and save copies of previous news releases. By using special programs, the sports information department can customize press releases to meet the format requirements of various news agencies. This increases compliance with guidelines and, ideally, increases the quality of press coverage.

Uses in the Physical Education Department   Educational settings can greatly benefit from the use of computer data bases. Many college students are familiar with the SCANTRON form, that little piece of paper covered with small boxes that can only be filled in with a #2 pencil. These testing forms are scanned by a computer and corrected. This allows teachers more time away from grading exams to attend to the special needs of students or to continue their own education.

Data storage systems can be used by educational departments to store and print exams, grades, and attendance records. Participant registration for workshops or other special events can be conducted more quickly and efficiently by computer. There are even software packages for storing information on physical testing and progress. Numerous high school strength coaches use software packages to store information about and evaluate student athletes' performance. Other software packages are available to assist in scouting, grading, and statistical evaluation.

A computer data base can also help in planning teachers' schedules. A file can be prepared for each teacher listing preferred class times, subjects, and teaching qualifications. A computer search can make the matching of classes offered and teacher assignments faster and more accurate.

Uses in Commercial Programs   In fitness centers, sports medicine clinics, and recreation programs, income depends on good customer service. Computerized information management can help to improve customer service. Mailing lists and client lists can be stored and retrieved in a variety of ways. For example, a computer can

Customer services are improved with computerized information management.

search for and print the names of all clients whose memberships are up for renewal in January. As another example, suppose a fitness center has four types of memberships: (1) weight control classes, (2) fitness evaluations and exercise, (3) exercise only/no fitness evaluations, and (4) junior memberships for ages thirteen through seventeen. By labeling each client's file with the type of membership he or she purchased, it is easier to target people for marketing specials, such as membership renewal at special rates.

In fitness or injury rehabilitation testing, computers can use numerical values and graphic displays to chart progress. In recent years, the manufacturers of testing and training equipment have integrated computers into their equipment. The time previously spent by exercise physiologists and physical therapists in manual calculation of data can now be used to better communicate goals and progress to the client. Manual manipu-

lation of equipment, such as spirometers or treadmills, has been replaced by automatic control by computers that allow selection of any type of protocol. Testing technologists thus have more time to attend to the needs of the patient or client being tested. Electrocardiograms can be programmed to record tracings at timed intervals or on demand.

Many people are already familiar with the variety of nutritional information software packages available today. This is yet another way that a fitness center can provide improved client services without the expense of a registered dietitian.

What to Look For Several special features of data base management systems lead to greater flexibility and ease of operation. A search feature allows the operator to call up all files with a certain label, such as zip code, membership code, or grade point average, thus enabling speedy report generation. Some software programs allow data to be exchanged with other programs. For example, using the Datastar program by MicroPro, files can be generated containing names, addresses, phone numbers, and other pertinent data. Then, these same files can be used with the Mailmerge function of Wordstar to create mass-mailing letters, envelopes, or mailing labels. This flexibility makes the stored information more useful.

When researching the purchase of data base packages, such as nutritional evaluations, exercise prescriptions, or fitness evaluations, a potential buyer should investigate the credentials of those who created the software. Is the information contained in the software valid? Have the theories upon which the data are based been scientifically tested and supported? Reliable data are crucial to the reputation of the fitness professional.

Some software allows the user to install data in the computer's memory using his or her own format for storage, while other software limits the user to the formats created for the program.

REPORT BY LAST NAME:

LAST NAME	FIRST NAME	LOCKER #	LOCK ID	COMBINATION
BELEW	ROBYN	607	MN34	14-16-34
BUCHHOLTZ	BARBARA	606	MN311	10-12-6
COHEN	KATHY	603	MN322	36-26-16
DAVIS	KAREN	604	MN211	30-8-30
GUILD	PAT	602	MN219	17-3-25
HARTMAN	TONI	605	MN456	24-2-28
JESSEE	LEE	601	MN214	18-20-6

REPORT BY LOCKER NUMBER:

LOCKER #	LOCK ID	COMBINATION	FIRST NAME	LAST NAME
601	MN214	18-20-6	LEE	JESSEE
602	MN219	17-3-25	PAT	GUILD
603	MN322	36-26-16	KATHY	COHEN
604	MN211	30-8-30	KAREN	DAVIS
605	MN456	24-2-28	TONI	HARTMAN
606	MN311	10-12-6	BARBARA	BUCHHOLTZ
607	MN34	14-16-34	ROBYN	BELEW

REPORT BY LOCK ID:

LOCK ID	COMBINATION	LOCKER #	FIRST NAME	LAST NAME
MN211	30-8-30	604	KAREN	DAVIS
MN214	18-20-6	601	LEE	JESSEE
MN219	17-3-25	602	PAT	GUILD
MN311	10-12-6	606	BARBARA	BUCHHOLTZ
MN322	36-26-16	603	KATHY	COHEN
MN34	14-16-34	607	ROBYN	BELEW
MN456	24-2-28	605	TONI	HARTMAN

REPORT BY COMBINATION:

COMBINATION	LOCK ID	LOCKER #	FIRST NAME	LAST NAME
10-12-6	MN311	606	BARBARA	BUCHHOLTZ
14-16-34	MN34	607	ROBYN	BELEW
17-3-25	MN219	602	PAT	GUILD
18-20-6	MN214	601	LEE	JESSEE
24-2-28	MN456	605	TONI	HARTMAN
30-8-30	MN211	604	KAREN	DAVIS
36-26-16	MN322	603	KATHY	COHEN

Figure 16.3   *Data Base Management*

Once the information is installed in files, a flexible program will allow the operator to change the format by adding or deleting information without losing information or beginning from scratch. When comparing data base management programs, reliability, flexibility, and ease of operation are key ingredients.

Insight through Illustration

Keeping track of locker assignments is one of many management tasks associated with a sport or recreation program. A simple data base listing categories such as last name, first name, locker number, lock identification number, and combination can be helpful in administering this task. Reports can be generated by arranging the columns of data in the desired order and then by sorting on the desired category. Also, with search capabilities, the identification number of a lost lock can be entered into the computer and instantly the owner can be identified. For example: [FIND: MN34] would produce the following record: BELEW ROBYN 607 MN34 14–16–34. Figure 16.3 illustrates how printed reports can be arranged several ways.

Planning, Organizing, and Controlling

Some may feel that using a computer for scheduling, organizing, and planning is impersonal. In contrast to this belief, many managers find that using a computer to handle this type of detail work allows them more free time to interact on a personal level with employees and clients. By filing away information on personnel, such as skills, interests, job assignments, and personal history, the manager can easily keep abreast of his or her staff.

Others find that a desktop computer can be used as a desktop organizer. Various software packages deal with time management. These allow tasks to be organized and prioritized according to personal and professional goals. Recurring tasks can be entered so they automatically are brought to the computer user's attention on specified days. How easy it would be to flip on the computer and have your daily or weekly schedule displayed on the screen! This information could also be made available to the secretary or administrative assistant to prevent scheduling conflicts. Software is also available to handle various other aspects of a manager's planning, organizing, and controlling functions.

Project Management   Project management software is available to chart and analyze progress on various projects. Features include cost analysis and charting of staff availability and scheduling considerations, to name a few. By using this type of program, managers can easily prepare reports

AND NOW I'D LIKE TO INTRODUCE
OUR NEW CHIEF OF STAFF...

for presentation to superiors, investors, and project staff. The system can also be used to analyze the impact of changes on the project as a whole.

Insight through illustration

Lisa Hastings was one of ten key members on the project for upgrading the football stadium at Smithtown College. She discovered an error in the original work plan that would cause construction to extend three weeks into the fall semester of classes. Using a computerized planning system, the committee determined which classes, club activities, athletic events, and band practices would be affected by this delay. Other considerations such as expenses and labor requirements were also analyzed using the planning system.

Scheduling   Almost every area of sports or fitness requires some type of scheduling. School officials schedule classes and athletic practices with respect to facilities, coaches, and teachers. A recreation director must schedule events to efficiently use all available resources. A fitness center must schedule staff and facilities for the most cost-effective use of each.

By computerizing scheduling, the complex task of matching instructors, participants, class subjects, and facilities to available times becomes easier. The computer organizes and analyzes all options and presents a plan free of personnel, time, and space availability conflicts. Teachers' preferences of subjects and times can also be considered so that, when possible, first preference will be honored. Printed schedules can easily be prepared. In clinical or consulting programs, clients can be scheduled to avoid overstaffing and understaffing, resulting in greater cost efficiency.

Traffic Flow   One recent advance in the health club industry is the use of computerized traffic flow monitoring. In many clubs and fitness centers, members receive an identification card bearing a bar code or "zebra sticker." When members enter the facility, they "sign in" by presenting their card to a receptionist for scanning by an electronic pen or device. This system is similar to the way grocery stores use a scanner to quickly check out groceries. When the bar code is read by the computer, the member's file is accessed and that visit is recorded in the file.

This information allows the sales staff and manager to track participants' activity history. For clubs that offer ten-visit or twenty-visit passes, the computer can track how many visits have been used, and notify the receptionist how many visits remain. This type of system can also notify the receptionist that a member's financial account is in arrears. The receptionist can then direct the delinquent member to the manager or sales staff to clear up any outstanding balance before working out.

Storing client data, schedules, project information, and employee data in a computerized system allows a variety of people at remote terminals to access the information without running up and down stairs or hallways to locate paper files. The use of security access codes prevents unauthorized personnel from finding out personal or confidential information by browsing through the memory banks.

*Computers facilitate improved communication about
scheduling sports events.*

Telecommunications

Computers talking to other computers—is this really necessary in sports and fitness? Why would an athletics director need to be concerned with telecommunications? The reason is that good communication is the basis for good management. If telecommunications can improve overall communication, then it is good for business.

Using telephone modems increases the manager's ability to communicate with business associates at remote locations. Consider the following case.

Insight through Illustration

The facility coordinator of a physical education department of a major university was having trouble scheduling facilities due to conflicts among physical education classes, athletic team demands, and recreational sports requirements. Due to the fact that although these three departments used the same fields, pools, and gymnasiums, each office was located in a different area of the large campus, excessive time was spent on the telephone or waiting for campus mail to deliver facility requests and availability information. To alleviate this problem, the facility coordinator investigated and proposed a plan to link the computers of all three departments by telephone. The facility coordinator could input changes to the facility schedules data base as requests were approved. At any time, the athletics department or recreational sports department could use telephone modems to call up the schedule for any facility by week, month, or quarter on their own computer terminal. This dramatically decreased the number of phone calls between departments and resulted in fewer denials of requests due to conflicts in scheduling.

There are other uses for telecommunications. Exchange of memos, agendas, and technical support documents by computer can decrease the volume of paper used and discarded. Public domain software can also be obtained directly through phone lines. Phone lines can bring public information systems such as MEDLARS (Medical Literature Analysis and Retrieval System), ERIC (Educational Resources Information Center) and INFO-BANK, a subsidiary of the *New York Times,* as close as a personal computer. For example, an athletics director can get airline schedules without waiting for a travel agent to research and return phone calls. Anyone who prepares articles or reports for publication in newspapers or magazines can save time in proofing and revising by sending the article by electronic mail to the printer or editor. Changes can be suggested and revisions made without spending days waiting for regular mail or the expense of overnight delivery.

We should note that in any form of telecommunications, it is imperative to make every word count and eliminate unnecessary information. Often when press releases are sent by electronic mail, the receiver views the abstract of the article initially to determine if the article is timely and newsworthy. The abstract must be attention-grabbing and must convey the essence of the story while keeping it brief. If the abstract is dull or confusing, the rest of the article will probably never make it to the editor's video screen.

Computers as Educators

Computers are being used in all areas of business and education to educate employees, clients, and students. Computers are excellent teachers because they can combine a self-paced instruction program with sound, text, graphics, and video technology to present data in a motivating and easy-to-comprehend fashion.

In training employees, computers are frequently used to convey goals and expectations of the organization or to teach precise skills such as conducting body composition evaluations. Many programs are available to tutor employees in computer use and usually are provided by vendors if requested.

Consultations can be performed by computer. By offering information followed by self-tests, the computer can teach the client or employee dietary information or new skills without the pressures of a classroom situation. A large network of health clubs uses video presentations to instruct employees in aerobic dance techniques. Computer consultations or video presentations allow employees to practice as much as necessary in a relaxed individual or small group atmosphere.

Businesses that educate the public can use video tapes and computers to convey information. A widely known example of this technique is the American Red Cross's multimedia cardiopulmonary resuscitation (CPR) instruction. An instruction book, video tape, and hands-on practice with mannequins are all used to reinforce proper CPR technique. Testing mannequins are equipped with a small computer sensor to monitor and report if proper force, compression, and timing are being applied by the CPR rescuer.

Nutritional education software can vary greatly, from simply counting up total calories to recommending dietary modifications. One of the most fun and easy-to-use systems is one that asks a client to use an electronic pen to simply touch the names and categories of foods presented on a video screen. The computer program then outlines a diet plan for a prescribed number of calories using the favorite foods chosen by the client.

HOW TO CHOOSE A COMPUTER

When considering any computer systems or accessories, the buyer should first list the functions in the organization that could be computerized, and then prioritize them. How frequently will the system be used when it is fully operational? If the time requirements and applications are small, a computer service bureau or timeshare system may be the best option. Are software and hardware available to meet the requirements? Can the system be upgraded as demands grow in the organization? All options should be examined before the system that is the most feasible, flexible, and best suited for the business or organization is chosen.

When purchasing a new system or upgrading a present computer system, cost is an important factor for most organizations, whether in education or private industry. As we touched upon in the first section of this chapter, costs for computers and accessories can vary dramatically. When considering costs, a buyer should be sure to examine *all* expenses—hardware, software, accessories, and training—as well as each area of the organization and its computer needs. Sometimes individual specialized systems are more feasible economically and operationally than an umbrella-type system that performs all functions.

When examining various options, it is necessary to research as many sources as possible. Current literature should be reviewed to see what recent advances have been made. Organizations currently using a system the buyer is considering should be visited. When possible, the buyer should talk to all who are in contact with the computer to see how well it works, how well it solves problems, and how easy it is to operate. Numerous dealers should be contacted for opinions on how best to meet the buyer's financial situation and computer needs.

A computer consultant can also be engaged to do the legwork and present the buyer with recommendations. The consultant's references should be checked to ensure adequate knowledge of computer systems and ability to communicate and negotiate with computer dealers. Consultants should have knowledge about several computer companies, hardware and software availability, and applications. They can also help in negotiating contracts once a decision has been made.

Considerations for Hardware Purchase and Update

Each component of the computer system should be considered in the buying decision, and the buyer should be sure to get hands-on experience with the equipment before buying it.

Central Processing Unit When purchasing or upgrading a system, it is crucial to determine that the size of the main memory is adequate to run the designed software and any peripheral data programs such as software buffers. Will the speed of processing provide data on demand, or will tasks be delayed while the CPU is processing and delivering data? If printers, modems, or other hardware accessories will be used, proper interface boards should be included. If these are not included in the CPU, the cost of purchasing them must be considered.

Video Display Terminal Selection of a video display terminal (VDT) should not be taken for granted. Numerous options in VDTs are available and today that means more than just cursor control, brightness, contrast and clarity. Screens that reduce glare will also reduce eye strain and headaches. A word processing specialist, who will be viewing a video display screen all day long, should consider a color monitor that can highlight areas of the screen in contrasting colors. A monitor stand or arm permits the height, distance, position and angle to be adjusted to the user. A VDT that permits viewing a full page may be appropriate for someone who uses a large spreadsheet or does mostly word processing applications.

Keyboard Some computers have fixed keyboards and number pads, while others have movable keyboards that are attached to the CPU by a cable. The user should try out the keyboard to see if it feels comfortable and if fingers are able to move easily among the character keys, the num-ber keys, and the special function keys. In addition to keyboards, the "mouse" has become a common keyboard accessory. Consideration should be given to the shape of the mouse, the speed (as slow as 20 dots per inch for precise control), and the mechanism (roller ball vs optical). There is also the choice of moving the mouse across a pad or rolling a ball in a track. Once again, each of these options should be tried since this is critical for comfort in prolonged use.

Printer The variety of printers available can be the most confusing aspect of buying a computer for many people. Speed, price, and document quality vary dramatically. The type of printer to purchase should be determined by the quality of document and speed of printing required. When checking the quality of printers, the buyer should take along a magnifying glass and examine the crispness of ink on the page. Does the printer accept a variety of paper types? The buyer must think ahead. Even if the initial use of a system will be adequately served by tractor-feed paper, in the future the printer may be required to print on single-feed paper or even envelopes. Will the printer accept these? Finally, a word about the noise level of printers. Some are very quiet while others can be distractingly loud. The buyer should consider the environment where the computer system will be used. If telephone or face-to-face conversations will be taking place nearby, a loud printer can become a nuisance.

In summary, when purchasing a computer system, the buyer should make sure that the hardware is adequate for the tasks at hand, but also that the system can be easily and inexpensively upgraded to accommodate expanding demands.

Software Considerations

Flexibility and expandability are as important to software as to hardware. The capabilities of the software should exceed the present needs and uses of the user, in order to allow for future expansion. The easier the program is to use, the more "user friendly" it is considered. Software should not be too complicated for the people who will be using it. The potential buyer should talk to others who have used the software to find out how adequately it performs.

In judging software's reliability and ease of operation, the buyer must use common sense. He or she should not think about how tasks are currently performed, but rather, should focus on the possibility for change. If possible, a hands-on trial using the software/hardware combination under consideration should be performed. The built-in controls, recovery, and backup systems should be checked. The buyer should try to mess up the data. Is the program "idiot proof"? Does it produce suitable documents? Vendor or manufacturer support should be readily available. Many manufacturers have toll-free phone numbers, which can come in handy for immediate assistance if necessary. Proper training should be provided if required.

When considering the cost of software, the buyer should remember that packaged software is less expensive than custom-designed programs. Only when all packaged software programs have been deemed inadequate should the buyer look toward custom programming. When the most cost-effective program is found, the buyer should consider if the price is reasonable for the job it will perform. A task should never be computerized just for the sake of computerization. Only when time and/or money can be saved should a task be changed.

One final word of caution: computer hardware and software should be thoroughly investigated. With the multitude of new programs available for sports and fitness applications, sometimes the consumer ends up being the research and development person for some companies. Claims made by manufacturers and dealers should not be accepted without some proof. If possible, a trial run or a service contract should be arranged for. If claims do not hold true, the consumer should be compensated in some form.

KEY WORDS AND PHRASES

Hardware	Microcomputer	Output device
Software	Timesharing	Data base management
Mainframe	Modem	Word processing
Minicomputer	Spreadsheets	Telecommunications

QUESTIONS FOR REVIEW

1. Compare and discuss the advantages and disadvantages of mainframe, minicomputer, microcomputer, and timeshare computer systems.

2. Compare and discuss the applications for three different types of printers.

3. Select a specific situation, such as athletics or sports rehabilitation, and discuss the fiscal applications for a computer system.

4. What are the advantages of using telecommunications?

5. Discuss in depth how computers can aid in employee training for a fitness club.

6. What is the most important consideration when purchasing software?

7. What is the most important consideration when purchasing or upgrading a computer hardware system?

8. Why should an administrator become knowledgeable about computer systems used by the organization's employees?

9. List and discuss three advantages and three disadvantages of computerization.

SELF-TEST

Corrected True-False

If the statement is true, mark it T. If the statement is false, mark it F and change it to a true statement by adding or deleting words.

_____ 1. Any business or organization will benefit from the purchase of a computer system.

_____ 2. The mainframe is the type of computer that started the computer age.

_____ 3. A time share computer system has the most flexible programs and output of any system.

_____ 4. In the authors' survey on computer usage, the minicomputer was the most popular system currently in use in sports, physical education, and fitness fields.

_____ 5. Computers require so much time for inputting data that an exercise physiologist using one may be unable to relate results to a client in a clear and timely manner.

_____ 6. Computerized scheduling is a tool that allows managers more time for personal interaction.

_____ 7. Computerized scheduling is an impersonal method for dealing with staff.

_____ 8. The bar code is a valuable feature for word processing.

Multiple Choice

_____ 9. Which telecommunications device increases the manager's ability to communicate with business associates at remote locations?
   a. telephone modem
   b. computerized memos
   c. telephone redial
   d. all of the above

_____ 10. Which is not an example of public domain software?
   a. MEDLARS
   b. ERIC
   c. INFOBANK
   d. SONICS

_____ 11. Computers are excellent teachers because they can use:
   a. text
   b. graphics
   c. sound
   d. all of the above

_____ 12. Which computer system is most cost efficient?
   a. umbrella-type
   b. individual specialized
   c. using outside system
   d. depends on individual needs

_____ 13. When purchasing computer equipment one needs to consider:
   a. video display terminal
   b. keyboard
   c. both a and b
   d. neither a nor b

_____ 14. Which of the following packaged software is least expensive?
   a. packaged software

   b. custom-designed software
   c. modem software
   d. all about the same

_____ 15. Copying commercially prepared software can result in:
   a. cheaply obtained software
   b. serious legal action
   c. both a and b
   d. neither a nor b

CASE 16.1 COMPUTERIZING INSTRUCTORS' SCHEDULES

Two years ago Betty Gee, class scheduler for the physical education department of Mid-State University, developed a data base management program for class and instructors' schedules. She created a schedule form that could be customized with the following information for each teacher: name, social security number, class teaching preferences, teaching responsibility for the year, non-teaching assignments, and hourly schedules for each of the three quarters of the academic year.

She spent close to sixty hours getting the initial forty-two teaching schedules prepared, but she believed that once the schedules were developed, numerous hours would be saved. She could make just a few changes on the computer each quarter, instead of starting from scratch as they had done for years with the old pencil and paper method.

However, she suffered a setback when making out these original schedules: She lost about six hours of work when she hit the wrong key and

exited the program improperly. All of the information she had recorded, even what had been saved on the diskette, disappeared when the file was recalled. After that, she began to update her backup diskette more frequently, but she still continued to lose hours of work because the program had no safety feature to make losing information by mistake more difficult. Finally, Betty decided that she was not saving time, even though the computerized forms had several advantages. She was considering going back to the old pencil and paper method of scheduling.

Your Response

1. Identify the problem(s).
2. What can you suggest as possible alternative solutions?
3. List two or three action guides that led you to your suggestions.

CASE 16.2 ARE COMPUTERS FOR SMALL OPERATIONS?

Stan Batts owned and operated a mobile fitness testing and exercise prescription business. He

ran a three-person operation and was considering an investment in some kind of computer system or service. He had heard of minicomputers and microcomputers, but he really didn't know whether either would be worth the investment. Neither he nor his two exercise physiologists knew how to operate a computer.

Your Response

1. What are Stan's problems?

2. What solutions do you suggest?

3. What are the bases for your suggestions?

BIBLIOGRAPHY

Danziger, George. "Scheduling with Computers" (three-part series). *Athletic Business* 8, 11, and 12 (1984–85).

Dougherty, Neil J., and Diane Bonanno. *Principles in Sport and Leisure Services.* Minneapolis: Burgess, 1985.

Falk, Howard. *Handbook of Computer Applications for the Small or Medium-Sized Business.* Radnor, PA: Chilton, 1983.

Gibson, Barbara. *Personal Computers in Business.* Cupertino, CA: Apple Computer, 1982.

Mohnsen, Bonnie. "Using Computers, Helping Physi-cal Education Administrators." *Journal of Physical Education, Recreation and Dance.* (January 1991).

Tontimonia, Thomas L. "Choosing a Computer to Fit Your Needs." *Athletic Business* 8, no. 10 (1984).

Watkins, David L. "Computers Can Streamline Your Program Operations." *Athletic Purchasing and Facilities* 8, no. 3 (1984).

Watkins, David L., and Judith M. Yorio. "Computers in Athletics: Promise and Reality." Lecture at the national convention of the American Alliance of Health, Physical Education, Recreation and Dance, Cincinnati, April 1986.

Index